CAREER OPPORTUNITIES
IN CASINOS AND
CASINO HOTELS

CAREER OPPORTUNITIES IN CASINOS AND CASINO HOTELS

S HELLY F IELD

Checkmark Books™

An imprint of Facts On File, Inc.

CAREER OPPORTUNITIES IN CASINOS AND CASINO HOTELS

Checkmark Books
An imprint of Facts On File, Inc.
11 Penn Plaza
New York NY 10001

Library of Congress Cataloging-in-Publication Data

Field, Shelly.
    Career opportunities in casinos and casino hotels: a comprehensive guide
to exciting careers in casinos and the gaming industry / by Shelly Field
        p.   cm.
    Includes bibliographical references and index.
    ISBN 0-8160-4122-9 (alk. paper)—ISBN 0-8160-4123-7 (alk. paper)
    1. Casinos—Employees—Vocational guidance—United States.
    2. Gambling—Employees—Vocational guidance—United States. I. Title.
HV6711.F54   2000
795′.023′73—dc21   99-047646

Checkmark books are available at special discounts when purchased in bulk quantities for businesses, associations, institutions or sales promotions. Please call our Special Sales Department in New York at
(212) 967-8800 or (800) 322-8755.

You can find Facts On File on the World Wide Web at http://www.factsonfile.com

Cover design by Nora Wertz

Printed in the United States of America

VB Hermitage 10 9 8 7 6 5 4 3 2 1
        (pbk) 10 9 8 7 6 5 4 3 2 1

This book is printed on acid-free paper.

This book is dedicated with love to
my parents, Ed and Selma;
my sisters, Jessica and Debbie;
Norman; Geoffrey; Susan; Honey; Quincy;
and all the aunts, uncles and cousins.
I hit the jackpot . . .
I couldn't pick a better family!

CONTENTS

HOW TO USE THIS BOOK

Over the years, the gaming industry has exploded and reaches into almost every corner of the country and many places throughout the world. Today, gaming is a booming business, and many job seekers want a piece of the action.

This book is designed to help you prepare for an interesting, exciting, fun, glamorous, and/or high-paying job. While many other industries are downsizing, the gaming industry is expanding. It is also one of the few industries where dedicated, hardworking employees can quickly move up the career ladder.

Thousands are currently working in the gaming industry, and many more are eager to enter but have no idea how to get a position. They have no concept of what career opportunities are available, where to find them, or what training and qualifications are required.

Career Opportunities in Casinos and Casino Hotels is the single most comprehensive source for learning about job opportunities in this growing field. This book was written for everyone who aspires to work in the gaming industry but does not know how to get in. The 94 jobs discussed in this book include careers not only on the gaming floor, but in the business, administration, and management areas; security and surveillance; entertainment, hotel management, and service; food and beverage service; health clubs and spas; retail; and more.

The gaming industry offers an array of opportunities and requires people with a variety of different skills and talents. It needs dealers, floorpeople, cashiers, hosts, slot repair technicians, publicists, marketing people, servers, desk clerks, health and fitness personnel, salespeople, secretaries, receptionists, administrative assistants, managers, human resources people, trainers, cooks, bakers, security and surveillance officers, executives, and more. The trick to locating the job you want is developing your skills and using them to enter this exciting and expanding industry. Once you have your foot in the door, you can climb the career ladder to success.

Sources of Information

Information for this book was obtained through interviews, questionnaires, and a variety of books, magazines, newsletters, other literature, television and radio programs, etc. Some information was gained as a result of personal experience in the industry. Other data were obtained from friends and business associates in various areas of the gaming industry.

Among the people interviewed were men and women engaged in all aspects of the gaming and hospitality industries in both the gaming and non-gaming areas. These include individuals working in the business, administration, and management end of the industry as well as frontline employees and support personnel.

Also interviewed were human resources directors and staff, training managers, publicists, marketing managers, bellpersons, servers, housekeepers, security and surveillance people, PBX operators, valets, concierges, marketing coordinators, public relations directors, hosts, tour and travel coordinators, desk personnel, convention managers, entertainers, slot managers, cashiers, dealers, floorpersons, pit managers, technicians, cooks, pastry chefs, bartenders, benefit coordinators, sales associates, secretaries, administrative assistants, and more.

Interviews included personnel from large luxury casinos as well as smaller land-based, docked and floating riverboat casinos, Indian gaming facilities, cruise line casinos, schools, colleges, unions, and trade associations.

Organization of Material

Career Opportunities In Casinos and Casino Hotels is divided into 10 general employment sections: Career Opportunities in Casino Operations and the Gaming Area; Career Opportunities in Casino and Casino Hotel Marketing, Public Relations, and Sales; Career Opportunities in Casino and Casino Hotel Security and Surveillance; Career Opportunities in Casino Hotels; Career Opportunities in Casino and Casino Hotel Entertainment; Career Opportunities in Casino and Casino Hotel Food and Beverage Service; Career Opportunities in Casino and Casino Hotel Human Resources Departments; Career Opportunities in Casino Hotel Health Clubs and Spas; Career Opportunities in Casino and Casino Hotel Retail Shops; and Career Opportunities in Casino and Casino Hotel Support Personnel. Within each of these sections are descriptions of individuals careers.

There are two parts to each job classification. The first part offers job information in chart form. The second part presents information in a narrative text. In addition to the basic career description, you will find additional information on unions and associations as well as tips for entry.

Ten appendixes are offered to help locate information you might want or need to get started looking for a job in the field. These appendixes include gaming academies and dealer schools; college and university degree programs in hospitality administration and management, hotel and restaurant management; trade associations, unions, and other organizations; American casinos; Canadian casinos; cruise lines; gaming conferences; seminars; and gaming Web sites. A bibliography of gaming and hospitality related books and periodicals is also included.

This book will help you take the first step toward preparing for a great career. Job opportunities exist throughout the country and the world, and will increase as more areas legalize gambling. Opportunities may be located in luxury casinos, casino hotels, docked and floating riverboat casinos, Indian gaming facilities, and cruise ships.

No matter which facet of the casino and casino hotel job market you choose to enter, you can find a career that is rewarding and fun. The jobs are out there waiting for you; you just have to go after them. Persevere and you will hit the jackpot in the job market.

—Shelly Field

ACKNOWLEDGMENTS

I thank every individual, casino, hotel, company, corporation, agency, association, and union that provided information, assistance, and encouragement for this book.

First and foremost, I acknowledge with appreciation James Chambers for his assistance, advice, and insight over the years. I also gratefully acknowledge the assistance of Ed and Selma Field for their ongoing support and encouragement in this project.

Others whose help was invaluable include: Academy of Casino Training, Inc.; Ellen Ackerman, Gem Communications; Terry Alexander, Ameristar Casino, Vicksburg; Harrison Allen; Julie Allen; American Federation of Musicians; Ameristar Casinos; Argosy Casinos; Barbara Ashworth, Beauty School of Middletown; Beth Ayjian; Lloyd Barriger; Allan Barrish; Linda Bernbach; Phil Berman, Catskill Development; Steve Blackman; Joyce Blackman; Robert Boone, Isle of Capri Casinos; Sam Boyd's California Hotel and Casino; Theresa Bull; Katrina Bull; Kim Butler, Trump Casino Resorts; Caryn Cammeyer, Advertising Research Foundation; Eileen Casey, Superintendent, Monticello Central Schools; Casino Career Center; Casino Career Institute; Atlantic City, NJ; Casino Employment Opportunities; Casino Management Association; Catskill Development; Anthony Cellini, Town of Thompson Supervisor; Brandi Cesario, Nevada Society of Certified Public Accountants; Patricia Claghorn; Andy Cohen; Bernard Cohen, Horizon Advertising; Dr. Jessica L. Cohen; Lorraine Cohen; Norman Cohen; Community General Hospital, Harris, NY; ConJel Company; Jan Cornelius; Crawford Memorial Library Staff; Margaret Crossley, Nevada Society of Certified Public Accountants; Meike Cryan; Gina Damato; Daniel Dayton; W. Lynne Dayton, Direct Mail/Marketing Association, Inc.; Carrie Dean, Gem Communications; Direct Marketing Educational Foundation, Inc.; Donna Dossey-Aust, American Airline Advantage Sales Reservationist; Scott Edwards; Dan England, UNLV; Cliff Ehrlich, Catskill Development; Ernest Evans; Deborah K. Field, Esq.; Greg Field; Lillian (Cooky) Field; Mike Field; Robert Field; Field Associates, Ltd.; Rob Fier; Finkelstein Memorial Library Staff; David Garthe, CEO, Graveyware.com; John Gatto; Sheila Gatto; Gem Communications; George Glantzis; Kaytee Glantzis; Sam Goldych; David Hernandez, Community College of Southern Nevada; Hermann Memorial Library Staff; Joan Howard; International Alliance of Theatrical Stage Employees (IATSE); Jimmy "Handyman" Jones; Howard Kaiser, Raleigh Hotel; Liberty Public Library Staff; Michael Madzy; Ginger Maher; Ernie Martinelli; Robert Masters, Esq.; Pat Matthews; Richard Mayfield; MGM Grand, Las Vegas, NV; Werner Mendel, New Age Health Spa; Phillip Mestman; Rima Mestman; Beverly Michaels, Esq.; Martin Michaels, Esq.; Monticello Central High School Guidance Department; Monticello Central High School Library Staff; Jennifer Morganti, Nevada Society of Certified Public Accountants; Earl Nesmith; Nevada Society of Certified Public Accountants; Marvin Newman; New York State Employment Service; New York State Nurses Association; Ellis Norman, UNLV; Peter Notarstefano; Christine Pearon, Casino Employment; Herb Perry; Public Relations Society of America; Doug Puppel, Business Editor, Las Vegas *Review Journal;* Ramapo Catskill Library System; Doug Richards; Martin Richman; John Riegler; Michele Roberts, Travel Planners; Diane Ruud, Nevada Society of Certified Public Accountants; Genice Ruiz; Bob Sertell; Bob Saludares, Community Employment Training Center, Las Vegas, NV; Matt Sjoquist; Stuart Slakoff, Professional Programs, Inc.; M.D. Smith, Slot Office Secretary, California Hotel and Casino; Raun Smith, Casino Career Center; Eve Steinberg; Matthew E. Strong; Sullivan County Community College; Thrall Library Staff; Turning Stone Casino; United States Department of Labor; Brian Vargas, Gem Communications; Marc Weiswasser, CMA; Bill Wilder, Academy of Casino Training; Carol Williams; John Williams; John Wolfe; Johnny World; WSUL Radio; WVOS Radio; and Ken Zeszutko, Turning Stone Casino.

In addition, because there is such mystique surrounding a great deal of the gaming industry, much of the material was provided by sources who wish to remain anonymous. My thanks to them, all the same.

FOREWORD

Gaming is currently enjoying a greater acceptance as an entertainment form than ever before, garnering attention nationwide. This booming industry and the hospitality industry growing along with it have generated a wealth of employment opportunities throughout the country and the world.

I have personally experienced the industry's expansion while working in the gaming trade show sector. Currently vice president of trade shows for Gem Communications, I oversee every aspect of the World Gaming Congress and Expo, the largest, most prominent, and prestigious gaming trade show in the world. The show continues to grow each year, currently bringing together more than 23,000 professionals in all facets of the gaming industry from more than 86 countries.

As a multibillion dollar business, the gaming industry is an economic force on all levels, and employment is no exception. The gaming and hospitality industries are closely intertwined, with the success of one sector depending closely on the other. Paramount to the success of both industries are employees. Opportunities abound—whether one works directly on the gaming floor, in the back of the house, the hotel, food and beverage services, support services, management, on the executive level, or as a vendor.

The explosion of the industry has resulted in excellent employment opportunities in all facets of the business. There has long been a need for a comprehensive guide detailing these career opportunities. Shelly Field, a consultant to casinos nationwide, has done a remarkable job of researching these opportunities and detailing them in this volume.

Career Opportunities in Casinos and Casino Hotels is an excellent source for those just starting in this exciting field. It also offers food for thought for professionals who aspire to move into other parts of the industry. The book gives people at all career levels the means to match their skills, talents, and interests to the vast arena of the gaming industry.

Whether guests come for vacations, business, to visit mega resorts and theme park settings, eat fine food, enjoy exciting entertainment or the casino itself, gaming is part of a total entertainment experience. This flourishing industry is now hungry for talented workers.

If you're seeking a career offering excitement, opportunity and future growth, I can think of no other industry in the world better than gaming. I urge everyone looking for a great career to read this book to learn more about joining this industry. I also look forward to seeing each and every one of you as professionals at the next World Gaming Congress and Expo!

Brian Vargas
Vice President of U.S. Trade Shows,
Gem Communications

INTRODUCTION

The gaming industry is a multibillion-dollar business. There are thousands of people working in the industry, and there is ample room for many more. One of them can be you.

Casinos and casino hotels resemble miniature cities and require the services of people with many skills. In addition to jobs in casino operations and gaming, a vast array of possibilities await you.

People are needed to handle marketing, public relations, and sales; provide security and surveillance; manage hotels; move luggage; open doors; greet people; provide guest services; clean rooms; answer phones; handle accounting services; develop special events; coordinate and implement activities; repair air-conditioning; entertain guests; prepare and serve food and beverages; hire, train, and pay employees; style guests' hair; teach guests how to use health club equipment; handle retail sales; provide clerical and secretarial support; and provide medical services.

In a world in which many industries are downsizing, the gaming industry is expanding dramatically. New casinos and casino hotels are under construction every year, and many in existence are expanding.

Casinos and casino hotels offer many high-paying jobs without requiring a great deal of prior education or training. For many jobs you need only a high school diploma or GED and a great attitude.

Most facilities offer flexible hours and liberal fringe benefit packages. Benefits may include health, dental, and life insurance; pension plans; profit-sharing programs; educational reimbursement; child care; and sick and vacation pay and more.

Whichever area you choose to work in, your gaining industry job will be a satisfying and rewarding career experience. Within each section of this book, you'll find information to acquaint you with job possibilities in casinos and casino hotels. A key to the organization of each entry follows:

Alternate Titles

Many jobs in the gaming industry have alternate titles. Job titles often vary from casino to casino. The duties these jobs consist of are similar, only the names are different.

Career Ladder

The career ladder illustrates a possible career path. Remember that in the gaming industry, there are no set rules. Advancement may occur in almost any manner. In some situations advancement may be in a totally different career area.

Position Description

Every effort has been made to give well-rounded job descriptions. Be aware that no two casinos are identically structured, so no two jobs will be precisely the same. For example, casinos might have various supervisors doing the same type of job or might eliminate certain positions entirely.

Salary Range

Salary ranges for the jobs titles in the book are as accurate as possible. Earnings for a job will depend on the size, location, and prestige of the casino as well as on the experience, education, training, and responsibilities of the individual. In jobs where employees receive tokens or tips, earnings will depend heavily on the customer service skills and personality of the individual. Annual salary ranges given for jobs usually paid on an hourly or other basis are estimates based on full-time employment.

Employment Prospects

If you choose a job that has an excellent, good, or fair rating, you are lucky. You will have an easier time finding employment. If, however, you would like to work at a job that has a poor rating, don't despair. The rating means only that it is difficult to obtain a job, not that finding one is totally impossible.

This section also discusses possible settings for jobs in each area. It should be noted that casino opportunities are available in many different locations throughout the country and the world. Because many states now host legalized gambling, the gambling capitals are just the beginning.

Since casinos are often open 24 hours a day, seven days a week, this section may also discuss available shift possibilities. Generally, the three main shifts are: the day shift from 8 A.M. to 4 P.M.; swing shift or evening shift from 4 P.M. to midnight; and graveyard shift or overnight shift from midnight to 8 A.M. Keep in mind that every casino may not have the same shift hours, and some may overlap shifts for effective employee coverage.

Advancement Prospects

Try to be as cooperative and helpful as possible in the workplace. Don't attempt to see how little work you can do.

Be enthusiastic, energetic, and outgoing. Go the step that no one expects. Learn as much as you can. When a job advancement possibility opens up, make sure that you're prepared to take advantage of it.

A variety of options for career advancement are included. However, as noted previously, there are no hard and fast rules for climbing the career ladder in the gaming industry. While work performance is important, advancement in many jobs is based on experience, education, training, employee attitude, and of course individual career aspirations.

Many casinos promote from within, so the best way to advance is to get your foot in the door and then climb the career ladder.

Education and Training

While this section presents the minimum educational and training requirements for each job area, this doesn't mean you should limit yourself. Try to get the best training and education possible.

As noted previously, many high-paying jobs in casinos and casino hotels do not require any formal education beyond a high school diploma. The requirements may also include attendance at dealers' and gaming schools and academies, technical and vocational schools, colleges and universities, or on-the-job training. Many casinos also offer their own in-house training programs.

Some casinos also offer programs to assist those who do not have a high school diploma to obtain a GED.

All states, areas, and casinos have a variety of rules and regulations that must be followed. This section also covers licensing or other credentials necessary for certain jobs. Casinos generally require those working in the gaming area to be licensed by the gaming authority in the specific state in which they work. Each area has its own licensing rules and regulations. These may include minimum age requirements, possession of sheriff's cards, and/or attendance of alcohol awareness programs.

Experience/Skills/Personality Traits

This section indicates which jobs require experience as well as specific skills and personality traits necessary for each job.

Best Geographic Location

While jobs in the gaming industry may be located throughout the country or the world, certain areas host more opportunities. As many states now host legalized gambling, the gambling capitals are just the beginning.

Unions/Associations

This section offers other sources for career information and assistance. Unions and trade associations offer valuable help in obtaining career guidance, support, and personal contacts. They may also offer training, continuing education, scholarships, fellowships, seminars, and other beneficial programs.

Tips for Entry

Use this section to gather ideas on how to get a job, gain entry into the area in which you are interested, and to excel in a current position.

When applying for any job always be as professional as possible. Dress neatly and conservatively Don't wear sneakers. Don't chew gum. Don't smoke. Don't wear heavy perfume or men's cologne.

Always have a few copies of your résumé with you. These, too, should look neat and professional. Have them typed and presented well, checked and rechecked for grammar, spelling, and content.

If asked to fill in an application, fill in the entire application even if you have a résumé with you. Print your information neatly.

When applying for jobs and filling in applications, be prepared. Make sure you know your Social Security number. Ask people *in advance* whether you can use them as references. Make sure you know their full names, addresses, and phone numbers. Secure at least three personal references and three professional references you can use.

The ability to go on-line, whether from your home computer or one in a school or public library, puts you at a great advantage. No matter which aspect of the gaming industry piques your interest, become computer literate. It is always a plus.

Many casinos, newspapers, and magazines now feature Web sites that may be helpful in your quest for that perfect job. You can obtain information about casinos and their current job opportunities, gaming news, or even the classified section from areas hosting gaming.

Be on time for everything. This includes job interviews, phone calls, meetings, work, and so forth. Habitual lateness will certainly have a negative effect on your prospects for career advancement.

The gaming industry is a mixture of the entertainment and hospitality industries. Customer service is essential to success in every job no matter what it is in this industry.

Imagine being able to love going to work every day! You have already taken the first step by picking up this book. Have fun reading it. Use it. It will help you prepare for a career you will enjoy and find rewarding for years to come.

Go after a job in this field, and you will find an exciting career that most only dream about. Good luck!

CAREER OPPORTUNITIES IN CASINO OPERATIONS AND THE GAMING AREA

CASINO MANAGER

CAREER PROFILE

Duties: Handling day-to-day casino operation; overseeing table games; supervising shift bosses and other casino management personnel; handling problems on the casino floor; taking care of customer complaints; promoting good customer service.

Alternative Titles(s): Manager

Salary Range: $65,000 to $150,000+

Employment Prospects: Fair

Best Geographical Location(s) for Position: Las Vegas, Reno, Laughlin, Lake Tahoe, Atlantic City, Biloxi, Baton Rouge, New Orleans, and Detroit offer most opportunities; other regions with land-based, riverboat, or Indian gaming facilities offer additional opportunities.

Prerequisites:

Education or Training—High school diploma or equivalent and dealers training; see text.

Experience and Qualifications—Extensive experience in gaming; state licensing required to work in gaming area.

Special Skills and Personality Traits—Supervisory skills; customer relations skills; organized; personable; knowledge of table games.

CAREER LADDER

```
┌──────────────────────────────────────┐
│   Casino Manager in Larger, More     │
│ Prestigious Casino or Vice President │
│       of Casino Operations           │
└──────────────────────────────────────┘

┌──────────────────────────────────────┐
│          Casino Manager              │
└──────────────────────────────────────┘

┌──────────────────────────────────────┐
│            Shift Boss                │
└──────────────────────────────────────┘
```

Position Description

The Casino Manager holds an important position in the casino. The individual is in charge of handling the day-to-day management of the gaming area.

In order to run efficiently, casinos have operating policies formulated by the board of directors, CEO, or president of the company with the assistance of the executive vice president and the vice president of casino operations. The Casino Manager helps administer these policies.

The Casino Manager is responsible for overseeing the management of the table games in the casino. The individual must make sure all games are played in accordance with federal and state governmental regulations. He or she must also assure that all casino procedures and rules are followed.

The Casino Manager is in charge of overseeing those working in the gaming area and supervising casino management personnel. Depending on the structure of the casino, these may include the assistant Casino Manager, casino operations manager, assistant casino operations manager, casino administrator, casino credit manager, and shift bosses.

The individual is expected to build a good working relationship with casino employees, an essential ability for maintaining employee loyalty to the casino.

Other responsibilities of the Casino Manager may include:

- Assuring the security and protection of casino bankroll
- Promoting customer relations
- Assisting in the implementation of credit policies
- Handling problems on the gaming floor
- Dealing with customer complaints

Salaries

There is a great range of salaries for casino managers depending on a number of variables. Individuals may earn between $65,000 and $150,000 or more annually. Factors affecting earnings include the experience, training, and responsibilities of the individual as well as the geographic location, size, and prestige of the specific casino. In some facilities, casino managers may also receive bonuses above their annual salary.

Employment Prospects

Most casinos employ Casino Managers. Those that do not usually have someone in a similar position with a different name handling the same responsibilities. Casino Managers often work the swing shift because that is the usually the busiest time in the casino. Individuals may be required to work other shifts when necessary as well as weekends and holidays.

Las Vegas, Reno, Laughlin, Lake Tahoe, Atlantic City, Biloxi, Baton Rouge, New Orleans, and Detroit offer the greatest number of job possibilities. Other employment settings may include casino hotels in other areas of Nevada, Mississippi, New York, Louisiana, Colorado, Connecticut, Illinois, Arizona, California, and other regions where gambling is legal.

Other regions hosting Indian gaming and land-based or riverboat gaming facilities offer additional opportunities. New casinos and casino hotels are constantly under construction. More casinos and casino hotels are also opening every year as areas legalize gambling.

Advancement Prospects

Casino Managers may climb the career ladder in a number of ways. Some individuals obtain experience and then locate similar jobs in larger or more prestigious casinos. Others are promoted to positions such as the vice president of casino operations.

Education and Training

As a rule, Casino Managers are expected to have a minimum of a high school diploma or the equivalent. Individuals usually are trained as dealers in dealers school or gaming academies. They then obtain on-the-job training and experience as they move up the career ladder as floorpersons, pit bosses, and shift bosses.

Experience/Skills/Personality Traits

Extensive experience working in the gaming industry is necessary for this position. As noted previously, most casino managers started out as dealers and then obtained experience as floorpersons, pit bosses, and shift bosses.

Casino Managers must have a total knowledge of table games. Supervisory skills are necessary. Communication skills are essential. Casino Managers must be personable people with the ability to promote good customer service. They must also be able to instill that ability in their employees.

Unions/Associations

There are no unions for Casino Managers. Individuals may obtain additional information from local gaming associations.

Tips for Entry

1. Job openings may be advertised in the classified sections of newspapers in areas hosting gaming. Look under classifications such as "Casinos/Gaming," "Casino Opportunities," "Casino Manager," or "Casinos."
2. Casinos often promote from within. Get experience as a floorperson, pit boss, and shift manager.
3. It is sometimes easier to seek employment as a Casino Manager in areas other than the gaming capitals.
4. Positions may be advertised on the Internet. They may be located via the home pages of casino hotels. They may also be found by doing a search of "Casino," "Casino Hotel," or "Gaming Job Opportunities."

DIRECTOR OF TABLE GAMES

CAREER PROFILE

Duties: Overseeing management of table games; supervising casino table staff; monitoring job performance of table staff; consulting and advising with management regarding casino.

Alternative Titles(s): Director of Games; Director of Tables

Salary Range: $60,000 to $95,000+

Employment Prospects: Fair

Best Geographical Location(s) for Position: Las Vegas, Reno, Laughlin, Lake Tahoe, Atlantic City, Biloxi, Baton Rouge, New Orleans, and Detroit offer most opportunities; other regions with land-based, riverboat, or Indian gaming facilities offer additional opportunities.

Prerequisites:

Education or Training—Training in table games and gaming; see text.

Experience and Qualifications—Supervisory experience in gaming; state licensing required to work in gaming area.

Special Skills and Personality Traits—Supervisory skills; management skills; communication skills.

CAREER LADDER

```
┌─────────────────────────────────┐
│  Director of Table Games at larger, │
│   more prestigious casino, or      │
│        Casino Manager              │
└─────────────────────────────────┘

┌─────────────────────────────────┐
│      Director of Table Games       │
└─────────────────────────────────┘

┌─────────────────────────────────┐
│           Pit Manager              │
└─────────────────────────────────┘
```

Position Description

The Director of Table Games is in charge of table gaming in the casino. This is an administrative position. Depending on the specific casino, the individual may also be referred to as the director of games or director of tables. Generally, there is one Director of Table Games in each casino.

The Director of Table Games is in charge of everything that goes on in the casino. The individual supervises the casino shift managers, who are directly under him or her, and has overall say involving the department. If there is a problem and it cannot be solved by the pit manager, the Director of Table Games must handle the situation.

The Director of Table Games is expected to supervise the casino table staff. He or she is also responsible for the scheduling and administration of the table game staff. As part of his or her job, the Director of Table Games must continually monitor job performance of the department staff.

There is a great deal of responsibility in this type of job. Some of the other responsibilities include:

- Consulting and advising management regarding the casino
- Handling employee problems
- Handling customer complaints
- Ensuring and maintaining that the gaming in the casino is within state regulations

Salaries

The Director of Table Games can earn between approximately $60,000 and $95,000 or more per year. Annual earnings for a Director of Table Games depend on the specific casino in which the individual is working, its size, prestige, and geographic location. Other variables might include the individual's experience and his or her responsibilities. Generally, individuals working in larger casinos in the gambling capitals will earn more than their counterparts in other areas.

Employment Prospects

Employment prospects are fair for those seeking positions as the Director of Table Games. The individual may find employment in casinos throughout the world. As noted previously, there is usually one Director of Table Games in each casino, so, while individuals may find employment in any casino in the world, most opportunities exist in areas where there are a large number of casinos.

Las Vegas, Reno, Laughlin, Lake Tahoe, Atlantic City, Biloxi, Baton Rouge, New Orleans, and Detroit offer the greatest number of job possibilities. Other employment settings may include casino hotels in other areas of Nevada, Mississippi, New York, Louisiana, Colorado, Connecticut, Illinois, Arizona, and California.

Other regions hosting Indian gaming and land-based or riverboat gaming facilities offer additional opportunities. New casinos and casino hotels are constantly under construction. More casinos and casino hotels are also opening every year as areas legalize gambling.

Advancement Prospects

A Director of Table Games in a casino may advance his or her career by locating a similar position in a larger or more prestigious casino. This would result in increased responsibilities and earnings. The individual might also climb the career ladder by either moving into a position as a general manager or a position in the corporate area.

Education and Training

As in many casino jobs, the Director of Table Games does not necessarily need a formal education in the profession. Many casinos just require a minimum of a high school diploma or a GED. However, they do require complete knowledge of the gaming industry. Many people who hold this job began as dealers. They started from the ground up and learned everything there was to know about table games.

Depending on the casino, some have their own training schools. In other situations, individuals can learn by attending a gaming institute. These are located throughout the country.

The Director of Table Games must be licensed in the state in which he or she works.

Experience/Skills/Personality Traits

The Director of Table Games must have a fair amount of experience in gaming with additional experience in a supervisory capacity. In many situations, the Director of Table Games had a prior job in the same casino as a shift manager.

Individuals need supervisory and administrative skills. In order to be effective, they also are required to have excellent verbal communications skills. Interpersonal skills are also needed. The Director of Table Games may be required to calm customers with complaints or deal with employee problems.

Unions/Associations

This is not a unionized position. The Director of Table Games may be a member of local gaming associations.

Tips for Entry

1. As most people in this type of position learn from the ground up, start off by getting skilled in dealing.
2. Casinos often recruit employees from gaming schools.
3. Positions for this type of job are often advertised in the newspaper classified section in areas where gaming is prevalent. Look under headings including "Director of Table Games," "Gaming," "Casinos," or "Table Games."
4. If you don't live in an area hosting gambling, consider subscribing to a newspaper in an area that does. You can also usually buy Sunday newspapers from different parts of the country in better bookstores and newspaper shops.

CREDIT MANAGER

CAREER PROFILE

Duties: Reviewing credit applications; creating and maintaining credit histories; supervising credit clerks; recommending credit limitations.

Alternative Titles(s): None

Salary Range: $25,000 to $45,000+

Employment Prospects: Good

Best Geographical Location(s) for Position: Las Vegas, Reno, Laughlin, Lake Tahoe, Atlantic City, Biloxi, Baton Rouge, New Orleans, and Detroit offer most opportunities; other regions with land-based, riverboat, or Indian gaming facilities offer additional opportunities.

Prerequisites:

Education or Training—Minimum of high school diploma or GED; training in general business and/or accounting may be required; see text.

Experience and Qualifications—Experience in credit or collections; state licensing required to work in gaming area.

Special Skills and Personality Traits—Supervisory skills; guest relations skills; communications skills; computer skills; diplomacy; tact.

CAREER LADDER

```
┌─────────────────────────────────┐
│ Casino Credit Supervisor or Director │
│        of Casino Credit          │
└─────────────────────────────────┘

┌─────────────────────────────────┐
│         Credit Manager           │
└─────────────────────────────────┘

┌─────────────────────────────────┐
│   Credit Clerk Shift Supervisor  │
└─────────────────────────────────┘
```

Position Description

A Credit Manager in a casino is in charge of various casino credit functions. This is an administrative position. Depending on the specific casino, the individual may also be referred to as a credit executive. The Credit Manager may report to the credit supervisor, the vice president of casino operations, or the assistant general manager or v.p. of general finance depending on the structure of the individual facility.

The structure of each casino is different. Sometimes there is one Credit Manager. In other facilities, there may be a Credit Manager for each shift.

When people visit casinos to gamble, they often request credit. They may, for example, ask for a certain amount of credit or a loan. The Credit Manager is expected to check out each person's credit rating or worthiness before extending a line of credit. This includes the available credit a person may have as well as a credit history. To do this, the Credit Manager may check computer credit sources, fax banks, or get information from other casinos. If the Credit Manager finds that an individual's credit is good, he or she will extend a line of credit to be used in the casino. The amount extended will depend on the credit manager's recommendations or evaluation. If the Credit Manager finds that an individual's credit is overextended, he or she must deny credit, and this must be done in a tactful manner.

There is a great deal of responsibility in this type of job. Some of the job functions include:

- Supervising credit clerks
- Monitoring job performance of the department staff
- Reviewing credit applications for completeness
- Creating and maintaining credit histories on guests

- Recommending credit limits based on credit checks
- Handling customer complaints regarding credit

Salaries

Casino credit managers can earn between $25,000 and $55,000 or more per year. Annual earnings depend on the specific casino the individual is working in, its size, prestige, and geographic location. Other variables include the individual's experience, responsibilities, training, and education. Generally, the larger or more prestigious the casino, the higher the earnings will be for this position.

Employment Prospects

Individuals may find employment in casinos throughout the world. Employment opportunities are good. This is an important job in every casino.

While individuals may find employment in any casino in the world, most opportunities exist in areas where there are a large number of casinos.

Las Vegas, Reno, Laughlin, Lake Tahoe, Atlantic City, Biloxi, Baton Rouge, New Orleans, and Detroit offer the greatest number of job possibilities. Other employment settings may include casino hotels in other areas of Nevada, Mississippi, New York, Louisiana, Colorado, Connecticut, Illinois, Arizona, and California.

Other regions hosting Indian gaming and land-based or riverboat gaming facilities offer additional opportunities. New casinos and casino hotels are constantly under construction. More casinos and casino hotels are also opening every year as areas legalize gambling.

Advancement Prospects

Casino Credit Managers can advance their careers by locating similar positions in larger or more prestigious casinos. They may also climb the career ladder by obtaining experience and becoming a credit supervisor or the director of casino credit.

Education and Training

Education and training requirements for Casino Credit Managers vary. In some positions, individuals need only have a high school diploma or GED and three to five years working in the credit or collection area. In other jobs, individuals may be required to have training in general business and/or accounting.

Many casino jobs also have on-the-job training programs. Some have their own in-house training programs. Community colleges, vocational technical schools, and gaming institutes throughout the country also offer training.

Individuals working in casinos must usually be licensed by the state in which they work.

Experience/Skills/Personality Traits

While the amount of experience varies, Casino Credit Managers are usually required to have a minimum of three to five years working in the credit or collection area. Supervisory experience is usually also required. Some facilities additionally require or prefer that applicants have cage or casino experience as well. There are Casino Credit Managers who started out working as slot booth cashiers and moved up to cage cashiers before working in the credit department. In other situations, the Credit Manager has worked as a credit clerk or credit clerk shift supervisor in the casino and been promoted from within.

Individuals need supervisory skills for this job. They must also have excellent verbal communication skills. Tact and diplomacy are also needed. Credit Managers should enjoy working with others and have good guest relations skills. Computer skills are necessary.

Unions/Associations

There are no bargaining unions for Casino Credit Managers. Individuals may belong to local gaming associations.

Tips for Entry

1. Look for a job as a credit clerk in a casino to obtain experience in this area.
2. Considering taking classes at a gaming institute to learn more about this job and to obtain a more thorough understanding of gaming.
3. If you do not live in an area hosting gambling and are thinking about moving, you might want to take a job working with a collection agency until you do. Ths will be good experience.
4. Positions for this type of job are often advertised in the newspaper classified section in areas where gaming is prevalent. Look under headings such as "Credit Manager," "Credit Executive," "Gaming," or "Casinos."
5. If you don't live in an area hosting gambling and are interested in looking for a job, consider subscribing to a newspaper in an area that does. You can also usually buy Sunday newspapers from different parts of the country in better bookstores and newspaper shops.
6. Positions are also advertised on the Internet. Put in search words including "Gaming," "Casinos," or the job title "Casino Credit Manager," or check out individual casino Web sites for employment listings.

CREDIT CLERK

CAREER PROFILE

Duties: Performing data entry; assisting in maintaining records; filing; answering phones.

Alternative Titles(s): Credit Person

Salary Range: $6.00 to $15.00+ per hour

Employment Prospects: Good

Best Geographical Location(s) for Position: Las Vegas, Reno, Laughlin, Lake Tahoe, Atlantic City, Biloxi, Baton Rouge, New Orleans, and Detroit offer most opportunities; other regions with land-based, riverboat, or Indian gaming facilities offer additional opportunities.

Prerequisites:

Education or Training—Minimum of high school diploma or GED; training requirements vary from no formal training to training in business and accounting; some casinos offer on-the-job training.

Experience and Qualifications—Experience in credit or financial environment helpful; state licensing required to work in gaming area.

Special Skills and Personality Traits—Computer skills; office skills; customer service skills; detail oriented; organized.

CAREER LADDER

```
┌─────────────────────────────┐
│    Credit Shift Manager      │
└─────────────────────────────┘

┌─────────────────────────────┐
│        Credit Clerk          │
└─────────────────────────────┘

┌─────────────────────────────┐
│  Credit or Collection Position in │
│       Other Industry         │
└─────────────────────────────┘
```

Position Description

The Casino Credit Clerk works in the casino's credit office. The individual is in charge of assisting others in the credit office perform their jobs. The Credit Clerk may report to the credit manager, Credit Clerk shift manager, or credit supervisor depending on the structure of the individual facility.

When people visit casinos to gamble, they often request a line of credit. In order to do this, they must visit the credit office and meet with a credit manager. The credit manager checks out each person's credit worthiness before extending a line of credit. There is often a great deal of paperwork involved in this task. The Credit Clerk takes care of this paperwork.

The individual is expected to handle general office duties. These include answering phones, filing, and typing correspondence. He or she may be required to organize incoming credit applications as well as perform data entry of information on credit applications.

Some of the other job functions include:

- Assisting credit manager with credit verifications
- Performing data entry of information for credit histories
- Processing completed credit applications
- Assisting in maintaining records and credit files

Salaries

As noted previously, credit clerks usually work on an hourly basis. They may earn between $6.00 and $15.00 per hour or more, depending on a number of variables. These include the specific casino in which the individual works as well as its size, prestige, and geographic location. Other factors may include the individual's responsibilities, training, and experience.

Generally, individuals working in larger casinos in the gambling capitals will earn higher salaries than their counterparts in smaller casinos or other geographic locations.

Employment Prospects

A Credit Clerk may find employment in casinos throughout the world. Employment opportunities are good. There are usually a number of credit clerks working in the credit office of every casino.

While individuals may find employment in any casino in the world, most opportunities exist in areas where there are a large number of casinos.

Las Vegas, Reno, Laughlin, Lake Tahoe, Atlantic City, Biloxi, Baton Rouge, New Orleans, and Detroit offer the greatest number of job possibilities. Other employment settings may include casino hotels in other areas of Nevada, Mississippi, New York, Louisiana, Colorado, Connecticut, Illinois, Arizona, and California.

Other regions hosting Indian gaming and land-based or riverboat gaming facilities or cruise ships offer additional opportunities. New casinos and casino hotels are constantly under construction. More casinos and casino hotels are also opening every year as areas legalize gambling.

Advancement Prospects

Credit Clerks working in casinos can climb the career ladder by obtaining experience. They may then land a position as a Credit Clerk shift supervisor. With more experience and training, individuals may also become a credit supervisor or the director of casino credit.

Education and Training

Education and training requirements for casino Credit Clerks vary. In some positions, individuals need only have a high school diploma or GED and three to five years working in the credit or collection area. In other jobs, individuals may be required to have training in general business and/or accounting. As in most jobs in casinos, experience may often be accepted in lieu of education.

Many casino jobs also have on-the-job training programs. Some have their own in-house training programs.

Community colleges, vocational technical schools, and gaming institutes throughout the country also offer training.

Individuals working in casinos must usually be licensed by the state in which they work.

Experience/Skills/Personality Traits

It is helpful for Credit Clerks to have some type of experience working in the credit or financial area. However, it is not always required.

Individuals need office and clerical skills for this position. They should be good on the phone and be able to use photocopy machines, faxes, and word processors. Data entry skills are essential. Organization is mandatory. Because individuals may deal with casino guests, customer relations skills are also important.

Unions/Associations

Casino Credit Clerks do not usually belong to any specific union. Contact a local community college offering courses in gaming, a gaming institute, or casino for more information on a job in this area.

Tips for Entry

1. The more you know and understand about the gaming industry and casinos in general, the more marketable you will be. Take a couple of classes at a gaming institute to learn more about the industry.
2. Positions for this type of job are often advertised in the newspaper classified section in areas hosting gaming. Look under headings such as "Credit Clerk," "Credit Department," "Gaming," or "Casinos."
3. If you don't live in an area hosting gambling and are interested in looking for a job, consider subscribing to a newspaper in an area that does. You can also usually buy Sunday newspapers from different parts of the country in better bookstores and newspaper shops.
4. Positions are also advertised on the Internet. Put in search words such as "Gaming," "Casinos," or the job title "Casino Credit Clerk."
5. Jobs in this area are often listed on casino job hotlines. These are frequently updated by recorded messages listing job availabilities. You can call each casino directly to get their job hotline phone number.

CAGE CASHIER

CAREER PROFILE

Duties: Perform accounting of casino cash and cash convertible inventory; redeem customers casino chips for cash; cash checks for customers; handle reconciliation of cage.

Alternative Titles(s): Cashier

Salary Range: $7.00 to $15.00+ per hour

Employment Prospects: Excellent

Best Geographical Location(s) for Position: Las Vegas, Reno, Laughlin, Lake Tahoe, Atlantic City, Biloxi, Baton Rouge, New Orleans, and Detroit offer most opportunities; other regions with land-based, riverboat, or Indian gaming facilities offer additional opportunities.

Prerequisites:
Education or Training—Minimum of high school diploma or GED; no formal training required.
Experience and Qualifications—Experience working in a bank or handling transactions with money is helpful. State licensing is required to work in the gaming area.
Special Skills and Personality Traits—Ability to count money accurately; money-handling skills; data entry skills; bookkeeping skills.

CAREER LADDER

```
┌─────────────────────────────────────┐
│ Casino Cage Cashier Supervisor or    │
│ Shift Manager                        │
└─────────────────────────────────────┘

┌─────────────────────────────────────┐
│ Cage Cashier                         │
└─────────────────────────────────────┘

┌─────────────────────────────────────┐
│ Entry Level Cashier in Other         │
│ Industry, or Employee in Bank        │
└─────────────────────────────────────┘
```

Position Description

The casino cage is similar to a bank. The Casino Cage Cashier position is similar to that of a teller in a bank. The cage is in charge of accounting for the financial activities that occur in the casino in each department for each shift.

The Cage Cashier issues money to the casino pits, hotel area restaurants, and bars. This money is used to handle customer sales in the gaming area, hotel, restaurants, and bars. Each department, in turn, sends their revenue to the Cage Cashier to be counted and verified. The Cage Cashiers then credit the correct department and place the monies in the cage cash inventory or a bank deposit.

Cage cashiers handle the issuance of credit to customers. They additionally are responsible for exchanging chips for money from customers who have won and want to "cash out" their chips.

The Casino Cage Cashier is responsible for a great deal of money. In addition to issuing money to casino departments the Casino Cage Cashier uses it to issue customer credits, to buy back chips, and to pay out jackpots.

The Casino Cage Cashier issues chips to the gaming tables. These transactions, too, must be recorded on fill slips or sheets so that the pit area can reimburse the cage to balance the transaction.

Casino Cage Cashiers are expected to count the casino bankroll or inventory as well as make an inventory of chips before and after each work shift. The Cage Cashier must perform an accounting *over* the entire casino bankroll or inventory. This includes money, chips, and markers, among other things. It also contains credits from those departments money has been issued to, debits from money received from other departments, and customer bank checks. All items that are cash or convertible back to cash are included when the accounting is taken.

Cage Cashiers record everything on paper. To do this, the individuals utilizes a cage cash count sheet as well as a bank control sheet. All information must be accounted for, recorded, and verified.

Other duties of the Cage Cashier may include:

- Redeeming chips or tokens that customers have won or have left over when they are done gambling
- Converting contents of Cage Cashier's drawer to cash currency in lieu of cash equivalents
- Obtaining currency fills from main banks if cage is running short
- Handling daily cage reconciliation for shift

Salaries

Hourly wages for casino Cage Cashiers can run from $7.00 to $15.00 or more depending on the specific casino in which the individual is working and the geographic location.

Employment Prospects

Because all casinos have Cage Cashiers, opportunities are excellent throughout the country, wherever casinos are located.

Cage Cashiers are usually hourly employees. Many casinos are open 24 hours a day and run in shifts. Individuals may work the day shift, swing shift or evening, graveyard shift, or overnight.

Shift hours may vary in different facilities. The day shift, for example, may run from 8 A.M. to 4 P.M., the swing shift from 4 P.M. to midnight, and the graveyard shift from midnight to 8 A.M. Some facilities may have overlapping shifts or different hours.

While individuals may find employment in any casino in the world, most opportunities exist in areas where there are a large number of casinos.

Las Vegas, Reno, Laughlin, Lake Tahoe, Atlantic City, Biloxi, Baton Rouge, New Orleans, and Detroit offer the greatest number of job possibilities. Other employment settings may include casino hotels in other areas of Nevada, Mississippi, New York, Louisiana, Colorado, Connecticut, Illinois, Arizona, and California.

Other regions hosting Indian gaming and land-based or riverboat gaming facilities or cruise ships offer additional opportunities. New casinos and casino hotels are constantly under construction. More casinos and casino hotels are also opening every year as areas legalize gambling.

Advancement Prospects

Casino Cage Cashiers can climb the career ladder by promotion to casino Cage Cashier supervisor or shift manager.

Education and Training

As in many jobs in casinos, the Casino Cage Cashier may receive on-the-job training. The individual might also attend gaming schools, academies, or institutes located throughout the country. These may be private or may be part of community colleges, four-year colleges, or universities. Many casinos also have their own training programs.

Cage Cashiers must be licensed in the state in which they work.

Experience/Skills/Personality Traits

Experience as a cashier or handling transactions with money is preferred for those seeking positions as Cage Cashiers. Money-handling and data entry skills are needed. The ability to count money accurately is essential.

Unions/Associations

While this may be a unionized position in a limited number of casinos, Cage Cashiers are not usually represented by any bargaining union. Individuals interested in a career in this field can get additional information by contacting casino human resources departments, gaming schools, institutes, or academies.

Tips for Entry

1. Stop by the human resources department of casinos to see if they have any job openings in this area.
2. Positions may be advertised in the classified section of newspapers in areas hosting gaming. Look under headings such as "Casinos/Gaming," "Casinos," or "Cage Cashier."
3. If you are not in an area hosting gaming, consider getting a short-term subscription to the newspaper in the area of your choice. The Sunday edition of many newspapers are also often available in larger bookstores.
4. Gaming is growing quickly throughout the country. You can often find an area building a gaming facility and get an application long before building is completed.
5. These jobs may be advertised on casino job hotlines. Call each casino to get their job hotline phone number.

HARD COUNT ATTENDANT

CAREER PROFILE

Duties: Collecting coins or electronic gaming device tokens; dropping coins into sorter; counting and accounting for coins; accounting for drop box contents.

Alternative Titles(s): Hard Count Specialists; Drop Box Counters

Salary Range: $8.00 to $16.00 per hour

Employment Prospects: Fair

Best Geographical Location(s) for Position: Las Vegas, Reno, Laughlin, Lake Tahoe, Atlantic City, Biloxi, Baton Rouge, New Orleans, and Detroit offer most opportunities; other regions with land-based, riverboat, or Indian gaming facilities offer additional opportunities.

Prerequisites:

Education or Training—No specialized training; high school diploma or equivalent preferred.

Experience and Qualifications—Experience requirements vary; state licensing required to work in casinos.

Special Skills and Personality Traits—Ability to count accurately; ability to lift heavy loads; ability to work in confined spaces; team player; money-handling skills.

CAREER LADDER

```
┌─────────────────────────────────┐
│  Assistant Hard Count or Hard   │
│      Count Supervisor           │
└─────────────────────────────────┘

┌─────────────────────────────────┐
│      Hard Count Attendant       │
└─────────────────────────────────┘

┌─────────────────────────────────┐
│          Entry Level            │
└─────────────────────────────────┘
```

Position Description

A great deal of money is gambled by customers every day in casinos. Thousands of coins are deposited daily in casino slot machines, games, and drop boxes. These coins must all be collected and counted. The employees who handle these duties are called Hard Count Attendants.

Hard Count Attendants may also be referred to as hard count specialists or drop box counters. They have a number of responsibilities. Hard count attendants must go to machines throughout the casino and empty the coins that have been deposited in them. Coins are collected in bags and placed on pushcarts. The Hard Count Attendants then move these into the count room or casino vault.

Once in the counting room, Hard Count Attendants lift the bags and drop them into coin sorters. Individuals then count all the coins.

Hard Count Attendants also are responsible for emptying drop boxes. Individuals usually record the contents of each

drop box separately. They then record other pertinent information such as the date, shift, and table number of each drop box. In this manner, an accurate report can be made of what was collected each day, from each box, the specific shift and table.

As in other areas of the casino, there are numerous security measures and controls associated with this type of job. Surveillance cameras constantly record workers to make sure Attendants count and account for every coin they collect. The count room is locked until the Hard Count Attendants bring in uncounted boxes. It is also locked when individuals are sorting and counting money. No unauthorized employees may enter the count room.

Hard Count Attendants usually work as part of a team. Individuals are required to empty the drop box in view of the surveillance cameras as well as in front of the other members of the team.

Hard Count Attendants count the total value of each coin denomination. Often, a second member of the team may recount. A third member must compare both numbers and verify they are the same. If they are not, attendants must recount until all numbers match.

In some casinos, electronic gaming device tokens are used in lieu of coins. In these settings, the hard count attendants are expected to perform similar duties with the electronic gaming device tokens instead of coins.

Additional duties of Hard Count Attendants include:

- Scaling wrapped coins
- Ensuring drop box contents are counted and accurately accounted for
- Signing reports to verify they are correct

Salaries

Hard Count Attendants are paid an hourly wage ranging from $8.00 to $16.00. Factors affecting earnings include the geographic location, size, and prestige of the specific casino or casino hotel as well as the experience of the individual.

Employment Prospects

Employment prospects are fair for this position. All casinos use Hard Count Attendants. Many casinos have only one daily count. To keep monies as secure as possible, this is usually done at night when fewer people are likely to be around. While various shifts may be available, the most common shift for this job is the graveyard or overnight shift.

While individuals may find employment in any casino in the world, most opportunities exist in areas where there are a large number of casinos.

Las Vegas, Reno, Laughlin, Lake Tahoe, Atlantic City, Biloxi, Baton Rouge, New Orleans, and Detroit offer the greatest number of job possibilities. Other employment settings may include casino hotels in other areas of Nevada, Mississippi, New York, Louisiana, Colorado, Connecticut, Illinois, Arizona, and California.

Other regions hosting Indian gaming and land-based or riverboat gaming facilities or cruise ships offer additional opportunities. New casinos and casino hotels are constantly under construction. More casinos and casino hotels are also opening every year as areas legalize gambling.

Advancement Prospects

Hard Count Attendants may advance their careers in a number of ways. Some individuals are promoted to supervisory positions such as the assistant hard count or hard count supervisor. Others may take one or more classes in accounting and move into the clerical end of the department. Hard Count Attendants may also move into cage cashier positions.

Education and Training

There is no specialized training for this position. Most casinos and casino hotels prefer their Hard Count Attendants have a high school diploma or equivalent. Many casinos will assist employees in obtaining a GED if they do not have the minimum education.

Experience/Skills/Personality Traits

Depending on the specific casino, this may be an entry level job or may require some experience in the hard count area. One of the most important qualifications of Hard Count Attendants is the ability to count coins accurately and precisely. Individuals must be able to lift heavy loads of coins. These are often 100 pounds or more. Hard Count Attendants should be team players. They must work easily with others.

Unions/Associations

Hard Count Attendants are usually not unionized. Those interested in learning more about careers in this field should contact the human resources department of casinos.

Tips for Entry

1. Stop by casino human resources departments to inquire about job openings.
2. Jobs may be advertised in the classified sections of newspapers in areas hosting gaming. Look under classifications such as "Casinos/Gaming," "Hard Count Attendant," "Hard Count Team Member," "Drop Box Counter," "Hard Count Specialist," or "Casino/Hotel Opportunities."
3. Openings are also often advertised on the Internet. They may be located via the home pages of casino hotels. Jobs may also be found doing a search of casino or casino hotel job opportunities. Look under key words in employment or career pages such as "Casinos," "Gaming," "Hospitality," "Entertainment," or "Hard Count Attendant."
4. Casino job fairs also may feature these jobs.

EXECUTIVE CASINO HOST

CAREER PROFILE

Duties: Greeting guests; answering questions regarding players' club memberships; developing special promotions to bring in groups.

Alternative Titles(s): Executive Host; Host

Salary Range: $25,000 to $55,000+

Employment Prospects: Good

Best Geographical Location(s) for Position: Las Vegas, Reno, Laughlin, Lake Tahoe, Atlantic City, Biloxi, Baton Rouge, New Orleans, and Detroit offer most opportunities; other regions with land-based, riverboat, or Indian gaming facilities offer additional opportunities.

Prerequisites:

Education or Training—Minimum of high school diploma or GED; see text.

Experience and Qualifications—Experience dealing with the public and working in casino environment; state licensing required to work in gaming area.

Special Skills and Personality Traits—Communications skills; organizational skills; promotional ability; interpersonal skills; customer relations skills; enthusiasm; enjoys dealing with public.

CAREER LADDER

```
┌─────────────────────────────────┐
│    Executive Casino Host at Larger, │
│  More Prestigious Casino, or Executive │
│     or Administrative Positions    │
│          Within Casino            │
└─────────────────────────────────┘

┌─────────────────────────────────┐
│       Executive Casino Host       │
└─────────────────────────────────┘

┌─────────────────────────────────┐
│           Casino Host             │
└─────────────────────────────────┘
```

Position Description

The gaming industry is in large part a people business. There are many casinos that people can visit. Each casino tries to be the most hospitable to their clientele. The Executive Casino Host is in charge of welcoming guests to the facility.

This is usually a salaried position. It is the perfect job for someone who is friendly, likes people, enjoys socializing, and is good at it. The Executive Casino Host meets and greet customers who come to the casino. The individual has a high-visibility job. He or she walks around the casino, talks to guests, and answers questions regarding the facility.

Casinos often welcome people who are known in the industry as "high rollers," people who spend a great deal of money gambling in the casino. The Executive Casino Host is in charge of meeting with these individuals. When people spend a lot of money in casinos, the facility often "comps" goods or services for these individuals. (Comp is short for complimentary and means that the casino provides these items or services free.) A casino may, for example, comp rooms, meals, or drinks, depending on how much an individual is spending in the casino. The Executive Casino Host is often responsible for tracking the high rollers, who are also known as high-limit customers. He or she can then authorize the complimentary amenities.

In addition to meeting with everyday casino customers and high-limit guests, the Executive Casino Host is in charge of meeting and greeting celebrities who visit the facility and gamble, stay at the hotel, or perform in the casino's showroom or nightclub.

In order to build up traffic in casinos, most facilities maintain players' clubs. These clubs offer various amenities and specials to people who are members. The Executive

Casino Host is expected to attend players' club functions and events designed to attract and keep members. As part of the duties of this job, the individual may explain players' club membership to new members.

The Executive Casino Host holds an important job in the casino. Some of the other job functions of the individual include:

- Assisting in the development of special promotions, events, and functions to attract new members to the players' club
- Assisting customers and players' club members with dinner and show arrangements
- Providing other guest services
- Answering questions regarding the casino

Salaries

Annual earnings vary from approximately $25,000 to $55,000 or more depending on a number of variables. These include the specific casino in which the individual works as well as its size, prestige, and geographic location. Other factors may include the individual's responsibilities, training, and experience.

Generally, individuals working in larger casinos in the major gambling capitals have higher earnings than their counterparts in smaller casinos or those in other geographic locations.

Employment Prospects

Casinos usually have a number of Executive Casino Hosts on staff. In many facilities there is one for each shift. Executive Casino Hosts may find employment in casinos throughout the world. Employment opportunities are good for qualified people.

While individuals may find employment in any casino in the world, most opportunities exist in areas where there are a large number of casinos.

Advancement Prospects

There are a number of different paths Executive Casino Hosts can take to career advancement. Some individuals obtain experience and move on to similar positions in larger or more prestigious facilities, resulting in increased responsibilities and earnings.

Other Executive Casino Hosts climb the career ladder by finding administrative or management positions in player development or other casino operations.

Education and Training

Education and training requirements for Executive Casino Hosts vary depending on the specific facility. The educational requirement for some positions is a high school diploma or GED. Other facilities prefer that their employees in this position have gone through some sort of formal training. As in most jobs in casinos, experience may often be accepted in lieu of education. In this instance, experience dealing with the public would be extremely helpful.

Many casinos have on-the-job training programs. Some have their own in-house training programs. Community colleges, vocational technical schools, and gaming institutes throughout the country also offer training useful to jobs in the gaming industry.

Individuals working in casinos must be licensed by the state in which they work.

Experience/Skills/Personality Traits

The ideal candidate for this job will have had extensive experience dealing with the public as well as experience working in casinos in some capacity. Many Executive Casino Hosts were promoted from the position of casino host. Others worked in other areas of gaming.

A variety of skills are needed to be successful in this area. Customer service skills top the list. Individuals should be friendly, enthusiastic people who enjoy socializing with guests.

Excellent communications skills are essential. Organization skills are also helpful. A good memory for faces and names can be useful.

Unions/Associations

Usually this is not a unionized position. Individuals interested in learning more about this type of job should contact casinos or a local gaming institute, academy, or college offering classes in gaming.

Tips for Entry

1. Get experience dealing with the public by working as a receptionist or host in a restaurant or in customer service in retail.
2. The more you know and understand about the gaming industry and casinos in general, the more marketable you will be. Take classes at a gaming institute to learn more about the industry.
3. Positions for this type of job are often advertised in the newspaper classified section in areas hosting gaming. Look under headings such as "Executive Casino Host," "Casino Host," "Gaming," "Player Development," or "Casinos."
4. If you don't live in an area hosting gambling and are interested in looking for a job, consider subscribing to a newspaper in an area that does. You can usually buy Sunday newspapers from different parts of the country in better bookstores and newspaper shops.

CASINO HOST

CAREER PROFILE

Duties: Greeting guests; issuing and awarding comps and amenities; handling customer requests; handling customer relations; giving special treatment to guests.

Alternative Titles(s): Host

Salary Range: $23,000 to $48,000+

Employment Prospects: Good

Best Geographical Location(s) for Position: Las Vegas, Reno, Laughlin, Lake Tahoe, Atlantic City, Biloxi, Baton Rouge, New Orleans, and Detroit offer most opportunities; other regions with land-based, riverboat, or Indian gaming facilities offer additional opportunities.

Prerequisites:

Education or Training—Minimum of high school diploma or GED; no formal training required; on-the-job training may be offered.

Experience and Qualifications—Experience dealing with the public and working in casino environment; state licensing required to work in gaming area.

Special Skills and Personality Traits—Communications skills; organizational skills; personable; customer service skills; interpersonal skills; enthusiastic; enjoys dealing with public.

CAREER LADDER

```
┌─────────────────────────────────────┐
│ Casino Host in Larger, More Prestigious │
│   Casino or Executive Casino Host    │
└─────────────────────────────────────┘

┌─────────────────────────────────────┐
│           Casino Host               │
└─────────────────────────────────────┘

┌─────────────────────────────────────┐
│ Other Position in Casino or Position in │
│  Other Industry Dealing With Public  │
└─────────────────────────────────────┘
```

Position Description

Many casino customers choose a facility by the type of service they receive. The gaming industry, like others in the hospitality industry, is a people business. Casinos cater to guests in order to attract and keep them.

Casino Hosts are individuals who offer a variety of services to guests to make their stay more enjoyable. Responsibilities of Casino Hosts vary, depending on the specific casino and its structure.

Casino Hosts are responsible for providing special treatment to preferred guests, high rollers, high-limit guests, VIPs and invited guests, and celebrities. They may also provide special services for day-to-day customers.

Casino Hosts meet and greet customers at the casino. In some casinos, an executive casino host handles VIP guests and celebrities who visit the casino.

Casino Hosts are highly visible. They walk around the casino, answer questions, and talk to guests to make them feel good about being there.

Sometimes customers call Casino Hosts before a visit and request they make room reservations for them. Hosts are then responsible for obtaining the type of rooms with the amenities needed for the guest.

It is imperative to the success of the casino to keep all guests happy, especially premium customers and high rollers. Casino Hosts may assist premium guests in any number of ways, including securing accommodation, making dinner reservations, obtaining tickets to entertainment events, coordinating visits to the health club or spa, and so forth.

When people spend a great deal of money in casinos, the facility often "comps" goods or services for these individuals. (*Comp* is short for *complimentary* and means that the casino provides these items or services free.) The Casino Host may comp an array of amenities, including rooms, meals, drinks, or tickets to shows. The comps generally depend on the amount an individual is spending in the casino. The Casino Host can track the amount being spent by customers in order to know what type of comps should be authorized.

Casinos often maintain players' clubs designed to bring in and keep customers and build traffic. Membership entitles guests to various amenities, specials, and promotions. Casino Hosts are expected to explain players' clubs to guests and answer any questions they may have regarding membership.

Successful Casino Hosts keep in contact with their customers. They may invite them to parties and other special functions at the casino. Casino Hosts may call or write to customers to tell them about special promotions. Individuals may also send notes to guests who have visited the casino, thanking them for their business. These activities keep contact with premium guests and make sure they come back to the facility.

Casino Hosts may also be responsible for:

- Attending players' club functions
- Meeting and greeting individual bus tours and other groups entering the casino
- Authorizing rim credit, credit issued at the rim of the gaming table, for premium guests
- Providing special guest services
- Obtaining reservations for guests at either their casino or another casino hotel's restaurants or entertainment facilities

Salaries

Annual earnings vary from approximately $23,000 to $48,000 or more depending on a number of variables, including the specific casino in which the individual works as well as its size, prestige, and geographic location. Other factors may include the individual's responsibilities and experience.

Generally, individuals working in larger casinos in the major gambling capitals have higher earnings than their counterparts in smaller casinos or those in other geographic locations.

Employment Prospects

Employment opportunities are good for enthusiastic, outgoing individuals interested in jobs as Casino Hosts. While individuals may find employment in any casino in the world, most opportunities exist in areas where there are a large number of casinos.

Advancement Prospects

There are a number of different paths Casino Hosts take to career advancement. Some individuals obtain experience

and move on to similar positions in larger or more prestigious facilities, resulting in increased earnings. Other Casino Hosts climb the career ladder by promotion to the position of casino executive host.

Education and Training

Education and training requirements for Casino Hosts vary depending on the specific facility. The educational requirement for most positions is a high school diploma or the equivalent. As in most jobs in casinos, experience may often be accepted in lieu of education.

Many casinos have on-the-job training programs. Some have their own in-house training programs. Community colleges, vocational technical schools, and gaming institutes throughout the country also offer training useful to jobs in this industry.

Experience/Skills/Personality Traits

In this position, experience dealing with the public is extremely helpful. Most Casino Hosts held prior jobs in the gaming industry.

Casino Hosts should be enthusiastic, friendly, personable people with customer service skills. Individuals should enjoy socializing with others. Hosts should be articulate people with good communications skills. The ability to remember names and faces is essential.

Individuals working in casinos must usually be licensed by the state in which they work.

Unions/Associations

Contact casinos or a local gaming institute, academy, or college offering classes in gaming for more information on a job in this area. Individuals might also belong to local gaming associations in their area.

Tips for Entry

1. The more you know and understand about the gaming industry, the more marketable you will be. Consider taking one or more classes at a gaming institute or academy to learn more about the industry.
2. Positions for this type of job are often advertised in the newspaper classified in areas hosting gaming. Look under "Casinos/Gaming," "Casino Hosts," "Gaming," or "Player Development."
3. If you don't live in an area hosting gambling and are interested in looking for a job, consider subscribing to a newspaper in an area that does.
4. Many casinos have job hotlines advertising job availabilities. Call each casino to get its job hotline number.

PIT MANAGER

CAREER PROFILE

Duties: Overseeing pit area; assuring games are run smoothly; supervising operation of games; mediating disputes; opening and closing table games.

Alternative Titles(s): Pit Boss

Salary Range: $35,000 to $75,000+

Employment Prospects: Good

Best Geographical Location(s) for Position: Las Vegas, Reno, Laughlin, Lake Tahoe, Atlantic City, Biloxi, Baton Rouge, New Orleans, and Detroit offer most opportunities; other regions with land-based, riverboat, or Indian gaming facilities offer additional opportunities.

Prerequisites:

Education or Training—Training at gaming academy, school, or institute.

Experience and Qualifications—Experience as floorperson or boxperson; state licensing required to work in gaming area; additional licensing requirements may be necessary.

Special Skills and Personality Traits—Supervisory skills; customer service skills; alert; knowledge of specific games in pit.

CAREER LADDER

```
┌─────────────────────────────────────┐
│   Pit Manager in Larger, More        │
│  Prestigious Casino, or Shift Manager│
└─────────────────────────────────────┘

┌─────────────────────────────────────┐
│            Pit Manager               │
└─────────────────────────────────────┘

┌─────────────────────────────────────┐
│      Floorperson or Boxperson        │
└─────────────────────────────────────┘
```

Position Description

There is a lot of action on the casino gaming floor. The gaming area is usually separated into pits or groups of tables. The person in charge of overseeing the pit is called the Pit Manager.

A pit may consist of tables of one specific game such as craps or blackjack, or may have tables of different types of games grouped together. The Pit Manager must have an understanding of the games he or she is overseeing.

The Pit Manager works under the direction of the shift manager. The individual has a variety of responsibilities. First and foremost, the Pit Manager is expected to supervise the games in the pit and be sure they run smoothly. Games must be run properly and according to the policies of the casino. The Pit Manager must assure that regulations and procedures of the games are followed.

Pit Managers are in charge of pit personnel. Individuals are responsible for the conduct of employees in their pit. Pit Managers are expected to watch dealers to make sure they are dealing properly and not making mistakes. Pit Managers watch for any cheating on the part of dealers or other employees in the pit. Pit Managers are additionally responsible for scheduling the breaks for all pit personnel.

The Pit Manager must be alert to players attempting to cheat the casino in any way. The individual watches players who seem more skilled than others, such as those who count blackjack cards.

Pit Managers deal with a certain amount of paperwork in the pit. This includes making out and authorizing cash-outs, fill, or credit slips. Individuals are also responsible for watching the play of high rollers and may award comps to players.

Other duties of the Pit Manager include:

- Settling disputes between players and casino employees
- Handling customer problems and complaints
- Calming down agitated customers
- Greeting players
- Opening and closing gaming tables

Salaries

Pit Managers are usually paid a weekly salary instead of an hourly wage. This can range between $35,000 and $75,000 or more annually. Factors affecting earnings include the geographic location, size, and prestige of the casino as well as the responsibilities and experience of the individual. Those with more experience working in large facilities in the gambling capitals may earn more than their counterparts in other areas.

Employment Prospects

Employment prospects are good for Pit Managers. Opportunities are available for qualified Pit Managers throughout the country or the world in a variety of settings. The greatest number of opportunities exist in areas where there are a large number of casinos.

Las Vegas, Reno, Laughlin, Lake Tahoe, Atlantic City, Biloxi, Baton Rouge, New Orleans, and Detroit offer the greatest number of job possibilities. Other employment settings may include casino hotels in other areas of Nevada, Mississippi, New York, Louisiana, Colorado, Connecticut, Illinois, Arizona, and California.

Other regions hosting Indian gaming and land-based or riverboat gaming facilities or cruise ships offer additional opportunities. New casinos and casino hotels are constantly under construction. More casinos and casino hotels are also opening every year as areas legalize gambling.

Advancement Prospects

Pit Managers can advance in two ways. After obtaining experience, some individuals locate similar positions in larger or more prestigious casinos, resulting in increased earnings. The other option for career advancement for Pit Managers is becoming a shift manager.

Education and Training

Pit Managers in casinos start out as dealers. They generally have gone through dealer training at gaming schools, academies, or institutes. Others have had similar training in community colleges, vocational technical schools, or casinos themselves. Some individuals have also taken casino-related training programs in-house to help prepare them for supervisory positions.

Pit Managers, like all others working in the gaming area, must be licensed by the state gaming agency in the specific state in which they work. They may also be required to meet additional licensing requirements.

Experience/Skills/Personality Traits

Experience in the gaming industry is necessary to become a Pit Manager. Individuals usually start out as dealers and move up to positions as boxpersons, floorpersons, or pit supervisors prior to becoming Pit Managers.

Pit Managers must be extremely alert so that they can watch everything that is going on in their pit. Supervisory and administrative skills are also necessary. A complete knowledge of the rules and procedures of the games in their pit is essential. Familiarity with the rules of the casino is also mandatory.

Unions/Associations

Individuals interested in learning more about careers in this area can contact gaming institutes, academies, and schools, as well as casino human resources departments. They may also belong to local gaming associations.

Tips for Entry

1. The more knowledgeable you are about a variety of games, and the more games you have experience with, the more marketable you will be.
2. Opportunities may be easier to obtain for individuals with less experience in casinos outside of the major gambling capitals of Las Vegas and Atlantic City.
3. Jobs are often advertised in the classified sections of newspapers in areas hosting gaming. Look under classifications such as "Casinos," "Casino Jobs," "Casino Opportunities," "Casino Executive," "Pit Manager," or "Gaming."
4. Visit the human resources department of casinos to inquire about job openings.
5. Look for new casinos under construction. Apply early.
6. Positions may be advertised on the Internet. Look under key words such as "Casinos," "Casino Jobs," "Gaming," or "Pit Manager." Many casino and casino hotel home pages also have employment opportunity sections.

PIT CLERK

CAREER PROFILE

Duties: Handling data entry; recording rim-credit transactions; communicating with cage, pit boss, and floor supervisors; updating players' credit standing; handling clerical duties.

Alternative Title(s): None

Salary Range: $13,000 to $19,000

Employment Prospects: Good

Best Geographical Location(s) for Position: Las Vegas, Reno, Laughlin, Lake Tahoe, Atlantic City, Biloxi, Baton Rouge, New Orleans, and Detroit offer most opportunities; other regions with land-based, riverboat, or Indian gaming facilities offer additional opportunities.

Prerequisites:

Education or Training—High school diploma or equivalent preferred; no formal training requirements; on-the-job training offered.

Experience and Qualifications—No experience necessary; state licensing required to work in gaming area; additional licensing requirements may be necessary.

Special Skills and Personality Traits—Data entry skills; clerical skills; detail-oriented.

CAREER LADDER

```
┌─────────────────────────────────────┐
│  Casino Cage Cashier or Pit Manager  │
└─────────────────────────────────────┘

┌─────────────────────────────────────┐
│              Pit Clerk               │
└─────────────────────────────────────┘

┌─────────────────────────────────────┐
│             Entry Level              │
└─────────────────────────────────────┘
```

Position Description

The gaming area is usually separated into pits or groups of tables. There are a number of different employees in the pit. These include dealers, pit bosses, supervisors, floorpeople, and Pit Clerks. The main function of the Pit Clerk is to sit in front of a computer terminal and input relevant data.

Pit Clerks handle a number of duties. They are responsible for recording rim-credit transactions. This type of credit is called rim because it is issued to players at the rim of a gaming table. Rim credit allows players to begin gambling without going to the cage to write a check to the casino. When rim credit is issued by a floorperson or pit boss, they notify the Pit Clerk to record the information in the pit terminal computer.

The casino must maintain records on the credit standings of individual casino customers. As new information becomes available, when customers request credit, the Pit Clerk is responsible for updating this data in the pit computer.

The individual often communicates with the cage cashier to get this and other information. Pit Clerks are expected to file all IOUs issued to players by casino executives. When players pay off IOUs at the cage, Pit Clerks are informed so they can input the new data into the terminal. In this way the documentation will balance at the end of the shift.

Other duties of the Pit Clerk may include:

- Tracking player ratings
- Reporting and keeping track of comps awarded by floorpersons or pit bosses
- Answering pit telephones
- Handling additional clerical duties

Salaries

Pit Clerks earn an hourly wage ranging from approximately $6.00 to $9.00, or roughly $13,000 to $19,000 for full-time clerks. Factors affecting earnings include the geographic location, size, and prestige of the casino as well as the experience of the individual.

Employment Prospects

Employment prospects are good for Pit Clerks. Opportunities are readily available in casinos throughout the country or the world. As casinos are often open 24 hours a day, individuals may work any shift. They may also be expected to work weekends or holidays.

While individuals may find employment in any casino in the world. the greatest number of opportunities exist in areas where there are a large number of casinos.

Las Vegas, Reno, Laughlin, Lake Tahoe, Atlantic City, Biloxi, Baton Rouge, New Orleans, and Detroit offer the greatest number of job possibilities. Other employment settings may include casino hotels in other areas of Nevada, Mississippi, New York, Louisiana, Colorado, Connecticut, Illinois, Arizona, and California.

Other regions hosting Indian gaming and land-based or riverboat gaming facilities or cruise ships offer additional opportunities. New casinos and casino hotels are constantly under construction. More casinos and casino hotels are also opening every year as areas legalize gambling.

Advancement Prospects

In many instances, Pit Clerks positions are entry-level jobs, a way to get a foot in the door of the casino. Individuals may move up to positions working in the cage of the casino handling money and chips. Pit Clerks may also be promoted to pit managers.

Education and Training

Casinos prefer that Pit Clerks have a high school diploma or the equivalent. Many casinos will help individuals who do not have either the diploma or the equivalent obtain a GED.

There is no formal training for Pit Clerks. However, casinos usually offer on-the-job training for this position.

Pit Clerks, like all others in the gaming industry, are licensed by the state gaming agency in the specific state in which they work.

Experience/Skills/Personality Traits

As noted previously, this is often an entry-level job, no experience is needed. Pit Clerks must have computer and data entry skills. A number of different computer software programs are used, so it is not necessary to be familiar with all software.

Unions/Associations

While there may be a limited number of casinos throughout the country where this is a unionized position, generally Pit Clerks are not represented by unions. Individuals interested in learning more about careers in this area can contact casino human resources departments. Pit Clerks may be members of local gaming associations.

Tips for Entry

1. Jobs are often advertised in the classified sections of newspapers in areas hosting gaming. Look under classifications such as "Casinos," "Casino Jobs," "Casino/Gaming Opportunities," or "Pit Clerk."
2. Visit the human resources department of casinos to inquire about job openings.
3. Most casinos have job hotlines. These are frequently updated messages listing job availabilities. You can call each casino directly to obtain its job hotline phone number.
4. Look for new casinos under construction. Apply early.
5. Positions may be advertised on the Internet. Look under key words such as "Casinos," "Casino Jobs," "Gaming," or "Pit Clerks." Many casino and casino hotel home pages also have employment opportunity sections.

FLOORPERSON

Duties: Overseeing table games and dealers.

Alternative Title(s): None

Salary Range: $30,000 to $40,000+

Employment Prospects: Fair

Best Geographical Location(s) for Position: Las Vegas, Reno, Laughlin, Lake Tahoe, Atlantic City, Biloxi, Baton Rouge, New Orleans, and Detroit offer most opportunities; other regions with land-based, riverboat, or Indian gaming facilities offer additional opportunities.

Prerequisites:

Education or Training—Dealer training at accredited gaming institute, academy, or college.

Experience and Qualifications—Experience as a dealer; state licensing required to work in casinos.

Special Skills and Personality Traits—Supervisory skills; alert; understanding of table games.

```
┌─────────────────────────────┐
│    Assistant Shift Boss      │
└─────────────────────────────┘

┌─────────────────────────────┐
│        Floorperson           │
└─────────────────────────────┘

┌─────────────────────────────┐
│          Dealer              │
└─────────────────────────────┘
```

Position Description

A great deal of overseeing and supervision makes certain that everything that occurs in the casino area is watched and videotaped by banks of surveillance cameras. This protects both the casino and the player from possible cheating, stealing, or mistakes. In addition to surveillance cameras, several individuals oversee the games and the people who run the action.

Dealers in casinos work in what are known as pits. A Floorperson is the first-level supervisor in a pit. This is a management position.

The Floorperson supervises and oversees the dealers in his or her pit. for example, a blackjack pit consists of four tables and utilizes five dealers. The Floorperson oversees the four tables and the five dealers. In a pit with 16 tables, there would be four floorpeople.

The individual is in charge of overseeing the conduct of the games and the dealers. The Floorperson makes sure the dealers are not making mistakes and are running the games fairly. He or she is expected to check that the dealers are operating properly, counting accurately, and giving the proper payoffs. The individual must also check to see that bets are in place at the correct time. As part of the job, the Floorperson is additionally required to be on the lookout for patrons who attempt to cheat.

If there are any disputes between customers and dealers, the Floorperson is responsible for arbitrating the problem. He or she may take customers names, as well track players' wins and losses. In some cases, the Floorperson may be required to go to a higher-level supervisor to settle the dispute. In other cases, the individual might just have to explain the rules of the game, the house, or the table to customers.

Depending on the specific casino, the Floorperson may have other duties. Dealers usually work for an hour and then break. The Floorperson is in charge of coordinating the scheduling of dealers. At times, the Floorperson may replace a dealer with a relief person if the dealer seems to be on a losing streak. Other responsibilities may include:

• Overseeing the conduct of games played at his or her tables

- Making sure rules and regulations of the gaming commission are followed
- Knowing the specific rules of the house and the table

Salaries

Because a Floorperson is considered part of the management team, he or she will usually be on salary. Individuals may have annual earnings ranging from $35,000 to $40,000 or more. Variables affecting salaries include the geographic location of the casino as well as the size and prestige of the facility. Other factors include the experience of the individual. While Floorpeople do not make tips, this position is the first step to a higher-paying management position.

Employment Prospects

Employment prospects are good for Floorpersons. Individuals are needed to oversee a variety of casino table games, including blackjack, craps, roulette, and keno. Positions may be located in all casinos hosting table games.

While individuals may find employment in any casino in the world, the greatest number of opportunities exist in areas where there are a large number of casinos.

Las Vegas, Reno, Laughlin, Lake Tahoe, Atlantic City, Biloxi, Baton Rouge, New Orleans, and Detroit offer the greatest number of job possibilities. Other employment settings include casino hotels in other areas of Nevada, Mississippi, New York, Louisiana, Colorado, Connecticut, Illinois, Arizona, and California.

Other regions hosting Indian gaming and land-based or riverboat gaming facilities offer additional opportunities. New casinos and casino hotels are constantly under construction. More casinos and casino hotels are also opening every year as areas legalize gambling.

Advancement Prospects

Floorpeople may advance their careers by obtaining experience and promotion to assistant shift boss, pit administrator, or pit boss, depending on the casino and game.

Education and Training

Floorpeople must usually be trained in dealing. Training requirements for Floorpeople vary depending on the specific state and casino. In certain areas, the Floorperson must be a graduate of an accredited gaming institute, academy, or dealer's school in order to get a job. In other areas, this training may not be required, but preferred. It is recommended that people interested in aspiring to a career in this field get formal training.

Floorpeople, like all others working in casinos, must be licensed in the state in which they work. Standards and regulations differ from state to state.

Experience/Skills/Personality Traits

The Floorperson must have prior dealing experience. Individuals should have supervisory skills. A complete knowledge and understanding of the rules of the games the individual supervises is essential.

Unions/Associations

Floorpeople do not usually belong to a union. Individuals may belong to local gaming associations and organizations geared to those in the casino industry.

Tips for Entry

1. Because Floorpeople must be dealers first, get trained in as many games as possible. This will make you more marketable.
2. Get job experience as a dealer. Many casinos promote from within.
3. Positions in this field are advertised in the newspaper classified section in areas hosting gambling facilities. Look under heading classifications such as "Floorperson," "Casinos," "Casino Jobs," or "Gaming."
4. Look for new casinos that are under construction. Get an application early.

BOXPERSON

CAREER PROFILE

Duties: Assuring crap game is run smoothly; supervising operation of craps table; overseeing conduct of craps dealers; mediating disputes; controlling chips.

Alternative Title(s): Boxman; Boxwoman

Salary Range: $30,000 to $55,000+

Employment Prospects: Good

Best Geographical Location(s) for Position: Las Vegas, Reno, Laughlin, Lake Tahoe, Atlantic City, Biloxi, Baton Rouge, New Orleans, and Detroit offer most opportunities; other regions with land-based, riverboat, or Indian gaming facilities offer additional opportunities.

Prerequisites:

Education or Training—Training at gaming academies, dealer schools or institutes; see text.

Experience and Qualifications—Experience as dealer and/or floorperson; state licensing required to work in gaming area.

Special Skills and Personality Traits—Supervisory skills; customer service skills; alert; knowledge of craps.

CAREER LADDER

```
┌─────────────────────────────────┐
│   Boxperson at Larger or More    │
│ Prestigious Casino or Pitboss    │
└─────────────────────────────────┘

┌─────────────────────────────────┐
│           Boxperson             │
└─────────────────────────────────┘

┌─────────────────────────────────┐
│      Dealer or Floorperson       │
└─────────────────────────────────┘
```

Position Description

Craps is a fast, interesting, and exciting game in casinos because it is one of the games in which people can win or lose a great deal of money in a very short time. Craps is a game in which dice are thrown. Players often become very loud when this is occurring.

Craps tables are staffed with four dealers, one of whom is a replacement dealer. The table also has a Boxperson. Sometimes the action at a craps table is so hot and heavy there may be two side-by-side Boxpersons required. In these cases, each Boxperson will be in charge of one side of the tables. Although women may be employed in the Boxperson position, the job has in the past been referred to as a boxman.

The Boxperson is a casino executive who holds an important job at the craps table. He or she is the only executive in the casino who works at a gaming table. The individual has a number of responsibilities. The Boxperson is responsible for assuring that the game is run smoothly. The individual is in charge of overseeing the entire operation of the craps table and supervising the game. While dealers are expected to wear uniforms, the Boxperson usually wears a suit or sports jacket.

Originally, the Boxperson sat on a wooden crate or box and thereby acquired the name. Today, the Boxperson sits on a stool in the center of the craps table and remains seated during the course of the game.

The chips are stored directly in front of the Boxperson, who controls the casino chips during the game, thus protecting the casino's bankroll. The Boxperson is responsible for supplying chips to the dealers. He or she will also take back chips from dealers when they accumulate in front of them, and put them back in the casino's bankroll.

When customers want to buy chips, the Boxperson is in charge of collecting and counting the money. He or she then puts the money in an opening in the table called the drop box, the place all money and markers that have been collected during the shift go. The Boxperson must be sure that players who have bought casino chips receive the right amount of chips for their cash.

If there is any dispute between players and dealers, the Boxperson is expected to mediate it, with his or her decision usually final. Disputes may involve situations such as incorrect or alleged wrong payoffs or bets.

Other duties of the Boxperson may include:

- Examining dice for tampering or imperfections after dice have fallen or been thrown off the craps table and maintaining the integrity of equipment
- Watching the moves of the dealers
- Making sure payoffs made to players are correct
- Accepting or rejecting call and finger bets

Salaries

As noted previously, the Boxperson is a casino executive. He or she is therefore paid a salary in relation to an hourly wage. Boxpersons may have annual earnings ranging from $30,000 to $55,000 or more. Factors affecting earnings include the geographic location, size, and prestige of the casino, as well as the experience of the individual. Those working in large facilities in the gambling capitals may earn more than their counterparts in other areas.

Employment Prospects

Employment prospects are good for Boxpersons and getting better as more and more casinos open throughout the country. Opportunities for a Boxperson may be found in any casino hosting craps tables. Because casinos are often open 24 hours a day, individuals may work during all shifts, including daytime, swing shift or evening, graveyard or overnight. Individuals may be expected to work weekends or holidays.

While individuals may find employment in any casino in the world, the greatest number of opportunities exist in areas where there are a large number of casinos.

Las Vegas, Reno, Laughlin, Lake Tahoe, Atlantic City, Biloxi, Baton Rouge, New Orleans, and Detroit offer the greatest number of job possibilities. Other employment settings include casino hotels in other areas of Nevada, Mississippi, New York, Louisiana, Colorado, Connecticut, Illinois, Arizona, and California.

Other regions hosting Indian gaming and land-based or riverboat gaming facilities or cruise ships offer additional opportunities. New casinos and casino hotels are constantly under construction. More casinos and casino hotels are also opening every year as areas legalize gambling.

Advancement Prospects

A Boxperson can advance his or her career by obtaining more experience and locating a similar position in a larger or more prestigious casino. Individuals may also move on to other management positions within the casino, including pit boss.

Education and Training

A Boxperson must have complete working knowledge of both the casino rules and the procedures of the game of craps. Depending on the specific casino, an individual in this position must be a graduate of an accredited gaming school, academy, or institute. In certain locations, community colleges, vocational technical schools, or the casinos themselves offer training.

Boxpersons, like all others working in the gaming area, must be licensed by the state gaming agency in the specific state in which they work.

Experience/Skills/Personality Traits

Experience as a dealer and/or a floorperson is necessary to become a Boxperson. The minimum amount of experience varies, but usually is approximately 1,200 to 1,500 hours.

A Boxperson must be extremely alert in order to watch everything that is going on at the table. Supervisory and administrative skills are also necessary.

Unions/Associations

Boxpersons working in casinos do not belong to a union. Individuals interested in learning more about careers in this area should contact gaming institutes, academies, and schools, as well as casino human resources departments.

Individuals may belong to local gaming associations and organizations.

Tips for Entry

1. Jobs are often advertised in the classified sections of newspapers in areas hosting gaming. Look under classifications such as "Casinos," "Casino Jobs," "Casino Opportunities," "Boxperson," "Boxman/woman," "Gaming."
2. Visit the human resources department of casinos to inquire about job openings.
3. Look for new casinos under construction. Apply early.
4. You may learn about job openings on casinos job hotlines. These are frequently updated messages listing job availabilities. You can call each casino directly to get its job hotline phone number.

CRAPS DEALER

CAREER PROFILE

Duties: Pushing dice to shooter; retrieving dice; calling game.

Alternative Title(s): Dealer; Stickman; Boxman; Stickperson; Boxperson

Salary Range: $13,000 to $21,000 plus tips.

Employment Prospects: Good

Best Geographical Location(s) for Position: Las Vegas, Reno, Laughlin, Lake Tahoe, Atlantic City, Biloxi, Baton Rouge, New Orleans, and Detroit offer most opportunities; other regions with land-based, riverboat, or Indian gaming facilities offer additional opportunities.

Prerequisites:

Education or Training—Training at gaming academy, school, or institute

Experience and Qualifications—Experience dealing craps obtained through training; state licensing required to work in gaming area.

Special Skills and Personality Traits—Manual dexterity; interpersonal skills; alert; knowledge of craps.

CAREER LADDER

```
┌─────────────────────────────────────┐
│   Craps Dealer at Larger, More      │
│  Prestigious Casino, Dealer of other │
│  Game, or Floorperson or Boxperson   │
└─────────────────────────────────────┘

┌─────────────────────────────────────┐
│            Craps Dealer              │
└─────────────────────────────────────┘

┌─────────────────────────────────────┐
│ Student at Dealer School or Academy  │
│   or Dealer in other Casino Game     │
└─────────────────────────────────────┘
```

Position Description

A craps crew is usually composed of two standing Dealers, another Dealer called the stickperson, and a replacement Dealer, as well as one or two boxpersons. The stickperson stands in the middle of the craps table, pushing the dice around the table to the shooters. The boxperson is the casino executive in charge of overseeing the craps table.

Dealers usually work for 40 minutes and then go on break and are replaced by another Dealer. The Dealers at the craps table generally rotate positions in a counterclockwise direction looking down at the table. In this manner, every Craps Dealer at the table handles the position of the base Dealer as well as the position of stickperson.

Dealers stand during play. As a rule, they are expected to wear uniforms. The two standing Craps Dealers are each located at the base of one side or the other of the table. Each Dealer is responsible for the players in his or her section of the craps table.

Individuals have a number of responsibilities. They are responsible for changing a player's cash into chips. This is done by giving the money to the boxperson. The Dealer may also change a player's chips during the course of play to those worth either a higher or lower denomination. This is called changing color.

The Stickperson is in charge of pushing the dice to the shooter before his or her roll. The shooter must choose two dice from a choice of four to eight that are offered. The Stickperson must then put the non-selected dice back in a box that is kept in view in front of the individual at all times.

Another responsibility of the Stickperson is to "call the game." This happens when the Stickperson announces what each roll of the dice is as well as whether it is a winner or loser. Every Stickperson has his or her own way of calling a game, so that enthusiasm and excitement are generated at the table at all times—when the shooter is shaking the dice, when the dice have been rolled, and when the winning or losing bets are announced.

The Stickperson takes or books the proposition bets placed in the center of the craps table. The individual must verbally acknowledge every proposition wager. This is sometimes called advertising the bets. He or she will then point out the customers who win the standing dealers and announce the correct payoff for each person.

Standing Dealers are responsible for handling all the place bets as well as keeping track of them. This must be done in the proper order so that the right players are paid correctly if their numbers come up again.

Dealers are expected to move a plastic disk to a corner box number after a point has been established on the come-out roll of a shooter. This disk is called a buck. It indicates that the number in which the disk has been placed is the point. The disk may have a black and a white side. The white side of the buck in a box number indicates that number is the point.

Sometimes when a new shooter is coming out, the Dealer will move the disk to the "don't come" box. If the disk is black and in the "don't come" box, it indicates that no point has been established and the roll is a come-out roll.

The Dealer is responsible for placing even bets and odd bets in the correct box when "come" or "don't come" bets have been made. Winning bets are then paid off. Chips for losing bets are taken off and given back to the casino.

Other duties of the standing Dealer may include:

- Giving players chips to play with after their credit has been approved
- Paying off winning bets
- Removing losing bets made on the section of the craps table he or she is responsible for

Salaries

Craps Dealers earn an hourly wage ranging between $6.00 and $10.00 plus tips. Tips may also be referred to as tokes. Players who win often tip the Dealer, pushing their hourly wage in some cases to $30 or more. Some Dealers working at tables with high limits may earn $50 to $100 or more per hour in tips. Some make $30,000 to $55,000 or more annually.

Employment Prospects

Employment prospects for Craps Dealers are good. Opportunities for Dealers may be located in any casino hosting craps tables. As casinos are often open 24 hours a day, individuals may work various shifts.

While individuals may find employment in any casino in the world, the greatest number of opportunities exist in areas where there are a large number of casinos.

Advancement Prospects

A Craps Dealer may take a number of different paths to career advancement. The individual can advance his or her career by obtaining more experience and finding a similar position in a larger or more prestigious casino, resulting in increased tips. Some Craps Dealers also obtain training and experience in dealing additional casino games. Individuals may also move on to management positions within the casino, including floorperson or boxperson.

Education and Training

A Craps Dealer must have complete working knowledge of both the casino rules and the procedures of the game of craps. According to many experts, craps is one of the most difficult casino games to work at as a Dealer. Individuals in this position should be trained in dealing craps at an accredited gaming school, academy, or institute. Community colleges, vocational technical schools, and casinos themselves also offer Dealer training.

Craps Dealers, like all others working in a gaming area, must be licensed in the state in which they work. There are also minimum age requirements in most states.

Experience/Skills/Personality Traits

Individuals should be personable people who enjoy being around others. Showmanship is helpful. An enthusiastic patter is essential. Math skills are also needed, as is manual dexterity.

Unions/Associations

Craps Dealers do not usually belong to a union. Individuals interested in learning more about careers in this area should contact gaming institutes, academies, and schools, as well as casino human resources departments.

Tips for Entry

1. Visit the human resources department of casinos to inquire about job openings.
2. Craps Dealers, like most other casino game Dealers, often must audition for jobs. Get as much experience as possible while in training.
3. Jobs are often advertised in the classifieds in areas hosting gaming. Look under classifications such as "Casinos," "Casino Jobs," or "Dealers."
4. Look for new casinos under construction. Job opportunities may exist. Apply early.
5. Gaming institutes and schools often offer job placement.
6. Most casinos have job hotlines. Call casinos directly to get job hotline phone numbers.

BLACKJACK DEALER

CAREER PROFILE

Duties: Dealing cards for game of blackjack in a casino.

Alternative Title(s): Dealer

Salary Range: $14,000 to $20,000 plus tips

Employment Prospects: Excellent

Best Geographical Location(s) for Position: Las Vegas, Reno, Laughlin, Lake Tahoe, Atlantic City, Biloxi, Baton Rouge, New Orleans and Detroit offer most opportunities; other regions with land-based, riverboat, or Indian gaming facilities offer additional opportunities.

Prerequisites:

Education or Training—Training at gaming academies, dealer schools, or institutes; see text.

Experience and Qualifications—Experience at dealing blackjack gained through training; state licensing required to work in gaming area.

Special Skills and Personality Traits—Dealing skills; math skills; manual dexterity; interpersonal skills.

CAREER LADDER

```
┌─────────────────────────────────────┐
│  Blackjack or other Dealer at Larger │
│    or More Prestigious Casino, or    │
│      Floorperson or Pit Manager      │
└─────────────────────────────────────┘

┌─────────────────────────────────────┐
│         Blackjack Dealer             │
└─────────────────────────────────────┘

┌─────────────────────────────────────┐
│  Student at Dealer School or Academy │
└─────────────────────────────────────┘
```

Position Description

Blackjack is one of the most common table games offered at casinos throughout the world. In this game, the Blackjack Dealer deals cards to the players at the table and the house. The house is the casino, and the dealer represents the house.

The object of blackjack is to get a "blackjack or 21." A blackjack is an ace and a picture card or 10. If the player does not get a blackjack, he or she must beat the house. In order to do this, the player must get closer to 21 than the house without going over. In blackjack, aces count as one or 11, numbered cards equal their value, and picture cards count as 10. A tie means everybody is even.

The Blackjack Dealer waits for the bets to be placed by the players. The individual goes around the table from left to right and deals each player a card facedown as well as dealing one to the house. He or she then deals each player a card faceup. The players will then indicate to the dealer whether they want any other cards either verbally or by motioning. The players and dealer turn their cards over and see who beat the house. If one or more of the players did, the dealer gives them the payoff.

Blackjack Dealers work in what is known as a pit. There are four tables in each pit and five dealers. Blackjack Dealers usually work for an hour and then break. The extra dealer is available to relieve the dealer who is on break.

Blackjack Dealers as well as everyone else in the casino are always being watched by others, including supervisors called floorpeople, pit clerks, and pit bosses. A supervisor may, for example, replace a dealer who is on a losing streak for the house. Everything that takes place in the gaming area is also screened and videotaped by banks of surveillance cameras. This procedure protects both the casino and the player from possible cheating or stealing.

The Blackjack Dealer must be able to deal from one or more decks of cards. He or she may also deal from a "shoe." This is a box that holds one or more decks of cards and dispenses them one by one. The individual must further understand the various options and procedures, including splitting pairs, doubling down, and insurance as it relates to the game.

The Blackjack Dealer is responsible for conducting the games at his or her table. In addition to mixing and dealing the cards, the individual is responsible for:

- Counting and tallying the cards of each player
- Determining the correct amount of chips the winner is entitled to
- Giving the payoff to the patron
- Knowing the specific rules of the house and the table
- Referring all customer problems to the floorperson

Salaries

Blackjack Dealers earn an hourly wage ranging between $6.50 and $9.00 or roughly $14,000 to $20,000 annually plus tips. Tips may also be referred to as tokes. Players who win often tip Blackjack Dealers, pushing their hourly wage in some cases to $30 or more. Blackjack Dealers working at tables with high limits may earn $50 to $100 or more an hour in tips.

Employment Prospects

Because blackjack is one of the most common table games offered at casinos, Blackjack Dealers are always in demand. Employment prospects are excellent.

While individuals may find employment in any casino in the world, the greatest number of opportunities exist in areas where there are a large number of casinos.

Las Vegas, Reno, Laughlin, Lake Tahoe, Atlantic City, Biloxi, Baton Rouge, New Orleans, and Detroit offer the greatest number of job possibilities. Other employment settings include casino hotels in other areas of Nevada, Mississippi, New York, Louisiana, Colorado, Connecticut, Illinois, Arizona, and California.

Other regions hosting Indian gaming and land-based or riverboat gaming facilities or cruise ships offer additional opportunities. New casinos and casino hotels are constantly under construction. More casinos and casino hotels are also opening every year as areas legalize gambling.

Advancement Prospects

Blackjack Dealers may advance their careers by learning more games. The more games that individuals learn, the more money they will be able to earn. Some Blackjack Dealers climb the career ladder by becoming floorpeople, supervisors, or pit clerks.

Education and Training

While formal training is not required to become a Blackjack Dealer, many casinos prefer to hire applicants who have gone through a gaming school or institute or at least taken classes in dealing blackjack. Gaming schools are located in areas hosting gambling casinos. Some casinos also have their own training facilities or offer on-the-job training.

Gaming schools offer classes during the day, evenings, and weekends to accommodate people working in the gaming industry. Some schools also offer classes after the midnight shift and on weekends to further accommodate workers.

Blackjack Dealers, like most other casino employees, must usually be licensed in the state in which they work. There are also minimum age requirements in most states.

Experience/Skills/Personality Traits

Blackjack Dealers should be personable people who enjoy being around others. The ability to count and add quickly and accurately is essential to this job. Because cards are mixed and dealt in a certain manner, manual dexterity is also required.

Unions/Associations

Blackjack Dealers are not usually unionized in most casinos. There are cases, however, in which individuals working on riverboats or cruises may be members of a union.

Dealers may be members of local gaming trade associations and organizations.

Additional information regarding this career can be obtained from gaming institutes, academies, and schools as well as casino human resources departments.

Tips For Entry

1. As noted previously, formal training is not required. However, classes at a gaming institute, academy, or college will give you an edge over someone who has not been trained.
2. Learn how to deal multiple games. This will make you more marketable.
3. Positions in this field are advertised in the newspaper classified section in areas hosting gambling facilities. Look under heading classifications such as "Blackjack Dealer," "Dealers," "Casinos," "Casino Jobs," or "Gaming."
4. Stop in at the human resources department of casinos in which you might be interested in working to see if there are any openings.

ROULETTE DEALER

CAREER PROFILE

Duties: Overseeing roulette game; selling chips; spinning roulette wheel; releasing ball; paying off winning bets; collecting losing bets.

PR:Alternative Title(s): Dealer

Salary Range: $14,000 to $21,000 plus tips

Employment Prospects: Good

Best Geographical Location(s) for Position: Las Vegas, Reno, Laughlin, Lake Tahoe, Atlantic City, Biloxi, Baton Rouge, New Orleans, and Detroit offer most opportunities; other regions with land-based, riverboat, or Indian gaming facilities offer additional opportunities.

Prerequisites:

Education or Training—Training at gaming academy, school, or institute; see text.

Experience and Qualifications—State licensing required to work in gaming area.

Special Skills and Personality Traits—Manual dexterity; interpersonal skills; alert; skilled at dealing roulette.

CAREER LADDER

```
┌─────────────────────────────────────┐
│  Roulette or other Dealer at Larger or │
│    More Prestigious Casino, or         │
│    Floorperson or Pitboss              │
└─────────────────────────────────────┘

┌─────────────────────────────────────┐
│         Roulette Dealer                │
└─────────────────────────────────────┘

┌─────────────────────────────────────┐
│  Student at Gaming School, Dealer     │
│      School, or Academy                │
└─────────────────────────────────────┘
```

Position Description

Roullete is a casino game played on a large felt table on which players place wagers. These wagers are placed on portions of the table corresponding to numbers on which people want to bet.

The game features a roulette wheel, which includes a 31- or 32-inch bowl-shaped base that sits outside of the wheel. The bowl has a track with a one-inch-wide groove running around the circumference. This is where the Dealer spins the roulette ball.

The wheel head spins counterclockwise. It has 38 pockets separated with metal separators or frets. Eighteen pockets are red, eighteen are black, and the other two are green. Pockets are numbered 0 through 36. In America, the extra pocket is numbered 00. Pockets are numbered so that high, low, odd, and even numbers and red and black colors alternate.

Roulette tables may have single layouts or double-end tables with two layouts. The number of roulette dealers depends on which type of table is in use. A single layout table is staffed by two Roulette Dealers or a Dealer and an assistant. They are also called croupiers. The double-end tables may have three or four dealers.

Dealers usually work for 40 minutes, then go on break and are replaced by another Dealer. They stand during play. As a rule, they are expected to wear uniforms.

The Roulette Dealer is responsible for staffing the roulette table. The individual is expected to oversee the conduct of the game. On a single layout table one Dealer is responsible for selling chips to players. The individual must keep track of the value of the chips each player has on the table. The Dealer does this near the wheel by placing numbered buttons also known as lammers next to each color chip to illustrate the value. This is especially important when the player wants to cash out. In this manner the Dealer knows how much to pay each player.

The Dealer is in charge of spinning the roulette wheel. The individual may be called a wheel roller. The Dealer is also responsible for taking the ball from the last pocket in which it falls. He or she pushes the wheel to make sure it keeps moving. The individual then releases the ball in a clockwise manner onto the track.

The Dealer's responsibility is to call out something to the effect of "no more bets" just as the ball is ready to fall from the back track. At that time, the Dealer and players watch the ball settle into a numbered pocket. The Dealer announces the winning number and color. The individual then pays off the winning bets as well as collecting all losing bets from the roulette table.

The other Dealer working the table is responsible for separating the losing chips. He or she must stack them after the other dealer sweeps them from the layout. This is done by stacking the chips in piles of 20 of the same color. These are then put into the chip rack on the apron of the roulette table.

Other duties of the Roulette Dealer may include:

- Placing a marker on the winning number of the felt
- Returning invalid bets to players

Salaries

The Roulette Dealer earns an hourly wage ranging between $6.50 and $10.00 or $14,000 to $21,000 annually plus tips. Tips may also be referred to as tokes. Players who win often tip the Dealer, pushing their hourly wage in some cases to $30 or more. Some Dealers working at tables with high limits may earn $50 to $100 or more per hour in tips.

Employment Prospects

Employment opportunities for Roulette Dealers are excellent and may be found in any casino hosting roulette tables. While individuals may find employment in any casino in the world, the greatest number of opportunities exist in areas where there are a large number of casinos.

Las Vegas, Reno, Laughlin, Lake Tahoe, Atlantic City, Biloxi, Baton Rouge, New Orleans, and Detroit offer the greatest number of job possibilities. Other employment settings include casino hotels in other areas of Nevada, Mississippi, New York, Louisiana, Colorado, Connecticut, Illinois, Arizona, and California.

Other regions hosting Indian gaming and land-based or riverboat gaming facilities or cruise ships offer additional opportunities. New casinos and casino hotels are constantly under construction. More casinos and casino hotels are also opening every year as areas legalize gambling.

Because casinos are often open 24 hours a day, individuals may work during the daytime, evening or swing shift, graveyard or overnight shift. Roulette Dealers may be expected to work weekends or holidays.

Advancement Prospects

A Roulette Dealer may take a number of different paths to career advancement. The individual can advance his or her career by obtaining more experience and locating a similar position in a larger or more prestigious casino, resulting in increased tips. Some Roulette Dealers also obtain training and experience in dealing additional casino games. Individuals may also get experience and move on to management positions within the casino, including floorpersons or pit bosses.

Education and Training

A Roulette Dealer must have complete working knowledge of both the casino rules and the procedures of the roulette game. Individuals in this position should be trained in dealing roulette at an accredited gaming school, academy, or institute. Community colleges, vocational technical schools, and casinos themselves may also offer Dealer training.

Gaming schools offer classes during the day, evenings, and weekends to accommodate people working in the gaming industry. Some schools also offer classes after the midnight shift and on weekends to further accommodate workers.

Roulette Dealers, like most other casino employees, must usually be licensed in the state in which they work. There are also minimum age requirements in most states.

Experience/Skills/Personality Traits

Roulette Dealers should be personable people who enjoy being around others. Interpersonal skills are necessary for success in this career. Showmanship is helpful. Manual dexterity is essential.

Unions/Associations

Roulette Dealers are not usually unionized in most casinos, although individuals working on riverboats or cruises may be members of various unions.

Dealers may belong to local gaming-related trade associations and organizations.

Tips for Entry

1. Gaming institutes and schools often offer job placement. Check out the placement rate of various schools in the area before making a choice.
2. Stop by the human resources department of casinos to inquire about job openings.
3. Roulette Dealers, like most other casino game dealers, often must audition for jobs. Get as much experience as possible while in training.
4. Look for new casinos under construction. Apply early.
5. Most casinos have job hotlines. These are frequently updated messages listing job availabilities. Positions as Dealers are often included.
6. Jobs are often advertised in the classified sections of newspapers in areas hosting gaming. Look under classifications such as "Casinos," "Casino Jobs," "Casino Opportunities," "Roulette Dealers," "Dealers," or "Gaming."

BACCARAT DEALER

CAREER PROFILE

Duties: Receiving baccarat cards; placing cards in correct boxes; determining whether a hand should stand or draw a card; paying off winning bets; collecting losing bets.

Alternative Title(s): Dealer; Croupier

Salary Range: $14,000 to $21,000 plus tips

Employment Prospects: Good

Best Geographical Location(s) for Position: Las Vegas, Reno, Laughlin, Lake Tahoe, Atlantic City, Biloxi, Baton Rouge, New Orleans, and Detroit offer most opportunities; other regions with land-based, riverboat, or Indian gaming facilities offer additional opportunities.

Prerequisites:

Education or Training—Training at gaming academies, schools, or institutes; see text.

Experience and Qualifications—Experience dealing baccarat gained through training; state licensing required to work in gaming area.

Special Skills and Personality Traits—Manual dexterity; math skills; interpersonal skills; alert; skilled at dealing baccarat.

CAREER LADDER

```
┌─────────────────────────────────┐
│  Baccarat Dealer at Larger or More │
│  Prestigious Casino, or Floorperson│
│         or Pit Boss              │
└─────────────────────────────────┘

┌─────────────────────────────────┐
│         Baccarat Dealer          │
└─────────────────────────────────┘

┌─────────────────────────────────┐
│     Student at Dealer School     │
└─────────────────────────────────┘
```

Position Description

Baccarat is a casino game played with cards. It was invented in Italy and became popular throughout Europe. Baccarat is a French word for the Italian term *baccarat* meaning zero. Zero refers to the face cards in a deck of jack, queen, king, and the 10 cards. In the game of baccarat these cards all have a zero value. Other cards, ace through nine, are valued according to their number.

A hand in baccarat consists of two or three cards. No hand can total more than nine. All hands totaling more than 10 have 10 subtracted from their value.

There are a number of versions of the game. In the American version of baccarat the casino plays against the participants at the gaming table. This includes the bet bank and the players. In the game of baccarat the player makes a bet on either the bank or the players.

Baccarat is a game that attracts bettors and high rollers. It is played on a large baccarat table. The baccarat area is often located in a separate area of the casino, roped off from other gaming tables.

Many people think baccarat is a glamorous game. Baccarat Dealers, like most other dealers in casinos, are expected to wear uniforms. However, the uniforms of these Dealers are often tuxedos, projecting a more glamorous image.

Baccarat is played at a special table on which numbers are printed. Fifteen people can participate at the table. The baccarat table is staffed by three Dealers.

At each table the rules are printed clearly, both for the participants' use as well as for the Dealers'. Dealers are in charge of knowing and enforcing the rules of the game. They make sure participants abide by the rules.

All three Dealers in baccarat cut, mix, and reshuffle the deck. One Dealer, referred to as the callman or callperson, stands between positions 1 and 15. Looking down at the table, this position is located at the bottom center of the table. This individual is responsible for receiving the cards. The callperson is also expected to place the cards in the appropriate boxes. The individual is also responsible, according to the written rules at the table, for deciding whether a hand should stand or draw a card. The callman or callperson is additionally expected to announce the winning hand after the final draw.

The other Dealers sit during play. After a winner is announced by the callman or callperson, the other Dealers pay off winning bets. They also must collect losing bets.

Other duties of Baccarat Dealers include:

- Keeping records of commissions due on wagers
- Collecting commissions when players leave the table or eight decks of cards are depleted

Salaries

A Baccarat Dealer earns an hourly wage ranging between $6.50 and $9.50 or approximately $14,000 to $21,000 annually plus tips. Tips may also be referred to as tokes. Players who win often tip the Dealer, pushing their hourly wage in some cases to $30 or more. Some Dealers working at tables with high limits may earn $50 to $100 or more per hour in tips.

Employment Prospects

Employment opportunities for Baccarat Dealers are good and may be found in most casinos. Because some casinos may be open 24 hours a day, Baccarat Dealers might work various shifts including daytime, swing shift, graveyard shift or overnight. Individuals may also be required to work weekends or holidays.

While individuals may find employment in any casino in the world, the greatest number of opportunities exist in areas where there are a large number of casinos.

Las Vegas, Reno, Laughlin, Lake Tahoe, Atlantic City, Biloxi, Baton Rouge, New Orleans, and Detroit offer the greatest number of job possibilities. Other employment settings include casino hotels in other areas of Nevada, Mississippi, New York, Louisiana, Colorado, Connecticut, Illinois, Arizona, and California.

Other regions hosting Indian gaming and land-based or riverboat gaming facilities or cruise ships offer additional opportunities. New casinos and casino hotels are constantly under construction. More casinos and casino hotels are also opening every year as areas legalize gambling.

Advancement Prospects

A Baccarat Dealer may take a number of different paths to career advancement. The individual can advance his or her career by obtaining more dealing experience and locating a similar position in a larger or more prestigious casino, resulting in increased tips. Baccarat Dealers may also obtain training and experience in dealing additional casino games, making them more marketable. Individuals may also get experience and move on to management positions within the casino, including floorpersons or pit bosses.

Education and Training

A Baccarat Dealer must have complete working knowledge of both the casino rules and the procedures of the baccarat game. Individuals should be trained in dealing baccarat at an accredited gaming school, academy, or institute. Community colleges and vocational technical schools in areas hosting gaming and casinos themselves may also offer dealer training.

Baccarat Dealers, like all others working in a gaming area, must be licensed in the state in which they work. There are also minimum age requirements in most states.

Experience/Skills/Personality Traits

Individuals should be personable people who enjoy being around others. The ability to deal with customers in a gracious, effective, and courteous manner is needed. Showmanship is helpful. Manual dexterity is also necessary.

Unions/Associations

Individuals may be members of local gaming-related trade associations and organizations.

Additional information regarding this career can be obtained from gaming institutes, academies, and schools, as well as casino human resources departments.

Tips for Entry

1. Baccarat Dealers, like most other casino game dealers, often must audition for jobs. Get as much experience as possible while being trained.
2. Gaming institutes and schools often offer job placement. Check out the placement rate of various schools in the area.
3. Stop by the human resources departments of casinos to inquire about job openings.
4. Look for new casinos under construction in gaming areas. Apply for jobs early.
5. Most casinos have job hotlines listing jobs available. These are frequently updated messages. You can call each casino directly to get its job hotline phone number.
6. Jobs are often advertised in the classified sections of newspapers in areas hosting gaming. Look under classifications such as "Baccarat," "Casinos," "Casino Jobs," "Casino Opportunities," "Baccarat Dealers," "Dealers," or "Gaming."

SLOT MANAGER

CAREER PROFILE

Duties: Formulating policies of slot department; overseeing slot operation; developing layout of floor; supervising slot personnel.

Alternative Title(s): None

Salary Range: $35,000 to $70,000+

Employment Prospects: Poor

Best Geographical Location(s) for Position: Las Vegas, Reno, Laughlin, Lake Tahoe, Atlantic City, Biloxi, Baton Rouge, New Orleans, and Detroit offer most opportunities; other regions with land-based, riverboat, or Indian gaming facilities offer additional opportunities.

Prerequisites:

Education or Training—Training requirements vary; see text.

Experience and Qualifications—Experience working in slot department; licensing as slot mechanic may be required; state licensing required to work in gaming area.

Special Skills and Personality Traits—Supervisory skills; administrative skills; marketing skills; analytical skills.

CAREER LADDER

```
┌─────────────────────────────────┐
│  Slot Manager in Larger, More   │
│   Prestigious Casino or Other   │
│      Supervisory Position       │
└─────────────────────────────────┘

┌─────────────────────────────────┐
│          Slot Manager           │
└─────────────────────────────────┘

┌─────────────────────────────────┐
│      Assistant Slot Manager     │
└─────────────────────────────────┘
```

Position Description

Slots generate a great deal of money for casinos. The person in charge overseeing the slot operation is called the Slot Manager. The individual holds an important administrative position and has a multitude of responsibilities.

The Slot Manager is responsible for formulating the policies and procedures used in the slot department. The individual is in charge of designing the layout for the slot floor. A lot of thought must go into this process. The Slot Manager must determine the width of aisles and location of booths, and decide where specific machines should physically be placed. The individual may also select the manufacturers and type and denominations of each machine used in the casino.

When designing the floor layout, the Slot Manager must find ways for machines to generate the maximum amount of business. Payoff schedules of machines must be developed to attract customers. The individual must decide which machines should have less frequent large payoffs and which should have smaller, more frequent jackpots.

The slot department has a number of employees. These may include an assistant slot manager, slot shift managers, attendant supervisors, slot attendants, slot repair managers, mechanics, floorpeople, cage cashiers, and change people. The Slot Manager is expected to oversee the slot employees and their activities.

The Slot Manager often works with the marketing and player development department designing promotions and special events to attract more players to the casino. These promotions may include events such as large slot tournaments.

Other duties of the Slot Manager may include:

• Attending staff and department head meetings
• Handling disputes on the floor between customers and employees
• Evaluating machines

Salaries

A Slot Manager may have annual earnings ranging from $35,000 to $70,000 or more. Factors affecting earnings include the geographic location, size, and prestige of the specific casino as well as the experience and responsibilities of the individual. Generally, those with the most experience working in larger, more prestigious casinos in the gambling capitals earn the highest salaries.

Employment Prospects

Employment prospects for Slot Managers may be limited in larger casinos located in the gambling capitals. In these facilities individuals may have to wait for an opening.

The greatest number of opportunities will be found in Las Vegas, Reno, Laughlin, Atlantic City, Biloxi, Baton Rouge, New Orleans, and Detroit. Other areas with land-based or riverboat gaming facilities offer additional job possibilities. As legalized gaming expands throughout the United States, opportunities in other locations will become available.

Advancement Prospects

Slot Managers can advance their careers by obtaining experience and locating similar positions in larger or more prestigious casinos. Individuals might also be promoted to other supervisory positions within the casino.

Education and Training

Training requirements vary at different casinos in various locations. Certain casinos require Slot Managers to have either completed an approved program in slot machine repair in at least two machines or be licensed as a slot mechanic in at least two types of machines. Other casinos may not have these requirements.

Courses or programs in casino-related training offered by gaming schools, academies, and institutes, as well as community colleges and vo-tech schools throughout the country may be useful.

Slot Managers, like others working in the gaming area, must also meet any additional state licensing requirements.

Experience/Skills/Personality Traits

Slot Managers are required to have from three to four years of experience working in the slot department prior to becoming Slot Managers. Some casinos require between 5,000 and 6,000 hours of experience working in the casino slot department to qualify for this job.

Supervisory skills, administrative skills, marketing skills, and analytical skills are necessary for success in this career.

Unions/Associations

Slot Managers in most casinos are not usually unionized. Individuals may belong to local gaming-related trade associations and organizations.

Additional information regarding this career can be obtained from gaming institutes, academies, and schools, as well as casino human resources departments.

Tips for Entry

1. Many casinos as well as gaming schools, academies, institutes, community colleges, and vo-tech schools in gaming areas offer casino-related training programs. These may not be necessary, but are helpful in attaining a high level of casino knowledge.
2. You may have to relocate to other gaming areas to find an opening as a Slot Manager.
3. Visit the human resources department of casinos and inquire about job openings.
4. Jobs are often advertised in the classified sections of newspapers in areas hosting gaming. Look under classifications such as "Slot Manager," "Casinos," "Casino Jobs," "Casino Opportunities," or "Gaming."
5. Check out specific casino Web sites. Many advertise employment openings directly on their sites.
6. New casinos under construction are a great place to look for employment. Stop at their human resources departments and ask for an application.
7. This is a position that is often promoted from within. Get your foot in the door and obtain as much as experience as possible in the slot department.

SLOT SHIFT MANAGER

CAREER PROFILE

Duties: Supervising slot personnel during shift.

Alternative Title(s): Shift Manager

Salary Range: $25,000 to $48,000+

Employment Prospects: Fair

Best Geographical Location(s) for Position: Las Vegas, Reno, Laughlin, Atlantic City, Biloxi, Baton Rouge, New Orleans, and Detroit offer most opportunities; other regions with land-based, riverboat, or Indian gaming facilities offer additional opportunities.

Prerequisites:

Education or Training—Training requirements vary; see text.

Experience and Qualifications—Experience working in slot department; licensing as slot mechanic may be required; additional state licensing required to work in gaming area.

Special Skills and Personality Traits—Supervisory skills; administrative skills; marketing skills; analytical skills; customer service skills.

CAREER LADDER

```
┌─────────────────────────────────┐
│  Slot Shift Manager in Larger, More │
│  Prestigious Casino or Assistant    │
│         Slot Manager                │
└─────────────────────────────────┘

┌─────────────────────────────────┐
│       Slot Shift Manager        │
└─────────────────────────────────┘

┌─────────────────────────────────┐
│        Slot Mechanic            │
└─────────────────────────────────┘
```

Position Description

Slots are a major moneymaker for casinos because it is easy for everyone to play. All people need to do is drop some coins into the machine and either pull a handle or press a button to start reels moving, then wait to see if they have won.

Many people work in the slot department. The Slot Shift Manager is responsible for supervising the slot personnel during the shift.

Slot personnel may include attendant supervisors, slot attendants, slot mechanics, floorpeople, cage cashiers, and change people. The Slot Shift Manager is expected to oversee the activities of these employees. The individual must make sure everyone is doing their job and assisting customers when needed. The Slot Shift Manager is also responsible for making sure employees take breaks when required.

Other duties of the Slot Shift Manager may include:

• Dealing with problems with employees
• Accounting for incidents during the shift
• Arbitrating decisions on payoffs

Salaries

Slot Shift Managers may have annual earnings ranging from $25,000 to $48,000 or more. Factors affecting earnings include the geographic location, size, and prestige of the specific casino, as well as the experience and responsibilities of the individual. Generally, those with the most experience working in larger, more prestigious casinos in the gambling capitals earn the highest salaries.

Employment Prospects

Employment opportunities for Slot Shift Managers may be limited in larger casinos located in the gambling capitals of Las Vegas and Atlantic City. In these facilities, individuals may have to wait for someone to leave and openings to occur. There may be more opportunities in some of the newer gaming areas located throughout the country. Other opportunities will be found as gaming expands throughout the United States.

Slot Shift Managers may work various shifts, including daytime, evening or swing shift, overnight or graveyard shift. Individuals may also be expected to work weekends and holidays.

Advancement Prospects

Slot Shift Managers can advance their careers by obtaining more experience and locating similar positions in larger or more prestigious casinos. Individuals might also be promoted to the position of assistant slot manager.

Education and Training

Training requirements vary at different casinos in various locations. Certain casinos require Slot Shift Managers to either complete an approved program in slot machine repair in at least two machines or qualify to be licensed as a slot mechanic in at least two types of machines. Depending on the casino, some may not have these requirements and accept on-the-job training and experience.

Courses or programs in casino-related training offered by gaming schools, academies, and institutes, as well as community colleges and vo-tech schools throughout the country may be useful.

Slot Shift Managers, like others working in the gaming area, must also meet specific state licensing requirements of the state gaming commission.

Experience/Skills/Personality Traits

Experience requirements, like training, vary. As noted previously, some casinos require that individuals complete an approved program in slot machine repair in at least two machines or be a licensed slot mechanic. Most positions require that Slot Shift Managers have at least two years or 2,500 to 3,000 hours of experience working in a casino slot department.

Slot Shift Managers should have both supervisory and administrative skills to be successful in this career. Marketing skills, analytical skills, and customer service skills are also essential.

Unions/Associations

Slot Shift Managers are not unionized. Individuals may be members of local gaming-related associations and organizations.

Additional information regarding this career can be obtained from gaming institutes, academies, and schools, as well as casino human resources departments.

Tips for Entry

1. Many casinos promote from within. Get your foot in the door and obtain as much as experience as possible in the slot department.
2. Stop by the human resources departments of casinos and inquire about job openings.
3. Some casinos as well as gaming schools, academies, institutes, community colleges, and vo-tech schools in gaming areas offer casino-related training programs. These may not be necessary, but are helpful in attaining a higher level of casino knowledge.
4. Jobs are often advertised in the classified sections of newspapers in areas hosting gaming. Look under classifications such as "Slot Shift Manager," "Slot Department," "Casinos," "Casino Jobs," "Casino Opportunities," or "Gaming."
5. New casinos under construction are a great place to look for employment. Visit their human resources departments as soon as they open and ask for an application.

SLOT FLOORPERSON

CAREER PROFILE

Duties: Supervising slot attendants; helping customers with jackpot payouts; handling customer complaints.

Alternative Title(s): Floorperson

Salary Range: $25,000 to $40,000+

Employment Prospects: Good

Best Geographical Location(s) for Position: Las Vegas, Reno, Laughlin, Lake Tahoe, Atlantic City, Biloxi, Baton Rouge, New Orleans, and Detroit offer most opportunities; other regions with land-based, riverboat, or Indian gaming facilities offer additional opportunities.

Prerequisites:

Education or Training—Minimum of high school diploma or GED; on-the-job training.

Experience and Qualifications—Experience working in slot department; state licensing required to work in gaming area; additional licensing may be necessary.

Special Skills and Personality Traits—Supervisory skills; administrative skills; knowledge of slot operation.

CAREER LADDER

```
┌──────────────────────────────────────┐
│   Slot Floorperson in Larger, More   │
│         Prestigious Casino or         │
│          Slot Shift Manager           │
└──────────────────────────────────────┘

┌──────────────────────────────────────┐
│           Slot Floorperson            │
└──────────────────────────────────────┘

┌──────────────────────────────────────┐
│     Slot Attendant or Slot Mechanic   │
└──────────────────────────────────────┘
```

Position Description

The Slot Floorperson is responsible for overseeing the slot machines in a specified area of the casino. The individual has an array of responsibilities. The Slot Floorperson may also be called the slot supervisor.

The Slot Floorperson is responsible for supervising the activities of the slot attendants. The individual makes sure that they are doing their jobs when on the floor. The Floorperson makes certain that customers in the slot area who need help are being assisted.

The Slot Floorperson is responsible for protecting the slots in his or her area. The individual must keep an eye out for patrons attempting to cheat at the slots.

Another function of the Slot Floorperson is to handle all problems regarding the specific bank of slots assigned to him or her. The individual must look out for machines that are not working properly or those with coin jams, and then call a slot mechanic to take care of them immediately.

The Slot Floorperson is additionally responsible for helping slot customers who have won jackpots. The individual is in charge of either paying off a jackpot or verifying the jackpot has been paid by the change person.

Other duties of the Slot Floorperson may include:

- Assisting customers with casino credit
- Handling customer complaints and problems regarding slot personnel, machines, and disputes over payoffs

Salaries

Slot Floorpersons earn between $25,000 and $40,000 or more annually. Some casinos pay their Slot Floorpersons an hourly wage instead of a weekly salary. This can range from $12.00 to $20.00 per hour. Slot Floorpersons may also receive tips.

Factors affecting earnings include the geographic location, size, and prestige of the specific casino, as well as the experience and responsibilities of the individual. Generally, those with the most experience working in larger, more prestigious casinos in the gambling capitals earn the highest salaries.

Employment Prospects

Employment prospects are good for Slot Floorpersons. While individuals may find employment in any casino in the world, the greatest number of opportunities exist in areas where there are a large number of casinos.

Las Vegas, Reno, Laughlin, Lake Tahoe, Atlantic City, Biloxi, Baton Rouge, New Orleans, and Detroit offer the greatest number of job possibilities. Other employment settings include casino hotels in other areas of Nevada, Mississippi, New York, Louisiana, Colorado, Connecticut, Illinois, Arizona, and California.

Other regions hosting Indian gaming and land-based or riverboat gaming facilities offer additional opportunities. New casinos and casino hotels are constantly under construction. More casinos and casino hotels are also opening every year as areas legalize gambling.

Many casinos are open 24 hours a day. These operations run in shifts. Individuals may work the day shift, evening or swing shift, overnight or graveyard shift.

Shift hours may vary in different facilities. The day shift, for example, may run from 8 A.M. to 4 P.M.; the swing shift from 4 P.M. to midnight; and the overnight or graveyard shift from midnight to 8 A.M. Some facilities may have overlapping shifts or different hours.

Advancement Prospects

Slot Floorpersons, like most others working in casinos, have excellent opportunities to advance their careers by obtaining more experience and locating similar positions in larger or more prestigious casinos. They might also be promoted to the position of slot shift manager.

Education and Training

Training requirements for Slot Floorpersons vary at different casinos in various locations. Certain casinos require that Slot Floorpersons complete an approved program in slot machine repair. Some casinos do not have these requirements and accept on-the-job training and experience.

Courses or programs in casino-related training offered by gaming schools, academies, and institutes, as well as community colleges and vo-tech schools throughout the country may be useful.

Slot Floorpersons, like others working in the gaming area, must also meet specific state licensing requirements of the state gaming commission.

Experience/Skills/Personality Traits

Experience requirements, like training requirements, vary for Slot Floorpersons. Most positions require or prefer that individuals have three to six months experience as either a slot attendant or slot mechanic.

Individuals in this position need supervisory and administrative skills. A knowledge of slot operations is mandatory. Customer service skills are also essential.

Unions/Associations

Slot Floorpersons in most casinos are not usually unionized. Individuals working on riverboats or cruises, however, may be members of various unions.

Slot Floorpersons may be members of local gaming-related trade associations and organizations.

Additional information regarding this career can be obtained from gaming institutes, academies, and schools, as well as casino human resources departments.

Tips for Entry

1. Most casinos have job hotlines. These are frequently updated messages listing jobs available. Call each casino directly to get its job hotline phone number.
2. Get your foot in the door in the slot department and obtain as much experience as possible. Most casinos promote from within.
3. Visit the human resources departments of casinos and inquire about job openings.
4. Jobs are often advertised in the classified sections of newspapers in areas hosting gaming. Look under classifications such as "Slot Floorperson," "Slot Department," "Casinos," "Casino Jobs," "Casino Opportunities," or "Gaming."
5. New casinos under construction are a great place to look for employment. Stop by their human resources departments as soon as you hear it is open and ask for an application.
6. Look for casino job and career fairs in areas hosting casinos. These offer good opportunities to find out about job openings.

SLOT REPAIR MANAGER

CAREER PROFILE

Duties: Overseeing and directing activities of slot mechanics; maintaining slot machines; converting machines; making recommendations for improvement of slots.

Alternative Title(s): Chief Slot Mechanic

Salary Range: $35,000 to $65,000+

Employment Prospects: Fair

Best Geographical Location(s) for Position: Las Vegas, Reno, Laughlin, Lake Tahoe, Atlantic City, Biloxi, Baton Rouge, New Orleans, and Detroit offer most opportunities; other regions with land-based, riverboat, or Indian gaming facilities offer additional opportunities.

Prerequisites:
Education or Training—Attend approved training program for slot machine repair.
Experience and Qualifications—Experience as slot mechanic or technician necessary; licensing as slot mechanic; state licensing required to work in gaming area.
Special Skills and Personality Traits—Supervisory skills; electronic skills; manual dexterity; detail-oriented.

CAREER LADDER

```
┌─────────────────────────────────────┐
│  Slot Repair Manager in Larger, More │
│  Prestigious Casino or Slot Manager  │
└─────────────────────────────────────┘

┌─────────────────────────────────────┐
│        Slot Repair Manager           │
└─────────────────────────────────────┘

┌─────────────────────────────────────┐
│          Slot Mechanic               │
└─────────────────────────────────────┘
```

Position Description

For many people who enjoy gambling, casinos mean slot machines. Casinos often have a great number of these electronic machines, which can be played with a nickel, quarter, dollar, and on up.

Slot machines, like all other electronic devices, sometimes break down. When machines are broken, they cannot be played and are not producing any revenue. Casinos, therefore, employ a staff of mechanics to keep the slots in working condition. The person in charge of overseeing the slot staff is called the Slot Repair Manager. Depending on the size of the casino and the number of slots, the Slot Repair Manager may supervise from eight to 20 employees or more. The individual may also be referred to as the chief slot mechanic.

The Slot Repair Manager has a number of duties in addition to supervising the slot staff. First and foremost, the individual is in charge of planning and directing activities within the slot department.

The Slot Repair Manager makes sure all machines within the casino are in working order. To do this, the individual makes sure regular maintenance is scheduled on all the machines.

Machines may not work properly for a number of reasons: programs may need readjusting; machines may have been tilted; slots may require a fill; or parts may malfunction. The Slot Repair Manager must also be sure those in need of repair are fixed promptly.

Another important function of the Slot Repair Manager may be converting machines to different denominations. For example, the casino may want to convert machines from quarters to dollars or from nickels to quarters.

Other duties of the Slot Repair Manager may include:

- Modifying, testing, and correcting existing programs in machines to make sure they work properly
- Making recommendations for improvements in slot machines

Salaries

Slot Repair Managers earn between $35,000 and $65,000 or more annually. Factors affecting earnings include the geographic location, size, and prestige of the specific casino, as well as the experience and responsibilities of the individual.

Generally, those with the most experience working in larger, more prestigious casinos in the gambling capitals earn the highest salaries.

Employment Prospects

Employment prospects are fair for Slot Repair Managers. While many Indian gaming facilities do not host slots, almost every other casino has slot machines. Slot Repair Managers may find employment in any of these settings. Experienced and capable Slot Repair Managers are an asset to casinos.

While individuals may find employment in any casino in the world, the greatest number of opportunities exist in areas where there are a large number of casinos.

Las Vegas, Reno, Laughlin, Lake Tahoe, Atlantic City, Biloxi, Baton Rouge, New Orleans, and Detroit offer the greatest number of job possibilities. Other employment settings include casino hotels in other areas of Nevada, Mississippi, New York, Louisiana, Colorado, Connecticut, Illinois, Arizona, and California.

Other regions hosting Indian gaming and land-based or riverboat gaming facilities or cruise ships offer additional opportunities. New casinos and casino hotels are constantly under construction. More casinos and casino hotels are also opening every year as areas legalize gambling.

Advancement Prospects

There is not a great deal of opportunity for advancement for Slot Repair Managers. Individuals may find similar jobs in larger casinos, resulting in increased earnings. If openings exist and the Slot Repair Manager has enough experience, he or she might also move into the position of a slot manager.

Education and Training

Slot Repair Managers are usually required to complete an approved slot machine repair program. The program offers fundamentals of troubleshooting and repairing all models of electro-mechanical, electronic, and microprocessor-controlled slot machines. Additional courses may cover advanced troubleshooting in specific brands of microprocessor slot machines.

Slot Repair Managers must usually be licensed as slot mechanics as well as meeting additional state licensing requirements necessary to work in the gaming area.

Experience/Skills/Personality Traits

Individuals must usually have approximately three years of experience as a slot mechanic prior to obtaining positions as Slot Repair Managers.

Slot Repair Managers should have supervisory and administrative skills. Manual dexterity is also needed.

Unions/Associations

Slot Repair Managers are not usually unionized. Individuals may belong to local gaming-related trade associations and organizations.

Those interested in learning more about careers in this area should contact gaming schools, academies, and community colleges offering training in slot machine repair, as well as human resources departments in casinos.

Tips for Entry

1. The more types of machines you are licensed in repairing, the more marketable you will be.
2. Continue taking classes in slot repair, advanced troubleshooting, and specific brands of slot machines.
3. Visit the human resources departments of casinos and inquire about job openings.
4. Jobs are often advertised in the classified sections of newspapers in areas hosting gaming. Look under classifications such as "Slot Repair Manager," "Chief Slot Mechanic," "Casinos," "Casino Jobs," "Casino Opportunities," or "Gaming."
5. Most casinos now have Web sites. Openings are often listed on their employment page.
6. New casinos under construction are a great place to look for employment. Stop at their human resources departments and ask for an application.

SLOT MECHANIC

CAREER PROFILE

Duties: Maintaining and repairing slot machines; resetting machines after jackpot.

Alternative Title(s): Slot Repair Mechanics; Slot Technicians

Salary Range: $25,000 to $54,000+

Employment Prospects: Good

Best Geographical Location(s) for Position: Las Vegas, Reno, Laughlin, Lake Tahoe, Atlantic City, Biloxi, Baton Rouge, New Orleans, and Detroit offer most opportunities; other regions with land-based, riverboat, or Indian gaming facilities offer additional opportunities.

Prerequisites:

Education or Training—Attend approved training program for slot machine repair.

Experience and Qualifications—Licensing as slot mechanic usually required; state licensing required to work in gaming area.

Special Skills and Personality Traits—Electronic skills; manual dexterity; detail-oriented; analytical skills.

CAREER LADDER

```
┌─────────────────────────────┐
│     Slot Repair Manager     │
└─────────────────────────────┘

┌─────────────────────────────┐
│        Slot Mechanic        │
└─────────────────────────────┘

┌─────────────────────────────┐
│ Student in Slot Machine Repair │
│ Program or Slot Technician Trainee │
└─────────────────────────────┘
```

Position Description

Casinos are often full of slot machines of various denominations. Some can be played for a nickel, others for a quarter or a dollar, or even higher. Every slot is a possible generator of income for the casino. In order for slots to generate monies, they must be kept in proper working condition.

Slot machines, like all other electronic devices, sometimes break or malfunction. When this occurs, they cannot be played and do not produce any revenue. Casinos employ a staff of mechanics to keep the slots in working condition. The individuals responsible for handling the physical repair of the machines are called Slot Mechanics. They may also be referred to as slot repair mechanics or slot technicians. Depending on the size of the casino and the number of slots housed, there may be from eight to 20 mechanics or more employed by the casino.

The Slot Mechanic has a number of duties. The individual works under the supervision of the slot repair manager.

The Slot Mechanic performs regular maintenance on slots in the casino and casino hotel area. Preventive maintenance keeps machines working longer with less extensive repair.

Slot Mechanics must also fix slots that are not working properly. Machines may not work correctly for a number of reasons: programs may need readjusting; machines might have been tilted; slots may require a fill; or parts may malfunction. The Slot Mechanic is responsible for fixing those machines that need repair promptly. This will often be done under the direction of the slot repair manager.

The Slot Mechanic may assist the slot repair manager in converting machines to different denominations. Casinos may find, for example, they want more quarter machines instead of nickel slots.

Other duties of the Slot Mechanic may include:

• Resetting machines after jackpots

Salaries

Slot Mechanics earn between $12.00 and $26.00 or more per hour or approximately $25,000 to $54,000 annually. Factors affecting earnings include the geographic location, size, and prestige of the specific casino, as well as the level of experience and responsibilities of the individual.

Generally, those with the most experience working in larger, more prestigious casinos in the gambling capitals earn the highest salaries.

Employment Prospects

A good Slot Mechanic is an asset to casinos. Opportunities are plentiful for skilled people. While individuals may find employment in any casino in the world, the greatest number of opportunities exist in areas where there are a large number of casinos.

Las Vegas, Reno, Laughlin, Lake Tahoe, Atlantic City, Biloxi, Baton Rouge, New Orleans, and Detroit offer the greatest number of job possibilities. Other employment settings include casino hotels in other areas of Nevada, Mississippi, New York, Louisiana, Colorado, Connecticut, Illinois, Arizona, and California.

Other regions hosting Indian gaming and land-based or riverboat gaming facilities or cruise ships offer additional opportunities. New casinos and casino hotels are constantly under construction. More casinos and casino hotels are also opening every year as areas legalize gambling.

Because many casinos are open 24 hours a day and machines must be fixed promptly, individuals may work various shifts. These include the day shift, evening or swing shift, overnight or graveyard shift.

Shift hours may vary in different facilities. The day shift, for example, may run from 8 A.M. to 4 P.M.; the swing shift from 4 P.M. to midnight; and the overnight or graveyard shift from midnight to 8 A.M. Some facilities may have overlapping shifts or different hours.

Advancement Prospects

Slot Mechanics can advance their careers by obtaining experience and locating similar positions in larger or more prestigious casinos. As casinos like to promote from within, with experience, Slot Mechanics also can advance to become slot repair managers.

Education and Training

Slot Mechanics must attend slot technicians school, a program in which individuals learn to repair and maintain slot machines. The program offers fundamentals of troubleshooting and repairing all models of electro-mechanical, electronic, and microprocessor-controlled slot machines. Additional courses may cover advanced troubleshooting in specific brands of microprocessor slot machines.

Individuals must be licensed as Slot Mechanics as well as having state licensing for working in a gaming area.

Experience/Skills/Personality Traits

Depending on the specific job, individuals may start out as slot technician trainees. They may then move up to become full-fledged Slot Mechanics.

Slot Mechanics have manual dexterity and an understanding of electronics.

Unions/Associations

Slot Mechanics in most casinos are not usually unionized. Individuals working on riverboats or cruises, however, may be members of various unions.

Slot mechanics may be members of local gaming-related trade associations and organizations.

Those interested in learning more about careers in this area should contact gaming schools, academies, and community colleges offering training in slot machine repair, as well as the human resources departments in casinos.

Tips for Entry

1. Visit the human resources departments of casinos and inquire about job openings.
2. Become more marketable by obtaining training and licensing in a range of types of machines.
3. Continue taking classes in slot repair, advanced troubleshooting, and specific brands of slot machines.
4. Jobs are often advertised in the classified sections of newspapers in areas hosting gaming. Look under classifications such as "Slot Technician," "Slot Mechanic," "Casinos," "Casino Jobs," "Casino Opportunities," or "Gaming."
5. Positions may also be advertised on individual casino Web sites under employment opportunities.
6. New casinos under construction are a great place to look for employment. Stop at their human resources departments and ask for an application.
7. Most casinos have job hotlines. These are frequently updated messages listing job availabilities. You can call each casino directly to get its job hotline phone number.

SLOT BOOTH CASHIER

CAREER PROFILE

Duties: Selling wrapped coins; redeeming coupons, tokens, and buckets of coins.

Alternative Title(s): Cashier

Salary Range: $14,000 to $30,000+

Employment Prospects: Excellent

Best Geographical Location(s) for Position: Las Vegas, Reno, Laughlin, Lake Tahoe, Atlantic City, Biloxi, Baton Rouge, New Orleans, and Detroit offer most opportunities; other regions with land-based, riverboat, or Indian gaming facilities offer additional opportunities.

Prerequisites:

Education or Training—Minimum of high school diploma or GED; no formal training required; see text.

Experience and Qualifications—Prior experience as cashier helpful, but not required; state licensing required to work in gaming area.

Special Skills and Personality Traits—Interpersonal skills; customer service skills; ability to count money accurately.

CAREER LADDER

```
┌─────────────────────────────────┐
│   Carousel or Cage Cashiers or  │
│        Cashier Supervisor       │
└─────────────────────────────────┘

┌─────────────────────────────────┐
│        Slot Booth Cashier       │
└─────────────────────────────────┘

┌─────────────────────────────────┐
│   Cashier in Other Industry or  │
│           Entry Level           │
└─────────────────────────────────┘
```

Position Description

The Slot Booth Cashier has a number of responsibilities. The individual sits in a booth in the casino and is in charge of handling and accounting for coins and cash in a number of different areas.

When customers come to the booth, the Slot Booth Cashier sells them wrapped coins. For example, a customer may want to exchange a ten dollar bill for quarters, and the Slot Booth Cashier will give the patron one roll or 40 quarters.

Many casinos use coupons that offer a certain amount of money in coins as an incentive to attract customers. The casinos may mail these coupons, give them out to groups coming off buses, or use them as part of newspaper ads. The Slot Booth Cashier takes the coupons, validates them, then redeems them for the correct amount of coins.

When customers are done gambling, they bring their buckets or cups of coins that they have won or have left over to the Slot Booth Cashier, who then drops them into a counting machine and gives the customer the correct amount of bills in return. The counting machines deposit the money in bags that must be sealed, marked, and accounted for.

Other duties of the Slot Booth Cashier may include:

- Redeeming chips or tokens that customers have won or have left over when they are done gambling
- Dealing with people who work on the casino floor making change

Salaries

Slot Booth Cashiers, who may earn $14,000 to $30,000 or more annually, are usually hourly employees. Hourly wages can run from $6.50 to $14.00 or more depending on the specific casino the individual is working in and the geographic location. In some cases, Slot Booth Cashiers also receive tips when people have won.

Employment Prospects

Employment prospects are excellent for Slot Booth Cashiers. Every casino needs Slot Booth Cashiers, and most employ a number of people in this position.

While individuals may find employment in any casino in the world, the greatest number of opportunities exist in areas where there are a large number of casinos.

Las Vegas, Reno, Laughlin, Lake Tahoe, Atlantic City, Biloxi, Baton Rouge, New Orleans, and Detroit offer the greatest number of job possibilities. Other employment settings include casino hotels in other areas of Nevada, Mississippi, New York, Louisiana, Colorado, Connecticut, Illinois, Arizona, and California.

Other regions hosting Indian gaming and land-based or riverboat gaming facilities or cruise ships offer additional opportunities. New casinos and casino hotels are constantly under construction. More casinos and casino hotels are also opening every year as areas legalize gambling.

Casinos that are open 24 hours a day run in shifts. Individuals may work the day shift, evening or swing shift, overnight or graveyard shift.

Shift hours may vary in different facilities. The day shift, for example, may run from 8 A.M. to 4 P.M.; the swing shift from 4 P.M. to midnight; and the overnight or graveyard shift from midnight to 8 A.M. Some facilities may have overlapping shifts or different hours.

Advancement Prospects

Slot Booth Cashiers, like most other employees working in casinos, have an excellent chance to advance their careers. Individuals can climb the career ladder by becoming carousel or cage cashiers. Others advance their careers by landing jobs as supervisors. This may require additional training and/or experience.

Education and Training

As in many jobs in casinos, the Slot Booth Cashier can receive on-the-job training or may attend any of the gaming schools, academies, or institutes located throughout the country. These may be private or may be part of community colleges, four-year colleges, or universities. Many casinos also have their own training programs or offer on-the-job training.

Often individuals who have received formal training from a gaming school, academy, or institute have an edge over their counterparts trained on the job.

Slot Booth Cashiers must be licensed in the state in which they work.

Experience/Skills/Personality Traits

Because the Slot Booth Cashier deals with the public, the individual must have good interpersonal skills. Customer service skills are necessary. Other skills needed for this job include the ability to handle and count money quickly and accurately.

Unions/Associations

Slot Booth Cashiers in most casinos are not usually unionized. Individuals working on riverboats or cruises, however, may be members of various unions.

Additional information regarding this career can be obtained from gaming institutes, academies, and schools, as well as casino human resources departments.

Tips for Entry

1. Stop by the human resources departments of casinos to see if they have any job openings in this area.
2. These jobs are often listed on casino job hotlines. These hotlines are frequently updated messages listing jobs available.
3. Positions may be advertised in newspaper classified sections in areas hosting gaming. Look under heading classifications such as "Gaming," "Casinos," or "Slot Booth Cashier."
4. If you are not in an area hosting gaming, consider getting a short-term subscription to the newspaper in the area of your choice. Sunday editions of many newspapers are also often available in larger bookstores.
5. Gaming is growing quickly throughout the country. You can often get an application for a gaming facility being built long before it is finished.

CHANGE PERSON

Duties: Exchanging bills for coins; calling into dispatch for jackpots or broken machines.

Alternative Title(s): Change Girl; Change Man

Salary Range: $14,000 to $20,000 plus tips

Employment Prospects: Good

Best Geographical Location(s) for Position: Las Vegas, Reno, Laughlin, Lake Tahoe, Atlantic City, Biloxi, Baton Rouge, New Orleans, and Detroit offer most opportunities; other regions with land-based, riverboat, or Indian gaming facilities offer additional opportunities.

Prerequisites:

Education or Training—High school diploma or equivalent; on-the-job training; see text.

Experience and Qualifications—Experience handling money may be helpful, but not always required; state licensing required to work in gaming area.

Special Skills and Personality Traits—Money-handling skills; math skills; customer relations; interpersonal skills; pleasant; physical stamina.

```
┌─────────────────────────────────────┐
│   Booth, Carousel, or Cage Cashiers  │
│        or Floor Supervisors          │
└─────────────────────────────────────┘

┌─────────────────────────────────────┐
│            Change Person             │
└─────────────────────────────────────┘

┌─────────────────────────────────────┐
│   Entry Level or Position in Other   │
│     Industry Handling Money          │
└─────────────────────────────────────┘
```

Position Description

For many people visiting casinos, slot machines are one of the most appealing ways to gamble. Casinos employ slot booth cashiers who sell wrapped coins in booths throughout the slot area. However, customers on a roll often do not want to leave their slot machines and go back to the booth to change bills for coins. In order to accommodate these customers, casinos hire Change Persons. Their main function is to give wrapped coins to patrons in exchange for bills.

The Change Person receives a bankroll of coins and bills. Depending on the casino, the bankroll may be worth from $200 to $2,000. Change Persons must sign a slip for the value of the bankroll they receive. They are totally responsible for this money. Individuals may store part of the bankroll in a drawer for which only they have a key.

The rest of the bankroll is placed either in a cart that the Change Person pushes or in an apron the individual wears as he or she walks around the slot area. When customers need coins, they motion to the Change Person, and the individual comes over and gives the patron the needed coins.

When customers hit small to medium jackpots, the Change Person may be called to issue the payoff. The individual signs and verifies that the customer is paid. In other situations, the individual signs and verifies that he or she observed a booth cashier issue the jackpot money to the customer. Usually two signatures are required. Larger jackpots are paid by slot supervisors or other casino executives.

In some settings, before the Change Person pays a winner, he or she slips blank jackpot sheets directly into the slot machine when a patron hits the jackpot. This is then stamped by the machine. In this manner the Change Person has a receipt stamped with needed information. The specialist must keep this receipt as proof the winner was paid.

The size of the bankroll the Change Person receives when signing in does not fluctuate throughout his or her shift because every transaction is always equally balanced in money or receipts. At the end of each individual's shift, the Change Person is expected to count down the bankroll with a shift manager or supervisor.

Other duties of the Change Person may include:

- Calling supervisors or dispatchers for jackpots
- Calling dispatchers to report malfunctioning machines
- Signing and verifying fill slips

Salaries

Change People earn between $6.50 and $9.50 per hour or roughly $14,000 to $20,000 annually. Individuals also receive tips also known as tokes from winning patrons whom they service. Factors affecting earnings include the geographic location, size, and prestige of the specific casino, as well as the experience of the individual.

Employment Prospects

Employment opportunities for Change People are good. Individuals may find openings in most casinos. Because casinos are often open 24 hours a day, individuals may work various shifts, including days, swing shift or evening, overnight or graveyard. Change People may work on weekends and holidays as well.

While individuals may find employment in any casino in the world, the greatest number of opportunities exist in areas where there are a large number of casinos.

Las Vegas, Reno, Laughlin, Lake Tahoe, Atlantic City, Biloxi, Baton Rouge, New Orleans, and Detroit offer the greatest number of job possibilities. Other employment settings include casino hotels in other areas of Nevada, Mississippi, New York, Louisiana, Colorado, Connecticut, Illinois, Arizona, and California.

Other regions hosting Indian gaming and land-based or riverboat gaming facilities or cruise ships offer additional opportunities. New casinos and casino hotels are constantly under construction. More casinos and casino hotels are also opening every year as areas legalize gambling.

Advancement Prospects

Change People may advance in a number of ways depending on career aspirations. Some individuals move to jobs as booth, carousel, or cage cashiers. Others advance their careers by landing jobs as supervisors. Some Change People find employment in other areas of the slot operation. This may require additional training and/or experience.

Education and Training

Most casinos prefer their Change People to hold a high school diploma or the equivalent, although work experience may be accepted in lieu of education.

Training may be obtained on the job or in casino-related training programs offered at gaming academies, institutes, or schools or vocational technical schools and community colleges in areas hosting gaming. Many casinos often also have in-house training programs for employees.

Change People working in casinos must be licensed by the state gaming commission in the specific state in which they work.

Experience/Skills/Personality Traits

Positions may or may not require prior experience handling money. Change People should enjoy working around people and have customer service skills. Money handling and math skills are also needed.

Unions/Associations

Individuals interested in learning more about careers in this area should contact gaming schools, academies, and community colleges offering casino-related training programs, as well as the human resources departments in casinos.

Tips for Entry

1. Any experience handling money such as being a cashier will be useful. Remember to mention this information when seeking a job.
2. Visit the human resources departments of casinos and inquire about job openings.
3. Jobs are often advertised in the classified sections of newspapers in areas hosting gaming. Look under classifications such as "Change Person," "Change Specialist," "Slot Change Person," "Casinos," "Casino Jobs," "Casino Opportunities," or "Gaming."
4. Positions may also be advertised on the Internet. Look under key words in employment sections of the Internet and World Wide Web such as "Casinos," "Casino Jobs," "Gaming," "Slot Change Person," "Change Person," or "Change Specialist."
5. New casinos under construction are a great place to look for employment. Stop by their human resources departments and ask for an application.
6. Most casinos have job hotlines listing jobs available. You can call each casino directly to get its job hotline phone number.

KENO SUPERVISOR

CAREER PROFILE

Duties: Supervising Keno operation; verifying winners; training staff.

Alternative Title(s): None

Salary Range: $25,000 to $38,000+

Employment Prospects: Fair

Best Geographical Location(s) for Position: Las Vegas, Reno, Laughlin, Lake Tahoe, Atlantic City, Biloxi, Baton Rouge, New Orleans, and Detroit offer most opportunities; other regions with land-based, riverboat, or Indian gaming facilities offer additional opportunities.

Prerequisites:

Education or Training—On-the-job training or Keno training at gaming school, academy, institute, or casino.

Experience and Qualifications—One to three years experience as Keno writer; state licensing required to work in gaming area.

Special Skills and Personality Traits—Supervisory skills; interpersonal skills; customer service skills; math skills.

CAREER LADDER

```
┌─────────────────────────────────────┐
│  Keno Supervisor in Larger, More    │
│  Prestigious Casino, or Supervisor in│
│      Other Part of the Casino       │
└─────────────────────────────────────┘

┌─────────────────────────────────────┐
│          Keno Supervisor            │
└─────────────────────────────────────┘

┌─────────────────────────────────────┐
│           Keno Writer               │
└─────────────────────────────────────┘
```

Position Description

Keno is played with 80 numbered Ping-Pong balls. The balls are mixed with circulated air in a large plastic bowl. Using air pressure, 20 balls are randomly forced up through tubes called gooses. Selected balls are referred to as the draw.

Keno is a fast-moving game. Participants buy Keno game tickets in which they select between one and 15 numbered spots. Certain games may allow players to choose up to 20 spots. Players win by having the numbered balls that are selected match the number they have chosen. The payout is related to the number of spots selected, the number of balls matching the spots, and the price of the ticket. The numbers that match the player's card are called catch spots. Once the balls are selected, the game is over and a new one begins.

Keno Supervisors are expected to oversee the Keno operation. They have a number of responsibilities. When people bring their winning tickets to Keno writers, the writers must

calculate the payoff. The Supervisor is responsible for checking the ticket to make sure it is valid and to verify the amount of the payoff.

Keno Supervisors are also responsible for the training of the Keno staff. Some staff members including runners and writers may have completed Keno training at gaming schools, institutes, or academies. Others may need on-the-job training. No matter where or how people were trained, the Supervisor trains the staff in the manner in which the specific casino runs its Keno operation.

A Keno Supervisor is also responsible for overseeing and supervising the Keno staff. If there are any problems with employees in this area, it is up to the Keno Supervisor to handle them appropriately.

Keno Supervisors sit at the Keno counter desk. They may also work on the floor. Supervisors collect the inside tickets from each of the Keno writers' bins. When doing this, individuals must check the floor and counters to be sure they have every inside ticket that was written. Tickets must be moved to the Keno counter desk after a game is closed and before numbers are drawn.

Other duties of the Keno Supervisor may include:

- Dealing with any customer problems or complaints
- Lighting the "closed" sign to indicate a game is closed and tickets will no longer be accepted for the current game
- Examining microfilm camera results to prevent fraud

Salaries

A Keno Supervisor can earn between $25,000 and $38,000 or more annually. Factors affecting earnings include the geographic location, size, and prestige of the specific casino, as well as the experience and responsibilities of the individual.

Employment Prospects

Employment prospects are fair for Keno Supervisors. Opportunities may be found in casinos hosting Keno. Because casinos are often open 24 hours a day, individuals may be expected to work the daytime, swing or evening, graveyard or overnight shift. Supervisors are also expected to work weekends and/or holidays.

While individuals may find employment in any casino in the world, the greatest number of opportunities exist in areas where there are a large number of casinos.

Las Vegas, Reno, Laughlin, Lake Tahoe, Atlantic City, Biloxi, Baton Rouge, New Orleans, and Detroit offer the greatest number of job possibilities. Other employment settings include casino hotels in other areas of Nevada, Mississippi, New York, Louisiana, Colorado, Connecticut, Illinois, Arizona, and California.

Other regions hosting Indian gaming and land-based or riverboat gaming facilities or cruise ships offer additional opportunities. New casinos and casino hotels are constantly under construction. More casinos and casino hotels are also opening every year as areas legalize gambling.

Advancement Prospects

Keno Supervisors may advance their careers by obtaining experience and/or additional training. Some may locate similar positions in larger or more prestigious casinos, resulting in increased earnings. Others move into other positions in the casino gaming area.

Education and Training

Most casinos require or prefer individuals to hold a minimum of a high school diploma or the equivalent. Work experience may be accepted in lieu of education. Some Keno Supervisors receive on-the-job training in Keno prior to becoming supervisors and move up the career ladder. Others have Keno training at gaming schools, academies, or institutes, as well as at community colleges, or vocational technical schools in areas hosting gaming, and in casinos themselves.

Keno Supervisors, like all others working in a gaming area, must usually be licensed in the state in which they work. There are also minimum age requirements in most states.

Experience/Skills/Personality Traits

Experience is required for this position. One to three years working in Keno is necessary to become a Keno Supervisor. Most Keno Supervisors have been Keno writers and were promoted.

Individuals should be personable people who enjoy being around others. Supervisory and training skills are necessary for this position. Excellent customer service skills are essential. Math skills are also needed.

Unions/Associations

There are no bargaining unions for Keno Supervisors. Individuals interested in learning more about careers in this area can contact gaming institutes, academies, and schools, as well as casino human resources departments.

Tips for Entry

1. Jobs are often advertised in the classified sections of newspapers in areas hosting gaming. Look under classifications such as "Casinos," "Casino Jobs," "Casino Opportunities," "Keno," "Keno Supervisors," "Casino Supervisory Opportunities," or "Gaming."
2. The human resources department of a casino is the place to visit to inquire about job openings. Stop by and fill out an application.
3. Look for new casinos under construction. There are a multitude of positions to fill.
4. Positions may be advertised on the Internet. Look under key words in employment sections of the Internet and World Wide Web such as "Casinos," "Casino Jobs," "Gaming," "Keno," or "Keno Supervisors."

KENO WRITER

CAREER PROFILE

Duties: Writing Keno tickets; collecting bets; making pay-offs.

Alternative Title(s): Writer

Salary Range: $11,000 to $16,000 plus tips

Employment Prospects: Good

Best Geographical Location(s) for Position: Las Vegas, Reno, Laughlin, Lake Tahoe, Atlantic City, Biloxi, Baton Rouge, New Orleans, and Detroit offer most opportunities; other regions with land-based, riverboat, or Indian gaming facilities offer additional opportunities.

Prerequisites:

Education or Training—On-the-job training or Keno training at gaming school, academy, institute, or casino.

Experience and Qualifications—Experience requirements vary; state licensing required to work in gaming area.

Special Skills and Personality Traits—Data entry skills; interpersonal skills; customer service skills; money-handling skills; math skills.

CAREER LADDER

```
┌─────────────────────────────────────┐
│ Keno Writer in Larger, More Prestigious │
│     Casino, or Keno Supervisor       │
└─────────────────────────────────────┘

┌─────────────────────────────────────┐
│            Keno Writer               │
└─────────────────────────────────────┘

┌─────────────────────────────────────┐
│    Entry Level or Keno Runner        │
└─────────────────────────────────────┘
```

Position Description

Keno is a casino game played with 80 numbered Ping-Pong balls that are mixed with air in a plastic or glass bowl. Twenty balls are forced up with air at random through tubes, much like procedures in bingo or state lotteries. The selected balls are known as the draw.

Participants buy Keno game tickets. On each ticket players select between one and 15 numbered spots. In some games players choose as many as 20 numbered spots. These will relate to the numbered balls they think will come up for the game. The payout is correlated to the number of spots selected, the number of balls that match the spots, and the price of the ticket. The numbers that match the player's card are called catch spots.

Keno Writers work at a Keno counter. They take the customer tickets, which are referred to as the inside tickets, mark them and make a copy. This is called writing Keno tickets. The copy called the outside ticket is given back to the player. Keno runners often deliver tickets from within the casino to Keno Writers to handle. Another responsibility of the Keno Writer is to collect bets from players. Depending on the ticket, players may place straight bets or combination tickets.

Keno Writers exchange winning tickets for the payoff. They calculate the payoff, stamp winning tickets "paid," and write the amount of the payoff on the outside of the ticket.

Salaries

The Keno Writer earns roughly $11,000 to $16,000 annually based on an hourly wage ranging between $5.50 and $9.00 per hour plus tips. Tips may also be referred to as tokes. Players who win often tip the Writer, pushing the hourly wage in some cases to $25 or more.

Employment Prospects

Employment prospects are good for Keno Writers. Opportunities may be found in all casinos hosting Keno. The greatest number of opportunities exist in areas where there are a large number of casinos.

Las Vegas, Reno, Laughlin, Lake Tahoe, Atlantic City, Biloxi, Baton Rouge, New Orleans, and Detroit offer the greatest number of job possibilities. Other employment settings include casino hotels in other areas of Nevada, Mississippi, New York, Louisiana, Colorado, Connecticut, Illinois, Arizona, and California.

Other regions hosting Indian gaming and land-based or riverboat gaming facilities or cruise ships offer additional opportunities. New casinos and casino hotels are constantly under construction. More casinos and casino hotels are also opening every year as areas legalize gambling.

Advancement Prospects

Keno Writers can advance their careers by obtaining experience and/or additional training. Some may locate similar positions in larger or more prestigious casinos, resulting in increased earnings and tips. Others may become Keno supervisors.

Education and Training

Most casinos require or prefer individuals to hold a minimum of a high school diploma or the equivalent. Work experience may be accepted in lieu of education. Some Keno Writers receive on-the-job training. Others take Keno training at gaming schools, academies, or institutes, as well as at community colleges, or vocational technical schools in areas hosting gaming, and in casinos themselves.

Keno Writers, like all others working in a gaming area, must usually be licensed in the state in which they work. There are also minimum age requirements in most states.

Experience/Skills/Personality Traits

Individuals should be personable people who enjoy being around others. Excellent customer service skills are essential. Data entry skills, the ability to handle money, and math skills are also necessary.

Experience requirements vary. In some situations, individuals move up from positions as Keno runners, while in others, this is an entry-level position.

Unions/Associations

Individuals interested in learning more about careers in this area can contact gaming institutes, academies, and schools, as well as casino human resources departments.

Tips for Entry

1. Jobs are often advertised in the classified sections of newspapers in areas hosting gaming. Look under classifications such as "Casinos," "Casino Jobs," "Casino Opportunities," "Keno Writers," or "Gaming."
2. Stop by the human resources departments of casinos to inquire about job openings.
3. These jobs are often listed on casino job hotlines. These are frequently updated messages listing jobs available. You may call each casino directly to get its job hotline phone number.
4. Look for new casinos under construction. Apply early.
5. Positions may be advertised on the Internet. Look under key words in employment sections of the Internet and World Wide Web such as "Casinos," "Casino Jobs," "Gaming," "Keno," or "Keno Writers." Opportunities may also be found on specific casino Web sites.

KENO RUNNER

Duties: Getting money for Keno tickets from customers; collecting tickets; bringing tickets back to customers; getting payoffs for winning tickets.

Alternative Title(s): None

Salary Range: $11,000 to $15,000 plus tips

Employment Prospects: Good

Best Geographical Location(s) for Position: Las Vegas, Reno, Laughlin, Lake Tahoe, Atlantic City, Biloxi, Baton Rouge, New Orleans, and Detroit offer most opportunities; other regions with land-based, riverboat, or Indian gaming facilities offer additional opportunities.

Prerequisites:

Education or Training—On-the-job training or Keno training at gaming school, academy, institute, or casino.

Experience and Qualifications—Experience requirements vary; state licensing required to work in casinos.

Special Skills and Personality Traits—Interpersonal skills; customer service skills; money-handling skills; physical stamina.

```
┌─────────────────────────────────┐
│   Keno Runner in Larger, More   │
│ Prestigious Casino, Keno Writer  │
│         or Supervisor           │
└─────────────────────────────────┘

┌─────────────────────────────────┐
│          Keno Runner            │
└─────────────────────────────────┘

┌─────────────────────────────────┐
│          Entry Level            │
└─────────────────────────────────┘
```

Position Description

Keno is a casino game that resembles state lotteries. Eighty numbered Ping-Pong balls are used in a Keno game. Twenty balls are chosen at random for each game. Balls are mixed by air and then forced up through tubes. Keno drawings are shown on electronic displays shown throughout the casino.

Players select between one and 15 or 20 spots on a Keno game ticket. The payout is related to the number of spots selected, the number of balls that match the spots, and the price of the ticket.

Casinos have Keno lounges. Players do not have to be in the Keno lounge to play or win this game. They must, however, turn in winning tickets before the next game is called or their prize will be forfeited.

Keno Runners service customers throughout the casino and casino hotel facilities. They do not usually handle customers within the casino lounge. Keno Runners increase the casino's Keno business by finding customers who are busy in other areas of the casino and then selling these people tickets. Players might be gambling at other games, sipping drinks at the bar, or eating in a restaurant.

Keno Runners have a number of responsibilities. Individuals get the money from customers to purchase Keno tickets. They must also collect the tickets from these players.

Keno Runners deliver the tickets to Keno writers. After the tickets are written, the runners return the outside tickets to the customers who purchased them. Players can then watch the game with their tickets.

Other duties of the Keno Runner may include:

- Collecting payoffs for winning customers
- Returning invalid bets to players

Salaries

The Keno Runner earns an hourly wage ranging between $5.50 and $8.50 plus tips, or approximately $11,000 to $15,000 annually. Tips may also be referred to as tokes. Players who win often tip the Runner, pushing their hourly wage in some cases to $25 or more.

Employment Prospects

Employment prospects are good for Keno Runners. Opportunities may be found in casinos hosting Keno. Because casinos are often open 24 hours a day, individuals may work during daytime, swing shift or evening, graveyard shift or overnight. Individuals may also be expected to work weekends or holidays.

The greatest number of opportunities exist in areas where there are a large number of casinos. Las Vegas, Reno, Laughlin, Lake Tahoe, Atlantic City, Biloxi, Baton Rouge, New Orleans, and Detroit offer the greatest number of job possibilities. Other employment settings include casino hotels in other areas of Nevada, Mississippi, New York, Louisiana, Colorado, Connecticut, Illinois, Arizona, and California.

Other regions hosting Indian gaming and land-based or riverboat gaming facilities offer additional opportunities. New casinos and casino hotels are constantly under construction. More casinos and casino hotels are also opening every year as areas legalize gambling.

Advancement Prospects

Keno Runners can advance their careers by obtaining experience and/or additional training. Some may locate similar positions in larger or more prestigious casinos, resulting in increased earnings and tips. Others may become Keno writers or supervisors.

Education and Training

Most casinos require or prefer individuals to hold a minimum of a high school diploma or the equivalent. Work experience may be accepted in lieu of education. Some Keno Runners receive on-the-job training. Others take Keno training at gaming schools, academies, or institutes, as well as at community colleges or vocational technical schools in areas hosting gaming, and in casinos themselves.

Keno Runners, like all others working in a gaming area, must usually be licensed in the state in which they work. There are also minimum age requirements in most states.

Experience/Skills/Personality Traits

Individuals should be personable people who enjoy being around others. Customer service skills are essential. Physical stamina is necessary. The ability to handle money is also needed.

Unions/Associations

Keno Runners are not usually unionized. Individuals interested in learning more about careers in this area can contact gaming institutes, academies, and schools, as well as casino human resources departments.

Tips for Entry

1. Stop by the human resources departments of casinos to inquire about job openings.
2. Look for new casinos under construction. Apply early.
3. Positions may be advertised on the Internet. Look under key words in employment sections of the Internet and World Wide Web such as "Casinos," "Casino Jobs," "Gaming," or "Keno Runners."
4. Call casino job hotlines. Most casinos have them. These are frequently updated messages listing jobs available. You can call each casino directly to get its job hotline phone number.
5. Jobs are often advertised in the classified sections of newspapers in areas hosting gaming. Look under classifications such as "Casinos," "Casino Jobs," "Casino Opportunities," "Keno Runners," or "Gaming."

POKER ROOM MANAGER

CAREER PROFILE

Duties: Developing and instituting policies of poker room; overseeing operation of poker room; supervising floor supervisors and shift supervisors.

Alternative Titles(s): None

Salary Range: $28,000 to $50,000+

Employment Prospects: Good

Best Geographical Location(s) for Position: Las Vegas, Reno, Laughlin, Lake Tahoe, Atlantic City, Biloxi, Baton Rouge, New Orleans, and Detroit offer most opportunities; other regions with land-based, riverboat, or Indian gaming facilities offer additional opportunities.

Prerequisites:

Education or Training—Training at gaming academy, school, or institute.

Experience and Qualifications—Four to seven years experience working in poker rooms; state licensing required to work in gaming area; additional licensing may be necessary.

Special Skills and Personality Traits—Supervisory skills; administrative skills; interpersonal skills; customer service skills; alert; knowledge of rules and procedures of card games.

CAREER LADDER

```
┌─────────────────────────────────────────┐
│  Poker Room Manager in Larger, More      │
│        Prestigious Casino or             │
│        Dealer or Supervisor              │
└─────────────────────────────────────────┘

┌─────────────────────────────────────────┐
│          Poker Room Manager              │
└─────────────────────────────────────────┘

┌─────────────────────────────────────────┐
│         Poker Room Supervisor            │
└─────────────────────────────────────────┘
```

Position Description

Most casinos have a separate room set off from the rest of the casino specifically for poker. The person in charge of overseeing the operation of the poker room is called the Poker Room Manager. There are a number of others employed in the poker room; these may include floor supervisors, dealers, and brushpersons.

A number of different types of poker are played in casinos. These include seven-card stud, pai gow poker, Caribbean stud, seven-card low, low-ball, Texas hold'em, Omaha hold'em, and high-low split. The Poker Room Manager must know the rules and regulations of each game in order to properly oversee the room.

The Poker Room Manager is in charge of developing and instituting policies in the poker room. The individual often works with other casino executives on this task.

The Poker Room Manager helps make the poker room profitable. In the game of poker, customers wager against each other instead of against the house. The casino makes money in the poker room by charging players for running the games. This may be done in a number of ways. One method takes a commission from each pot, commonly referred to as taking a rake of the chips. Another method the casino uses to make money in poker rooms is by charging a specific amount of money for each player as a time charge. This method is usually used in high-limit or no-limit games. The Poker Room Manager may develop programs to assure the room will be full of games and players. In this manner, the profitability of the room can be increased.

The Poker Room Manager is responsible for overseeing the employees of the poker room. On a day-to-day basis, the individual provides administrative supervision over the floor supervisor, who in turn oversees the rest of the employees.

Other duties of the Poker Room Manager may include:

- Overseeing floor supervisors
- Handling customer problems and disputes
- Ensuring rules and regulations are followed

Salaries

Poker Room Managers are usually part of the executive staff and therefore receive a weekly salary instead of an hourly wage. Individuals may earn between $30,000 and $50,000 or more annually depending on a number of factors. These include the geographic location, size, and prestige of the specific casino, size of the room, and the experience and responsibilities of the individual.

Employment Prospects

Employment prospects for qualified individuals are good. Poker Room Managers may find positions throughout the country in areas hosting card rooms, land-based casinos, dockside or floating riverboat casinos, and Indian gaming facilities.

Advancement Prospects

Poker Room Managers may obtain more experience and find similar positions in larger or more prestigious facilities. This will result in increased responsibilities and earnings. As with other jobs in casinos, advancement depends to a great extent on the area in which the individual wishes to work. Poker Room Managers with training and experience in other areas of gaming may find other executive-type positions.

Education and Training

A Poker Room Manager must have complete knowledge of the procedures of the poker games. The individual should also have an understanding and knowledge of the casino rules and regulations.

The best training can be obtained at an accredited gaming school, academy, or institute. Community colleges, vocational technical schools, and casinos themselves may also offer training in this area.

Poker Room Managers, like all others working in a gaming area, must usually be licensed in the state in which they work. There may also be specific licensing and age requirements.

Experience/Skills/Personality Traits

Experience requirements for Poker Room Managers can range from four to seven years, depending on the specific casino. Usually, larger, more prestigious casinos prefer more experience.

Individuals should have supervisory and administrative skills. They should be personable people who enjoy being around others. Interpersonal and customer service skills are mandatory.

Unions/Associations

Poker Room Managers are not unionized. Those interested in learning more about careers as Poker Room Managers should contact gaming institutes, academies, and schools, as well as casino human resources departments.

Tips for Entry

1. Jobs may be advertised in the classified sections of newspapers in areas hosting gaming. Look under classifications such as "Casinos/Gaming," "Poker Room Manager," "Poker Room," or "Casino Opportunities."
2. Visit the human resources departments of casinos and inquire about job openings.
3. Check out specific casino Web sites to see what employment opportunities casinos offer.

POKER BRUSHPERSON

CAREER PROFILE

Duties: Calling out available poker games to customers; posting game information; explaining rules to customers.

Alternative Titles(s): Brushman

Salary Range: $13,000 to $15,000 plus tips.

Employment Prospects: Good

Best Geographical Location(s) for Position: Las Vegas, Reno, Laughlin, Lake Tahoe, Atlantic City, Biloxi, Baton Rouge, New Orleans, and Detroit offer most opportunities; other regions with land-based, riverboat, or Indian gaming facilities offer additional opportunities.

Prerequisites:

Education or Training—Training at gaming academy, school, or institute.

Experience and Qualifications—State licensing required to work in gaming area; additional licensing may be necessary.

Special Skills and Personality Traits—Interpersonal skills; customer service skills; alert; knowledge of rules of poker game.

CAREER LADDER

```
┌─────────────────────────────────────┐
│   Poker Brushperson in Larger, More │
│        Prestigious Casino or         │
│        Dealer or Supervisor          │
└─────────────────────────────────────┘

┌─────────────────────────────────────┐
│          Poker Brushperson           │
└─────────────────────────────────────┘

┌─────────────────────────────────────┐
│             Entry Level              │
└─────────────────────────────────────┘
```

Position Description

Poker is a card game. There are a number of different types of poker played in casinos. One of the most popular is called seven-card stud. Other popular games include seven-card low, low-ball, Texas hold'em, Omaha hold'em, and high-low split.

Poker is the only game in the casino in which customers wager against each other instead of against the house. The casino charges customers for running the games. This may be done by taking a commission from each pot, sometimes referred to as taking a rake of the chips. Sometimes, with high-limit or no-limit games, the casino charges a specific amount of money to each player for a time charge.

Most casinos have a separate room set off from the rest of the casino specifically for poker. A number of different employees in the poker room may include the poker room manager, floor supervisor, dealers, and Brushpersons.

The Brushperson has a number of responsibilities. The individual keeps poker seats filled. In order to accomplish this, the Brushperson waits for potential customers to walk by the poker room and then calls out the games that are available. This often may occur, for example, after the showroom breaks. The Poker Brushperson may also post poker game information for guests so that they know about games.

The individual is responsible for explaining the rules of the various games to customers. This is important so that new players will understand the games.

The Poker Brushperson will seat customers, and this is often done at the direction of the floor supervisor, who may direct customers to games. In some settings, the Poker Brushperson may handle the exchange of chips and money. In other situations, this function may be done by another employee.

Other duties of the Poker Brushperson may include:

• Ordering drinks for players
• Handling customer problems and disputes

Salaries

Poker Brushpersons may earn between $6.50 and $9.00 or more per hour plus tips or approximately $13,000 to $15,000 annually. Factors affecting earnings include the geographic location, size, and prestige of the specific casino, as well as the experience and responsibilities of the individual.

Employment Prospects

Employment prospects for Poker Brushpersons are good. Opportunities are abundant in Las Vegas, Reno, Atlantic City, Biloxi, Baton Rouge, and New Orleans. Other regions with land-based or riverboat gaming and Indian gaming facilities offer additional job prospects.

Because casinos often are open 24 hours a day, individuals may work any shift. Employees in these positions often are scheduled to work on weekends and holidays.

Advancement Prospects

Individuals may climb the career ladder in a number of ways. Some obtain experience and find similar positions in larger or more prestigious facilities. Others may move up to other positions in the card room, such as dealers or floor supervisors. With the proper training, individuals may work in other areas of the casino as well.

Education and Training

The Poker Brushperson must have a complete knowledge of the procedures of the poker games. The individual should also have an understanding and knowledge of the casino rules and regulations.

The best training can be found at an accredited gaming school, academy, or institute. Community colleges, vocational technical schools, and casinos themselves may also offer training in this area.

Poker Brushpersons, like all others working in a gaming area, must usually be licensed in the state in which they work. There may also be additional licensing and age requirements.

Experience/Skills/Personality Traits

Experience requirements for Poker Brushpersons vary depending on the casino. More prestigious casinos may prefer more experience.

Individuals should be personable people who enjoy being around others. Interpersonal and customer service skills are essential.

Unions/Associations

Those interested in learning more about careers as Poker Brushpersons should contact gaming institutes, academies, and schools, as well as casino human resources departments.

Tips for Entry

1. Call casino job hotlines. Most casinos have these and update them regularly with current job openings. You can call each casino directly to get its job hotline phone number.
2. Get your foot in the door of a casino. Most promote from within. Obtain experience and move up the career ladder.
3. Jobs may be advertised in the classified sections of newspapers in areas hosting gaming. Look under classifications such as "Casinos/Gaming," "Poker Brushperson," "Poker Room Employees," or "Casino Opportunities."
4. Stop by the human resources departments of casinos and inquire about job openings.
5. Look for new casinos under construction. Apply early.
6. Check out casino job fairs. These offer an opportunity to interview and be hired quickly.

BINGO MANAGER

CAREER PROFILE

Duties: Overseeing bingo operation; supervising bingo employees; assuring compliance with gaming regulations.

Alternative Title(s): Manager

Salary Range: $30,000 to $40,000+

Employment Prospects: Fair

Best Geographical Location(s) for Position: Indian gaming facilities and bingo halls throughout the country offer most opportunities; regions with land-based or riverboat gaming facilities offering additional opportunities.

Prerequisites
Education and Training—On-the-job training.
Experience/Qualifications—Experience working in gaming industry; state licensing required.
Special Skills and Personality Traits—Supervisory skills; interpersonal skills; knowledge of bingo game rules and regulations.

CAREER LADDER

```
┌─────────────────────────────────┐
│   Assistant Bingo Hall Manager  │
└─────────────────────────────────┘

┌─────────────────────────────────┐
│         Bingo Manager           │
└─────────────────────────────────┘

┌─────────────────────────────────┐
│   Bingo Floor Supervisor or Other│
│     Supervisory Gaming Position │
└─────────────────────────────────┘
```

Position Description

Bingo, a game used for fund-raising purposes throughout the country in many not-for-profit institutions such as churches, synagogues, and schools, is also featured in many casinos. The game attracts a variety of people who enjoy games that can be played for a minimum amount and for an extended period of time.

Players buy one or more bingo cards to participate in a game. Each card has five rows of five squares each. One letter, either B, I, N, G, or O is printed above each vertical column. Each square has a number with the exception of the center square. The center square is known as a free square or free play.

Casinos hosting bingo usually have large rooms known as bingo parlors. The bingo operation employs a number of staff people. These include bingo floor workers, floor supervisors, paymasters, callers, and package preparers. The individual who is in charge of overseeing the bingo operation is called the Bingo Manager. He or she also has an assistant to help with the duties of the job.

The Bingo Manager supervises the bingo staff. He or she is responsible for overseeing training of employees within the department. The individual may pass this duty on to the assistant bingo manager.

The Bingo Manager is expected to develop and formulate policies and procedures used within the bingo area. The individual further develops programs that will help maximize the profits of the bingo operation within the casino.

Other duties of the Bingo Manager may include:

• Handling customer problems or complaints
• Attending department head meetings
• Recommending promotions within the bingo operation
• Implementing programs and policies within department

Salaries

The Bingo Manager's salary can range from approximately $30,000 to $40,000 annually. Factors affecting earnings include the geographic location, size, and prestige of the specific casino, as well as the experience and responsibilities of the individual.

Employment Prospects

Employment prospects are fair for Bingo Managers. Individuals may find employment at casinos hosting bingo. It should be noted, however, that every casino does not have this game. Individuals may find employment in settings such as casinos, dockside and floating riverboat casinos, and Indian gaming facilities.

Advancement Prospects

Bingo Managers may advance their careers by obtaining experience. They may then locate similar positions in other more prestigious casinos, resulting in increased earnings.

Education and Training

Most casinos require or prefer individuals to hold a minimum of a high school diploma or the equivalent. Work experience may be accepted in lieu of education. Bingo Managers are usually trained within the casino. Much of the training is picked up as individuals move up the career ladder in the bingo area. Most have worked as floor workers, floor supervisors, and assistant bingo managers.

Bingo Managers must be licensed by the gaming commission in the state in which they work.

Experience/Skills/Personality Traits

Experience is required for Bingo Managers. Depending on the casino, individuals may need four to six years of experience working in gaming. Some of that experience needs to be working in the bingo area. One to two years supervisory experience is also required.

Individuals must have a total understanding and knowledge of the rules, regulations, and procedures of the casino and those of bingo operations.

Unions/Associations

Bingo Managers are not represented by a union. Additional information regarding this career can be obtained from casino human resources departments.

Tips For Entry

1. Jobs are often advertised in the classified sections of newspapers in areas hosting gaming. Look under classifications such as "Casinos," "Casino Jobs," "Casino Opportunities," "Bingo Manager," "Bingo Operations," or "Gaming."
2. Casinos often promote from within when openings exist. Keep up with what is happening in the bingo operations area.
3. Visit the human resources departments of casinos to find out about job openings.
4. Look for new casinos under construction. Stop at their human resources departments and ask for an application. Apply early.
5. Positions may be advertised on the Internet. Look under key words in employment sections of the Internet and World Wide Web such as "Casinos," "Casino Jobs," "Gaming," or "Bingo Managers."

BINGO FLOOR SUPERVISOR

CAREER PROFILE

Duties: Oversee bingo activities on floor; supervise games; handle customer problems.

Alternative Title(s): Supervisor

Salary Range: $23,000 to $26,000+

Employment Prospects: Fair

Best Geographical Location(s) for Position: Indian gaming facilities and bingo halls throughout the country offer most opportunities; regions with land-based or riverboat gaming facilities offer additional opportunities.

Prerequisites:
Education or Training—On-the-job training.
Experience and Qualifications—Experience working in bingo operation necessary; state licensing required to work in gaming area.
Special Skills and Personality Traits—Supervisory skills; interpersonal skills; knowledge of bingo game rules and regulations.

CAREER LADDER

```
┌─────────────────────────────────────┐
│     Assistant Bingo Hall Manager     │
└─────────────────────────────────────┘

┌─────────────────────────────────────┐
│       Bingo Floor Supervisor         │
└─────────────────────────────────────┘

┌─────────────────────────────────────┐
│ Bingo Caller, Assistant Floor Supervisor │
└─────────────────────────────────────┘
```

Position Description

Casinos with bingo parlors have a number of employees to run the operation. These include bingo managers, assistant bingo managers, floor workers, paymasters, bingo callers, package preparers, and Floor Supervisors.

The Bingo Floor Supervisor oversees everything that occurs on the bingo floor. This includes supervising floor workers as well as the bingo paymaster. The individual may assign floor workers to various parts of the bingo room. The Floor Supervisor also makes sure the floor workers are doing their job and assisting players when needed. The individual must be sure the floor workers go to players who have winning cards when they shout "Bingo."

Another duty of the Bingo Floor Supervisor is to make sure the bingo paymaster goes to winning players and pays them the correct amounts.

The Bingo Floor Supervisor works under the direction of the assistant bingo manager. The individual assists in carrying out programs that help maximize the profits of the casino. Within the scope of the job, the individual is in charge of supervising the games. The Floor Supervisor makes sure all gaming rules and regulations are complied with on the bingo floor.

Other duties of the Bingo Floor Supervisor may include:

• Handling customer problems or complaints
• Scheduling workers

Salaries

Bingo Floor Supervisors earn between $23,000 and $26,000 or more annually. Factors affecting earnings include the geographic location, size, and prestige of the specific casino, as well as the experience and responsibilities of the individual.

Employment Prospects

Employment prospects for Bingo Floor Supervisors are fair. Individuals may find employment opportunities at casinos with bingo games. Depending on when casinos hold bingo sessions, individuals may work shifts, including daytime, swing shift or evening, graveyard or overnight. Bingo Floor Supervisors may also have to work weekends and holidays.

Advancement Prospects

With experience, Bingo Floor Supervisors may advance their careers through promotion to the job of assistant bingo manager.

Education and Training

Generally, casinos require or prefer individuals to hold a minimum of a high school diploma or the equivalent. Work experience may be accepted in lieu of education.

Bingo Floor Supervisors usually receive on-the-job training within the casino. A great deal of the training needed is picked up in prior jobs in bingo operations.

Bingo Floor Supervisors must be licensed by the gaming commission in the state in which they work.

Experience/Skills/Personality Traits

Experience working in bingo operations is necessary to become a Bingo Floor Supervisor. Depending on the specific casino, this may range from one to three years. Supervisory experience in some capacity is also usually required. Individuals must have total understanding and knowledge of the rules, regulations, and procedures of bingo operations.

Unions/Associations

Bingo Floor Supervisors are not unionized. Additional information regarding this career can be obtained from gaming schools, as well as from casino human resources departments.

Tips For Entry

1. Visit the human resources departments of casinos to find out about job openings.
2. Many casinos promote from within. If you are working in the bingo area as a floor worker, keep up with developments in your department.
3. Jobs are often advertised in the classified sections of newspapers in areas hosting gaming. Look under classifications such as "Casinos," "Casino Jobs," "Casino Opportunities," "Bingo Floor Supervisor," "Bingo Operations," or "Gaming."
4. Positions may also be advertised on the Internet and World Wide Web. Look under key words in employment sections of the Internet such as "Casinos," "Casino Jobs," "Gaming," or "Bingo Floor Supervisors."
5. Look for new casinos under construction. Stop at their human resources departments and ask for an application.
6. These positions may be listed on casino job hotlines. These are frequently updated messages listing jobs available. You can call each casino directly to get its job hotline phone number.

BINGO PAYMASTER

CAREER PROFILE

Duties: Paying bingo prizes to winners; recording winnings.

Alternative Title(s): Paymaster

Salary Range: $18,000 to $21,000

Employment Prospects: Fair

Best Geographical Location(s) for Position: Indian gaming facilities and bingo halls throughout the country offer most opportunities; regions with land-based or riverboat gaming facilities offer additional opportunities.

Prerequisites

Education and Training—On-the-job training.

Experience/Qualifications—Cashier experience helpful; state licensing required.

Special Skills and Personality Traits—Money-handling skills; cashier skills; math skills; knowledge of bingo game rules and regulations.

CAREER LADDER

```
┌──────────────────────────────────────┐
│ Other Positions in Bingo Hall or Casino │
└──────────────────────────────────────┘

┌──────────────────────────────────────┐
│          Bingo Paymaster             │
└──────────────────────────────────────┘

┌──────────────────────────────────────┐
│       Entry Level or Cashier         │
└──────────────────────────────────────┘
```

Position Description

The game of bingo is popular in many casinos due to its simplicity of play and the fact that every game has at least one winner. As bingo callers announce more and more numbers and the game progresses, excitement builds. For the players at least, the most exciting part of a bingo game is hearing the last number needed for winning.

When a player covers all the required numbers on his or her card and shouts "Bingo," a floor worker reads the numbers on the card and verifies it is a winner. Once the card is declared a winner, the floor person indicates the individual to a staff member called the Bingo Paymaster.

The Bingo Paymaster is responsible for paying the lucky winner. If there is more than one winner, the Bingo Paymaster must determine what the prize will be for each person.

The Paymaster pays each winner the correct amount of money. The individual is responsible for recording each bingo prize paid out.

Other duties of the Bingo Paymaster may include:

• Accounting for cash and winnings at the end of each shift

Salaries

Bingo Paymasters earn between $8.50 and $12.00 or more per hour or about $18,000 to $21,000 annually. They may also receive tips. Factors affecting earnings include the geographic location, size, and prestige of the specific casino, as well as the experience of the individual.

Employment Prospects

Employment prospects are fair for Bingo Paymasters. Individuals may find employment opportunities at casinos hosting bingo games. Depending on when casinos hold bingo sessions, individuals may work daytime, swing or evening, graveyard or overnight shifts. Bingo Paymasters may be expected to work weekends and holidays.

Advancement Prospects

Depending on career aspirations, Bingo Paymasters can obtain experience and move into other areas of the bingo operation or other areas of the casino for advancement opportunities.

Education and Training

Generally, casinos require or prefer individuals to hold a minimum of a high school diploma or the equivalent. Work experience may be accepted in lieu of education.

Bingo Paymasters usually receive on-the-job training within the casino. They must be licensed by the gaming commission in the state in which they work.

Experience/Skills/Personality Traits

Depending on the specific position, casinos may require from six months to one year of cashier experience.

Individuals must have math and money-handling skills. The ability to record prizes in an accurate fashion is also necessary. Knowledge of the rules, regulations, and procedures of bingo operations is needed.

Unions/Associations

Bingo Paymasters are not represented by a union. Additional information regarding this career can be obtained from gaming schools as well as from casino human resources departments.

Tips for Entry

1. Stop by the human resources departments of casinos and inquire about job openings.
2. Jobs are often advertised in the classified sections of newspapers in areas hosting gaming. Look under classifications such as "Casinos," "Casino Jobs," "Casino Opportunities," "Bingo Paymaster," "Bingo Operations," or "Gaming."
3. Positions may also be advertised on the Internet. Look under key words in employment sections of the Internet and World Wide Web such as "Casinos," "Casino Jobs," "Gaming," or "Bingo Paymasters."
4. New casinos under construction are a great place to look for employment. Stop at their human resources departments and ask for an application.
5. Experience working as a cashier is often necessary. This experience can be obtained anywhere in or out of the casino.
6. Most casinos have job hotlines. These are frequently updated messages listing job available. You can call each casino directly to get its job hotline phone number.

BINGO CALLER

CAREER PROFILE

Duties: Calling letter and number of bingo balls during bingo games; verifying winners.

Alternative Title(s): Caller

Salary Range: $11,000 to $20,000

Employment Prospects: Fair

Best Geographical Location(s) for Position: Indian gaming facilities and bingo halls throughout the country offer most opportunities; regions with land-based or riverboat gaming facilities offer additional opportunities.

Prerequisites:

Education or Training—On-the-job training.

Experience and Qualifications—No experience necessary; state licensing required to work in gaming area.

Special Skills and Personality Traits—Clear speaking voice; ability to speak in public; manual dexterity; personable.

CAREER LADDER

```
┌─────────────────────────────────────┐
│   Bingo Caller at Larger or More     │
│  Prestigious Casino, or Paymaster,   │
│  Floorperson, or Floor Supervisor    │
└─────────────────────────────────────┘

┌─────────────────────────────────────┐
│            Bingo Caller              │
└─────────────────────────────────────┘

┌─────────────────────────────────────┐
│            Entry Level               │
└─────────────────────────────────────┘
```

Position Description

Many casinos offer bingo as an attractive gambling game. Bingo does not have difficult rules to follow, and there is always at least one if not more winners in every game. In order to induce players, many casinos offer large super jackpots or special bingo promotions.

Players buy one or more bingo cards to participate in a game. Depending on the casino and game, these may be made of cardboard, paper, or plastic. Each card has five rows of five squares each. One letter, either B, I, N, G, or O is printed above each vertical column. Each square has a number with the exception of the center square, which is known as a free square or free play.

There are a number of ways to win in bingo, depending on the game. Players might play a game in which five numbers in a straight vertical, horizontal, or diagonal line must be covered. Other games require players to cover four numbers at the four corners of their bingo card, to cover eight numbers surrounding the center square, or to cover all the numbers on the card.

Bingo uses 75 Ping-Pong balls, each imprinted with a number from one to 75 and lettered with one of the letters B, I, N, G, or O. The balls are placed in a bingo bowl, cage, or bingo blower. Some casinos have a special colored ball in the mix, which can be used as a wild ball when a number is needed to win. Randomly, one by one, balls are chosen or forced out by air into a pocket or the neck of a tube.

The Bingo Caller is responsible for taking the ball that has been selected and showing it to the audience. The individual must then announce the number and letter of the ball. The Bingo Caller places each announced ball onto a board that corresponds to the number and letter that have been called. The Bingo Caller continues selecting and announcing ball numbers and letters until someone shouts "Bingo," indicating a winner. Electronic numbered boards are often used that light up when a number is selected so that the playing audience can clearly see the numbers that have been picked.

A Bingo Caller is responsible for verifying the winning ticket. This is done by a floorperson going to the winning player and reading out loud the numbers that have been covered. The Bingo Caller checks the numbers that are read against the numbers that have been selected. He or she may also verify the ticket number. The Bingo Caller announces a winner and the payoff.

The Bingo Caller may be responsible for operating the bingo equipment. He or she may turn the machine on and off. In some games there may be two Callers. One turns on the machine and hands the ball that comes out to the second Bingo Caller. In other games one Bingo Caller handles both functions.

Other duties of the Bingo Caller may include:

- Releasing balls back into machine after end of game
- Announcing type of game, rules, and payoffs before game begins.

Salaries

A Bingo Caller is paid an hourly wage ranging from $5.50 to $10.00 or about $11,000 to $20,000 annually. Factors affecting earnings include the geographic location, size, and prestige of the specific casino, as well as the experience of the individual.

Employment Prospects

Employment prospects for Bingo Callers are fair. Opportunities may be located in casinos hosting bingo parlors. Because casinos are often open 24 hours a day, individuals may be asked to work during various shifts including daytime, evening or swing shift, graveyard or overnight. Individuals may also work weekends or holidays.

Advancement Prospects

Bingo Callers may advance their careers by obtaining experience and/or additional training. They may then locate similar positions in larger or more prestigious casinos, resulting in increased earnings. Depending on training, experience, and qualifications, individuals may move into other positions in this area such as bingo paymasters, floorpersons, or floor supervisors.

Education and Training

Most casinos require or prefer individuals to hold a minimum of a high school diploma or the equivalent. Work experience may be accepted in lieu of education. On-the-job training is usually offered at casinos.

Bingo Callers, like others working in a gaming area, must be licensed in the state in which they work. There are also minimum age requirements in most states.

Experience/Skills/Personality Traits

In most positions, no prior experience is necessary for this job. An individual should have a clear speaking voice, and the ability to speak into a microphone and talk in front of an audience is necessary.

Unions/Associations

Bingo Callers are not represented by a union. Additional information regarding this career can be obtained from gaming schools as well as from casino human resources departments.

Tips For Entry

1. While experience isn't usually required, it never hurts and might give you an edge over another applicant. You might want to obtain experience volunteering at church, synagogue, or school bingo games as a Bingo Caller.
2. Jobs are often advertised in the classified sections of newspapers in areas hosting gaming. Look under classifications such as "Casinos," "Casino Jobs," "Casino Opportunities," "Bingo Callers," or "Gaming."
3. Visit the human resources departments of casinos to inquire about job openings.
4. Read newspapers from areas where gaming is legal. Look for articles on new casinos under construction. Apply early.

BINGO FLOOR WORKER

CAREER PROFILE

Duties: Listening for shouts of "Bingo"; selling bingo cards to players; reading numbers to bingo caller to verify winning card; assisting and servicing bingo players.

Alternate Title(s): Floorperson

Salary Range: $11,000 to $16,000

Employment Prospects: Fair

Best Geographical Location(s) for Position: Indian gaming facilities and bingo halls throughout the country offer most opportunities; regions with land-based or riverboat gaming facilities offer additional opportunities.

Prerequisites:

Education or Training—On-the-job training.

Experience and Qualifications—No experience necessary; state licensing required.

Special Skills and Personality Traits—Interpersonal skills; customer service skills; physical stamina.

CAREER LADDER

```
┌─────────────────────────────┐
│   Bingo Floor Supervisor    │
└─────────────────────────────┘

┌─────────────────────────────┐
│     Bingo Floor Worker      │
└─────────────────────────────┘

┌─────────────────────────────┐
│  Bingo Caller or Entry Level │
└─────────────────────────────┘
```

Position Description

Bingo is offered in many casinos. The game often attracts players who enjoy gambling with a relatively minimum amount of money for a long period of time. The game has simple rules, is easy to play, and guarantees one or more winners every time. Bingo in casinos is played like bingo games in not-for-profit facilities throughout the country such as churches, synagogues, and schools.

Players buy one or more bingo cards to participate in a game. Each card has five rows of five squares each. One letter, either B, I, N, G, or O. is printed above each vertical column. Each square has a number with the exception of the center square, which is known as a free square or free play.

Bingo parlors are often large rooms. Bingo Floor Workers are assigned a section of the room and are responsible for assisting players in their area.

Bingo Floor Workers may also be called bingo floor attendants, bingo attendants, or bingo floorpeople in different casinos. Responsibilities vary depending on the specific casino. A Bingo Floor Worker explains to participants the various games and how they are played.

Bingo games may be won in various ways. It might be a game in which five numbers in a straight vertical, horizontal, or diagonal line must be covered. Other games might require players to cover four numbers at the four corners of their bingo card, to cover eight numbers surrounding the center square, or to cover all the numbers on the card. Players may, for example, need an explanation of what a small round robin looks like.

As the bingo caller announces numbers and the game progresses, players cover the designated spots on their cards. The Bingo Floor Workers walk around their designated area, listening for a player to call out "Bingo!" When that occurs, the Floor Worker takes the card from the player, reads the numbers that have been covered aloud to the bingo caller, and verifies the card as a winner. The individual may also verify the ticket or card number. Once a card is declared a winner, the floorperson indicates the individual to the bingo paymaster, who pays the lucky person.

Bingo Floor Workers in some casinos may be responsible for selling additional bingo cards, packages, and specials to players in their areas. In other casinos, other workers handle this function.

Other duties of the Bingo Floor Worker may include:

- Seating players
- Assisting and servicing players throughout games

Salaries

The Bingo Floor Worker is paid an hourly wage ranging from $5.50 to $7.50 plus tips or about $11,000 to $16,000 per year. Factors affecting earnings include the geographic location, size, and prestige of the specific casino.

Employment Prospects

Employment prospects for Bingo Floor Workers are fair. Individuals may work at any casino hosting bingo parlors. It should be noted, however, that all casinos do not have bingo. A number of Bingo Floor Workers are needed for each game. Bingo Floor Workers work various shifts, depending on when the casino schedules games. These may include daytime, swing shift or evening, graveyard or overnight. Individuals may also work weekends or holidays.

Advancement Prospects

Bingo Floor Workers may advance their careers by obtaining experience and/or additional training. Some may move into other positions in the bingo area such as bingo floor supervisors. Others may locate positions in other areas of the casino.

Education and Training

Most casinos require or prefer individuals to hold a minimum of a high school diploma or the equivalent. Work experience may be accepted in lieu of education. On-the-job training is usually offered for this type of position at casinos hosting bingo parlors. Bingo Floor Workers must be licensed by the gaming commission in the state in which they work.

Experience/Skills/Personality Traits

In most positions, no prior experience is necessary for this job. Individuals should be personable, friendly people. Interpersonal skills and customer service skills are mandatory. Physical stamina and the ability to stand for periods of time are necessary.

Unions/Associations

Bingo Floor Workers are not represented by a union. Additional information regarding this career can be obtained from casino human resources departments.

Tips For Entry

1. As noted previously, experience is not usually necessary, but it can't hurt. Experience working on the bingo floor at a church, synagogue, or school should be noted when applying for jobs.
2. Jobs are often advertised in the classified sections of newspapers in areas hosting gaming. Look under classifications such as "Casinos," "Casino Jobs," "Casino Opportunities," "Bingo Floor Workers," "Bingo Floor People," or "Gaming."
3. Visit the human resources departments of casinos to find out about job openings. You might want to check newspapers first to see which casinos in the area offer bingo.
4. Look for new casinos under construction. Stop at their human resources departments and ask for an application. Apply early.

CAREER OPPORTUNITIES IN CASINO AND CASINO HOTEL MARKETING, PUBLIC RELATIONS, AND SALES

DIRECTOR OF CASINO MARKETING

CAREER PROFILE

Duties: Developing and implementing casino's marketing plan; finding innovative ways to attract new business; increasing market share; increasing casino profitability.

Alternative Titles(s): Marketing Director

Salary Range: $65,000 to $120,000 +

Employment Prospects: Poor

Best Geographical Location(s) for Position: Las Vegas, Reno, Laughlin, Lake Tahoe, Atlantic City, Biloxi, Baton Rouge, New Orleans, and Detroit offer most opportunities; other regions with land-based, riverboat, or Indian gaming facilities offer additional opportunities.

Prerequisites:

Education or Training—College degree preferred; see text.

Experience and Qualifications—Experience in gaming and casino marketing.

Special Skills and Personality Traits—Creativity; writing skills; communication skills; marketing skills; ability to conceptualize; sales skills.

CAREER LADDER

```
┌─────────────────────────────────┐
│   Vice President of Marketing or │
│   Director of Casino Marketing   │
│ at Larger, More Prestigious Casino│
└─────────────────────────────────┘

┌─────────────────────────────────┐
│   Director of Casino Marketing   │
└─────────────────────────────────┘

┌─────────────────────────────────┐
│  Assistant Director of Marketing │
└─────────────────────────────────┘
```

Position Description

Those interested in visiting casinos have numerous choices depending on the location, size, and atmosphere they are seeking. In order to increase their market share, therefore increasing profitability, casinos develop programs to market their facilities.

The Director of Casino Marketing is in charge of the development and implementation of the casino's marketing plan. The individual often works under the direction of the vice president of marketing for the entire facility.

The Director of Casino Marketing develops different promotions designed to attract business, brings in new customers, and brings back those who have previously visited the facility. The individual often works in conjunction with staff people in the public relations, publicity, advertising, and sales departments to attain the goals.

As part of the job, the Director of Casino Marketing must not only conceptualize and plan innovative programs, promotions, and special events, but implement them as well.

These might include a variety of promotions as well as tournaments, bus tour programs, and junkets. The individual is responsible for taking these projects from inception to fruition. It is essential that these marketing efforts build customer loyalty and increase the existing player base.

The Director of Casino Marketing is responsible for developing the concepts and campaigns that detail how the casino lets potential customers know about the facility and its programs. He or she decides how much and what type of advertising, promotion, public relations, and selling will be most effective.

The individual also determines the most effective techniques to market the casino and its services. The Director will often determine the viability of introducing new promotions, games, clubs, or markets to the casino. In some cases, after attempting to market a new promotion, the Director of Casino Marketing may find the idea is not financially viable. In these cases the Director scraps the particular program in favor of another.

The Director of Casino Marketing may direct marketing efforts toward various segments of the population — those who visit casinos on bus tours or junkets, and those who play the slots or other popular games at the casino.

The Director of Casino Marketing often works on marketing programs involving special events and functions for customers, bringing new players into the casino and keeping prior guests coming back.

Other duties of the Director of Casino Marketing include:

- Overseeing the casino marketing staff
- Handling player development
- Developing direct mail marketing
- Coordinating database marketing efforts
- Performing research for marketing efforts and results

Salaries

Directors of Casino Marketing earn between $65,000 and $120,000 or more annually. Factors affecting earnings include the geographic location, size, and prestige of the specific casino, as well as the track record, experience, education, and responsibilities of the individual. Generally, those with a proven track record working in larger, more prestigious casinos in the gambling capitals earn the highest salaries.

Employment Prospects

Employment prospects for the Director of Casino Marketing are limited because each casino has only one person in this position. Because casinos promote from within, jobs can be secured by talented and creative individuals who move up the career ladder.

The largest number of opportunities can be found in Las Vegas, Reno, Laughlin, Atlantic City, Biloxi, Baton Rouge, New Orleans, and Detroit. Other regions with land-based or riverboat gaming facilities offer additional opportunities. As other areas begin to host gaming, more positions will become available.

Advancement Prospects

The Director of Casino Marketing may climb the career ladder by promotion to vice president of marketing. However, a more common method of advancement is finding a similar position in a larger or more prestigious facility. This results in increased responsibilities and earnings.

Education and Training

Most casinos and casino hotels prefer their Director of Casino Marketing to hold a bachelor's degree in marketing, public relations, communications, business management, or a related field.

Courses, workshops, and seminars in marketing, sales, and the gaming and hospitality industries are also useful.

Experience/Skills/Personality Traits

Casinos expect their Director of Casino Marketing to have a proven track record and marketing credentials in the casino gaming and hospitality industry.

The Director of Casino Marketing needs a wide array of skills. The individual must be a self-starter. He or she should also be creative, with the ability to develop innovative ideas for marketing casinos. Excellent writing and communication skills are essential. Marketing, public relations, and sales skills are necessary in this position. Strategic-planning skills are also needed.

A complete knowledge and understanding of the gaming and hospitality industries are mandatory.

Unions/Associations

Those interested in learning more about careers as the Director of Casino Marketing can obtain additional information by contacting the Hotel Sales and Marketing Association International (HSMA), the Public Relations Society of America (PRSA), or the human resources departments in casino hotels.

Tips for Entry

1. Some employment agencies and recruitment firms deal specifically in the field of marketing, as well as in the hospitality industry.
2. Get your foot in the door of a casino hotel. Most promote from within. Start out in the marketing or sales department, obtain experience, and climb the career ladder.
3. Jobs may be advertised in the classified sections of newspapers in areas hosting gaming. Look under classifications such as "Casino/Gaming Opportunities," "Director of Casino Marketing," "Casino Marketing Director," "Marketing," or Casino Opportunities."
4. Read trade journals and the business news in areas hosting gaming. Look for articles on people who have been promoted. This often means job openings.

CASINO MARKETING COORDINATOR

CAREER PROFILE

Duties: Sending out mailings; answering phones; making phone calls; inputting information into computers; assisting in handling details for special events, parties, and functions; assisting in coordinating details for junkets and bus programs.

Alternative Titles(s): Marketing Assistant

Salary Range: $15,000 to $30,000

Employment Prospects: Good

Best Geographical Location(s) for Position: Las Vegas, Reno, Laughlin, Lake Tahoe, Atlantic City, Biloxi, Baton Rouge, New Orleans, and Detroit offer the greatest number of job possibilities. Other employment settings include casino hotels in other areas of Nevada, Mississippi, New York, Louisiana, Colorado, Connecticut, Illinois, Arizona and California.
Other regions hosting Indian gaming and land-based or riverboat gaming facilities offer additional opportunities.

Prerequisites:
Education or Training—High school diploma or equivalent; on-the-job training.
Experience and Qualifications—Experience in gaming, hospitality, or marketing helpful, but not required.
Special Skills and Personality Traits—Customer service skills; computer literate; telephone skills; communications skills; detail-oriented.

CAREER LADDER

```
┌─────────────────────────────────┐
│   Casino Marketing Supervisor   │
└─────────────────────────────────┘

┌─────────────────────────────────┐
│   Casino Marketing Coordinator  │
└─────────────────────────────────┘

┌─────────────────────────────────┐
│          Entry Level            │
└─────────────────────────────────┘
```

Position Description

Casinos put a great deal of emphasis on their marketing programs to increase their market share and profitability. The casino director of marketing is expected to develop programs to market the facility effectively. The marketing program often consists of a great many promotions, special events, player parties, and tournaments. Marketing efforts also include bus programs, junkets, and player development promotions.

Casino Marketing Coordinators assist in handling many of the details of these events and programs. For example, Casino Marketing Coordinators help set up the parties and other functions held for high rollers, slot tournaments, or V.I.P. guests.

Individuals work under the direction of marketing managers, supervisors, and administrators. Marketing Coordinators are required to handle a great deal of the clerical work associated with this department. For example, they may be responsible for collating direct mail brochures and letter responses directed toward prior or potential customers. Individuals must also prepare direct mail pieces for distribution.

Marketing Coordinators are responsible for inputting a variety of data into computers for use in the marketing office. This may include names, addresses, and phone numbers of customers who call, visit, or fill in forms from advertisements.

Marketing Coordinators may be required to input and tabulate data regarding specific programs and promotions the marketing department has held. This information will then be used to analyze and track those that have been effective or ineffective.

The Casino Marketing Coordinator handles the phones in the marketing office. The individual answers questions from callers regarding upcoming promotions and special events in the casino. The Coordinator additionally is responsible for sending callers information and mailings on specific promotions upon request. The Coordinator might also be required to make calls to customers to see if they are attending functions or to tell them about upcoming events in the facility.

Other duties of the Casino Marketing Coordinator include:

- Tabulating questionnaires and other research
- Inputting data regarding player tracking
- Assisting in player tracking
- Sending invitations to customers for events, promotions, parties, and other functions

Salaries

Casino Marketing Coordinators earn an hourly wage ranging from $8.00 to $15.00 or approximately $15,000 to $30,000 annually. Factors affecting earnings include the geographic location, size, and prestige of the specific casino, as well as the experience and responsibilities of the individual.

Employment Prospects

Every casino, no matter how small, has Casino Marketing Coordinators. Casino marketing is extremely important to all casinos, so employment opportunities are good for Casino Marketing Coordinators. The greatest number of jobs are located in the gambling capitals and other areas hosting larger casinos, including cities such as Las Vegas, Reno, Laughlin, Lake Tahoe, Atlantic City, Biloxi, Baton Rouge, New Orleans, and Detroit. Other areas with land-based or riverboat gaming facilities offer additional job possibilities. As legalized gaming expands throughout the United States, opportunities in other locations will become available.

Advancement Prospects

Casinos like to promote from within. This is a great position to start with if you are interested in casino marketing.

Casino Marketing Coordinators may climb the career ladder by promotion to casino marketing supervisors or marketing office administrators. With additional education and experience, individuals may move into other positions in the casino marketing area.

Education and Training

Casino Marketing Coordinators are often trained on the job. Most casinos and casino hotels prefer their Marketing Coordinators to hold a minimum of a high school diploma or its equivalent. Many casinos help individuals who do not have the minimum education obtain a GED. Work experience may be accepted in lieu of education.

Experience/Skills/Personality Traits

In most casinos, this is an entry-level job. Any experience in marketing, gaming, or the hospitality industry will be helpful.

There is a great deal of customer service needed in this job. Marketing coordinators should be detail-oriented individuals. Excellent telephone and communication skills are necessary. Office skills such as data entry and typing are also mandatory. Individuals should also have computer skills.

Unions/Associations

Additional information regarding this career can be obtained from gaming institutes, academies, and schools, as well as casino and casino human resources departments.

Tips for Entry

1. This is a good position to get your foot in the door of casino marketing. Learn what you can, get some experience, and move up the career ladder.
2. Jobs are often advertised on casino job hotlines. These are recorded messages put out by casinos announcing current job openings as well as required skills. Call individual casinos to get their job hotline phone numbers.
3. Openings may be also advertised in the classified sections of newspapers in areas hosting gaming. Look under classifications such as "Casino/Gaming Opportunities," "Casino Marketing," "Casino Marketing Coordinator," "Marketing," or "Casino Opportunities."
4. Stop by casino human resources departments and inquire about job openings.

PUBLIC RELATIONS DIRECTOR

CAREER PROFILE

Duties: Publicizing and promoting casino and casino hotel as well as their theaters, showrooms, and restaurants; publicizing promotional and special events.

Alternative Titles(s): Director of Public Relations

Salary Range: $35,000 to $80,000+

Employment Prospects: Fair

Best Geographical Location(s) for Position: Las Vegas, Reno, Laughlin, Lake Tahoe, Atlantic City, Biloxi, Baton Rouge, New Orleans, and Detroit offer most opportunities; other regions with land-based, riverboat, or Indian gaming facilities offer additional opportunities.

Prerequisites:

Education or Training—Bachelor's degree preferred; see text.

Experience and Qualifications—Experience in public relations or the hospitality industry helpful.

Special Skills and Personality Traits—Writing skills; communication skills; marketing skills; creativity; organization; interpersonal skills; customer service skills.

CAREER LADDER

```
┌─────────────────────────────────────┐
│  Public Relations Director in Larger, │
│     More Prestigious Casino,          │
│  V.P. of Public Relations, or Director│
│          of Marketing                 │
└─────────────────────────────────────┘

┌─────────────────────────────────────┐
│     Public Relations Director         │
└─────────────────────────────────────┘

┌─────────────────────────────────────┐
│    Public Relations Coordinator,      │
│   Assistant Director of Public        │
│    Relations, or Publicist            │
│        in Other Industry              │
└─────────────────────────────────────┘
```

Position Description

Casinos and casino hotels employ a Public Relations Director to publicize the facility. The individual is responsible for promoting everything in the resort including the hotel, casino, showrooms, nightclubs, restaurants, and theaters. The Public Relations Director also publicizes any promotional and special events held at the casino or hotel.

The P.R. Director tries to develop various angles and conceive different methods to promote the facility. The P.R. Director often has a staff that assists in many of the individual's responsibilities.

The Public Relations Director is responsible for developing and writing press releases for media distribution. Targets include print, television, and radio. Stock press releases must be prepared, as well as releases on hotel and casino news and events. The P.R. Director must also make sure fact sheets on all areas of the casino and hotel are prepared. These might include interesting facts such as the number of eggs or steaks or shrimp served per year in one of the restaurants, the ratio of employees to rooms, or the amount of quarters won in slots annually.

The difference between advertising and publicity is that advertising has a cost factor. A full page ad in a major newspaper or magazine, or a commercial on national television can cost thousands of dollars. While it often costs money to generate publicity, there generally is no charge to get feature stories and articles written in the print media or have stories appear on television. The Public Relations Director generates publicity ideas so that editors and producers find the concepts interesting and want to do articles or stories.

The Public Relations Director acts as a liaison between the casino hotel and the media. A great many events occur at any one time in a casino hotel. A big slot tournament might be scheduled, as well as the opening of a well-known celebrity act in the showroom, a major boxing show, interesting new slot machines, or a major convention. The Public

Relations Director must know which media to call for specific events—sports editors, entertainment writers, gaming media, and hotel or hospitality columnists. The P.R. Director must have a good working relationship with all media, print as well as television, cable, and radio.

The casino hotel P.R. Director works with the facility's marketing and advertising department. Together, they may develop and implement a variety of special events designed to promote the facility and its activities. These might include press conferences, parties, extravaganzas, promotions, or tournaments.

Because guests often travel to casinos and casino hotels from other areas, the Public Relations Director must generate both local and national media exposure.

Other duties of the casino hotel Public Relations Director may include:

- Supervising the public relations staff
- Developing special projects and promotional events to promote the facility
- Building relationships with media editors, producers, and writers

Salaries

Casino and casino hotel Public Relations Directors earn $35,000 and $80,000 or more annually. Factors affecting earnings include the geographic location, size, and prestige of the specific casino hotel, as well as the experience and responsibilities of the individual. Generally, those with the most experience working in larger, more prestigious casinos hotels, in the gambling capitals earn the highest salaries.

Employment Prospects

Employment prospects for casino and casino hotel Public Relations Directors are fair. Jobs can be found throughout the country in locations hosting casinos.

The greatest number of opportunities exist in areas where there are a large number of casinos. Las Vegas, Reno, Laughlin, Lake Tahoe, Atlantic City, Biloxi, Baton Rouge, New Orleans, and Detroit offer the greatest number of job possibilities. Other employment settings include casino hotels in other areas of Nevada, Mississippi, New York, Louisiana, Colorado, Connecticut, Illinois, Arizona, and California. Other regions hosting Indian gaming and land-based or riverboat gaming facilities offer additional opportunities.

Advancement Prospects

Individuals may climb the career ladder in a number of ways. Some people gain experience and professional reputations and locate similar positions in larger or more prestigious facilities. This results in increased responsibilities and earnings.

Public Relations Directors may also advance their careers by being promoted to positions such as vice president of P.R., Corporate Public Relations Director, or Director of Marketing.

Education and Training

Generally, most casinos and casino hotels prefer their Public Relations Directors to have a bachelor's degree. Good majors include public relations, marketing, communications, journalism, English, or liberal arts.

Courses, workshops, and seminars in publicity, writing, and the hospitality industry are useful.

Experience/Skills/Personality Traits

Experience working in public relations is required to become a casino or casino hotel Public Relations Director. Some individuals start out as journalists or publicists. They then move up to positions as assistant directors of public relations prior to their appointment as P.R. Director. Experience working in the hospitality industry, hotels, or casinos is required or preferred.

Public Relations Directors are creative individuals with excellent writing and communication skills. They enjoy working with the public and are outgoing and articulate.

Unions/Associations

Those interested in learning more about careers as casino hotel publicists can obtain additional information by contacting the Hotel Sales and Marketing Association International (HSMA), the Public Relations Society of America (PRSA), or the human resources departments in casino hotels.

Tips for Entry

1. You might also want to check out recruitment and search firms dealing in the public relations or hospitality industries.
2. Get your foot in the door of a casino hotel. Most promote from within. You might have to start as a publicist, but you can obtain experience and move up the career ladder.
3. Jobs may be advertised in the classified sections of newspapers in areas hosting gaming. Look under classifications such as "Hotel Public Relations Director," "Casino Hotel Public Relations Director," "Director of Public Relations," "Public Relations," "Communications," or "Casino Opportunities."
4. Skills are transferable. If you have worked as a P.R. Director in another industry, you might have a good shot if you are in the right place at the right time.

HOTEL PUBLICIST

CAREER PROFILE

Duties: Publicizing facility; writing press releases; working on promotional events.

Alternative Titles(s): Publicist

Salary Range: $20,000 to $45,000+

Employment Prospects: Fair

Best Geographical Location(s) for Position: Las Vegas, Reno, Laughlin, Lake Tahoe, Atlantic City, Biloxi, Baton Rouge, New Orleans, and Detroit offer most opportunities; other regions with land-based, riverboat, or Indian gaming facilities offer additional opportunities.

Prerequisites:

Education or Training—Bachelor's degree.

Experience and Qualifications—Experience in public relations, publicity, marketing, and the hospitality industry is helpful.

Special Skills and Personality Traits—Writing skills; communication skills; marketing skills; organization; creativity.

CAREER LADDER

```
┌─────────────────────────────────────┐
│  Publicity Manager or Assistant Director │
│       of Public Relations            │
└─────────────────────────────────────┘

┌─────────────────────────────────────┐
│       Casino Hotel Publicist         │
└─────────────────────────────────────┘

┌─────────────────────────────────────┐
│    Publicist in other industry,      │
│      Journalist or Intern            │
└─────────────────────────────────────┘
```

Position Description

Casino hotels usually have public relations and marketing departments. Depending on the facility, there may be one or more Hotel Publicists working within the department, as well as Publicists who handle the publicity for the casino.

The Casino Hotel Publicist has varied duties. The major function, of course, is to publicize the facility. This often overlaps with the duties of the casino publicist or marketing people.

The individual is responsible for developing and writing informative press releases about the facility. The Publicist also prepares press releases regarding special events and promotions of the casino hotel.

The Publicist may also be responsible for either taking photographs or arranging for photos of the hotel, as well as special events and promotions that take place at the facilities.

The Hotel Publicist also puts together fact sheets and develops press kits about the facility. These will be provided to the various media.

The casino Hotel Publicist also works with travel agents. The individual may work with others in the department, setting up "FAM" or familiarization programs. These are designed so travel agents visit the facility and then recommend the hotel to their clients.

The casino Hotel Publicist is generally responsible for publicizing events and celebrities that bring bookings to the facility or just keep the name of the hotel in the public eye. The casino Hotel Publicist often works with publicists for entertainers appearing in the facility's showroom. They also work with publicists of sports figures, such as world champion fighters starring in boxing shows at the hotel.

Other duties of the casino Hotel Publicist may include:

- Developing relationships with print feature editors, television and radio producers, and other media personnel
- Compiling media lists for the travel and gaming trade, as well as for the general press
- Working on special projects and promotional events within the casino hotel

Salaries

Casino Hotel Publicists earn between $20,000 and $45,000 or more annually, depending on a number of factors, including the geographic location, size, and prestige of the specific casino hotel, as well as the experience and responsibilities of the individual. Generally, those with the most experience working in larger, more prestigious casinos hotels in the gambling capitals earn the highest salaries.

Employment Prospects

Employment prospects for casino Hotel Publicists are fair. Jobs can be found throughout the country. The greatest number of employment opportunities are be found in Las Vegas, Reno, Laughlin, Lake Tahoe, Atlantic City, Biloxi, Baton Rouge, New Orleans, and Detroit. Other regions hosting Indian gaming and land-based or riverboat gaming facilities offer additional opportunities.

As more areas begin to legalize gambling, more opportunities will become available.

Advancement Prospects

Casino Hotel Publicists may advance their careers in a number of ways. Depending on career aspirations, individuals may find positions as the assistant director of public relations, public relations manager, special events assistant director, or director. Some individuals may also move into the casino marketing area. Experience and additional training are generally required for career advancement.

Education and Training

Educational requirements vary at different casino hotels. While every position does not require a college degree, one is recommended. Good majors include journalism, public relations, marketing, communications, English, or liberal arts.

Courses, workshops, and seminars in publicity, writing, and the hospitality industry are useful.

Experience/Skills/Personality Traits

Experience requirements, like educational requirements, vary. Most employers require or prefer individuals to have some sort of experience writing or handling publicity or public relations. Some casino hotels may have training programs or internships for those with no experience.

Casino Hotel Publicists should have excellent writing and communication skills. They should enjoy working with the public and be outgoing, articulate individuals.

Unions/Associations

Those interested in learning more about careers as casino Hotel Publicists can obtain additional information by contacting the Hotel Sales and Marketing Association International (HSMA), the Public Relations Society of America (PRSA), or the human resources departments in casino hotels.

Tips for Entry

1. Get your foot in the door of a casino hotel. Most promote from within. You might have to start as a trainee, but if you work hard, you will move up the career ladder.
2. Stop by the human resources departments of casinos and inquire about job openings. You might also consider sending a résumé and a short cover letter.
3. Jobs may be advertised in the classified sections of newspapers in areas hosting gaming. Look under classifications such as "Hotel Publicist," "Casino Hotel Publicist," "Publicist," "Public Relations," or "Casino Opportunities."

ADVERTISING COORDINATOR

CAREER PROFILE

Duties: Assisting in the development of advertising campaigns; creating promotional ads, sales pieces, and commercials; supporting casino's marketing and public relations efforts.

Alternative Titles(s): Advertising Assistant; Media Coordinator

Salary Range: $22,000 to $33,000+

Employment Prospects: Fair

Best Geographical Location(s) for Position: Las Vegas, Reno, Laughlin, Lake Tahoe, Atlantic City, Biloxi, Baton Rouge, New Orleans, and Detroit offer the greatest number of opportunities; other regions hosting Indian gaming and land-based or riverboat gaming facilities offer additional opportunities.

Prerequisites:

Education or Training—Bachelor's degree preferred, but not always required.

Experience and Qualifications—Experience in advertising, marketing, or public relations necessary; experience in the gaming or hospitality industry a plus.

Special Skills and Personality Traits—Creativity; communication skills; copywriting skills; ability to work on multiple projects at one time; knowledge of graphics and typefaces.

CAREER LADDER

```
┌─────────────────────────────────────┐
│  Advertising Director or Other Position │
│  in Marketing or Public Relations    │
│  Department                          │
└─────────────────────────────────────┘

┌─────────────────────────────────────┐
│  Advertising Coordinator             │
└─────────────────────────────────────┘

┌─────────────────────────────────────┐
│  Advertising Assistant in Other Industry │
│  or Advertising Intern               │
└─────────────────────────────────────┘
```

Position Description

More and more casinos are being constructed every year. Casinos and casino hotels are different sizes, have different atmospheres, and offer an array of amenities, games, foods, entertainment, and themes. Casinos market and advertise their facilities to attract customers.

The marketing department constantly develops different promotions designed to attract new customers and keep those who have previously visited the facility. Within this department are sub areas such as public relations, publicity, and advertising. These departments work in conjunction with marketing to help attain the goals. The Advertising Coordinator creates themes, campaigns, and single advertisements that support the casino and casino hotel's marketing efforts. This individual may also be referred to as an advertising assistant.

The Advertising Coordinator assists in the creation of advertising campaigns. The individual works with an advertising director or under the supervision of the director of marketing. In some settings, casinos and casino hotels utilize the services of outside advertising agencies. In these cases, the Advertising Coordinator often acts as a liaison between the agency and the facility in developing advertising campaigns.

In addition to working on the advertising campaigns, the Coordinator also creates individual promotional ads that may be needed for special promotions and events in both the casino and the casino hotel. These may include hotel and restaurant specials, entertainment events, slot parties and tournaments, nationally televised attractions, sporting events, and many other promotions.

Keeping these goals in mind, the Advertising Coordinator must reach the proper markets. The Coordinator must know in which geographic area it is best to advertise, as well as the proper media. This may include radio, television, newspapers, consumer and business publications, and billboards.

The Advertising Coordinator also prepares direct mail advertising pieces aimed at former customers and potential guests. This type of advertising is often used in casinos to promote specials and giveaways during slow seasons.

The Advertising Coordinator performs a variety of research projects in the job. The individual must determine the most effective type of ads, as well as media and locations in which to place them in order to reach the market the facility is aiming for.

The Advertising Coordinator might be required to do the actual copywriting, graphics, and audiovisual components of advertising, or to farm out some of these duties to freelance people. If the facility is working with an outside advertising agency, the Coordinator may develop the ideas instead of doing the actual writing and artwork.

Other duties of a casino or casino hotel Advertising Coordinator may include:

- Obtaining current demographics and rate information from media
- Assisting in the development of the advertising budget
- Helping develop other marketing pieces

Salaries

Advertising Coordinators working in casinos and casino hotels earn between $22,000 and $33,000 or more annually. Factors affecting earnings include the geographic location, size, and prestige of the specific casino or casino hotel, as well as the education, experience, and responsibilities of the individual.

Employment Prospects

Employment prospects are fair for people seeking this position and will increase as gaming expands throughout the country. Opportunities exist in the marketing departments of many gaming facilities. As noted, some facilities utilize the services of independent advertising agencies. However, these casinos and hotels often employ an Advertising Coordinator to work with the outside agency.

Advancement Prospects

One of the great things about working in casinos and casino hotels is that they like to promote from within. Once you're in, if you are a good employee, your opportunities are limitless.

The Advertising Coordinator may take a number of different steps toward advancement depending on career aspirations. Individuals may become the advertising director of the casino or casino hotel if the facility has such a position. With experience, education, and training advertising coordinators may also be promoted to other jobs in the marketing and public relations area.

Education and Training

Educational requirements vary for Advertising Coordinators at casinos and casino hotels. Most prefer candidates to hold a bachelor's degree with a major in advertising, marketing, public relations, communications, or liberal arts. In some cases, work experience is accepted in lieu of education.

Experience/Skills/Personality Traits

Experience working in advertising, marketing, public relations, or a related field is usually necessary. Any experience in the hospitality or gaming industry is a plus.

Advertising Coordinators should be creative individuals with copywriting and graphics skills. An understanding of the hospitality and gaming industries is needed. Good communication skills are also necessary. The Advertising Coordinator must have the ability to work on several multiple projects at one time without getting flustered.

Unions/Associations

Those interested in learning more about careers in this field can contact the Hotel Sales and Marketing Association (HMA) and the American Advertising Federation (AAF).

Tips for Entry

1. Many casinos have job hotlines for available jobs. Call casinos directly to obtain their job hotline phone numbers.
2. Get your foot in the door of a casino hotel. Most promote from within. If you have experience in advertising or marketing, see what positions are open, then move up the career ladder.
3. Jobs may be advertised in the classified sections of newspapers in areas hosting gaming. Look under classifications such as "Casino/Casino Hotel Advertising Coordinator," "Casino/Casino Hotel Advertising Assistant," "Advertising," "Marketing," or "Casino/Hotel Opportunities."
4. Openings are often advertised on the Internet. They may be located via the home pages of casino hotels.

PROMOTIONS COORDINATOR

CAREER PROFILE

Duties: Assisting in development and implementation of promotions in the casino and casino hotel; handling details of promotions to ensure success; supporting casino's marketing and public relations efforts.

Alternative Titles(s): Promotions Assistant

Salary Range: $24,000 to $40,000+

Employment Prospects: Good

Best Geographical Location(s) for Position: Las Vegas, Reno, Laughlin, Lake Tahoe, Atlantic City, Biloxi, Baton Rouge, New Orleans, and Detroit offer most opportunities; other regions with land-based, riverboat, or Indian gaming facilities offer additional opportunities.

Prerequisites:

Education or Training—Bachelor's degree preferred, but not always required; work experience may be accepted in lieu of education; see text.

Experience and Qualifications—Experience in marketing, public relations, or entertainment industry necessary.

Special Skills and Personality Traits—Creativity; communication skills; detail-oriented; organization; writing skills; supervisory skills.

CAREER LADDER

```
┌─────────────────────────────────┐
│  Promotions Coordinator in Larger, │
│    More Prestigious Casino, or    │
│      Special Events Manager       │
└─────────────────────────────────┘

┌─────────────────────────────────┐
│     Promotions Coordinator        │
└─────────────────────────────────┘

┌─────────────────────────────────┐
│  Promotions, Marketing, or Special │
│          Events Staffer           │
└─────────────────────────────────┘
```

Position Description

Casinos often plan a multitude of special events and promotions to attract new customers. The programs are designed to keep those who have already visited the facility as well as to generate publicity for the casino. The Promotions Coordinator is employed by the casino to assist with the development and implementation of promotions and special events.

Depending on the specific facility and its structure, the Promotions Coordinator works in conjunction with the marketing director, special events director, or manager of entertainment.

Casinos generally plan promotions well in advance. Most casinos prepare an annual calendar of events and attractions for customers via direct mail, as well as promotion in the casino and casino hotel and media advertising.

In order to be successful, promotions must be novel, workable ideas. The individual assists in the development of innovative promotions for the facility. In some settings these promotions are the result of brainstorming efforts of others in the marketing, public relations, special events, entertainment, and advertising departments.

The Promotions Coordinator assists in working out the details of the promotion. The individual is often responsible for putting together a basic outline of the event. He or she is expected to locate people, places, and items necessary for making the promotion a success.

The Promotions Coordinator must be extremely organized, and every detail of the promotion must be coordinated. The Promotions Coordinator is responsible for notifying all department heads of the promotion and explaining what, if any, their participation will be. The individual must also coordinate all activities in the casino necessary to execute promotions.

The Promotions Coordinator is expected to work with the media by arranging interviews, articles, feature stores, photo opportunities, and broadcasts to garner publicity and media attention for the promotion and therefore the facility.

The individual may also be required to prepare press releases and other publicity on upcoming events or on parts of a promotion that have already occurred.

Other duties of a casino or casino hotel Promotions Coordinator may include:

- Assisting in the preparation of a budget for the promotion
- Working with advertising department creating promotional ads and direct mail advertising pieces
- Helping develop marketing materials such as ads and brochures

Salaries

Promotions Coordinators working in casinos and casino hotels earn between $24,000 and $40,000 or more annually. Factors affecting earnings include the geographic location, size, and prestige of the specific casino or casino hotel, as well as the education, experience, and responsibilities of the individual.

Employment Prospects

Employment prospects are good for Promotions Coordinators. Opportunities exist in most gaming facilities. The greatest number of opportunities exist in areas where there are a large number of casinos.

Las Vegas, Reno, Laughlin, Lake Tahoe, Atlantic City, Biloxi, Baton Rouge, New Orleans, and Detroit offer the greatest number of job possibilities. Other employment settings include casino hotels in other areas of Nevada, Mississippi, New York, Louisiana, Colorado, Connecticut, Illinois, Arizona, and California.

Other regions hosting Indian gaming and land-based or riverboat gaming facilities offer additional opportunities. New casinos and casino hotels are constantly under construction. More casinos and casino hotels are also opening every year as areas legalize gambling.

Advancement Prospects

The Promotions Coordinator may take a number of different steps toward advancement depending on career aspirations. Individuals may climb the career ladder through promotion to positions such as entertainment and special events coordinator or manager. Others may move into another area of the marketing or public relations department.

Education and Training

Educational requirements vary for Promotions Coordinators at casinos and casino hotels. Most prefer candidates to hold a bachelor's degree with a major in marketing, public relations, communications, or liberal arts. In some cases, work experience is accepted in lieu of education.

Experience/Skills/Personality Traits

Experience working in marketing, public relations, entertainment, or a related field is usually necessary. Any experience in the hospitality or gaming industry is a plus.

Promotions Coordinators should be creative, detail-oriented, organized individuals. They must have the ability to work on a variety of projects at one time without becoming confused. Excellent communication skills, both verbal and written, are needed. An understanding of the hospitality and gaming industries is helpful.

Unions/Associations

Those interested in learning more about careers in this field can contact the Public Relations Society of America (PRSA). Other information may be obtained by contacting the human resources departments of casino hotels.

Tips for Entry

1. Jobs may be advertised in the classified sections of newspapers in areas hosting gaming. Look under classifications such as "Casino/Casino Hotels," "Casino/Gaming," "Casino Promotions Coordinator," "Promotions Coordinator," or "Marketing."
2. Many casinos have job hotlines for jobs available. Call casinos to get the job hotline phone number.
3. Get your foot in the door of a casino hotel. Most promote from within. If you have experience in marketing, public relations, entertainment, special events, or promotions, see what positions are open, then move up the career ladder.
4. Openings are often advertised on the Internet. They may be located via the home pages of casinos and casino hotels.

GROUP/CONVENTION SALES MANAGER

CAREER PROFILE

Duties: Soliciting and booking convention and group sales; negotiating rates; assigning leads to salespeople; maintaining wholesale accounts.

Alternative Titles(s): Sales Manager

Salary Range: $45,000 to $75,000+

Employment Prospects: Good

Best Geographical Location(s) for Position: Las Vegas, Reno, Laughlin, Lake Tahoe, Atlantic City, Biloxi, Baton Rouge, New Orleans, and Detroit offer most opportunities; other regions with land-based, riverboat, or Indian gaming facilities offer additional opportunities.

Prerequisites:

Education or Training—Bachelor's degree preferred; see text.

Experience and Qualifications—Experience in convention or group sales.

Special Skills and Personality Traits—Sales ability; communication skills; organization; detail-oriented; administrative ability; interpersonal skills; customer service skills; aggressive; negotiation skills.

CAREER LADDER

```
┌─────────────────────────────────────┐
│  Group/Convention Sales Manager in   │
│   Larger, More Prestigious Casino    │
│     Hotel or Director of Sales       │
└─────────────────────────────────────┘

┌─────────────────────────────────────┐
│   Group/Convention Sales Manager     │
└─────────────────────────────────────┘

┌─────────────────────────────────────┐
│  Group Sales Manager in Other Industry │
└─────────────────────────────────────┘
```

Position Description

Convention sales can substantially increase business in casino hotels during slow periods at the facilities. In order to keep rooms filled, casino hotels often market their facilities to conventions, conferences, and other groups. Many hotels have constructed their own private convention facilities. Some areas hosting gaming also have centrally located major convention centers. As a result, casino hotels have become important convention destinations.

The Convention or Group Sales Manager is responsible for seeking out groups looking for locations to hold their meetings. The hotel often sells rooms at a reduced price to these groups because they are buying blocks of rooms. In addition to selling rooms, the Sales Manager offers groups food and beverage service for meetings and banquets, meeting rooms, ballrooms, and convention facilities.

The Sales Manager is responsible for maintaining established accounts. He or she must also look for new business by contacting representatives of government, business, or social groups to solicit convention or conference business for the casino hotel. The individual is responsible for analyzing the requirements of the group. He or she will then develop a proposal outlining the services and quoting prices the casino hotel can offer.

The Sales Manager is responsible for developing marketing packages, telemarketing, and direct mail promotions to attract new group business. The individual may work with others in advertising, marketing, and public relations on these projects.

The individual works closely with other departments to make sure groups that are booked receive proper service. Once a group is booked, the Sales Manager alerts the convention services manager about the contract to assure that groups' needs are taken care of and that they are satisfied with their visit.

The Group or Convention Sales Manager may be required to go on the road on occasion to make contact with groups, to meet important clients, and to attend trade shows and sales meetings.

The Sales Manager makes calls to prospective clients or has sales packages sent to potential clients. The individual works with hotel sales representatives in closing deals.

Other duties of a Casino Hotel Convention or Group Sales Manager may include:

- Conducting training seminars and workshops for salespeople
- Assigning leads to salespeople
- Drawing up contracts and obtaining required signatures

Salaries

Group/Convention Sales Managers working in casino hotels earn between $45,000 and $75,000 or more annually. Individuals in some facilities may earn bonuses or commissions on business brought into the hotel or business over and above that which has been forecast.

Factors affecting earnings include the geographic location, size, and prestige of the specific casino or casino hotel, as well as the experience, responsibilities, and professional reputation of the individual.

Employment Prospects

Employment prospects for talented Group Sales Managers are good. Casino hotels, like others in the hospitality industry, are always on the lookout for individuals who can produce.

The greatest number of opportunities can be found in Las Vegas, where countless casino hotels and new mega resorts are being built. Other good opportunities can be found in Reno, Laughlin, Lake Tahoe, Atlantic City, Biloxi, Baton Rouge, New Orleans, and Detroit. Other regions hosting Indian gaming and land-based or riverboat gaming facilities offer additional job possibilities.

Advancement Prospects

Group/Convention Sales Managers may advance their careers by locating similar positions in larger, more prestigious casino hotels. Some individuals may be promoted to the position of director of sales if the facility has such a job. Depending on the career aspirations and training of the individual, he or she may also move into the marketing department.

Education and Training

A bachelor's degree is usually required or preferred by most casino hotels for Group or Convention Sales Managers. In some settings, work experience may be accepted in lieu of formal education.

Good choices for majors include marketing, sales, public relations, communications, or hotel management and administration.

Experience/Skills/Personality Traits

Group/Convention Sales Managers need experience in hotel sales, group or convention sales, or tours and travel. Some individuals also have held similar positions with hotels not involved in the gaming industry prior to being employed at a casino hotel.

Sales Managers should be personable, pleasantly aggressive people with sales ability. Communication skills are necessary. Individuals should be organized and detail-oriented. The ability to negotiate is mandatory.

Unions/Associations

Those interested in learning more about careers as Group/Convention Sales Managers may obtain additional information from the American Hotel and Motel Association (AH&MA).

Tips for Entry

1. Casinos often promote from within. If you have sales ability, start as a sales representative and work your way up the career ladder.
2. Send, fax, or visit the human resources departments of casino hotels to inquire about job openings. You might also consider sending or faxing a résumé and a short cover letter.
3. Jobs may be advertised in the classified sections of newspapers in areas hosting gaming. Look under classifications such as "Casino/Gaming Opportunities," "Convention Sales Manager," "Group Sales Manager," "Hotel Sales," or "Casinos/Casino Hotels."
4. Openings are often advertised on the Internet. They may be located via the home pages of casino hotels. They may also be found by doing a search of "Casino," "Casino Hotel," or "Gaming Job Opportunities."

HOTEL SALES REPRESENTATIVE

CAREER PROFILE

Duties: Contacting groups; soliciting and booking convention and group sales; preparing proposals; negotiating rates; servicing groups.

Alternative Titles(s): Sales Rep; Convention Sales Representative

Salary Range: $23,000 to $45,000+

Employment Prospects: Good

Best Geographical Location(s) for Position: Las Vegas, Reno, Laughlin, Lake Tahoe, Atlantic City, Biloxi, Baton Rouge, New Orleans, and Detroit offer most opportunities; other regions with land-based, riverboat, or Indian gaming facilities offer additional opportunities.

Prerequisites:

Education or Training—Educational requirements vary; see text.

Experience and Qualifications—Experience in convention hotel sales preferred, but not always required.

Special Skills and Personality Traits—Sales ability; communication skills; organization; detail-oriented; interpersonal skills; negotiation skills; persuasiveness; customer service skills.

CAREER LADDER

```
┌─────────────────────────────────────┐
│ Advertising Director or Other Position in │
│   Marketing or Public Relations     │
│            Department               │
└─────────────────────────────────────┘

┌─────────────────────────────────────┐
│  Casino Hotel Sales Representative  │
└─────────────────────────────────────┘

┌─────────────────────────────────────┐
│   Sales Position in Other Industry  │
│          or Entry Level             │
└─────────────────────────────────────┘
```

Position Description

Casino hotels seek out groups looking for locations to hold meetings, conferences, and conventions. The facility often sells rooms at a reduced price to these groups because they are buying blocks of rooms as well as food and beverage service, meeting rooms, ballrooms, and/or convention facilities.

Casino Hotel Sales Representatives are responsible for soliciting and booking groups, conferences, and conventions into the facility. These groups often substantially increase the business of a casino hotel, especially during slow periods of the year.

In order to attract group business, Casino Hotel Sales Representatives actively seek out and contact groups. They contact groups that have previously visited the facility, or they are assigned leads by the convention and group sales manager.

Sales Representatives deal with potential customers on the telephone or set up and meet with prospective clients at the facility. Some Sales Representatives also meet outside the hotel with clients.

Sales Representatives must have complete knowledge of the casino hotel and all the services and amenities it offers. They must be able to discuss every detail of the facility comfortably and knowledgeably. While doing this, the Casino Hotel Sales Representative is responsible for explaining how the services and facilities offered meet the potential client's needs. For example, the Sales Representative may be required to discuss availability of types of rooms and packages, as well as options in catering meals, breaks, and meetings.

The individual is also expected to answer any questions the client may have. While doing this, the Sales Representative attempts to overcome objections or problems of potential clients, persuading these customers to choose their hotel instead of another.

The Sales Representative often gives tours of the facility to prospective customers. He or she shows rooms, convention facilities, the gaming area, health clubs, and restaurants. The Sales Representative may also show customers sample menus for food service.

The Casino Hotel Sales Representative must constantly follow up. He or she schedules additional visits, writes additional letters, or makes more phone calls to prospective customers.

The Sales Representative negotiates rates and services with groups. Generally, individuals have some sort of leeway in handling these negotiations, although they may need approval from the sales manager.

Other duties of Casino Hotel Sales Representatives may include:

- Servicing groups
- Preparing proposals
- Obtaining required signatures
- Sending sales packages to clients

Salaries

Casino Hotel Sales Representatives earn between $23,000 and $45,000 or more annually. Individuals may be compensated in a variety of ways, ranging from straight salary, salary plus commissions, or salary plus bonuses on business brought into the hotel over and above what was forecast.

Factors affecting earnings include the geographic location, size, and prestige of the specific casino or casino hotel, as well as the experience, responsibilities, and professional reputation of the individual.

Employment Prospects

Employment opportunities for Casino Hotel Sales Representatives are very good. Casino hotels, like all others in the hospitality industry, are always on the lookout for talented people who can produce sales.

Sales Representatives work in various settings, including land-based casino hotels, Indian gaming facilities with on-site hotels, and dockside or floating riverboat casinos with hotel facilities.

Advancement Prospects

Casino Hotel Sales Representatives may climb the career ladder by locating similar positions in larger, more presti-

gious casino hotels. Others may advance through promotion to the position of convention sales manager.

Education and Training

Educational requirements vary for Casino Hotel Sales Representatives. Some facilities require just a high school diploma or the equivalent. Others prefer a college background or degree. Good choices for majors include marketing, sales, public relations, communications, or hotel management and administration. Work experience may be accepted in lieu of formal education. In many casino hotels, the convention or group sales manager conducts training seminars and workshops for Sales Representatives.

Experience/Skills/Personality Traits

Experience requirements, like education requirements, vary. In some casino hotels, this may be an entry-level position. Others require experience in hotel sales.

Sales Representatives should be pleasantly aggressive, personable people with sales ability. Communication and phone skills are necessary. Individuals should be organized, detail-oriented, and have the ability to negotiate.

Unions/Associations

Those interested in learning more about careers as Casino Hotel Sales Representatives can obtain additional career information from the American Hotel and Motel Association (AH&MA) or casino hotel human resources departments.

Tips for Entry

1. Send or fax your résumé to the human resources departments of casino hotels with a short cover letter inquiring about job openings. Include any sales experience you have had in any capacity on your résumé.

2. You can also stop by the human resources departments of casino hotels with this same information.

3. Many casinos offer these jobs on their job hotlines. These are recorded messages giving jobs available at the casino hotel. Call the casino to get its job hotline phone number.

4. Jobs are often advertised in the classified sections of newspapers in areas hosting gaming. Look under classifications such as "Casino/Gaming Opportunities," "Convention Sales," "Group Sales," "Casino Hotel Sales," "Casinos/Casino Hotels," or "Sales Rep."

CONVENTION SERVICES MANAGER

CAREER PROFILE

Duties: Coordinating needs and requirements of meeting planners and group representatives for conventions or group meetings.

Alternative Titles(s): None

Salary Range: $30,000 to $55,000+

Employment Prospects: Fair

Best Geographical Location(s) for Position: Las Vegas, Reno, Laughlin, Lake Tahoe, Atlantic City, Biloxi, Baton Rouge, New Orleans, and Detroit offer most opportunities; other regions with land-based, riverboat, or Indian gaming facilities offer additional opportunities.

Prerequisites:

Education or Training—High school diploma or equivalent; college background preferred.

Experience and Qualifications—Experience in hotel or hospitality industry.

Special Skills and Personality Traits—Supervisory skills; communication skills; detail-oriented; service-oriented; organization; interpersonal skills; customer service skills.

CAREER LADDER

```
┌─────────────────────────────────┐
│  Convention Services Manager in  │
│    Larger, More Prestigious      │
│  Casino Hotel or Positions in    │
│  Convention or Group Sales       │
└─────────────────────────────────┘

┌─────────────────────────────────┐
│  Convention Services Manager     │
└─────────────────────────────────┘

┌─────────────────────────────────┐
│ Assistant Convention Services Manager │
└─────────────────────────────────┘
```

Position Description

Organizations, corporations, and associations often plan group meetings and annual conventions at casino hotels. These groups have a variety of needs and requirements. The person in charge of coordinating all the details for these groups is called the Convention Services Manager.

The individual has a wide array of duties. His or her job starts when a group is booked. The Convention Services Manager talks to the group's representative or meeting planner to discuss special needs, such as display space, meeting rooms, stages, podiums, audio-visual equipment, food service, and break schedules. The Convention Services Manager also arranges for special permits from fire and/or health departments. The individual also may have to deal with the various unions whose members may work in a hotel setting.

The Convention Services Manager is responsible for notifying other departments in the hotel of arrangements being made or requirements that must be met.

The Convention Services Manager directs workers in preparing special rooms for guests. These may include meeting rooms, banquet halls, and convention rooms. The individual also supervises workers or exhibition companies in erecting displays and exhibits for conventions. The Convention Services Manager inspects rooms and displays to make sure they conform to the needs and desires of the group.

The Convention Services Manager may arrange publicity for the group and/or their meeting. The individual handles this function directly or assigns the task to the hotel's public relations or publicity department.

Convention Services Managers meet with the group's representatives before and during their stay to assure that everything is going as scheduled and that any problems are taken care of. The Convention Services Manager may also contact the group's representative after their stay to be sure the group was satisfied, helping to secure the group's return business.

Other duties of Convention Services Manager may include:

- Promoting good will between the hotel and the group
- Handling complaints and problems
- Arranging special functions

Salaries

Convention Services Managers in casino hotels work on salary. Individuals have annual earnings ranging from $30,000 to $55,000 or more. Factors affecting earnings include the geographic location, size, and prestige of the facility. Other variables include the experience and responsibilities of the individual. Those working in large facilities in the gambling capitals usually earn more than their counterparts in other hotels.

Employment Prospects

Employment prospects are fair for Convention Services Managers. Individuals can find employment in areas hosting casino hotels. The largest number of opportunities are available in areas with more casino hotels: Las Vegas, Reno, Laughlin, Lake Tahoe, Atlantic City, Biloxi, Baton Rouge, New Orleans, and Detroit. Other regions with land-based, riverboat, or Indian gaming facilities offer additional opportunities.

Advancement Prospects

Convention Services Managers working in casino hotels can advance their careers in a number of ways. Individuals may find similar jobs in larger or more prestigious hotels, resulting in increased responsibilities and earnings. Depending on career aspirations, education, and experience, Convention Services Managers may also move on to positions in convention or group sales.

Education and Training

Education and training requirements vary from job to job. For some positions, a high school diploma or its equiva-lent is required. For others, a college background or degree may be needed. Work experience is often accepted in lieu of education.

Experience/Skills/Personality Traits

Depending on the specific casino hotel, this job may require from three to 10 years' experience working in a hotel or other area of the hospitality industry. Some individuals gain experience working in the convention services office in various positions, including assistant convention services manager. Others may have prior experience in other departments of the hotel.

Unions/Associations

Individuals interested in learning more about careers in this area can contact the human resources departments of casino hotels. Other information may be available from the American Hotel and Motel Association (AH&MA).

Tips for Entry

1. Jobs are often advertised in the classified sections of newspapers in areas hosting gaming. Look under classifications such as "Casino," "Casino Hotels," "Hotels," "Convention Services," "Convention Services Manager," "Casino Hotel Opportunities," or "Hospitality."
2. If you are still in school, consider an internship offered by a hotel to obtain experience and make contacts.
3. Stop by the human resources departments of casino hotels to inquire about job openings.
4. Send your résumé to directors of human resources at casino hotels.
5. Look for new casino hotels that are under construction. Apply early.
6. Check out casino home pages to see if the casino hosts an employment site. Openings may be listed.

TOUR AND TRAVEL MANAGER

CAREER PROFILE

Duties: Developing programs to attract bus business; creating promotions.

Alternative Titles(s): Travel Manager

Salary Range: $38,000 to $65,000+

Employment Prospects: Fair

Best Geographical Location(s) for Position: Las Vegas, Reno, Laughlin, Lake Tahoe, Atlantic City, Biloxi, Baton Rouge, New Orleans, and Detroit offer most opportunities; other regions with land-based, riverboat, or Indian gaming facilities offer additional opportunities.

Prerequisites:

Education or Training—College degree preferred; see text.

Experience and Qualifications—Experience working in tour and travel, marketing, or other related area.

Special Skills and Personality Traits—Communication skills; marketing skills; creativity; organization.

CAREER LADDER

```
┌─────────────────────────────────────┐
│  Tour and Travel Manager in Larger,  │
│      More Prestigious Casino         │
│  or Position in Marketing or Sales   │
└─────────────────────────────────────┘

┌─────────────────────────────────────┐
│       Tour and Travel Manager        │
└─────────────────────────────────────┘

┌─────────────────────────────────────┐
│  Tour and Travel Coordinator or      │
│  Assistant or Public Relations,      │
│     Marketing, or Convention         │
│         Sales Position               │
└─────────────────────────────────────┘
```

Position Description

Bus tour trade for casinos grows annually. Each facility vies for customers by offering promotions, giveaways, and special prices for bus customers.

Some casinos themselves own buses, which leave from a central location on a scheduled basis and bring excited guests to the facility. Many bus lines also work in conjunction with casinos, scheduling daily trips to the various casinos. Some groups of people and organizations charter buses for visits to the gaming area.

The individual responsible for developing bus programs to attract customers to the casino is called the Tour and Travel Manager. Bus promotions have become very popular with casinos. For many guests, the bus is an ideal method of visiting a casino. To garner bus customers for their casino, Tour and Travel Managers must constantly create new promotions.

These promotions, for example, provide guests with some sort of monetary reimbursement, such as a roll of quarters or equivalent coupon to use for slots, food, or enter-

tainment. They may also include coupons for reduced prices on meals in casino restaurants and entertainment in showrooms. In order to assure repeat business, promotions may also involve coupons for future trips. Some promotions involve contests, giveaways, or entertainment. Promotions might include books of coupons for a wide array of items such as free souvenirs, slot machine pulls, or drinks.

Most bus customers are slot players. Therefore, the Tour and Travel Manager also works with the slot and marketing departments on slot promotions designed to attract bus customers. Together the departments create, market, and implement bus tour programs.

The Tour and Travel Manager may work with private bus lines as well as charter groups in order to develop new markets for service to the casino.

With a successful bus program, the casino may have 100 or more buses pulling up to the facility daily. The Tour and Travel Manager must create a working operating system so that total mayhem does not occur at the casino hotel's arrival and departure area.

The individual must work out a reservation system for charter buses, as well as a timetable for daily scheduled bus lines. The Tour and Travel Manager must also develop procedures for bus drivers regarding discharging arriving passengers, loading them at departure time, and parking.

Other duties of the casino Tour and Travel Manager may include:

• Overseeing and training tour and travel staff
• Developing promotional literature for bus programs

Salaries

Tour and Travel Managers working in casinos earn between $38,000 and $65,000 or more annually. Factors affecting earnings include the geographic location, size, and prestige of the casino, as well as the importance placed on its bus program. Other variables include the experience and responsibilities of the individual.

Employment Prospects

Employment prospects for Tour and Travel Managers are fair. Casinos are always looking for talented, creative people who can produce in this job. Opportunities for Tour and Travel Managers can be found in facilities hosting bus programs. Areas with a large number of casinos hosting bus programs have more opportunities. These include land-based casinos, dockside and floating riverboat casinos, and Indian gaming facilities.

Advancement Prospects

Advancement opportunities for Tour and Travel Managers depend to a great extent on the area in which the individual desires to work. Some Tour and Travel Managers climb the career ladder by locating similar positions in larger casinos or properties placing more emphasis on bus programs. Depending on career aspirations and training, the individual may also move into an administrative position in a marketing or convention sales department.

Education and Training

A bachelor's degree is usually required or preferred by most casinos for the position of Tour and Travel Manager. In some settings, work experience may be accepted in lieu of formal education.

Good choices for majors include marketing, public relations, communications, liberal arts, or hotel management and administration. Courses and seminars on various aspects of casinos administration and marketing are offered in many areas hosting gaming.

Experience/Skills/Personality Traits

Two to four years' experience working in tour and travel or marketing, public relations, travel, or hospitality are necessary for most positions in casinos as a Tour and Travel Manager. Individuals must be creative with good marketing and communication skills. An understanding of the gaming and tour and travel industries is essential.

Unions/Associations

Those interested in learning more about careers in this area can obtain additional information by contacting the American Hotel and Motel Association (AH&MA) or the human resources departments of casinos.

Tips for Entry

1. Many casinos promote from within. If you are interested in this type of job, see what openings exist in the department. Learn what you can and move up the career ladder.
2. Jobs may be advertised in the classified sections of newspapers in areas hosting gaming. Look under classifications such as "Casino/Gaming Opportunities," "Casino Tour and Travel," or "Tour and Travel Manager."
3. Send, fax, or visit the human resources departments of casino hotels to inquire about job openings. You might also send or fax a résumé and a short cover letter.
4. Call casinos job hotline numbers. These offer current job opportunities available at the facility. You can call casinos directly to obtain their job hotline phone numbers.
5. Check out individual casino web sites. Many casinos now list job openings on an employment page within their web sites.

TOUR HOST

CAREER PROFILE

Duties: Welcoming and greeting guests coming in on buses; orienting guests to property; answering questions.

Alternative Titles(s): Bus Greeter

Salary Range: $15,000 to $25,000

Employment Prospects: Good

Best Geographical Location(s) for Position: Las Vegas, Reno, Laughlin, Lake Tahoe, Atlantic City, Biloxi, Baton Rouge, New Orleans, and Detroit offer most opportunities; other regions with land-based, riverboat, or Indian gaming facilities offer additional opportunities.

Prerequisites:

Education or Training—High school diploma or equivalent.

Experience and Qualifications—No experience necessary.

Special Skills and Personality Traits—Communication skills; customer service skills; guest relations skills; personable; enthusiastic.

CAREER LADDER

```
┌─────────────────────────────────────┐
│      Positions in Tour and          │
│  Travel Department, VIP Host,       │
│  or Other Position within Casino    │
└─────────────────────────────────────┘

┌─────────────────────────────────────┐
│            Tour Host                │
└─────────────────────────────────────┘

┌─────────────────────────────────────┐
│           Entry Level               │
└─────────────────────────────────────┘
```

Position Description

Every day people pile on buses for scheduled trips to casinos. While there are bus trips that include overnight stays, most visitors stay only for the day. Guests who take these trips are often called day-trippers.

In keeping with their goal of providing excellent customer service, casinos often employ Tour Hosts to meet incoming buses. Tour Hosts wait in the area where buses pull up. The Hosts either get on the bus to say hello to guests, or greet each guest as he or she gets off the bus.

Tour Hosts provide brochures, literature, and other written material on the facility and its restaurants, games, and other amenities. Tour Hosts also give out coupons for coin reimbursement, meals, and other giveaways.

Tour Hosts orient the guests to the property, including directing guests to the gaming area, restaurants, gift shops, and rest rooms. They also answer questions regarding the casino, hotel, or any of the facilities located on the property.

Individuals often escort guests to specific parts of the casino such as the slot area. Tour Hosts show guests where

the various denominations of slots can be played. They also escort patrons to change booths and cages.

In some cases, bus tour leaders make arrangements for meals in one of the casino restaurants. The Tour Host escorts the group to the restaurant, makes sure they are seated and that everything moves along satisfactorily. During the meal, the individual talks to guests to see if they need anything. After the meal, the Tour Host escorts guests to the gaming area.

Other duties of the casino bus Tour Host may include:

• Telling guests when and where to meet the bus for departure
• Wishing guests well on departure
• Promoting good customer service to guests

Salaries

Casino Tour Hosts are usually paid an hourly wage. This can range between $7.50 and $12.00 or more, approximately $15,000 to $25,000 annually. Individuals may also receive tips. Factors affecting earnings include the geographic location, size, and prestige of the specific casino hotel, as well as the experience and responsibilities of the individual.

Employment Prospects

Employment prospects are good for casino Tour Hosts. Opportunities can be found in casinos with active bus programs. Some larger casinos bring in over 100 buses or more daily. Individuals may work either full or part time.

Land-based casinos, dockside and floating riverboat casinos, and Indian gaming facilities all use active bus programs and are potential employment possibilities.

Advancement Prospects

Advancement opportunities depend to a great extent on the area in which the individual desires to work. This is often an entry-level position and a good way to get in the door of the casino. Individuals can then move into a variety of other areas with experience and the proper training. Some Tour Hosts go into public relations or marketing.

Some Tour Hosts obtain additional training or education and experience and are promoted within the tour and travel department. Others move into other areas of customers service such as VIP hosts, slot hosts, and other hosting positions.

Education and Training

Most casinos and casino hotels prefer Tour Hosts to have a minimum of a high school diploma or the equivalent. Many facilities help those who do not have a high school diploma obtain a GED.

Experience/Skills/Personality Traits

As noted, this job is usually an entry-level position. Any experience in the hospitality industry will be helpful, as well as experience dealing with the public.

Tour Hosts should be personable, enthusiastic, outgoing people who enjoy being around others. They should be articulate with good communication skills. Customer and guest service skills are mandatory.

Unions/Associations

Those interested in learning more about careers as casino Tour Hosts can obtain additional information by contacting the human resources departments in casinos and casino hotels.

Tips for Entry

1. While experience is not necessary in most situations, it is always useful. Be sure to mention any retail sales experience or any experience in hospitality or food service when seeking a job.
2. Many casinos have job hotline numbers. These offer current job opportunities available at the facility. Call each casino directly to obtain its job hotline phone number.
3. This is a great job to get your foot in the door of a casino. Most promote from within. Obtain experience and move up the career ladder.
4. Jobs may be advertised in the classified sections of newspapers in areas hosting gaming. Look under classifications such as "Casino/Gaming Opportunities," "Casino Tour Host," "Bus Tour Host," "Travel/Tour Program Host," "Casino Bus Program," or "Tour Host."
5. Stop by the human resources departments of casinos and inquire about job openings. You might also send or fax a résumé and a short cover letter.
6. Look for casino job or career fairs. These jobs are often available at fairs.
7. This a great job for college students on summer vacation or retired people looking for part-time employment.

CAREER OPPORTUNITIES IN CASINO AND CASINO HOTEL SECURITY AND SURVEILLANCE

SECURITY OFFICER

CAREER PROFILE

Duties: Patrolling, inspecting, and protecting casino and casino hotel property, guests, and employees; enforcing regulations; handling loss prevention.

Alternative Titles(s): Security Guard

Salary Range: $17,000 to $35,000

Employment Prospects: Good

Best Geographical Location(s) for Position: Las Vegas, Reno, Laughlin, Lake Tahoe, Atlantic City, Biloxi, Baton Rouge, New Orleans, and Detroit offer most opportunities; other regions with land-based, riverboat, or Indian gaming facilities offer additional opportunities.

Prerequisites:

Education or Training—High school diploma or equivalent; on-the-job training; additional training may be required; see text.

Experience and Qualifications—Clean criminal record; good moral character. State licensing required to work in gaming area.

Special Skills and Personality Traits—Good judgment; responsible; interpersonal skills; leadership; alert; deals well with others; customer relations skills; communication skills.

CAREER LADDER

```
┌─────────────────────────────────────────┐
│ Security Shift Commander or Seargent     │
└─────────────────────────────────────────┘

┌─────────────────────────────────────────┐
│ Security Officer                         │
└─────────────────────────────────────────┘

┌─────────────────────────────────────────┐
│ Entry-Level or Private Security Officer, │
│ Police Officer,                          │
│ Member of the Military                   │
└─────────────────────────────────────────┘
```

Position Description

Casinos and casino hotels take security very seriously. These facilities are among the safest places to visit. Properties have large security departments to assure the safety and protection of customers, guests, and employees.

Security Officers protect the casino and casino property. The security department should not be confused with the surveillance department, whose main responsibility is monitoring the activities in the gaming area, count rooms, and cages. One of the major ways security officers can be distinguished from surveillance officers is that Security Officers are usually visible. While there may be some plainclothes or non-uniformed security employees, security officers generally wear uniforms and can be identified. Surveillance officers, on the other hand, are not identifiable. They are not usually seen by those outside the surveillance office.

Security Officers are responsible for patrolling the casino and the rest of the facility. They walk around the casino and maintain a presence. Security Officers are assigned designated areas to patrol. It is up to them to identify potentially dangerous situations and act on them in an effective manner.

Security Officers keep the peace. Individuals are responsible for calming situations if customers become loud or boisterous. They may be required to evict guests acting in a disorderly fashion. Individuals also handle any other disturbances within the casino gaming areas and hotel.

Security Officers are responsible for protecting against theft and vandalism. Individuals must be alert to everything going on around them. They must observe the actions and activities of both customers and employees. Individuals may have to handle thefts in the casino area, as well as in any retail or food establishments in the facility. Security Officers patrol the common areas of the hotel as well to assure guest safety.

Individuals must be alert for unusual situations. This may include players who are attempting to cheat the house or employee improprieties such as embezzlement.

Gaming is a regulated industry. Security Officers are required to enforce all casino rules, as well as state gaming regulations and controls.

Some Security Officers are armed, while others are not. In the event of problems requiring police assistance, security officers may be required to detain people until the outside law enforcement agency arrives.

Security Officers often use two-way radios to keep in contact with their supervisor and vice versa. Individuals must be able to handle emergency situations such as holdups, power outages, and weather problems.

Security Officers file daily shift reports detailing any incidents or accidents that occur during shifts. All unusual activities within the casino complex must be documented.

Other duties of the casino or casino hotel Security Officer may include:

- Escorting casino employees when money or chips are being transferred
- Transporting cash and chips to designated areas
- Answering guests' questions regarding the facility
- Following state-regulated security duties
- Providing for loss prevention within the casino

Salaries

Security Officers working in casinos and casino hotels earn between $8.00 and $17.00 or more per hour or $17,000 to $35,000 annually. Factors affecting earnings include the geographic location, size, and prestige of the specific casino or casino hotel, as well as the education, experience, and responsibilities of the individual.

Employment Prospects

Employment prospects for Security Officers in casinos are good. The greatest number of opportunities exist in areas where there are a large number of casinos.

Advancement Prospects

With experience and/or additional training, Security Officers may be promoted to supervisory positions within the security department. Individuals may, for example, advance to positions such as shift commander or sergeant.

Education and Training

Most casinos and casino hotels prefer their Security Officers to have a high school diploma or the equivalent. Training requirements vary from state to state. In house, on-the-

job training is usually provided. Individuals with no experience may start out on the graveyard shift and learn the ropes.

Certain states require individuals working as Security Officers in casinos to complete either an in-house training program or another specified training program offered in the area. Some states or casinos require an annual in-service course to refresh or update officers in changes in the security field or gaming regulations.

Armed officers must complete a firearms training course, usually involving both classroom instruction and a specified number of hours on the firing range.

Experience/Skills/Personality Traits

In some casinos, entry-level positions may be open. However, experience working in private security, the military, or civil service police is useful.

Many states require that Security Officers working in casinos be registered with the state. Security Officers who are armed usually also must be registered with the state to carry arms.

Security Officers require many skills. Individuals should be responsible people with good judgment. Interpersonal and customer relations skills are essential. Communication skills are mandatory.

Unions/Associations

Those interested in learning more about careers in this field can contact casino human resources departments.

Tips for Entry

1. Some community colleges, universities, and vocational technical schools offer courses for Security Officers interested in working in casinos and casino hotels. These courses may be useful in career advancement.
2. Jobs may be advertised in the classified sections of newspapers in areas hosting gaming. Look under classifications such as "Casinos/Gaming," "Casino Security," "Gaming Security," "Security Officer/Gaming," or "Casino/Hotel Opportunities."
3. Most casinos have job hotlines. These are updated messages listing jobs available. Call each casino directly to obtain its job hotline phone number.
4. Get your foot in the door of a casino hotel. Most promote from within. If you have experience in security, whether in the military or civil service, see what positions are open, get in, and then move up the career ladder.

SURVEILLANCE OFFICER

CAREER PROFILE

Duties: Monitoring closed-circuit video systems; observing and videotaping activities of games, slots, cashier cages, booths, count rooms, and other areas of casino property to identify cheating, stealing, embezzlement, or other potential problems.

Alternative Titles(s): Surveillance Observer

Salary Range: $18,000 to $37,000

Employment Prospects: Good

Best Geographical Location(s) for Position: Las Vegas, Reno, Laughlin, Lake Tahoe, Atlantic City, Biloxi, Baton Rouge, New Orleans, and Detroit offer most opportunities; other regions with land-based, riverboat, or Indian gaming facilities offer additional opportunities.

Prerequisites:

Education or Training—Dealer and surveillance school training; see text.

Experience and Qualifications—Background in games necessary; state licensing required to work in gaming area.

Special Skills and Personality Traits—Alertness; good judgment; responsible; knowledge of casino games and policies.

CAREER LADDER

```
Surveillance Supervisor
```

```
Surveillance Officer
```

```
Dealer or Floorperson
```

Position Description

The gaming industry must adhere to strict state and government regulations. In addition, casinos deal with a great many customers and employees and a great deal of money. In order to keep everything legal, casinos have very extensive security and surveillance departments.

The security department makes a casino one of the safest places in the world to visit. This department ensures the safety and protection of customers, guests, and employees. Security officers are visible in the casino, and most are uniformed and readily identifiable.

Members of the surveillance department work in an isolated area of the casino, apart from other employees and customers. Surveillance Officers, also called surveillance observers, are not usually seen by those outside the surveil-

lance office and are not identifiable in the casino. The main responsibility of the surveillance department is to observe the activities in the gaming areas, count rooms, and cages.

The most visible part of surveillance are the closed-circuit video cameras located throughout the property. Surveillance Officers monitor these cameras to determine if there are any wrongdoings, illegal activities, or problems occurring in the casino.

Many casinos build catwalks above the gaming tables, where surveillance can be conducted, as well as the observation of the action in the gaming areas via the closed-circuit screens. Surveillance Officers are responsible for extensive game protection. They must watch for cheating at all table games, including roulette, craps, blackjack, and baccarat. Individuals look for cheating by both customers and employees. For example, a customer may have a $50 bet down in blackjack, looks at the hand, sees it is not good, and tries to take back some chips when a dealer looks away. An employee may try to steal chips or money from the drop box, the betting area, or other locations. Surveillance Officers also watch over the activity at the slots, Bingo, Keno, and all other gaming activities.

Surveillance Officers must be alert for unusual situations. They must be on the lookout for the various ways people attempt to cheat. Individuals also watch for errors made by dealers in the ways games are dealt, played, or paid off.

Surveillance Officers monitor the activities of the cages and cashiers. They look for improprieties like embezzlement or errors such as giving out incorrect amounts of money or chips.

Surveillance Officers must observe employees entering, working in, and leaving the count room. This is the area where the contents of drop boxes as well as the money from slots and cashiers are counted and accounted for.

Other duties of casino Surveillance Officers include:

- Reporting illegal activities of employees and customers
- Initiating enforcement procedures
- Observing to assure all casino rules and state gaming regulations and controls are followed

Salaries

Surveillance Officers working in casinos earn between $9.00 and $19.00 per hour or more or about $18,000 to $37,000 a year. Factors affecting earnings include the geographic location, size, and prestige of the specific casino, as well as the experience and responsibilities of the individual.

Generally, Surveillance Officers working in larger, more prestigious casinos in the gaming capitals earn more than their counterparts working in other settings.

Employment Prospects

Employment prospects for Surveillance Officers in casinos are good. The greatest number of opportunities exist in areas where there are a large number of casinos. Las Vegas, Reno, Laughlin, Lake Tahoe, Atlantic City, Biloxi, Baton Rouge, New Orleans, and Detroit offer the greatest number of job possibilities. Other employment settings include casino hotels in other areas of Nevada, Mississippi, New York, Louisiana, Colorado, Connecticut, Illinois, Arizona, and California.

Other regions hosting Indian gaming and land-based or riverboat gaming facilities offer additional opportunities. New casinos and casino hotels are constantly under construction. More casinos and casino hotels are also opening every year as areas legalize gambling.

Surveillance Officers work various shifts and may be expected to work weekends and holidays.

Advancement Prospects

With experience, Surveillance Officers may be promoted to supervisory positions in the surveillance department. Individuals can also find similar positions in larger, more prestigious casinos.

Education and Training

Most casinos and casino hotel prefer Surveillance Officers to have a high school diploma or the equivalent. Individuals must also be formally trained in at least one if not more casino games, usually at a dealers or gaming school. Additional training requirements vary from state to state. In most areas, Surveillance Officers must complete an approved surveillance school course of study. These are offered in gaming schools as well as in some community colleges, vo-tech, and trade schools in areas hosting gaming. In some areas, especially those new to gaming, casinos may offer surveillance training programs themselves.

Experience/Skills/Personality Traits

Experience as a dealer is usually necessary for this position. Casinos may prefer some supervisory experience, such as that of a floorperson.

Surveillance Officers must undergo a complete background check. Individuals must be licensed by the specific state gaming authority in which they work.

Surveillance Officers should be alert, responsible people with good judgment. They must have total understanding and knowledge of the rules of the casino and its games, as well as government regulations. Individuals must also be aware of cheating techniques and methods used by employees and casino customers.

Unions/Associations

Those interested in learning more about careers in this field should contact gaming institutes, academies, and schools, as well as casino human resources departments.

Tips for Entry

1. Prior experience in surveillance, police work, or security may be helpful.
2. Jobs may be advertised in the classified sections of newspapers in areas hosting gaming. Look under classifications such as "Casinos/Gaming," "Casino/Hotel Opportunities," "Casino Surveillance," "Gaming Surveillance," "Surveillance Officer/Gaming," or "Surveillance Observer."
3. Openings are often advertised on the Internet. They may be located via the home pages of casino hotels. They may also be found by doing a search of "Casino," "Casino Hotel," or "Gaming Job Opportunities."
4. Make sure you are trained in as many table games as possible, making you more marketable.

CAREER OPPORTUNITIES
IN CASINO HOTELS

CASINO HOTEL GENERAL MANAGER

CAREER PROFILE

Duties: Overseeing operations of hotel; supervising staff; assigning tasks to department heads; developing budgets.

Alternative Titles(s): Manager

Salary Range: $55,000 to $95,000+

Employment Prospects: Fair

Best Geographical Location(s) for Position: Las Vegas, Reno, Laughlin, Lake Tahoe, Atlantic City, Biloxi, Baton Rouge, New Orleans, and Detroit offer most opportunities; other regions with land-based, riverboat, or Indian gaming facilities offer additional opportunities.

Prerequisites:

Education or Training—Educational requirements vary; college degree in hotel management preferred; see text.

Experience and Qualifications—Administrative and supervisory experience working in hospitality industry.

Special Skills and Personality Traits—Administrative skills; supervisory skills; management skills; communication skills; organization.

CAREER LADDER

```
┌─────────────────────────────────────┐
│  Hotel General Manager in a Larger,  │
│    More Prestigious Casino Hotel     │
└─────────────────────────────────────┘

┌─────────────────────────────────────┐
│      Hotel General Manager           │
└─────────────────────────────────────┘

┌─────────────────────────────────────┐
│        Assistant Manager             │
└─────────────────────────────────────┘
```

Position Description

There are many types of casino hotels. Some, in Las Vegas for example, have hundreds of rooms, while others have accommodations for thousands. Many are like cities unto themselves. Others are smaller. A large number of casino hotels have themes or special attractions that touch upon every part of the hotel operation. The one thing all casino hotels have in common is a casino on-site.

People visit casino hotels for a number of reasons—many come to gamble, some to watch others gamble or to be a part of the excitement. Guests schedule stays at casino hotels for the lavish entertainment, the food, and the fun.

The Casino Hotel General Manager has an important job. He or she is responsible for overseeing the day-to-day operation of the facility. Specific duties vary depending on the job. The individual's main functions, however, are to make sure the establishment runs smoothly, efficiently, and profitably.

Hotels run 24 hours a day. The General Manager is responsible for supervising other managers in the facility. Depending on the specific hotel, there may be one or more assistant managers, shift managers, customer service managers, and guest service managers in the hotel. Every hour is covered. All managers and administrative personnel report to the General Manager.

Most casino hotels are part of corporate conglomerates. In some the General Manager works in conjunction with the corporate structure, setting room rates, and developing services for guests and standards for housekeeping and food service. In others these responsibilities are handled by the president, chief executive officer (CEO), chief operating officer (COO), or executive vice president. Whoever formulates the standards, once they are set, the General Manager makes sure everything is continually up to par.

While casino hotels, like other large facilities in the hospitality industry, employ customer service and guest service managers, the General Manager has ultimate responsibility in dealing with problems or complaints. Maintaining good customer relations is important to every hotel, but especially to casino hotels where repeat business both in the hotel and the casino is imperative.

The General Manager often works with other departments, including food and beverage, marketing, public relations, promotions, and sales to find ways to bring in new customers as well as to maintain a repeat business.

The General Manager develops budgets for the entire facility or specific departments for approval by the CEO, COO, president, or executive vice president. The General Manager has the power to authorize certain expenses and approve expenditures.

Individuals in this position work long, hard hours. All problems that occur in the hotel become his or her responsibility. The individual must constantly monitor activities in the facility and take care of any problems or situations that crop up. Other responsibilities of the General Manager may include:

- Representing the hotel at public or private functions
- Participating in community affairs
- Evaluating performance of supervisory and administrative staff

Salaries

Annual earnings can range from $55,000 to $95,000 or more for Casino Hotel General Managers. Factors affecting earnings include the geographic location, size, and prestige of the specific casino hotel. Other variables include the experience, education, and responsibilities of the individual. Those working in larger, more prestigious facilities in the gambling capitals usually earn more than their counterparts in other hotels.

Employment Prospects

Employment prospects are fair for those seeking positions as Casino Hotel General Managers. Individuals can find employment in all areas hosting gaming. Individuals may work in large, luxury casino hotels, smaller casino hotels, and theme casino hotels.

Regions hosting Indian gaming and land-based or riverboat gaming facilities offer additional opportunities. New casinos and casino hotels are constantly under construction.

Advancement Prospects

Casino Hotel General Managers can advance their careers by obtaining experience and landing jobs in larger or more prestigious casino hotels, resulting in increased responsibilities and earnings. Depending on experience, education, and career aspirations, individuals may also be promoted to other administrative positions.

Education and Training

While educational requirements vary from job to job, recommended education for Casino Hotel General Managers is a bachelor's degree in hotel administration or management. In some cases, experience will be accepted in lieu of education requirements.

Some individuals move through the ranks in hotels owned by major corporations to General Manager positions, as do those who have participated in management training programs sponsored by hotels.

Experience/Skills/Personality Traits

Casino Hotel General Managers must have a fair amount of experience working in administrative and supervisory positions within the hospitality industry. Experience working in the casino industry is also useful.

Some Casino Hotel General Managers obtain prior experience as hotel assistant managers or as General Managers in smaller hotels.

Casino Hotel General Managers should be well-spoken, articulate people with good communication skills. Supervisory, management, and administrative skills are essential. Complete understanding of the hospitality industry is mandatory.

Individuals should be organized and have the ability to prioritize projects.

Unions/Associations

Individuals interested in pursuing careers in casino hotel management can obtain additional information by contacting the American Hotel and Motel Association (AH&MA) or the Educational Institute of the American Hotel & Motel Association (EIAH&MA) for more information.

Tips for Entry

1. Many hotel chains offer training programs in this field. These are excellent ways to get training, and experience.
2. Jobs are often advertised in the classified sections of newspapers in areas hosting gaming. Look under classifications such as "Casino Hotels," "Casino Hotel General Manager," "Hotel General Manager," "Hospitality Careers," or "Management-Casino Hotels."
3. Contact recruitment firms specializing in the hospitality or gaming industries.

RESERVATIONS MANAGER

CAREER PROFILE

Duties: Overseeing reservations department; supervising and scheduling reservations clerks.

Alternative Titles(s): None

Salary Range: $25,000 to $48,000+

Employment Prospects: Fair

Best Geographical Location(s) for Position: Las Vegas, Reno, Laughlin, Lake Tahoe, Atlantic City, Biloxi, Baton Rouge, New Orleans, and Detroit offer most opportunities; other regions with land-based, riverboat, or Indian gaming facilities offer additional opportunities.

Prerequisites:

Education or Training—High school diploma or equivalent; see text.

Experience and Qualifications—Experience in reservations or front desk departments.

Special Skills and Personality Traits—Supervisory skills; computer skills; customer service skills; organization; data-entry skills.

CAREER LADDER

```
┌─────────────────────────────────────┐
│ Reservations Manager in Larger, More │
│      Prestigious Casino Hotel        │
└─────────────────────────────────────┘

┌─────────────────────────────────────┐
│        Reservations Manager          │
└─────────────────────────────────────┘

┌─────────────────────────────────────┐
│ Assistant Reservations Manager or    │
│       Front Desk Supervisor          │
└─────────────────────────────────────┘
```

Position Description

The reservations department of a casino hotel is responsible for making sure rooms are available for guests when they arrive. Guests of casino hotels usually make reservations prior to arriving at the facilities. The Reservations Manager of a casino hotel is in charge of overseeing the entire reservations department. The individual has a vast array of duties.

The Reservations Manager supervises and coordinates the activities of the reservations clerks in the front office. The individual makes sure room clerks answer phones to take, record, and, if necessary, cancel reservations.

The Reservations Manager trains new clerks in reservations methods used by the hotel. This may include training clerks in the correct method for taking telephone reservations, as well as operating computer terminals and printers. The individual may also pass these training duties on to an assistant.

Some reservations arrive by mail. Room Reservations Managers are in charge of sorting reservations received and giving them to clerks so that this information may be input into the computer system.

The Reservations Manager is given information from sales representatives or the sales director regarding contracts detailing room allotments for conventions. This information, too, must be input into the computer system.

The Reservations Manager makes sure that room clerks at the front desk have daily printouts listing arriving guests. The individual must also verify that guests' folios are given to the front desk personnel.

The Reservations Manager devises schedules for reservations clerks. The individual may also reschedule workers to accommodate arrivals of large conventions and other groups.

Other duties of Reservations Managers may include:

- Recommending promotion and/or termination of reservations clerks
- Corresponding with individuals, groups, and travel agents to answer special requests for rooms and rates
- Handling guest problems or complaints about room reservations

Salaries

Reservations Managers working in casino hotels are usually on salary. Annual earnings range from $25,000 to $48,000 or more. Factors affecting earnings include the geographic location, size, and prestige of the facility. Other variables include the experience and responsibilities of the individual. Those working in facilities with a large number of rooms in the gambling capitals usually earn more than their counterparts in other hotels.

Employment Prospects

Employment prospects are fair for Reservations Managers in casino hotels. Individuals have more opportunities in areas with larger numbers of casino hotels.

Las Vegas, Reno, Laughlin, Lake Tahoe, Atlantic City, Biloxi, Baton Rouge, New Orleans, and Detroit offer the greatest number of job possibilities. Other employment settings include casinos and casino hotels in other areas of Nevada, Mississippi, New York, Louisiana, Colorado, Connecticut, Illinois, Arizona, and California.

Other regions hosting Indian gaming and land-based or riverboat gaming facilities offer additional opportunities. New casinos and casino hotels are constantly under construction. More casinos and casino hotels are also opening every year as areas legalize gambling.

Advancement Prospects

Reservations Managers working in casino hotels can advance their careers by finding similar positions in larger casino hotels, resulting in increased responsibilities and earnings.

Education and Training

Education and training requirements for Reservations Managers vary from job to job. Usually, a high school diploma or its equivalent is required. However, work experience may be accepted in lieu of education.

Experience/Skills/Personality Traits

Reservations Managers must have experience in either the reservations or front desk departments of hotels. The length of experience needed varies from two to three years depending on the specific hotel. Individuals must have supervisory experience as well, often obtained through positions as assistant reservations manager or supervisor.

Complete knowledge of the front office and/or reservations departments is needed. Additionally, individuals should be computer competent.

Unions/Associations

Individuals interested in learning more about careers in this area can contact the human resources departments of casino hotels. Other information may be available from the American Hotel and Motel Association (AH&MA).

Tips for Entry

1. Jobs are often advertised in the classified sections of newspapers in areas hosting gaming. Look under classifications such as "Casinos," "Casino Hotels," "Hotels," "Reservations," "Casino Hotel Opportunities," "Reservations Manager," "Room Reservations," or "Hospitality."
2. If you are still in school, consider an internship offered by a hotel to obtain experience and to make contacts.
3. Stop by the human resources departments of casino hotels to inquire about job openings.
4. Send your résumé to the directors of human resources at casino hotels.
5. Look for new casino hotels that are under construction. Apply early.
6. Positions may be advertised on the Internet. Look under keywords such as "Hospitality," "Hotels," and "Casinos." Also check out casino hotel home pages for employment listings.

ROOM RESERVATIONS CLERK

CAREER PROFILE

Duties: Answering telephone calls from potential guests regarding hotel rates and availability; taking, making, and processing reservations; canceling room reservations.

Alternative Titles(s): Reservations Attendant

Salary Range: $11,000 to $20,000

Employment Prospects: Excellent

Best Geographical Location(s) for Position: Las Vegas, Reno, Laughlin, Lake Tahoe, Atlantic City, Biloxi, Baton Rouge, New Orleans, and Detroit offer most opportunities; other regions with land-based, riverboat, or Indian gaming facilities offer additional opportunities.

Prerequisites:

Education or Training—High school diploma or equivalent and on-the-job training.

Experience and Qualifications—Understanding of hotel reservations and front office operation helpful, but not always required.

Special Skills and Personality Traits—Phone skills; interpersonal skills; customer service skills; organization; data-entry skills.

CAREER LADDER

```
┌─────────────────────────────────────┐
│    Assistant Reservations Manager    │
└─────────────────────────────────────┘

┌─────────────────────────────────────┐
│ Casino Hotel Room Reservations Clerk │
└─────────────────────────────────────┘

┌─────────────────────────────────────┐
│   Entry Level or Room Reservations   │
│    Clerk for Non-Casino Hotel        │
└─────────────────────────────────────┘
```

Position Description

Potential guests of casino hotels usually make reservations prior to arriving at facilities. Room Reservations Clerks are in charge of taking, recording, and canceling these reservations.

Room Reservations Clerks have a number of duties. They answer incoming calls from people who are interested in knowing about room rates and availability. Individuals may also be asked about specials, promotions, activities, or other events being held in the hotel or casino. Room Reservations Clerks also answer questions regarding conventions and meetings scheduled at the hotel.

Reservations Clerks retrieve information regarding room rates and availabilities. With this information Clerks can help guests choose the type of room and room rates needed.

When people decide to make reservations, the Room Reservations Clerk must obtain certain information, such as names, addresses, and phone numbers. Other information includes the number of people in the party, the date guests are arriving, and the number of nights they expect to stay. Reservations Clerks must also find out if there are any special requests, such as king-size beds, cribs, smoking, or nonsmoking sections.

Reservations Clerks then input all information into the computer, including credit card information to guarantee reservations. Clerks then usually provide confirmation numbers to guests.

Some people call to cancel reservations made previously. After Room Reservations Clerks cancel a guest's reservation, they give the individual a confirmation cancellation number to use in case they are inadvertently charged on their credit card.

Often when people call hotels, they request brochures or other written information on the facility. Room Reservations

Clerks take people's names and addresses so that requested material may be forwarded to them.

Other duties of Room Reservations Clerks may include:

• Performing any additional clerical duties regarding making and canceling room reservations
• Referring guest problems or complaints about room reservations to the reservations assistant manager, manager, or supervisor

Salaries

Room Reservations Clerks working in casino hotels are paid an hourly salary. Individuals earn $11,000 to $20,000 annually or between $5.50 and $10.00 or more per hour. Factors affecting earnings include the geographic location, size, and prestige of the facility. Other variables include the experience and responsibilities of the individual. Those working in larger or more prestigious facilities in the gambling capitals usually earn more than their counterparts in other hotels.

Employment Prospects

Employment prospects for Room Reservations Clerks are excellent. Individuals can find employment in locations where casino hotels are located. The number of Reservation Clerks employed by each hotel depends on the size of the facility.

Reservation Clerks work various shifts depending on the structure of the hotel. Las Vegas, Reno, Laughlin, Lake Tahoe, Atlantic City, Biloxi, Baton Rouge, New Orleans, and Detroit offer the greatest number of job possibilities. Other employment settings include casino hotels in other areas of Nevada, Mississippi, New York, Louisiana, Colorado, Connecticut, Illinois, Arizona, and California.

Other regions hosting Indian gaming and land-based or riverboat gaming facilities offer additional opportunities. New casinos and casino hotels are constantly under construction. More casinos and casino hotels are also opening every year as areas legalize gambling.

Advancement Prospects

Reservations Clerks can advance their careers by obtaining experience working in the reservations or front desk department of the hotel. Individuals may be promoted to assistant reservations managers, reservations managers, or room reservations supervisors.

Education and Training

Education and training requirements vary from job to job. Usually, a high school diploma or its equivalent is required. However, work experience may be accepted in lieu of education. On-the-job training is often available for this position.

Experience/Skills/Personality Traits

Experience requirements, like education, vary for Reservations Clerks. In some hotels, this is an entry-level position. In others, prior experience in the reservations department is required or preferred. General understanding of the workings of the front office and/or reservations department is helpful.

Reservations Clerks should have data-entry and retrieval skills. A pleasant phone manner and customer service skills are essential.

Unions/Associations

This may or may not be a unionized position, depending on the specific casino hotel. In unionized casino hotels in Las Vegas, for example, Reservations Clerks may be members of the Teamsters Local #995 union.

Individuals interested in learning more about careers in this area can contact the human resources departments of casino hotels. Other information may be available from the American Hotel and Motel Association (AH&MA).

Tips for Entry

1. While experience may not be required, experience usually gives one applicant an edge over another. Any experience working with reservations, whether it be with a hotel, travel agent, or airline, is useful.
2. Stop by the human resources departments of casino hotels to inquire about job openings.
3. Jobs are often advertised in the classified sections of newspapers in areas hosting gaming. Look under classifications such as "Casinos," "Casino Hotels," "Hotels," "Reservations," "Casino Hotel Opportunities," "Reservations Clerk," "Room Reservations Clerk," or "Hospitality."

FRONT OFFICE MANAGER

Duties: Overseeing front office; supervising employees; estimating volume of reservations; overseeing guests' check-in and check-out.

Alternative Titles(s): None

Salary Range: $35,000 to $60,000+

Employment Prospects: Fair

Best Geographical Location(s) for Position: Las Vegas, Reno, Laughlin, Lake Tahoe, Atlantic City, Biloxi, Baton Rouge, New Orleans, and Detroit offer most opportunities; other regions with land-based, riverboat, or Indian gaming facilities offer additional opportunities.

Prerequisites:

Education or Training—Bachelor's degree preferred; see text.

Experience and Qualifications—Experience working in front office operation.

Special Skills and Personality Traits—Organized; communication skills; administrative and supervisory skills; customer service skills.

```
┌─────────────────────────────────────┐
│   Front Office Manager at Larger,    │
│      More Prestigious Casino         │
│    Hotel or Director of Rooms        │
└─────────────────────────────────────┘

┌─────────────────────────────────────┐
│       Front Office Manager           │
└─────────────────────────────────────┘

┌─────────────────────────────────────┐
│   Assistant Front Office Manager     │
└─────────────────────────────────────┘
```

Position Description

On any given day, successful casino hotels have a large volume of guests checking in and out. It is essential that the hotel have a system for making sure that guests who are arriving can check in easily, and those who are departing can leave in a timely manner without incident. The person in charge of overseeing these functions is the Front Office Manager.

This individual has a great deal of responsibility. The Front Office Manager oversees everything that occurs in the department, including supervising the front office staff. Employees in the front office include an assistant front office manager, front desk managers, front office shift supervisors, front office agents or representatives, front office cashiers, mail and information clerks, reservation and assistant reservations managers, and reservations clerks. In some hotels the Front Office Manager is also responsible for customer relations managers, concierges, and the bell staff.

The Front Office Manager trains the front desk staff to make sure they deal with guests in a courteous and efficient manner.

The Front Office Manager coordinates reservations and room assignments. It is imperative that the individual know how many of each room type are available at all times. The Front Office Manager must also know approximately how many reservations are firm, assuring that hotel rooms are not overbooked.

The Front Office Manager develops systems for guest information. In most hotels, information is entered into a computer system. The hotel must know exactly who is registered in each room, the number of guests, and the length of their stay.

The Front Office Manager sees that departments are in contact with one another to make sure rooms are available when needed.

Other duties of the casino hotel Front Office Manager may include:

- Resolving guest complaints and problems
- Handling guests' requests for special services

Salaries

A Front Office Manager earns between $35,000 and $60,000 or more annually. Factors affecting earnings include the geographic location, size, and prestige of the specific casino hotel, as well as the experience and responsibilities of the individual. Generally, those with the most experience working in larger or more prestigious casinos hotels in the gambling capitals earn the highest salaries.

Employment Prospects

Employment prospects for casino hotel Front Office Managers are fair and may be found throughout the country. Las Vegas, Reno, Laughlin, Lake Tahoe, Atlantic City, Biloxi, Baton Rouge, New Orleans, and Detroit offer the greatest number of job possibilities.

Other employment settings include casinos and casino hotels in other areas of Nevada, Mississippi, New York, Louisiana, Colorado, Connecticut, Illinois, Arizona, and California.

Other regions hosting Indian gaming and land-based or riverboat gaming facilities offer additional opportunities. New casinos and casino hotels are constantly under construction. More casinos and casino hotels are also opening every year as areas legalize gambling.

Advancement Prospects

Casino hotel Front Office Managers may climb the career ladder by obtaining more experience and/or training. Individuals may find similar positions in larger, more prestigious casino hotels, resulting in increased earnings. A casino hotel Front Office Manager may also advance his or her career by locating a position as a director of rooms.

Education and Training

Educational requirements vary at different casino hotels. While every position does not require college, a bachelor's degree is recommended. Good majors include hotel management, marketing, sales, or liberal arts. Some hotels accept experience in lieu of education.

Courses, workshops, and seminars in the hospitality and gaming industry are useful.

Experience/Skills/Personality Traits

Prior to hiring someone as a Front Office Manager, casino hotels usually require three to four years experience working in various areas of the front office.

Casino hotel Front Office Managers should be very organized and have administrative and supervisory skills. Communication skills and customer service skills are essential.

Unions/Associations

Those interested in learning more about careers as casino hotel Front Office Managers can obtain additional information by contacting the Council on Hotel, Restaurant and Institutional Education (CHRIE), Hotel Sales and Marketing Association International (HSMA), or the human resources departments in casino hotels.

Tips for Entry

1. Get your foot in the door of a casino hotel. Most promote from within. You might have to start out as a trainee, but if you work hard, you will move up the career ladder.
2. Stop by the human resources departments of casino hotels and inquire about job openings. You might also consider sending a résumé and a short cover letter.
3. Jobs may be advertised in the classified sections of newspapers in areas hosting gaming. Look under classifications such as "Hotel Front Office Manager," "Casino Hotel Front Office Manager," "Front Office Manager," "Front Office," or "Casino Opportunities."
4. A number of search firms deal exclusively with positions in the hospitality industry. A few deal with jobs in gaming related to the hospitality industry.

FRONT DESK MANAGER

CAREER PROFILE

Duties: Overseeing front desk clerks.

Alternative Titles(s): None

Salary Range: $25,000 to $42,000+ annually; see text.

Employment Prospects: Fair

Best Geographical Location(s) for Position: Las Vegas, Reno, Laughlin, Lake Tahoe, Atlantic City, Biloxi, Baton Rouge, New Orleans, and Detroit offer most opportunities; other regions with land-based, riverboat, or Indian gaming facilities offer additional opportunities.

Prerequisites:

Education or Training—High school diploma or equivalent; on-the-job training; see text.

Experience and Qualifications—Experience working in front office operation.

Special Skills and Personality Traits—Organization; supervisory skills; communication skills; computer skills; customer service skills.

CAREER LADDER

```
┌─────────────────────────────────┐
│   Front Desk Manager in Larger, │
│   More Prestigious Casino or    │
│   Assistant Front Office Manager│
└─────────────────────────────────┘

┌─────────────────────────────────┐
│      Front Desk Manager         │
└─────────────────────────────────┘

┌─────────────────────────────────┐
│   Front Desk Shift Supervisor   │
└─────────────────────────────────┘
```

Position Description

The front desk is the place in the casino hotel where guests check in and check out. To run this area in an efficient manner, the hotel employs front office or front desk clerks. The individual responsible for overseeing these employees is called the Front Desk Manager. In some casino hotels the person is called the front desk supervisor.

The Front Desk Manager supervises all activities of the front desk clerks. He or she is responsible for making sure the clerks are properly trained. The Front Desk Manager makes certain that clerks welcome guests when they arrive and treats each one in a courteous and pleasant manner.

The Front Desk Manager is responsible for handling problems that may occur with guests' reservations. This might include, for example, a reservation that somehow is not in the computer. The Front Desk Manager does everything possible to keep guests happy. This can mean upgrading a room or offering some type of amenity. In some cases, these decisions may have to be authorized by the front office manager.

The Front Desk Manager assists clerks in solving difficulties with credit cards or in handling check cashing or other monetary transactions.

The Front Desk Manager assists clerks with guests' problems at checkout. These might include charges guests think are incorrect or were supposed to be "comped" or provided at no charge.

Other duties of the casino hotel Front Desk Manager may include:

• Handling customer complaints and problems
• Recommending front office clerks for promotion

Salaries

Depending on the specific casino hotel, Front Desk Managers are paid an hourly wage or a weekly salary. Individuals may earn between $12.00 and $20.00 or more per hour or be paid annual salaries ranging from $25,000 and $42,000 plus.

Factors affecting earnings include the geographic location, size, and prestige of the specific casino hotel, as well as the experience and responsibilities of the individual.

Employment Prospects

Employment opportunities for casino hotel Front Desk Managers are fair. Las Vegas, Reno, Laughlin, Lake Tahoe, Atlantic City, Biloxi, Baton Rouge, New Orleans, and Detroit offer the greatest number of job possibilities. Other employment settings include casinos and casino hotels in other areas of Nevada, Mississippi, New York, Louisiana, Colorado, Connecticut, Illinois, Arizona, and California.

Other regions hosting Indian gaming and land-based or riverboat gaming facilities offer additional opportunities. New casinos and casino hotels are constantly under construction. More casinos and casino hotels are also opening every year as areas legalize gambling.

Advancement Prospects

Casino hotel Front Desk Managers may climb the career ladder by obtaining more experience and/or training. They may then locate similar positions in larger, more prestigious casino hotels, resulting in increased earnings. With additional experience and training an individual may also be promoted to the job of assistant front office manager.

Education and Training

Most hotels require individuals to hold a high school diploma or the equivalent. Experience may be accepted in lieu of education. Individuals are usually trained on the job for this position.

Experience/Skills/Personality Traits

Generally, Front Desk Managers must have at least one year of experience working in the front office of a hotel. Individuals must be organized, detail-oriented, and have supervisory skills. Computer skills and customer service skills are essential in this job.

An understanding of the front office and the hospitality industry is also necessary.

Unions/Associations

Those interested in learning more about careers as casino hotel Front Desk Managers can obtain additional information by contacting the Council on Hotel, Restaurant and Institutional Education (CHRIE), Hotel Sales and Marketing Association International (HSMA), or the human resources departments in casino hotels.

Tips for Entry

1. If you do not live in a gaming area and aspire to work in a casino hotel, get experience in the front office of a luxury hotel before you move.
2. The human resources departments of casino hotels will tell you of any job openings.
3. Most casinos have job hotlines. These are frequently updated messages listing jobs available. You can call each casino directly to get its job hotline phone number.
4. Jobs are often advertised in the classified sections of newspapers in areas hosting gaming. Look under classifications such as "Hotel Front Desk Manager," "Casino Hotel Front Desk Manager," "Front Desk Manager," "Hospitality Industry," or "Casino Hotel Opportunities."

FRONT OFFICE CLERK

CAREER PROFILE

Duties: Registering guests; assigning rooms; issuing room keys.

Alternative Titles(s): Desk Clerk

Salary Range: $14,000 to $25,000

Employment Prospects: Excellent

Best Geographical Location(s) for Position: Las Vegas, Reno, Laughlin, Lake Tahoe, Atlantic City, Biloxi, Baton Rouge, New Orleans, and Detroit offer most opportunities; other regions with land-based, riverboat, or Indian gaming facilities offer additional opportunities.

Prerequisites:

Education or Training—High school diploma or equivalent; on-the-job training; see text.

Experience and Qualifications—Experience working in front office operation preferred, but not always required.

Special Skills and Personality Traits—Organization; communication skills; data-entry skills; customer service skills.

CAREER LADDER

```
┌─────────────────────────────────┐
│  Front Office Clerk in Larger, More │
│     Prestigious Casino Hotel    │
│  or Front Office Shift Superviso │
└─────────────────────────────────┘

┌─────────────────────────────────┐
│       Front Office Clerk        │
└─────────────────────────────────┘

┌─────────────────────────────────┐
│  Front Office Clerk in Non-Casino │
│       Hotel or Entry Level      │
└─────────────────────────────────┘
```

Position Description

When guests arrive at a casino hotel, they usually expect to check in quickly and efficiently. Front Office Clerks are the individuals responsible for making sure this happens. Front Office Clerks may also be called front office agents or front desk clerks.

Front Office Clerks welcome guests and check their reservations, often by computer. Information regarding the reservation is retrieved from the computer by the Front Office Clerk, who then registers the guest.

The Front Office Clerk usually asks the guest for identification such as a driver's license or credit card. In many situations the individual makes an imprint of the guest's credit card to guarantee payment.

The Front Office Clerk checks the computer to see what type of room has been reserved and assigns the guest to his or her room. Information regarding guests must also be input into the computer system.

The Front Office Clerk issues the guest one or more room keys. In some situations, hotels use computerized cards instead of keys. The Front Office Clerk may be responsible for explaining how such cards work.

The Front Office Clerk assists guests when they check out. The individual asks if the guest had a pleasant stay. During this time, the Front Office Clerk brings up the necessary computer information regarding guest charges.

The Front Office Clerk must deal with guests in a courteous and efficient manner at all times.

Other duties of the casino hotel Front Office Clerk may include:

• Cashing checks or handling other monetary transactions for guests
• Accepting payment for guest charges, including rooms, room service, restaurant and bar bills, and other amenities

Salaries

Casino hotel Front Office Clerks are paid an hourly wage. Individuals may earn between $7.00 and $12.00 or more per hour or about $14,000 to $25,000 annually. Factors affecting earnings include the geographic location, size, and prestige of the specific casino hotel, as well as the experience and responsibilities of the individual. In some hotels, Front Office Clerks may also receive tips.

Employment Prospects

Employment opportunities for casino hotel Front Office Clerks are plentiful. They may be found throughout the country.

Las Vegas, Reno, Laughlin, Lake Tahoe, Atlantic City, Biloxi, Baton Rouge, New Orleans, and Detroit offer the greatest number of job possibilities. Other employment settings include casinos and casino hotels in other areas of Nevada, Mississippi, New York, Louisiana, Colorado, Connecticut, Illinois, Arizona, and California.

Other regions hosting Indian gaming and land-based or riverboat gaming facilities offer additional opportunities. New casinos and casino hotels are constantly under construction. More casinos and casino hotels are also opening every year as areas legalize gambling.

Advancement Prospects

Casino hotel Front Office Clerks may climb the career ladder by obtaining more experience and/or training. They may then locate similar positions in larger, more prestigious casino hotels, resulting in increased earnings. With additional experience and training, individuals may also be promoted to front office shift supervisor.

Education and Training

Educational requirements vary with different casino hotels. Most hotels require individuals to hold a high school diploma or the equivalent. Experience may be accepted in lieu of education. Individuals are usually trained on the job for this position.

Experience/Skills/Personality Traits

Depending on the hotel, this may be an entry-level position. Individuals must be organized and detail-oriented. Customer service and interpersonal skills are essential.

Understanding of hotel front office activities and the hospitality industry is useful.

Unions/Associations

Depending on the specific casino, this may or may not be a unionized position. In unionized hotels in Las Vegas, for example, Front Office Clerks may be members of the Teamsters Local #995.

Those interested in learning more about careers as casino hotel Front Office Clerks can obtain additional information by contacting the Council on Hotel, Restaurant and Institutional Education (CHRIE), Hotel Sales and Marketing Association International (HSMA), or the human resources departments in casino hotels.

Tips for Entry

1. This is a good job to get your foot in the door of a casino hotel. Remember that most facilities promote from within. Learn as much as you can and work hard to move up the career ladder.
2. Visit the human resources departments of casino hotels and inquire about job openings.
3. At casino job fairs in areas hosting gaming these types of positions are often available.
4. Jobs may be advertised in the classified sections of newspapers in areas hosting gaming. Look under classifications such as "Hotel Front Office Clerk," "Casino Hotel Front Office Clerk," "Front Office Clerk," "Front Office," or "Casino Opportunities."
5. Most casinos have job hotlines. These are frequently updated messages listing jobs available. You can call each casino directly to get its job hotline phone number.
6. Openings are often advertised on the Internet. They may be located via the home pages of casino hotels. They may also be found by doing a search of "Casino," "Casino Hotel," or "Gaming Job Opportunities."

CONCIERGE

CAREER PROFILE

Duties: Providing special assistance and service to casino hotel guests.

Alternative Titles(s): None

Salary Range: $20,000 to $45,000

Employment Prospects: Good

Best Geographical Location(s) for Position: Las Vegas, Reno, Laughlin, Lake Tahoe, Atlantic City, Biloxi, Baton Rouge, New Orleans, and Detroit offer most opportunities; other regions with land-based, riverboat, or Indian gaming facilities offer additional opportunities.

Prerequisites:

Education or Training—High school diploma or equivalent; on-the-job training; see text.

Experience and Qualifications—Experience working in hospitality industry.

Special Skills and Personality Traits—Customer service skills; service-oriented; communication skills; personable; detail-oriented; ingenuity; articulate.

CAREER LADDER

```
┌─────────────────────────────────────┐
│  Concierge in Larger, More Prestigious │
│      Casino Hotel or Guest           │
│        Services Manager              │
└─────────────────────────────────────┘

┌─────────────────────────────────────┐
│              Concierge               │
└─────────────────────────────────────┘

┌─────────────────────────────────────┐
│  Position at Front Desk or Guest Services │
└─────────────────────────────────────┘
```

Position Description

Casino hotels, especially the larger, more luxurious ones, pride themselves on customer service. The more the hotel staff can do to accommodate guests' needs, the better. These hotels employ a person called the Concierge to provide special assistance and service to hotel guests.

The Concierge performs a variety of services. He or she may, for example, help a guest obtain tickets to a show either in the hotel or at another hotel's showroom. Sometimes the Concierge is asked to obtain tickets to sold-out events or shows for which tickets are no longer available.

Guests may be looking for a restaurant that serves a specific type of food. The Concierge tells the guests about the restaurants in the area and may recommend one or two. He or she may even get a sample menu for guests to look over before they visit the restaurant.

The Concierge may be asked to find babysitters, nannies, or other child care services for guests. The individual might also make arrangements for guests to take a tour of the casino, the area, or special attractions nearby.

The Concierge assists guests who need courier services, cell phone or beeper rentals, fax or computer rentals, or secretarial services.

The Concierge helps guests requiring other types of special services. For example, a guest wants to talk to a casino representative who speaks another language so that the rules of a game can be explained in the guest's native tongue.

The Concierge may be asked to find a shop that sells a specific brand of clothing or to find an-after hours pharmacy. The individual might additionally be required to recommend a physician, dentist, or optician close by.

The Concierge gives information to guests when they are looking for something interesting to do in the area. The individual may make arrangements for transportation such as limos or car service, or recommend various entertainment activities.

Depending on the hotel, the concierge may be responsible for attending to the needs of VIP guests or may be expected to handle the special needs of all guests. The individual sometimes has an office on a special floor of the hotel, or may be found at a desk in the lobby.

In order to be effective, Concierges must have a great many contacts both in and out of the casino hotel. They must know every inch of the area or city in which they are located.

Other duties of the casino hotel Concierge may include:

- Introducing hotel guests to casino personnel
- Assisting guests with other services

Salaries

Depending on the specific casino hotel, Concierges are usually paid an hourly wage ranging from $10.00 to $22.00 plus tips or roughly $20,000 to $45,000 annually.

Factors affecting earnings include the geographic location, size, and prestige of the specific casino hotel, as well as the experience and responsibilities of the individual.

Employment Prospects

Employment opportunities for casino hotel Concierges are good. Jobs may be found throughout the country in larger, prestigious, and luxury casino hotels, as well as in many of the smaller ones.

Las Vegas, Reno, Laughlin, Lake Tahoe, Atlantic City, Biloxi, Baton Rouge, New Orleans, and Detroit offer the greatest number of job possibilities. Other employment settings include casinos and casino hotels in other areas of Nevada, Mississippi, New York, Louisiana, Colorado, Connecticut, Illinois, Arizona, and California.

Other regions hosting Indian gaming and land-based or riverboat gaming facilities offer additional opportunities. New casinos and casino hotels are constantly under construction. More casinos and casino hotels are also opening every year as areas legalize gambling.

Advancement Prospects

Casino hotel Concierges may climb the career ladder by obtaining more experience and locating similar positions in larger or more prestigious hotels, resulting in increased earnings. With additional training and experience Concierges can be promoted to customer relations managers.

Education and Training

Most hotels require Concierges to hold a minimum of a high school diploma or the equivalent. Experience may be accepted in lieu of education. College training in hotel management is a plus. Concierges are usually trained on the job for this position.

Experience/Skills/Personality Traits

Generally, Concierges working in a casino hotel are required to have some experience working in a hotel. Some individuals have worked in guest services or at the front desk.

To be successful, Concierges must have customer service skills, be personable, and like to help people. Individuals should have a great deal of ingenuity and creativity in order to "do the impossible." They should also be organized and detail-oriented.

Understanding of the hospitality industry is also necessary.

Unions/Associations

Those interested in learning more about careers as Concierges can obtain additional information by contacting the Council on Hotel, Restaurant and Institutional Education (CHRIE) or the human resources departments in casino hotels.

Tips For Entry

1. If you are not currently living in a gaming area and aspire to work in such a region, get experience in some capacity working in a luxury hotel before you move.
2. Stop by the human resources departments of casino hotels to learn of job openings.
3. Jobs may be advertised in the classified sections of newspapers in areas hosting gaming. Look under classifications such as "Hotels," "Concierge," "Hospitality Industry," "Casino Hotels," or "Casino Hotel Opportunities."
4. Look for new casino hotels under construction. Apply early for the best positions.

BELL CAPTAIN

CAREER PROFILE

Duties: Supervising bellpersons, baggage handlers, and front door staff.

Alternative Titles(s): None

Salary Range: $14,000 to $30,000

Employment Prospects: Fair

Best Geographical Location(s) for Position: Las Vegas, Reno, Laughlin, Lake Tahoe, Atlantic City, Biloxi, Baton Rouge, New Orleans, and Detroit offer most opportunities; other regions with land-based, riverboat, or Indian gaming facilities offer additional opportunities.

Prerequisites:

Education or Training—High school diploma or equivalent.

Experience and Qualifications—Understanding of service and hospitality industry.

Special Skills and Personality Traits:—Interpersonal skills; customer service skills; supervisory skills; organization; friendly; courteous; ability to carry heavy baggage.

CAREER LADDER

```
┌─────────────────────────────────┐
│   Bell Captain in Larger, More  │
│   Prestigious Casino Hotel or   │
│   Superintendent of Services    │
└─────────────────────────────────┘

┌─────────────────────────────────┐
│          Bell Captain           │
└─────────────────────────────────┘

┌─────────────────────────────────┐
│          Bellperson             │
└─────────────────────────────────┘
```

Position Description

Thousands of guests check in and out of casino hotels every day. Those who help guests carry their luggage in and out of the hotel are called bellpersons or bellhops. The person who supervises these individuals is called the Bell Captain.

Depending on the hotel, the Bell Captain reports to the customer relations manager or the superintendent of services. In some hotels, the Bell Captain also handles the duties of a superintendent of services.

Bell Captains have a number of responsibilities. They are in charge of the bellhops. When guests arrive at a casino hotel and are given rooms, the Bell Captain assigns a bellperson to escort guests to their rooms, transporting their luggage as well.

When guests are ready to depart, they often make a call to the service desk, requesting a bellperson. Bell Captains assign bellpersons to go to guests' rooms to bring luggage to the checkout area or to transport it to the guests' vehicles.

Bell Captains may also be responsible for supervising the hotel's front door staff, the employees who assist arriving and departing guests, open doors, welcome guests, call taxis, and help guests with public transportation needs.

Casino hotel guests arrive by car, limo, public transportation, or by chartered or scheduled bus. The Bell Captain is additionally responsible for overseeing the baggage handlers who load, unload, and sort guests' luggage for movement to and from rooms.

Bell Captains answer questions regarding activities and facilities in the casino and hotel, as well as questions about attractions in the area, and public transportation.

Bell Captains must have an understanding of the duties of the bellpersons, door attendants, and baggage handlers. When these employees are busy with guests leaving, arriving, or in need of service, the Bell Captain may be required to step in to perform their duties.

Other duties of the Bell Captain may include:

- Scheduling bell persons, door attendants, and baggage handlers
- Handling special requests for guests
- Taking care of guest complaints regarding bellpersons, door people, and baggage handlers.

Salaries

Bell Captains working in hotel casinos are usually paid an hourly salary. Individuals may earn between $7.00 and $15.00 per hour or more plus tips or approximately $14,000 to $30,000 annually. Factors affecting earnings include the geographic location, size, and prestige of the casino hotel. Other variables include the experience and responsibilities of the individual. Those working in larger or more prestigious facilities in the gambling capitals usually earn more than their counterparts in other hotels.

Some Bell Captains receive a salary instead of an hourly wage.

Employment Prospects

Employment prospects are good for Bell Captains in casino hotels. Individuals can find employment wherever casino hotels are located. There usually is one Bell Captain per shift. Because casinos hotels operate 24 hours a day, individuals may work the day shift, swing or evening shift, overnight or graveyard shift.

Las Vegas, Reno, Laughlin, Lake Tahoe, Atlantic City, Biloxi, Baton Rouge, New Orleans, and Detroit offer the greatest number of job possibilities. Other employment settings include casinos and casino hotels in other areas of Nevada, Mississippi, New York, Louisiana, Colorado, Connecticut, Illinois, Arizona, and California.

Other regions hosting Indian gaming and land-based or riverboat gaming facilities offer additional opportunities. New casinos and casino hotels are constantly under construction. More casinos and casino hotels are also opening every year as areas legalize gambling.

Advancement Prospects

There are a number of ways Bell Captains can advance their careers. Individuals can find similar positions in larger or more prestigious hotels, resulting in increased responsibilities and earnings. Bell Captains may also be promoted to other supervisory positions, including superintendent of services, or customer relations manager. These promotions usually require that the individual obtain additional experience.

Education and Training

Education and training requirements vary from job to job. Usually, a high school diploma or its equivalent is required. However, work experience may be accepted in lieu of education.

Experience/Skills/Personality Traits

Experience requirements, like education, vary for Bell Captains. In many positions, Bell Captains are promoted from the ranks of bellpersons.

To be successful, Bell Captains should be friendly, courteous individuals with excellent customer service and interpersonal skills. Ability to carry heavy baggage is necessary, as is understanding of the service and hospitality industries.

Unions/Associations

Individuals interested in learning more about careers in this area can contact the human resources departments of casino hotels. Other information may be available from the American Hotel and Motel Association (AH&MA).

Tips for Entry

1. Get experience as a bellperson in a casino hotel. Management often promotes from within.
2. Stop by human resources departments to inquire about job openings.
3. Jobs are often advertised in the classified sections of newspapers in areas hosting gaming. Look under classifications such as "Casinos," "Casino Hotels," "Hotels," "Bell Captain," "Casino Hotel Opportunities," and "Gaming."

BELLPERSON

CAREER PROFILE

Duties: Escorting hotel guests to rooms; assisting with luggage; inspecting guests' rooms to ensure guest satisfaction.

Alternative Titles(s): Bellman; Bellwoman; Bellhop; Bell Attendant

Salary Range: $10,000 to $17,000

Employment Prospects: Excellent

Best Geographical Location(s) for Position: Las Vegas, Reno, Laughlin, Lake Tahoe, Atlantic City, Biloxi, Baton Rouge, New Orleans, and Detroit offer most opportunities; other regions with land-based, riverboat, or Indian gaming facilities offer additional opportunities.

Prerequisites:

Education or Training—High school diploma or equivalent; see text.

Experience and Qualifications—Experience in hospitality industry useful.

Special Skills and Personality Traits—Interpersonal skills; customer service skills; friendly; courteous; ability to carry heavy baggage.

CAREER LADDER

```
┌─────────────────────────────────────┐
│ Bellperson in Larger, More Prestigious │
│   Casino Hotel or Bell Captain        │
└─────────────────────────────────────┘

┌─────────────────────────────────────┐
│            Bellperson                 │
└─────────────────────────────────────┘

┌─────────────────────────────────────┐
│           Entry Level                 │
└─────────────────────────────────────┘
```

Position Description

Casino hotels, like all other hotels, are part of the hospitality industry. In order to make guests happy, hotels provide a great deal of service. Bellpersons, also known as Bell Attendants or Bellhops, are the individuals who escort incoming hotel guests to their rooms after they check in.

Bellpersons serve casino hotel guests in a variety of ways. Individuals load luggage onto carts. They also assist with hand luggage. While escorting guests to their rooms, the bellperson answers any questions regarding the hotel and its facilities.

Once the Bellperson gets to the correct room with a guest, he or she opens the door, shows the guest in, and inspects the room. The individual must be sure the room is in order and the guest is satisfied. Sometimes after guests see a room, they decide they want a king-size bed instead of a queen or that they want a room with a different view. The

Bellperson calls down to the desk to get the guest a more satisfactory room.

The Bellperson explains the features of the room, such as the operation of the locks, thermostat, air conditioner, or in-room Jacuzzi. The Bellperson also shows guests where exits are located.

Bellpersons may also deliver packages, additional luggage, trunks, and flowers to guest rooms.

Bellpersons in many casino hotel assist guests with local information about points of interest and entertainment attractions.

When guests are ready to depart, they often call the service desk to request that a Bellperson bring their luggage downstairs. Individuals may transport luggage to the checkout area or to guests' vehicle.

Other duties of the Bellperson may include:

• Delivering messages to guests

- Handling special requests for guests
- Bringing guests room keys

Salaries

Bellpersons earn an hourly salary ranging from minimum wage to approximately $8.00 or more plus tips or about $10,000 to $17,000 annually. Factors affecting earnings include the geographic location, size, and prestige of the casino hotel. Those working in larger or more prestigious facilities usually earn more than their counterparts in other hotels.

Employment Prospects

Employment opportunities for Bellpersons are excellent. Individuals can find employment wherever casino hotels are located. Usually a number of Bellpersons work each shift. Because casino hotels operate 24 hours a day, individuals may work various shifts.

Las Vegas, Reno, Laughlin, Lake Tahoe, Atlantic City, Biloxi, Baton Rouge, New Orleans, and Detroit offer the greatest number of job possibilities. Other employment settings include casinos and casino hotels in other areas of Nevada, Mississippi, New York, Louisiana, Colorado, Connecticut, Illinois, Arizona, and California.

Other regions hosting Indian gaming and land-based or riverboat gaming facilities offer additional opportunities. New casinos and casino hotels are constantly under construction. More casinos and casino hotels are also opening every year as areas legalize gambling.

Advancement Prospects

Bellpersons may move up the career ladder by locating similar positions in larger or more prestigious hotels, resulting in increased earnings and tips. If a position opens up, and individuals have experience, they may also be promoted to bell captain.

Education and Training

Usually casino hotels prefer applicants to hold a high school diploma or its equivalent. Many casinos assist people who do not hold a high school diploma to get a GED. Work experience may be accepted in lieu of education.

Experience/Skills/Personality Traits

In most casino hotels this is an entry-level position. Any experience in the hospitality or service industries will be useful.

Bellpersons must be able to carry heavy luggage. Individuals should be friendly, courteous, and personable. Excellent customer service and interpersonal skills are mandatory in this job.

Unions/Associations

Individuals interested in learning more about careers in this area can contact the human resources departments of casino hotels. Other information may be available from the American Hotel and Motel Association (AH&MA).

Tips for Entry

1. Human resources departments in casino hotels are good places to find out about job openings.
2. Call each casino directly to obtain its job hotline phone number.
3. Jobs are also advertised in the classified sections of newspapers in areas hosting gaming. Look under classifications such as "Casinos," "Casino Hotels," "Hotels," "Bellperson," "Bellhop," "Bell Attendant," and "Casino Hotel Opportunities."

DOORPERSON

CAREER PROFILE

Duties: Helping guests get in and out of their cars; welcoming guests to facility; opening doors; loading and unloading guests' luggage from vehicles; calling taxis.

Alternative Titles(s): Doorman; Doorwoman

Salary Range: $11,000 to $18,000 plus tips

Employment Prospects: Good

Best Geographical Location(s) for Position: Las Vegas, Reno, Laughlin, Lake Tahoe, Atlantic City, Biloxi, Baton Rouge, New Orleans, and Detroit offer most opportunities; other regions with land-based, riverboat, or Indian gaming facilities offer additional opportunities.

Prerequisites:

Education or Training:—High school diploma or equivalent preferred; see text.

Experience and Qualifications—Experience in hospitality industry preferred, but not required.

Special Skills and Personality Traits—Interpersonal skills; customer service skills; friendly; courteous.

CAREER LADDER

```
┌─────────────────────────────────────┐
│ Doorperson in Larger, More Prestigious │
│    Casino Hotel, Bellperson or        │
│         Bell Supervisor               │
└─────────────────────────────────────┘

┌─────────────────────────────────────┐
│             Doorperson               │
└─────────────────────────────────────┘

┌─────────────────────────────────────┐
│            Entry Level               │
└─────────────────────────────────────┘
```

Position Description

Casinos and casino hotels are very customer-oriented. When guests arrive at a casino, a Doorperson is often one of the first people to greet and welcome them.

Sometimes called a door attendant, the individual opens guests' car doors and helps them out of the vehicle.

The Doorperson is stationed near the main casino or casino hotel door so the individual can open the door for guests each time they enter and depart from the facility.

The Doorperson assists guests with hand luggage, packages, and other items. The individual also unloads guests' luggage onto a cart. In some facilities, the Doorperson moves the luggage inside the hotel. In others, baggage handlers or bellhops handle interior luggage movement.

Doorperson duties extend to assisting guests when they are leaving as well as upon arrival. Individuals load luggage into guests' vehicles. They also open the patrons' car doors, help them in, and close the doors. Doorpersons converse with guests on departure, asking if they enjoyed their stay and inviting them back to the facility.

Other duties of the Doorperson may include:

- Assisting guests with local information
- Calling or hailing taxis
- Helping guests with public transportation

Salaries

Doorpersons earn an hourly salary ranging from $5.50 to $8.50 or more plus tips or approximately $11,000 to $18,000 annually. Tips can be good for personable, customer-oriented individuals. Factors affecting earnings include the geographic location, size, and prestige of the casino hotel. Those working in larger or more prestigious facilities usually earn more than their counterparts in other hotels.

Employment Prospects

Employment opportunities for Doorpersons are good for customer- and guest-oriented individuals. Because casinos and casino hotels operate 24 hours a day, individuals may work various shifts.

Las Vegas, Reno, Laughlin, Lake Tahoe, Atlantic City, Biloxi, Baton Rouge, New Orleans, and Detroit offer the greatest number of job possibilities. Other employment settings include casinos and casino hotels in other areas of Nevada, Mississippi, New York, Louisiana, Colorado, Connecticut, Illinois, Arizona, and California.

Other regions hosting Indian gaming and land-based or riverboat gaming facilities offer additional opportunities. New casinos and casino hotels are constantly under construction. More casinos and casino hotels are also opening every year as areas legalize gambling.

Advancement Prospects

Doorpersons may move up the career ladder in a number of ways. Some individuals move into the guest service area, while others become bellpersons or bell supervisors.

Education and Training

Usually casino hotels prefer applicants to hold a high school diploma or its equivalent. Casinos often assist employees who do not hold either of these to obtain a GED.

Experience/Skills/Personality Traits

In many casinos and hotels this job is an entry-level position. However, experience in the hospitality industry is useful.

Doorpersons must be personable, friendly, and courteous individuals who like being around others. Customer service skills are essential to this type of job.

Unions/Associations

Depending on the specific casino, this may or may not be a unionized position. Individuals interested in learning more about careers in this area can contact the human resources departments of casino hotels.

Tips for Entry

1. Most casinos have job hotlines. These are frequently updated messages listing jobs availables. You can call each casino directly to get its job hotline phone number.
2. Stop by the human resources departments in casino hotels to inquire about job openings.
3. Jobs are advertised in the classified sections of newspapers in areas hosting gaming. Look under classifications such as "Casinos/Gaming," "Casino Hotels," "Hotels," "Doorperson," "Door Attendant," and "Casino Hotel Opportunities."
4. Attend casino job fairs in areas hosting gaming.

VALET ATTENDANT

CAREER PROFILE

Duties: Parking and retrieving guest vehicles.

Alternative Titles(s): Valet

Salary Range: $12,000 to $18,000 plus tips

Employment Prospects: Excellent

Best Geographical Location(s) for Position: Las Vegas, Reno, Laughlin, Lake Tahoe, Atlantic City, Biloxi, Baton Rouge, New Orleans, and Detroit offer most opportunities; other regions with land-based, riverboat, or Indian gaming facilities offer additional opportunities.

Prerequisites:

Education or Training—High school diploma or equivalent; see text.

Experience and Qualifications—Valid, clean driver's licence.

Special Skills and Personality Traits—Ability to drive; customer service skills; pleasant; interpersonal skills; friendly; courteous.

CAREER LADDER

```
┌─────────────────────────────┐
│      Valet Supervisor       │
└─────────────────────────────┘

┌─────────────────────────────┐
│      Valet Attendant        │
└─────────────────────────────┘

┌─────────────────────────────┐
│        Entry Level          │
└─────────────────────────────┘
```

Position Description

Guests who drive to casinos and casino hotels often prefer valet parking so that they do not have to park their own cars in a distant lot or garage and walk back to the facility.

With valet parking, guests get out of their cars at the main entrance of the casino, leave their keys in the vehicles, and have their cars parked for them.

As guests drive up to the facility, Valet Attendants welcome them, opening car doors for guests and helping them out of their vehicles.

The Valet Attendant ascertains the length of a guest's stay to determine where the vehicle should be parked. Many facilities have different parking areas for guests just staying for the day and for those staying overnight.

Two-piece tickets with numbers are usually used in valet parking. One side of the ticket is given to the customer to retrieve the automobile later. The other portion is either placed on the windshield of the auto or kept with the guest's keys. In some casinos, the Valet Attendant may be expected to write information on the parking ticket, stating the make, model, color, and license of the guest's automobile, as well

as the location in which the car is to be parked. In others, a valet supervisor handles this responsibility. The Valet Attendant or supervisor also stamps the ticket with the time and date. This information is used to determine any parking charges levied by the facility.

The Valet Attendant is responsible for driving the guest's car to the correct lot and parking the car. The individual will then bring the keys back to the valet parking office for storage.

When guests are ready to leave, they give their valet ticket to the valet supervisor. The Valet Attendant must then go to the parking area, retrieve the car, and drive it back to the casino hotel and turn it over to the guest.

Other duties of the casino or casino hotel Valet Attendant may include:

- Retrieving items for guests from their parked cars
- Bringing vehicles to a garage or service center to be cleaned or serviced
- Giving directions to guests
- Directing customers to spaces to park their own vehicles

Salaries

Valet Attendants working in casinos and casino hotels are paid an hourly wage ranging between $6.00 and $8.50 or more plus tips or approximately $12,000 to $18,000 annually. In unionized casinos, the union will negotiate minimum wages.

Many Valet Attendants earn $40,000 or more annually with tips.

Employment Prospects

Employment prospects for Valet Attendants in casinos and casino hotels are excellent. There are usually openings at most facilities. Individuals may work full-time or part-time during various shifts.

Las Vegas, Reno, Laughlin, Lake Tahoe, Atlantic City, Biloxi, Baton Rouge, New Orleans, and Detroit offer the greatest number of job possibilities. Other employment settings include casinos and casino hotels in other areas of Nevada, Mississippi, New York, Louisiana, Colorado, Connecticut, Illinois, Arizona, and California.

Other regions hosting Indian gaming and land-based or riverboat gaming facilities offer additional opportunities. New casinos and casino hotels are constantly under construction. More casinos and casino hotels are also opening every year as areas legalize gambling.

Advancement Prospect

Valet Attendants may be promoted to supervisory positions within the valet department. These may include valet supervisor or valet cashier. Individuals may also find similar jobs at larger or more prestigious facilities, resulting in increased earnings and tips.

Education and Training

Casinos and casino hotels usually prefer Valet Attendants to have a high school diploma or the equivalent. Many hotels assist individuals who do not have this education in obtaining a GED.

Experience/Skills/Personality Traits

In many casino hotels, no experience is required for this position. In others, experience working in a valet department may be preferred.

Valet Attendants must hold a valid driver's license. Individuals should be careful drivers with clean driving records. Valets should be courteous, personable people with good customer service skills.

Unions/Associations

Depending on the specific hotel and its location, Valets may be represented by a union. Unionized casino hotels in different parts of the country have different union representation. In Las Vegas, for example, Valets may be represented by the Teamsters Local #995.

Those interested in learning more about jobs in this area should contact the human resources departments of casinos and casino hotels to learn about specific opportunities.

Tips for Entry

1. Visit the human resources departments of casinos and casino hotels to learn of job openings.
2. Most casinos have job hotlines. These are frequently updated messages listing jobs available. You can call each casino directly to obtain its job hotline phone number.
3. Jobs are often advertised in the classified sections of newspapers in areas hosting gaming. Look under classifications such as "Casinos/Gaming," "Casinos/Hotels," "Valet Attendants," or "Valet Department."
4. If you don't like being confined to an office and enjoy dealing with people and moving around during your shift, this job may be a good opportunity.

BAGGAGE HANDLER

Duties: Unloading and loading guests' luggage from cars and buses; sorting luggage; transporting luggage to rooms.

Alternative Titles(s): None

Salary Range: $10,000 to $17,000 plus tips

Employment Prospects: Good

Best Geographical Location(s) for Position: Las Vegas, Reno, Laughlin, Lake Tahoe, Atlantic City, Biloxi, Baton Rouge, New Orleans, and Detroit offer most opportunities; other regions with land-based, riverboat, or Indian gaming facilities offer additional opportunities.

Prerequisites:

Education or Training—High school diploma or equivalent; see text.

Experience and Qualifications—No experience necessary.

Special Skills and Personality Traits—Ability to lift and carry heavy baggage; interpersonal skills; customer service skills; courteous.

```
┌──────────────────────────────┐
│   Doorperson or Bellperson   │
└──────────────────────────────┘

┌──────────────────────────────┐
│      Baggage Handler         │
└──────────────────────────────┘

┌──────────────────────────────┐
│        Entry Level           │
└──────────────────────────────┘
```

Position Description

A great many guests arrive daily at casino hotels. Some come by cars or limos. Others arrive on bus tours or in vans from airport junkets. Baggage Handlers are responsible for loading and unloading guests' luggage from vehicles.

After Baggage Handlers unload guests' luggage, they bring it into the hotel. Bellhops can then transport the luggage to the correct room.

When guests arrive in groups on buses or vans, Baggage Handlers are responsible for sorting the luggage, tagging it with the guests' names.

In some situations, Baggage Handlers are required to get guests' room assignments and bring their luggage to the rooms. In other situations, Baggage Handlers just carry luggage into the hotel. Bellhops are then responsible for getting the correct luggage to the proper rooms.

Other duties of the Baggage Handler may include:

• Loading baggage back into vehicles

• Transporting trunks, packages, and other baggage to loading areas, using luggage cart or handtruck

Salaries

Baggage Handlers earn an hourly salary ranging from minimum wage to approximately $8.00 or more plus tips or about $10,000 to $17,000 annually. Factors affecting earnings include the geographic location, size, and prestige of the casino hotel. Those working in larger or more prestigious facilities usually earn more than their counterparts in other hotels.

Employment Prospects

Employment prospects for Baggage Handlers in casino hotels are good. Individuals may find employment whereever casino hotels are located. Hotels usually hire a number of Baggage Handlers per shift.

Las Vegas, Reno, Laughlin, Lake Tahoe, Atlantic City, Biloxi, Baton Rouge, New Orleans, and Detroit offer the greatest number of job possibilities. Other employment settings include casinos and casino hotels in other areas of Nevada, Mississippi, New York, Louisiana, Colorado, Connecticut, Illinois, Arizona, and California.

Other regions hosting Indian gaming and land-based or riverboat gaming facilities offer additional opportunities. New casinos and casino hotels are constantly under construction. More casinos and casino hotels are also opening every year as areas legalize gambling.

Advancement Opportunities

Baggage Handlers may be promoted to either doorpersons or bellpersons. These positions often provide increased earnings through tips.

Education and Training

Casino hotels prefer applicants to hold a high school diploma or its equivalent. Work experience may be accepted in lieu of education.

Experience/Skills/Personality Traits

This is an entry-level position. No experience is necessary. Individuals must be able to carry heavy luggage. They should also be friendly, courteous, and personable. Excellent customer service and interpersonal skills are essential.

Unions/Associations

Individuals who want to know more about careers in this field should contact the human resources departments of casino hotels. Additional information may be available from the American Hotel and Motel Association (AH&MA).

Tips for Entry

1. Visit the human resources departments in casino hotels and ask about job openings.
2. Jobs are often advertised in the classified sections of newspapers in areas hosting gaming. Look under classifications such as "Casinos," "Casino Hotels," "Hotels," "Hospitality," "Baggage Handler," and "Casino Hotel Opportunities."
3. Most casino hotels have job hotlines that are updated frequently. You can call each casino directly to obtain its job hotline phone number.

EXECUTIVE HOUSEKEEPER

CAREER PROFILE

Duties: Supervising housekeeping staff; making sure guest rooms, banquet rooms, and public areas are clean and well maintained; training staff; inspecting rooms.

Alternative Titles(s): None

Salary Range: $35,000 to $75,000+

Employment Prospects: Fair

Best Geographical Location(s) for Position: Las Vegas, Reno, Laughlin, Lake Tahoe, Atlantic City, Biloxi, Baton Rouge, New Orleans, and Detroit offer most opportunities; other regions with land-based, riverboat, or Indian gaming facilities offer additional opportunities.

Prerequisites:

Education or Training—Bachelor's degree in hotel administration preferred; experience may be accepted in lieu of education.

Experience and Qualifications—Experience in hotel housekeeping.

Special Skills and Personality Traits—Supervisory skills; management skills; communication skills; detail-oriented; organized.

CAREER LADDER

```
┌─────────────────────────────────────┐
│   Executive Housekeeper in Larger,   │
│    More Prestigious Casino Hotel     │
└─────────────────────────────────────┘

┌─────────────────────────────────────┐
│       Executive Housekeeper          │
└─────────────────────────────────────┘

┌─────────────────────────────────────┐
│          Floor Supervisor            │
└─────────────────────────────────────┘
```

Position Description

It is essential to the success of hotels that guests feel comfortable and find their stay enjoyable and pleasant. The first thing guests often notice at hotels is the cleanliness or lack of cleanliness of their room. The Executive Housekeeper at a casino hotel is in charge of keeping guest rooms, meeting rooms, banquet rooms, and public areas of the hotel clean, orderly, and well maintained. The individual has a number of responsibilities depending on the specific hotel, and its size and structure.

An Executive Housekeeper may be expected to physically clean rooms on occasion. Most of the time, however, the Executive Housekeeper supervises others on the housekeeping staff. The individual inspects rooms that others in the staff have cleaned, making sure everything is up to hotel standards. When inspecting rooms, the Executive House-keeper must check the condition of the rooms to make sure needed repairs are made.

The Executive Housekeeper is responsible for training all other housekeeping personnel. The individual explains cleaning procedures and hotel policies.

The Executive Housekeeper is also responsible for devising work schedules for housekeepers, as well as for assigning individual rooms to clean. The Executive Housekeeper must keep an accurate record of which rooms are clean and ready for guests.

Casino hotels usually provide a number of amenities to guests such as shampoos. bubble baths, body lotions, shower caps, mouthwash, soaps, chocolates, stationery, and postcards. The Executive Housekeeper makes sure that there is an adequate supply of these amenities and that they are distributed to each guest room. The individual must also ensure that room service menus and other literature regarding the hotel, casino, and restaurants are stocked and distributed to each guest room.

In many casino hotels, the Executive Housekeeper also must supervise laundry and valet services provided by the facility for guests.

Other duties of the Executive Housekeeper might include:

- Ordering cleaning supplies
- Making sure there are enough clean linens and towels for guest rooms
- Making sure uniforms for housekeeping staff are cleaned and distributed
- Preparing budget for department

Salaries

Annual earnings for Executive Housekeepers working in casino hotels can range from $35,000 to $75,000 or more annually. Factors affecting earnings include the specific hotel, number of rooms, prestige, and geographic location. Other variables include the individual's responsibilities, education, and experience. In addition to salaries, Executive Housekeepers may also receive annual bonuses.

Individuals with the most education, working in the largest, most prestigious hotels generally make the most money.

Employment Prospects

Employment prospects for Executive Housekeepers in casino hotels are fair. All hotels large or small require housekeepers, and most utilize an Executive Housekeeper.

Las Vegas, Reno, Laughlin, Lake Tahoe, Atlantic City, Biloxi, Baton Rouge, New Orleans, and Detroit offer the greatest number of job possibilities. Other employment settings include casinos and casino hotels in other areas of Nevada, Mississippi, New York, Louisiana, Colorado, Connecticut, Illinois, Arizona, and California.

Other regions hosting Indian gaming and land-based or riverboat gaming facilities offer additional opportunities. New casinos and casino hotels are constantly under construction. More casinos and casino hotels are also opening every year as areas legalize gambling.

Advancement Prospects

Executive Housekeepers can advance their careers by obtaining experience. They may then locate similar positions in larger or more prestigious hotels, resulting in increased responsibilities and earnings. Individuals may also climb the career ladder by finding employment in hotels in other supervisory positions.

Education and Training

Educational requirements for Executive Housekeepers vary. While some hotels accept experience in lieu of educa-

tion, individuals with a formal college education usually are more marketable.

Recommended education for this position is a four-year college degree. A good major is hotel administration. There are also a number of technical schools, community, and junior colleges offering majors or courses in hotel housekeeping. The National Executive Housekeepers Association (NEHA) works with schools and colleges, putting together courses in this area.

Continuing education as well as home study courses are also offered through the Educational Institute of the American Hotel and Motel Association (AHMA).

Experience/Skills/Personality Traits

Executive Housekeepers need excellent supervisory and administrative skills. They must have the ability to work well with others while directing their activities.

In order to be successful in this field, individuals should have excellent communication skills. They need to be organized, detail-oriented, and have a great deal of pride in their work.

Executive Housekeepers are usually required to have several years' experience in supervisory housekeeping. This is often obtained through prior positions as assistant executive housekeepers, or as night or evening housekeeping supervisors.

Unions/Associations

Organizations that provide additional information regarding a career as Executive Housekeeper include the National Executive Housekeepers Association (NEHA) and the American Hotel and Motel Association (AHMA).

Tips for Entry

1. Continue your education. Contact trade associations to see what courses or seminars are offered in your area.
2. Positions in this field are advertised in the newspaper classified sections in the casino capitals of the country. Look under headings such as "Casino Hotels," "Casinos," "Hotels," and "Executive Housekeeper."
3. Subscribe to newspapers in Atlantic City, Las Vegas, Reno, Laughlin, Lake Tahoe, Detroit, or any other city where there are casino hotels. Don't forget other areas hosting gambling throughout the country. Your local newspaper or bookstore can often get you Sunday newspapers from various areas in the country. Look in the classified section to see what openings are available.
4. If you can't get Sunday newspapers from areas hosting gaming, check out newspapers on the Web. Some have their classified section on-line.

GUEST ROOM ATTENDANT

Duties: Cleaning and preparing hotel guest rooms; replenishing supplies and amenities.

Alternative Titles(s): Housekeeper

Salary Range: $13,000 to $28,000 plus tips

Employment Prospects: Excellent

Best Geographical Location(s) for Position: Las Vegas, Reno, Laughlin, Lake Tahoe, Atlantic City, Biloxi, Baton Rouge, New Orleans, and Detroit offer most opportunities; other regions with land-based, riverboat, or Indian gaming facilities offer additional opportunities.

Prerequisites:
Education or Training—On-the-job training.
Experience and Qualifications—Prior experience in service industry helpful.
Special Skills and Personality Traits—Detail-oriented; organized; physical stamina.

```
┌─────────────────────────────────┐
│   Floor Supervisor or Guest Room │
│   Attendant in Larger, More      │
│   Prestigious Casino Hotel       │
└─────────────────────────────────┘

┌─────────────────────────────────┐
│      Guest Room Attendant        │
└─────────────────────────────────┘

┌─────────────────────────────────┐
│  Guest Room Attendant in Non-Casino │
│       Hotel or Entry Level       │
└─────────────────────────────────┘
```

Position Description

Guest Room Attendants are responsible for cleaning guest rooms in casino hotels. They also clean and maintain public areas such as hallways on guest floors.

Guest Room Attendants have a number of duties. Individuals are usually assigned rooms to clean. Their responsibilities include changing linens and making the beds in guest rooms. They also are expected to dust, wipe up any spills, and vacuum.

The Guest Room Attendant must thoroughly clean the bathroom shower, tub, and toilet, as well as make sure counters and floor are spotless. The individual also clears any room service dishes and trays from the room.

The Guest Room Attendant empties waste baskets and cleans ashtrays in the rooms. He or she replenishes drinking glasses as well as stationery, postcards, matches, room service menus, and magazines. Casino hotels usually offer an array of cosmetic amenities including shampoos, soaps, shower caps, body creams, conditioners, and bubble baths. The Guest Room Attendant makes sure each room is fully supplied with the required amenities. The individual also places clean towels in the bathroom and replenishes any other bathroom supplies.

The Guest Room Attendant makes sure the room is well maintained. He or she must check to see no light bulbs are out, that blankets and bedspreads are clean and not worn, and that drapes are not ripped.

Guest Room Attendants' responsibilities may also include:

• Turning down beds in the evening
• Placing candy or cookies on turned-down beds
• Bringing guests extra towels, pillows or other requested amenities
• Transporting trash to disposal area
• Stocking housekeeping cart

Salaries

Guest Room Attendants earn between $6.50 and $15.00 per hour plus tips or about $13,000 to $28,000 annually. Factors affecting earnings include the geographic location, size, type, and prestige of the specific casino hotel, as well as the experience and responsibilities of the individual.

In unionized settings, the union may negotiate minimum earnings.

Employment Prospects

Employment opportunities for Guest Room Attendants are abundant. Las Vegas, Reno, Laughlin, Lake Tahoe, Atlantic City, Biloxi, Baton Rouge, New Orleans, and Detroit offer the greatest number of job possibilities. Other employment settings include casinos and casino hotels in other areas of Nevada, Mississippi, New York, Louisiana, Colorado, Connecticut, Illinois, Arizona, and California.

Other regions hosting Indian gaming and land-based or riverboat gaming facilities offer additional opportunities. New casinos and casino hotels are constantly under construction. More casinos and casino hotels are also opening every year as areas legalize gambling.

Advancement Prospects

Guest Room Attendants working in casino hotels can advance their careers by locating similar jobs in larger, more prestigious facilities. This may result in increased earnings and/or tips.

Some Guest Room Attendants climb the career ladder through promotion to positions such as floor supervisor.

Education and Training

On-the-job training is usually provided for Guest Room Attendants. Individuals who have prior experience in this area may be preferred.

Experience/Skills/Personality Traits

Experience requirements vary. In many casino hotels this is an entry-level position. As noted, some hotels prefer or require applicants to have prior experience working in either the service or hospitality industry.

Unions/Associations

Depending on the specific hotel and its location, Guest Room Attendants may be represented by a union. Casinos in different parts of the country have different union representation. In Las Vegas, for example, Guest Room Attendants may be members of the Culinary Workers Local #226 union. In Atlantic City casino hotels, Guest Room Attendants are represented by Local 54 of the Hotel Employees and Restaurant Employees International Union. It is important to note that many casinos in the country are not unionized.

Individuals interested in jobs as Guest Room Attendants may obtain additional career information by contacting human resource directors of casino hotels. Additional information may be obtained by writing to the National Executive Housekeepers Association (NEHA).

Tips for Entry

1. While this is often an entry-level position, the ability to demonstrate a stable work history will be helpful.
2. Jobs are often advertised in the classified sections of newspapers in areas hosting gaming. Look under classifications such as "Guest Room Attendants," "Hotel Housekeepers," "Hospitality Industry Jobs," and "Casino Hotels."
3. Call casino job hotlines for openings in this area. These are frequently updated messages listing jobs available. Call each casino directly to get its job hotline phone number.
4. Visit the human resources departments of casino hotels to inquire about job openings.
5. Look for casino job fairs. They often have openings in this area.

PBX OPERATOR

Duties: Handling incoming calls; supplying information to callers; routing incoming calls to correct party; connecting outgoing calls.

Alternative Titles(s): Operator; PBX Attendant

Salary Range: $14,000 to $28,000

Employment Prospects: Good

Best Geographical Location(s) for Position: Las Vegas, Reno, Laughlin, Lake Tahoe, Atlantic City, Biloxi, Baton Rouge, New Orleans, and Detroit offer most opportunities; other regions with land-based, riverboat, or Indian gaming facilities offer additional opportunities.

Prerequisites:

Education or Training—High school diploma or equivalent.

Experience and Qualifications—Prior PBX experience preferred.

Special Skills and Personality Traits—Clear speaking voice; phone skills; courteous; pleasant; customer service skills.

```
┌─────────────────────────────────────┐
│   Lead Operator or PBX Supervisor    │
└─────────────────────────────────────┘

┌─────────────────────────────────────┐
│            PBX Operator              │
└─────────────────────────────────────┘

┌─────────────────────────────────────┐
│   Entry Level or PBX Operators in    │
│          Different Setting           │
└─────────────────────────────────────┘
```

Position Description

The first contact many people have with casinos or casino hotels is the telephone operator who answers calls. The individual is referred to as the PBX Operator, PBX Attendant, or Operator.

PBX stands for private branch exchange. These are the type of switchboards used in casinos and casino hotels. PBX Operators answer calls and connect them to the correct party. Individuals are often responsible for determining the specific department or individual to which a caller should be transferred.

In order to connect callers to the proper person, PBX Operators are responsible for finding room numbers of guests, as well as extensions of departments and personnel. This may be accomplished by retrieving data from computers or consulting lists or other written information.

The success of casinos and casino hotels depends on good customer service skills. Operators in these facilities should be very pleasant and helpful in making customers feel good about calling. Individuals answer questions, give directions, and provide a great deal of information regarding the hotel, and casino facilities.

PBX Operators are responsible for connecting interoffice or house calls. They also relay or connect outgoing calls.

Other duties of casino or casino hotel PBX Operators may include:

• Assisting guests in placing calls
• Handling related clerical duties

Salaries

PBX Operators working in casinos and casino hotels earn between $7.00 and $14.00 or more per hour or about $14,000 to $28,000 annually. In unionized situations, the union will negotiate minimum earnings. Factors affecting earnings include the geographic location, size, and prestige of the specific casino or casino hotel, as well as the training, experience, and responsibilities of the individual.

Employment Prospects

Employment opportunities for PBX operators in casinos are good. Individuals work various shifts, including daytime, swing shift or evening, or graveyard or overnight shift.

Las Vegas, Reno, Laughlin, Lake Tahoe, Atlantic City, Biloxi, Baton Rouge, New Orleans, and Detroit offer the greatest number of job possibilities. Other employment settings include casinos and casino hotels in other areas of Nevada, Mississippi, New York, Louisiana, Colorado, Connecticut, Illinois, Arizona, and California.

Other regions hosting Indian gaming and land-based or riverboat gaming facilities offer additional opportunities. New casinos and casino hotels are constantly under construction. More casinos and casino hotels are also opening every year as areas legalize gambling.

Advancement Prospects

With experience and/or additional training, PBX Operators may be promoted to supervisory positions within the communications department. Individuals may advance to positions such as lead operator or PBX supervisor.

Education and Training

Most casinos and casino hotels prefer PBX Operators to have a high school diploma or the equivalent. Many facilities assist individuals who do not have this education in obtaining a GED.

On-the-job training in handling routine calls and equipment is usually provided for PBX Operators. Individuals are also usually trained in providing customer service to callers.

Experience/Skills/Personality Traits

In some casinos, entry-level positions may be open. Many facilities, however, prefer to hire individuals with prior PBX experience.

PBX Operators must have a clear speaking voice and good telephone skills. Individuals must be courteous, and pleasant and have good customer service skills.

Unions/Associations

Depending on the specific hotel and its location, this may or may not be a unionized position. In unionized casinos and casino hotels in Las Vegas, for example, PBX Operators may be members of the Teamsters Local #995 union.

Those interested in learning more about careers in as PBX Operators can obtain information from the Communications Workers of America (CWA) as well as the human resources departments of casinos.

Tips For Entry

1. Get experience as a PBX operator at an office, large retail establishment, or hotel.
2. Jobs may be advertised in the classified sections of newspapers in areas hosting gaming. Look under classifications such as "Casinos/Gaming," "PBX Operator," "PBX Clerk," "Operator," "Comminations Department," or "Casino/Hotel Opportunities."
3. Openings are often advertised on the Internet via the home pages of casino hotels. They may also be found by doing a search of "Casino," "Casino Hotel," or "Gaming Job Opportunities."
4. Get your foot in the door of a casino hotel. Most promote from within.
5. Stop by the human resources departments of casinos and casino hotels to learn about job openings.
6. Most casinos have job hotlines. These are frequently updated messages listing jobs available. You can call each casino directly to obtain its job hotline phone number.
7. Look for new casinos under construction. Some may need PBX operators before opening.

CAREER OPPORTUNITIES IN CASINO AND CASINO HOTEL ENTERTAINMENT

STAGE MANAGER

CAREER PROFILE

Duties: Overseeing and supervising activities occurring onstage and backstage during performances.

Alternative Titles(s): None

Salary Range: $24,000 to $48,000+

Employment Prospects: Poor

Best Geographical Location(s) for Position: Las Vegas, Reno, Laughlin, Lake Tahoe, Atlantic City, Biloxi, Baton Rouge, New Orleans, and Detroit offer the greatest number of opportunities; other regions hosting Indian gaming and land-based or riverboat gaming facilities offer additional opportunities.

Prerequisites:

Education or Training—No formal educational requirements.

Experience and Qualifications—Experience working backstage.

Special Skills and Personality Traits—Supervisory skills; organizational skills; knowledge of lighting and sound technology.

CAREER LADDER

```
┌─────────────────────────────────┐
│  Stage Manager in Larger, More  │
│      Prestigious Casino         │
└─────────────────────────────────┘

┌─────────────────────────────────┐
│         Stage Manager           │
└─────────────────────────────────┘

┌─────────────────────────────────┐
│  Assistant Stage Manager, Sound │
│     Technician, Intern or       │
│          Apprentice             │
└─────────────────────────────────┘
```

Position Description

Many casinos and casino hotels have big showrooms where a variety of entertainment is presented. The Stage Manager is in charge of supervising and overseeing everything occurring onstage and backstage during a performance. This is an important job in the entertainment end of the casino industry. The Stage Manager performs a vast array of duties and usually has one or more assistants. He or she is responsible for supervising the backstage staff, including sound people, lighting people, and electricians.

The Stage Manager is required to attend sound checks, rehearsals, and performances. Individuals in this position do not work normal business hours. Instead, they generally work split shifts.

The Stage Manager works closely with the entertainers and artists appearing at the facility. In some cases, the casino or casino hotel produces its own elaborate stage shows. In other situations, entertainers and artists are booked to appear at the facility. The Stage Manager works closely with all of these people. He or she works with the crew of the artists and entertainers appearing at the facility. When performers travel with their own sound and light crews, the Stage Manager assists and advises them.

Backstage areas be kept as clear as possible. The Stage Manager must find out ahead of time who is allowed backstage. This list can be obtained from the performer's management or road manager. In addition to performers, singers, musicians, and crew members, others on a backstage list might include business associates, journalists, friends and/or family members. The Stage Manager issues backstage passes to each person authorized to be in that area before and during a performance. The individual is in charge of making sure that everyone backstage has proper permission.

This is a job with a great deal of responsibility. During a performance, the Stage Manager makes sure everyone does their job properly. Before the show begins, the Stage Manager determines the length of the show, when any intermissions will be held and when the curtain must be opened and closed. Additional information may also be needed to cue sound and lighting people.

Other duties of the Stage Manager may include:

- Assigning dressing rooms
- Making sure any required amenities are available
- Advising performers how much time remains before they must appear
- Advising performers exactly what time they must go onstage
- Handling all emergencies and problems occurring during shows
- Documenting accidents or injuries that take place before or during a performance

Salaries

Annual earnings for Stage Managers in casinos and casino hotels can range from $24,000 to $48,000 or more. Factors affecting earnings include the size, prestige, and location of the specific facility, as well as the responsibilities, qualifications, and experience of the individual. In unionized settings, Stage Managers' salaries are negotiated by a union.

Employment Prospects

Employment prospects for Stage Managers are poor. While jobs may be available in casinos throughout the country, only the larger facilities have more than one individual in this position. That doesn't mean jobs aren't available at all; it just means you may have to look a little harder to find one.

Look for jobs in Las Vegas, Reno, Laughlin, Lake Tahoe, Atlantic City, Biloxi, Baton Rouge, New Orleans, and Detroit. Other employment settings include casinos and casino hotels in other areas of Nevada, Mississippi, New York, Louisiana, Colorado, Connecticut, Illinois, Arizona, and California.

Other regions hosting Indian gaming and land-based or riverboat gaming facilities offer additional opportunities. Casino hotels are constantly under construction. More casinos and casino hotels are opening every year as new areas legalize gambling.

Advancement Prospects

Stage Managers can advance their careers by locating similar positions in larger, more prestigious facilities, resulting in increased earnings and responsibilities. Some Stage Managers climb the career ladder by going into other types of facilities and becoming facility managers or directors.

Others make contacts and move to positions in other areas in the entertainment industry.

Education and Training

There is no formal education or training for Stage Manager positions. Individuals often work as apprentices, interns, or assistant stage managers to obtain training. Others acquire training by watching others or working in sound, lighting, and/or electronics.

Experience/Skills/Personality Traits

Experience as an assistant stage manager is helpful. Some people obtain experience in school or local community theater and performing arts productions.

Stage Managers should be very organized, detail-oriented people. Supervisory and interpersonal skills are necessary to be successful.

Knowledge of lighting, sound, and electronics is important.

Unions/Associations

Depending on the specific casino, this may or may not be a unionized position. Individuals interested in becoming Stage Managers can obtain additional information by contacting the International Alliance of Theatrical Stage Employees (IATSE).

Tips for Entry

1. Look for internships in this field to give you on-the-job training. You will also make valuable contacts.
2. Positions may be advertised in newspaper classified sections. Look under headings such as "Stage Manager," "Casinos," "Casino Hotels," "Stage Director," or "Entertainment."
3. Get experience by offering to act as the Stage Manager in your school or community theater, music, or performing arts production.
4. Consider getting other experience in small clubs and facilities. These venues usually experience a high employee turnover rate as people often move on quickly for career advancement.
5. A summer or part-time job assisting a Stage Manager will also give you good hands-on experience, as well as additional opportunities to make contacts.
6. Send your résumé and a short cover letter to human resources directors of casinos and casino hotels. Inquire about openings and ask that your résumé be kept on file.
7. Take as many workshops, seminars, and courses as you can regarding lighting, sound, electronics, and staging techniques. The more skills you have, the more marketable you will be.

SOUND TECHNICIAN

CAREER PROFILE

Duties: Overseeing sound requirements of showroom or club.

Alternative Titles(s): Sound Person; Soundman/woman; Sound Tech

Salary Range: $20,000 to $42,000+

Employment Prospects: Good

Best Geographical Location(s) for Position: Las Vegas, Reno, Laughlin, Lake Tahoe, Atlantic City, Biloxi, Baton Rouge, New Orleans, and Detroit offer the greatest number of opportunities; other regions hosting Indian gaming and land-based or riverboat gaming facilities offer additional opportunities.

Prerequisites:

Education or Training—Formal or self-taught electronic or sound training.

Experience and Qualifications—Experience using sound equipment and working soundboards.

Special Skills and Personality Traits—Ability to use soundboard; knowledge of electronics; dependable.

CAREER LADDER

```
┌─────────────────────────────────┐
│  Sound Technician in Larger, More │
│     Prestigious Casino or         │
│       Stage Manager               │
└─────────────────────────────────┘

┌─────────────────────────────────┐
│        Sound Technician           │
└─────────────────────────────────┘

┌─────────────────────────────────┐
│  Sound Technician in Other Setting │
│         or Apprentice             │
└─────────────────────────────────┘
```

Position Description

Casinos and casino hotels host a wide array of showrooms and nightclubs. The individual responsible for overseeing the sound requirements of these rooms is called the Sound Technician. The individual has a multitude of responsibilities and duties.

Every room has different sound requirements depending on the size and structure. Different types of performances also require varying sound requirements. The Sound Technician oversees the setup of the sound equipment. If there are acoustical problems, the Sound Technician determines what they are and finds solutions including moving equipment to different spots in the room or adjusting controls on the soundboard.

One of the most important duties of the Sound Technician is running the sound control board during performances. The individual sits at the board during a performance and makes adjustments so the sound is properly balanced and regulated. The Technician also adjusts the board for any special sound effects required.

In some cases, performers bring their own sound equipment. In these situations the resident Sound Technician works with the performers' sound people, advising and assisting them. Sound Technicians must attend rehearsals, sound checks, and performances. Working with performers and their crews, individuals can determine the type of sound required.

Other duties of the Sound Technician include:

- Keeping the sound equipment in perfect working condition
- Checking equipment after each performance for problems
- Advising supervisors if equipment cannot be repaired

Salaries

Earnings for resident Sound Technicians range from $20,000 to $42,000 or more annually. Factors affecting earnings include the specific hotel or casino, its facility, size, prestige, and geographic location. Other variables include the experience and responsibilities of the individual.

Sound Technicians working in unionized settings may have their minimum earnings negotiated by the union.

Employment Prospects

Employment prospects are good for Sound Technicians aspiring to work in casinos and casino hotels. Opportunities can be found in all gaming facilities hosting entertainment.

Las Vegas, Reno, Laughlin, Lake Tahoe, Atlantic City, Biloxi, Baton Rouge, New Orleans, and Detroit offer the greatest number of job possibilities. Other employment settings include casinos and casino hotels in other areas of Nevada, Mississippi, New York, Louisiana, Colorado, Connecticut, Illinois, Arizona, and California.

Other regions hosting Indian gaming and land-based or riverboat gaming facilities offer additional opportunities. New casinos and casino hotels are constantly under construction. More casinos and casino hotels are also opening every year as new areas legalize gambling.

Advancement Prospects

Advancement prospects for Sound Technicians include locating similar positions in larger, more prestigious casinos or casino hotels. Some Sound Technicians obtain experience and become a facility's stage manager. As the Sound Technician works with a variety of performers, he or she may climb the career ladder by making contacts and locating a position on the road with a major touring artist.

Education and Training

Sound Technicians must have some type of training in electronics and sound. This may be obtained through attendance at vocational and technical schools or may be self-taught. Many people pick up the skills of the trade by apprenticing or watching others.

Experience/Skills/Personality Traits

Sound Technicians should have complete knowledge of electronics and sound. Experience working the soundboards and other sound equipment is required.

Unions/Associations

Depending on the specific casino or casino hotel, this position may or may not be unionized. Those interested in learning more about this job can contact the International Alliance of Theatrical Stage Employees (IATSE).

Tips for Entry

1. Find an apprenticeship in this area by contacting clubs, halls, theaters, and other facilities. Ask a sound technician if you can apprentice with him or her.
2. Offer to handle the sound requirements for a local musical group. It will provide good experience.
3. Another way to learn skills and gain experience is by taking part in your school or local community theater productions. Volunteer to work with people handling the sound requirements.
4. Stop in at casino and casino hotel human resources departments to inquire about job openings in this area.
5. If you don't live in a gaming area and are interested in finding employment in a casino or casino hotel, send your résumé with a short cover letter.
6. Job openings are often advertised in the newspaper classified section in areas hosting gaming. Look under headings such as "Sound Technician," "Audio Technician," "Sound Engineer," "Casinos," "Casino Hotels," or "Entertainment."

LIGHTING TECHNICIAN

CAREER PROFILE

Duties: Working light board during performances in main showroom or nightclub.

Alternative Titles(s): Lighting Person; Light Man/woman; Lighting Tech.

Salary Range: $18,000 to $90,000+

Employment Prospects: Good

Best Geographical Location(s) for Position: Las Vegas, Reno, Laughlin, Lake Tahoe, Atlantic City, Biloxi, Baton Rouge, New Orleans, and Detroit offer the greatest number of opportunities; other regions hosting Indian gaming and land-based or riverboat gaming facilities offer additional opportunities.

Prerequisites:

Education or Training—No formal educational requirements; training through internships, apprenticeships, or hands-on training as assistant.

Experience and Qualifications—Experience working with lighting.

Special Skills and Personality Traits—Electronics skills; communication skills; reliable.

CAREER LADDER

```
┌─────────────────────────────────────┐
│ Lighting Technician in Larger, More │
│      Prestigious Casinos or         │
│        Lighting Designer            │
└─────────────────────────────────────┘

┌─────────────────────────────────────┐
│        Lighting Technician          │
└─────────────────────────────────────┘

┌─────────────────────────────────────┐
│ Lighting Technician in Other Industry│
│           or Apprentice             │
└─────────────────────────────────────┘
```

Position Description

Casino hotels are often known for their entertainment. In large facilities there may be a showroom featuring major entertainment and one or more small nightclubs hosting lesser-known acts. Smaller facilities may have just one club. Many productions in large casino showrooms are elaborately staged with dramatic lighting and special effects.

Lighting Technicians are responsible for handling the lighting requirements for a facility's entertainment. Some lighting requirements are fairly simple and just involve spotlights and other lighting so the audience can see the entertainers better. In other situations, elaborate lighting plans have been developed by a lighting designer to increase the excitement of shows. These are often documented in writing so the Lighting Technician can follow them precisely. The documentation describes exactly what the Lighting Technician must do in order to duplicate the lighting effects created by the lighting designer. Various lights, filters, and colors create an array of lighting effects.

The Lighting Technician is responsible for working the lighting control board during the performance. The individual follows the cue schedule provided by the lighting designer. These cues alert the lighting technician to which lights are used at specific times during the performance.

Other responsibilities of the Lighting Technician include:

- Performing lighting checks before each performance
- Making sure all lights and equipment are working properly
- Checking that all lights, bulbs, and filters are in the proper position
- Discussing lighting changes or requirements with entertainers if there is no lighting designer

Salaries

Earnings for lighting people range from $350 to $1,800 or more weekly or from $18,000 to $90,000 annually. In some casino hotels, this is a union position. Depending on the specific situation, those working in a unionized setting have their minimum weekly earnings negotiated and set by the International Alliance of Theatrical Stage Employees (IATSE), the United Scenic Artists (USA), or the International Brotherhood of Electrical Workers (IBEW). Individuals working in nonunionized settings negotiate their own salaries.

Factors affecting earnings include the specific facility, its size, prestige, and geographic location. Other factors include the specific responsibilities, experience, and professional reputation of the Lighting Technician. Additionally, earnings depend on the type of stage productions the individual handles.

Employment Prospects

Employment prospects are good for Lighting Technicians. As noted previously, many casino hotels host showrooms as well as nightclubs. Usually there are a number of Lighting Technicians working in all but the smallest facilities.

Las Vegas, Reno, Laughlin, Lake Tahoe, Atlantic City, Biloxi, Baton Rouge, New Orleans, and Detroit offer the greatest number of job possibilities. Other employment settings include casinos and casino hotels in other areas of Nevada, Mississippi, New York, Louisiana, Colorado, Connecticut, Illinois, Arizona, and California.

Other regions hosting Indian gaming and land-based or riverboat gaming facilities offer additional opportunities. New casinos and casino hotels are constantly under construction. More casinos and casino hotels are opening every year as new areas legalize gambling.

Advancement Prospects

Lighting Technicians can advance their careers in a couple of ways. Individuals may either locate similar jobs in larger facilities or handle lighting for more elaborate productions. Some Lighting Technicians climb the career ladder by becoming lighting designers for major stage extravaganzas.

Education and Training

There are no educational requirements necessary to become a Lighting Technician, though some individuals opt for a college degree in theater or music.

While formal education is not required, training is necessary and can be acquired through apprenticeships, internships, or work as an assistant to other Lighting Technicians or lighting designers. Other valuable training includes classes in lighting and electronics often offered in school or through vocational programs.

Experience/Skills/Personality Traits

Experience in lighting is necessary in this job. As noted previously, experience can be obtained through apprenticeships, internships, or work as an assistant to a Lighting Technician or lighting designer. Experience may also be acquired by assisting lighting people handle lights in school or community theater productions.

Some Lighting Technicians work in the music industry handling lighting requirements for entertainers on the road before they settle down for a career in one place. Others work in small nightclubs as lighting people prior to jobs in casino hotels.

Knowledge of lighting, staging, and electronics is imperative.

Unions/Associations

Depending on the casino, this position may or may not be unionized. Individuals interested in becoming a Lighting Technician can obtain additional information by contacting the International Alliance of Theatrical Stage Employees (IATSE), the United Scenic Artists (USA), or the International Brotherhood of Electrical Workers (IBEW).

Tips for Entry

1. Consider breaking into the field on a small scale. Get experience working the lights in a local club.
2. Consider a short stint handling lights for a local rock group.
3. Obtain experience is by volunteering to handle the lighting for school and community theater productions.
4. Take workshops and seminars in theatrical and entertainment lighting and staging. You can hone skills, learn new ones, and make valuable contacts.
5. Watch lighting people at work, take classes, and read relevant books. The more you know, the more marketable you will be.
6. Contact hotels, clubs, theaters, and production companies to find internships and apprentice or training programs.
7. Jobs may be advertised in trade papers or local newspapers in areas hosting gaming. Look under heading classifications such as "Lighting Technician," "Lighting," "Lighting Person," "Lightman/woman," "Entertainment," "Showroom," or "Nightclubs."
8. Call casino human resources offices to see if they have openings in this area.

ENTERTAINER

CAREER PROFILE

Duties: Performing in casino or casino hotel nightclubs, lounges, or showrooms.

Alternative Titles(s): Singer; Comedian; Dancer; Magician; Musician; Show Group

Salary Range: Impossible to determine due to nature of the job.

Employment Prospects: Good

Best Geographical Location(s) for Position: Las Vegas, Reno, Laughlin, Lake Tahoe, Atlantic City, Biloxi, Baton Rouge, New Orleans, and Detroit offer the greatest number of opportunities; other regions hosting Indian gaming and land-based or riverboat gaming facilities offer additional opportunities.

Prerequisites:

Education or Training—No formal educational or training requirements.

Experience and Qualifications—Prior performing experience.

Special Skills and Personality Traits—Talent; ability to perform in front of audience; stage presence; charisma.

CAREER LADDER

```
┌─────────────────────────────────┐
│  Entertainer in Bigger Showrooms│
│  or Larger, More Prestigious     │
│  Casinos                         │
└─────────────────────────────────┘

┌─────────────────────────────────┐
│         Entertainer             │
└─────────────────────────────────┘

┌─────────────────────────────────┐
│  Entertainer in Different Setting│
└─────────────────────────────────┘
```

Position Description

Entertainment is a big attraction at many casinos and casino hotels. Facilities may have a variety of entertainment venues. These include showrooms, lounges, and nightclubs of different sizes utilizing various types of entertainment.

A wide array of Entertainers are booked at casinos and casino hotels, including singers, magicians, dancers, jugglers, and comedians.

While showrooms often host big-name entertainers and/or major extravaganzas to attract patrons, lounges and nightclubs feature a combination of talent to entertain guests. Some Entertainers are well known through television, movies, radio, and records. However, lesser-known people may be equally talented.

Entertainers put together a show to entertain a seated audience. The set may be any combination of music, songs, dancing, jokes, ad libs, and skits.

Entertainers may also utilize light shows, special effects, and costumes to create elaborate productions or shows with a great deal of excitement.

Other duties of Entertainers performing in a casino hotel showroom, lounge, or nightclub may include:

• Involving the audience in the show
• Obtaining bookings

Salaries

It is difficult to determine earnings of Entertainers. The range can be tremendous. Earnings depend to a great extent on the popularity and reputation of the entertainer. A popular singer or singing group earns more than a singer or group that is lesser known. In certain areas, minimum earnings are set by the presiding union.

Employment Prospects

Employment opportunities for Entertainers in casinos and casino hotels are good. As noted previously, these facilities utilize a wide variety of Entertainers.

In addition to working in nightclubs, lounges, and showrooms, Entertainers may be booked to work in other settings, including special events, players' club parties, VIP parties, or corporate events.

Las Vegas, Reno, Laughlin, Lake Tahoe, Atlantic City, Biloxi, Baton Rouge, New Orleans, and Detroit offer the greatest number of job possibilities. Other employment settings include casinos and casino hotels in other areas of Nevada, Mississippi, New York, Louisiana, Colorado, Connecticut, Illinois, Arizona, and California.

Other regions hosting Indian gaming and land-based or riverboat gaming facilities offer additional opportunities. New casinos and casino hotels are constantly under construction. More casinos and casino hotels are opening every year as new areas legalize gambling.

Advancement Prospects

Entertainers working in casinos and casino hotels can climb the career ladder by earning more popularity and building a following. Entertainers who are professional and exciting can find employment in larger and more prestigious casinos and casino hotels.

Education and Training

There is no formal educational or training requirement for Entertainers. Individuals may have music, voice, or dance training, or may be self-taught.

Experience/Skills/Personality Traits

Generally, Entertainers working in casinos and casino hotels have had prior experience performing. Often individuals or groups perform in other venues before finding employment in these facilities.

In order for Entertainers to be successful, they must be talented, energetic, charismatic individuals with a great deal of stage presence.

Unions/Associations

Entertainers working in casinos may be members of various unions, including the American Federation of Musicians (AFM).

Those interested in learning more careers in entertainment at casinos and casino hotels should contact the directors of entertainment, house bookers, or musical directors at these facilities.

Tips for Entry

1. You often are required to be a member of the appropriate union to perform in a casino.
2. Contact casino and casino hotel house bookers and directors of entertainment.
3. Openings are often advertised in the classified sections of newspapers in areas hosting gaming. Look under classifications such as "Entertainment," "Casinos/Casino Hotels," "Casino Hotel Entertainment," "Singer," "Comedian," "Dancer," "Entertainer," "Magician," and so on.
4. Jobs may also be located in trade publications such as *Billboard.*
5. Make sure you have professional 8 X 10 glossy photographs, bios, and press kits.
6. Retain an agent to help you find work.
7. Get booking commitments in writing. You might want to engage an attorney to put together a standard contract.

CAREER OPPORTUNITIES IN CASINO AND CASINO HOTEL FOOD AND BEVERAGE SERVICE

HOTEL FOOD AND BEVERAGE MANAGER

CAREER PROFILE

Duties: Overseeing kitchen operations in food service outlets in facility; supervising sous chefs and pastry chefs; creating menus; devising recipes; developing budgets.

Alternative Titles(s): None

Salary Range: $35,000 to $120,000+

Employment Prospects: Fair

Best Geographical Location(s) for Position: Las Vegas, Reno, Laughlin, Lake Tahoe, Atlantic City, Biloxi, Baton Rouge, New Orleans, and Detroit offer most opportunities; other regions with land-based, riverboat, or Indian gaming facilities offer additional opportunities.

Prerequisites:

Education or Training—Education and training requirements vary; see text.

Experience and Qualifications—Supervisory experience in hotel and food service necessary; complete knowledge of food and beverage departments.

Special Skills and Personality Traits—Detail-oriented; organization; management and administrative skills; budgeting; negotiating skills; communication skills; supervisory skills.

CAREER LADDER

```
┌─────────────────────────────────────┐
│ Food and Beverage Manager in Larger,│
│     More Prestigious Casino         │
│        or Casino Hotel              │
└─────────────────────────────────────┘

┌─────────────────────────────────────┐
│     Food and Beverage Manager       │
└─────────────────────────────────────┘

┌─────────────────────────────────────┐
│    Assistant Food and Beverage      │
│         Manager or Chef             │
└─────────────────────────────────────┘
```

Position Description

Hotels and hotel casinos realize a great deal of their profits in their food and beverage departments. The Food and Beverage Manager holds the important position of being in charge of directing the food services of the hotel. Within the scope of the job, there is a vast array of responsibilities.

The Food and Beverage Manager is ultimately responsible for the quality of the service in all food establishments in the facility. He or she oversees the operation of all the hotel's restaurants, room service, cocktail lounges, and bars. The individual is additionally responsible for the food and beverage service for banquets, meeting facilities, conferences, and receptions.

As part of the job, the Food and Beverage Manager is responsible for monitoring the supervisory staff in charge all the food and beverage preparation. The Food and Beverage Manager works with a staff that includes assistants, managers, and other service workers. He or she may be responsible for hiring and scheduling them or may assign this task to an assistant. The individual may also be responsible for training staff or developing training programs.

Generally, each restaurant or bar within the facility has a separate manager. The Food and Beverage Manager is responsible for the service and profits in each establishment, making sure they are the best possible. The individual schedules meetings on a regular basis to discuss these and other topics.

The Food and Beverage Manager and the managerial staff of the various food establishments in the hotel are responsible for planning menus, including those for special celebrations, events, or hotel happenings and promotions, as well as those for special foods and drinks. They may develop themes within the food establishments, including decorations and wait staff costumes, as well as related food and drink items.

To make sure the food establishments are as profitable as possible the Food and Beverage Manager must know how to estimate food costs. The individual often deals with food suppliers, negotiating prices. Menus may then be adjusted to reflect seasonal and bountiful foods.

This position carries a great deal of responsibility and it is not usually a nine-to-five job. The Food and Beverage Manager is on call whenever a problem arises and he or she is needed.

As part of this job, the Food and Beverage Manager is responsible for:

- Working closely with various food establishment managers
- Establishing standards for each restaurant in the facility
- Working with managers on any emergencies that arise
- Keeping in close contact with all managers to make sure everything is taking place as scheduled and problems are solved as they occur

Salaries

Earnings for Food and Beverage Managers in these settings can range from approximately $35,000 to $120,000 or more, depending on a number of variables. These include the specific facility, type, size, and geographic location. Other factors affecting earnings include the responsibilities, training, and experience of the individual. Many employment settings provide an annual bonus in addition to salary, depending on profits.

Employment Prospects

More states are allowing gambling facilities every year. Establishments and locations where people can gamble are on the increase. Employment opportunities are fair for quality people seeking this position. The best-trained individuals will be the most marketable.

Advancement Prospects

Food and Beverage Managers can advance their careers by locating similar positions in larger or more prestigious facilities. This results in increased responsibilities and earnings. Some individuals also climb the career ladder by moving into other hotel management positions.

Education and Training

As noted previously, the better an individual's training, the more marketable he or she will be. A number of different educational paths lead to this position.

A bachelor's degree in hotel management or hotel and restaurant administration is often required or preferred.

Some individuals have moved into this position with a liberal arts degree coupled with related hotel and restaurant experience.

There are also programs offered at community and junior colleges leading to associates' degrees, as well as formal programs at technical institutes, vocation and trade schools, and other institutions in hotel and restaurant management. These programs plus experience in food service and hotel management may also be acceptable.

Some Food and Beverage Managers are trained in food preparation at culinary institutes or have worked as apprentices in food service.

Experience/Skills/Personality Traits

Individuals interested in pursuing a career in this field should have a vast amount of experience working in food service. Ideally, but not always, this includes experience in management and cooking. Some Food and Beverage Managers worked as chefs prior to their current position. Others worked in a variety of hotel management jobs.

Depending on the specific position and an individual's education, applicants may be required to have from five to 15 years of experience working in the hospitality industry before landing a job such as this.

Successful individuals need the ability to deal with a variety of people on different levels. They should be organized and detail-oriented. Administrative and management skills are necessary. Problem-solving skills are mandatory. A tremendous wealth of knowledge of every area of food service and management is necessary to be successful in this career.

Unions/Associations

Additional career information may be obtained by contacting the Council on Hotel, Restaurant and Institutional Education, the American Hotel and Motel Association (AHMA), the American Culinary Federation (ACF), and the American Institute of Wine and Food (AIWF).

Tips for Entry

1. If you are still in school, look for an internship to learn skills, make contacts, and network.
2. Positions in this field are advertised in newspaper classified sections under the headings such as "Food and Beverage Manager," "Casino Hotels," "Casino Restaurants," "Food Service," and "Food and Beverage."
3. Join trade associations. They usually hold annual conferences that are invaluable for learning and making contacts.
4. Look for executive search firms specializing in the hospitality and gaming industry.

CASINO HOTEL EXECUTIVE CHEF

Duties: Overseeing kitchen operations in food service outlets in facility; supervising sous chefs and pastry chefs; creating menus; devising recipes; developing budgets.

Alternative Titles(s): Restaurant Outlet Manager

Salary Range: $45,000 to $120,000+

Employment Prospects: Poor

Best Geographical Location(s) for Position: Las Vegas, Reno, Laughlin, Lake Tahoe, Atlantic City, Biloxi, Baton Rouge, New Orleans, and Detroit offer most opportunities; other regions with land-based, riverboat, or Indian gaming facilities offer additional opportunities.

Prerequisites:

Education or Training—Training in culinary school, academy, institute, or apprenticeship.

Experience and Qualifications—Prior experience required; see text.

Special Skills and Personality Traits—Supervisory skills; culinary skills; administrative skills; organization; budgeting skills; knowledge of a variety of cuisines; food creativity.

```
┌─────────────────────────────────┐
│   Executive Chef in Larger, More │
│   Prestigious Casino/Casino Hotel│
└─────────────────────────────────┘

┌─────────────────────────────────┐
│         Executive Chef           │
└─────────────────────────────────┘

┌─────────────────────────────────┐
│  Executive Chef in Other Setting or│
│      Executive Sous Chef         │
└─────────────────────────────────┘
```

Position Description

Casinos and casino hotels host a variety of restaurants serving different types of food. The Executive Chef in a casino or casino hotel is responsible for the kitchen operations of all the food outlets in the facility. The individual sets the mood for each of the restaurants in the facility and is responsible for their culinary reputation.

The Executive Chef has a variety of responsibilities. He or she is responsible for hiring and training the kitchen staff. The individual is further responsible for directing the training and apprenticeship programs of chefs and other cooks working in the hotel. The Executive Chef handles this alone, or may assign this duty to an executive sous chef.

The individual must be a talented Chef with excellent culinary skills. He or she makes sure that food is appetizing and prepared in an attractive, efficient, and profitable manner. The Executive Chef plans menus by knowing the probable number of guests or customers and the popularity of various dishes, thus being able to estimate food consumption and requisition the necessary food and kitchen supplies from the purchasing manager.

The Executive Chef creates new and special recipes. These menus and recipes often reflect the theme or flavor of the particular casino, casino hotel, or restaurant. They may also take things into account such as food surpluses, local specialities, or seasonal items. Once recipes and dishes are created for inclusion on the menu, the Executive Chef develops recipe specifications. Sous chefs must then be trained in the preparation of each dish.

The Executive Chef also reviews menus, analyzes recipes, and determines food, labor, and overhead costs. With this information in mind, the Chef may be responsible for assigning prices to various items on the menu.

While the Executive Chef may on occasion prepare dishes, this job is mostly an administrative position. The individual supervises the culinary skills of the other chefs. The Executive Chef, for example, may taste food in various stages of preparation to make sure the food preparation is in line with his or her specifications.

The Executive Chef is additionally responsible for the following functions:

- Representing casino or hotel in food-related benefit functions
- Coordinating the activities of the sous chefs and pastry chefs in the kitchen
- Developing budgets for food and payroll

Salaries

Executive Chefs in casinos and casino hotels earn from $45,000 to $120,000 or more depending on a number of factors, including the geographic location, size, and prestige of the specific facility. Other variables include the experience, training, professional reputation, and responsibilities of the individual. Those working in larger, more prestigious facilities in the gambling capitals usually earn more than their counterparts in other hotels.

Employment Prospects

Employment prospects are fair for Executive Chefs seeking employment in casinos and casino hotels.

Las Vegas, Reno, Laughlin, Lake Tahoe, Atlantic City, Biloxi, Baton Rouge, New Orleans, and Detroit offer the greatest number of job possibilities. Other employment settings include casino hotels in other areas of Nevada, Mississippi, New York, Louisiana, Colorado, Connecticut, Illinois, Arizona, and California.

Other regions hosting Indian gaming and land-based or riverboat gaming facilities offer additional opportunities. New casinos and casino hotels are constantly under construction. More casinos and casino hotels are also opening every year as areas legalize gambling.

Advancement Prospects

Executive Chefs working in this area can advance their careers by locating similar positions in larger or more prestigious facilities. This is often accomplished after the individual obtains experience and develops a professional reputation.

Education and Training

Recommended training for this position is attendance at a culinary school, institute, or academy. One of the most

well known in the country is the Culinary Institute of America (CIA). Other training options include apprenticeships. The American Culinary Federation (ACF) as well as the Culinary Institute of America (CIA) offer apprenticeship programs. Other apprenticeships are available through hotel and restaurant chains.

Experience/Skills/Personality Traits

Executive Chefs in casinos and casino hotels need a great deal of experience in restaurants. Prior experience as sous chefs, executive sous chefs, and/or executive chefs in other setting are helpful.

Individuals must extremely talented in culinary skills. They also need management and administrative skills. The ability to teach others is necessary.

Unions/Associations

Individuals interested in pursuing careers as Executive Chefs can obtain additional career information by contacting the American Culinary Federation (ACF), the International Association of Culinary Professionals, or a culinary academy or institute.

Tips for Entry

1. A hotel apprenticeship program in this field is an excellent way of obtaining training and experience.
2. The better your training and skills the more marketable you will be. Get the best training you possibly can.
3. You may have to "audition" for this type of job. The facility can see how you deal with situations in the kitchen.
4. Send your résumé and a short cover letter to the human resources departments of casinos and casino hotels to inquire about job openings.
5. Jobs may be advertised in the classified sections of newspapers in areas hosting gaming. Look under classifications such as "Chef," "Executive Chef," "Casino Hotels," and "Food and Beverage."
6. Many executive search firms and headhunters place people in these positions.
7. Contact an Executive Chef whose work you admire and inquire about apprenticeship possibilities.

RESTAURANT SOUS CHEF

CAREER PROFILE

Duties: Working under direction of executive chef; preparing dishes, sauces, and other recipes; assisting in supervision of kitchen staff.

Alternative Titles(s): Sous Chef; Chef

Salary Range: $25,000 to $50,000+

Employment Prospects: Good

Best Geographical Location(s) for Position: Las Vegas, Reno, Laughlin, Lake Tahoe, Atlantic City, Biloxi, Baton Rouge, New Orleans, and Detroit offer most opportunities; other regions with land-based, riverboat, or Indian gaming facilities offer additional opportunities.

Prerequisites:

Education or Training—Apprentice program or training at culinary institute or academy; see text.

Experience and Qualifications—Supervisory experience in culinary setting.

Special Skills and Personality Traits—Cooking skills; supervisory skills; organization; ability to follow style of executive chef; familiarity with variety of cuisines.

CAREER LADDER

```
┌─────────────────────────────────────┐
│  Sous Chef in Larger, More Prestigious │
│  Restaurant or Executive Sous Chef   │
└─────────────────────────────────────┘

┌─────────────────────────────────────┐
│       Restaurant Sous Chef          │
└─────────────────────────────────────┘

┌─────────────────────────────────────┐
│      Sous Chef in Non-Casino        │
│       Restaurant Setting            │
└─────────────────────────────────────┘
```

Position Description

Casinos and casino hotels have a variety of restaurants serving different types of food, some more domestic, others more international. The executive chef decides what recipes and dishes should be included on the menu in each casino hotel restaurant. Once this is determined, the executive chef develops recipe specifications. Sous Chefs are then trained in the preparation of each dish on the menu.

The Restaurant Sous Chef is responsible for cooking the recipes exactly as the casino hotel executive chef instructs. Variations or experimenting on the recipes must usually be approved by the executive chef.

The Sous Chef maintains the quality and style of food preparation in the kitchen. It is essential that the Sous Chef prepares recipes exactly as the executive chef has instructed so that dishes consistently taste the same no matter which chef cooks them.

The Sous Chef is responsible for assisting the executive chef in areas other than cooking. Responsibilities vary depending on the specific restaurant. For example, the Sous Chef may take inventory of food in the kitchen, order supplies, and accept and check deliveries.

Other duties of the Restaurant Sous Chef may include:

- Assisting in the training of apprentices and other kitchen workers
- Supervising kitchen staff

Salaries

Sous Chefs working in casinos and casino hotel restaurants are compensated in two ways. Some individuals are paid an hourly wage, others a weekly salary. Annual earnings range from $25,000 to $50,000 or more.

Factors affecting earnings include the geographic location, size, and prestige of the specific casino hotel and type of restaurant. Other variables include the experience, training, and responsibilities of the individual.

Employment Prospects

Employment opportunities are good for Sous Chefs. Qualified individuals can find employment in casino and casino hotel restaurants throughout the country and the world. Restaurants in gaming areas are often open 24 hours a day. Depending on the restaurant outlet, individuals work various shifts.

Las Vegas, Reno, Laughlin, Lake Tahoe, Atlantic City, Biloxi, Baton Rouge, New Orleans, and Detroit offer the greatest number of job possibilities. Other employment settings include casinos and casino hotels in other areas of Nevada, Mississippi, New York, Louisiana, Colorado, Connecticut, Illinois, Arizona, and California.

Other regions hosting Indian gaming and land-based or riverboat gaming facilities offer additional opportunities. New casinos and casino hotels are constantly under construction. More casinos and casino hotels are opening every year as areas legalize gambling.

Advancement Prospects

Sous Chefs can climb the career ladder in a number of ways. They might locate a similar position in a larger or more prestigious casino hotel restaurant, resulting in increased responsibilities and earnings, or may be promoted to executive sous chef.

With experience, sous chefs can advance to executive chefs.

Education and Training

Training requirements for Sous Chefs vary, depending on the specific facility. Training is available at culinary schools, institutes, and academies throughout the country.

Some casino hotels require or prefer that Sous Chefs complete a training or apprentice program from one of the major culinary institutes such as the Culinary Institute of America (CIA). Other training options include apprentice-ships with the American Culinary Federation (ACF). Apprenticeships may also be available through hotel and restaurant chains.

Experience/Skills/Personality Traits

Culinary experience is necessary to obtain a job as Sous Chef in a casino hotel restaurant. In many facilities, individuals must have experience as sous chef in other restaurants or hotels.

Supervisory experience as well as culinary expertise is also necessary for this job. A familiarity with a variety of cuisines in useful.

Unions/Associations

Individuals interested in pursuing careers as Sous Chefs can obtain additional career information by contacting the American Culinary Federation (ACF), the International Association of Culinary Professionals, or a culinary academy or institute.

Tips for Entry

1. Jobs may be advertised in the classified sections of newspapers in areas hosting gaming. Look under classifications such as "Chef," "Sous Chef," "Casino Hotels Opportunities," and "Food and Beverage,"
2. Send or fax your résumé with a short cover letter to the human resources director of casino hotels.
3. If you live in an area hosting casino hotels, stop by the human resources departments to inquire about openings.
4. The better your training, the more marketable you will be. Get the best training possible.
5. You may have to "audition" for this job. The facility can see how you deal with situations in the kitchen.
6. Contact an executive chef whose work you admire and inquire about apprenticeship possibilities.
7. Some headhunters and search firms specialize in placing individuals seeking these types of positions.

PASTRY CHEF

CAREER PROFILE

Duties: Preparing desserts on menu; creating special desserts; decorating desserts.

Alternative Titles(s): None

Salary Range: $25,000 to $75,000+

Employment Prospects: Fair

Best Geographical Location(s) for Position: Las Vegas, Reno, Laughlin, Lake Tahoe, Atlantic City, Biloxi, Baton Rouge, New Orleans, and Detroit offer most opportunities; other regions with land-based, riverboat, or Indian gaming facilities offer additional opportunities.

Prerequisites:

Education or Training—Formal training through culinary school or vocational tech or trade school; on-the-job training; self-taught or cooking, baking, and pastry classes.

Experience and Qualifications—Experience as pastry trainee or apprentice helpful.

Special Skills and Personality Traits—Creative; artistic; detail-oriented; baking skills; decorating skills; ability to work in chocolate, sugar, and pastillage.

CAREER LADDER

```
┌─────────────────────────────────────┐
│  Pastry Chef in Larger, More Prestigious │
│       Casino or Casino Hotel         │
└─────────────────────────────────────┘

┌─────────────────────────────────────┐
│           Pastry Chef               │
└─────────────────────────────────────┘

┌─────────────────────────────────────┐
│   Pastry Chef in Other Setting      │
│         or Apprentice               │
└─────────────────────────────────────┘
```

Position Description

Dessert is the grand finale of a meal. Many restaurants are remembered for their spectacular desserts and dessert specialties. The individual in charge of preparing desserts in a restaurant is called the Pastry Chef.

This individual has a number of responsibilities. He or she is expected to prepare all the desserts on the restaurant's menu. The Pastry Chef may handle this task alone or may have helpers, including pastry trainees. Depending on the size and structure of the hotel and the number of restaurants, the Pastry Chef may be responsible for preparing the desserts for all the restaurants on-site or just one.

While the name of the position implies that the individual makes pastries, he or she is responsible for making an array of desserts and components, including pies, cakes, tortes, tarts, custards, flans, ice cream, petit fours, strudels, fruit concoctions, cookies, confections, sauces, fillings, and frostings. The Pastry Chef working in this type of environment must know everything about both domestic desserts and those with an international flavor. A full working knowledge of sugar, pastillage, and chocolate is also required for full desserts and decorating.

The Pastry Chef makes desserts that are on the menu on a regular basis. It is essential that desserts not be stale or taste old. The Pastry Chef may also be responsible for creating dessert specials that use seasonal or local ingredients such as fruits or nuts or have holiday themes. The individual may also develop dessert specials low in calories or fat. Some Pastry Chefs are known for specialties they have created using chocolate.

The Pastry Chef also maintains a supply of certain basic dessert components such as puff pastry, meringues, genoise layers, and ice creams.

The Pastry Chef must create desserts that have a consistent taste, often using standardized recipes. If the Pastry

Chef has assistants or trainees, he or she is responsible for suggesting methods and procedures to assure a consistent product.

The Pastry Chef is responsible for fashioning table and pastry decorations. These can include ornaments from sugar paste and icings. The individual must know how to properly use a cream bag, spatula, and other tools to decorate desserts.

The Pastry Chef may work varied hours. The individual usually bakes early at a time when the restaurant is closed and other cooks don't need the ovens.

After baking pastries and making any necessary sauces or fillings, the Pastry Chef assembles and decorates the desserts. Presentation of desserts is essential to the success of the Pastry Chef. In some restaurants the Pastry Chef decorates each plate for each dessert. In others, this task is left to others under the direction of the Pastry Chef.

Other responsibilities of the Pastry Chef may include:

- Determining what supplies are needed
- Ordering supplies
- Scheduling employees
- Training assistants

Salaries

Earnings for Pastry Chefs range from $25,000 to $75,000 or more depending on a number of factors. These include the size, type, prestige, and geographic location of the specific restaurant. Other variables include the training, responsibilities, and reputation of the individual.

Employment Prospects

While this is a competitive field, employment prospects are fair for skilled Pastry Chefs in casino and casino hotel restaurants. Individuals may work for one restaurant or be responsible for the desserts in all the hotel's eateries. Pastry Chefs may also find part-time opportunities.

Las Vegas, Reno, Laughlin, Lake Tahoe, Atlantic City, Biloxi, Baton Rouge, New Orleans, and Detroit offer the greatest number of job possibilities. Other employment settings include casinos and casino hotels in other areas of Nevada, Mississippi, New York, Louisiana, Colorado, Connecticut, Illinois, Arizona, and California.

Other regions hosting Indian gaming and land-based or riverboat gaming facilities offer additional opportunities. New casinos and casino hotels are constantly under construction. More casinos and casino hotels are also opening every year as areas legalize gambling.

Advancement Prospects

Pastry Chefs working in casino and hotel restaurants can climb the career ladder by obtaining experience and locating similar positions in larger, more prestigious facilities. Depending on training, the Pastry Chef may move to other food-related positions such as sous chef.

Some Pastry Chefs move out on their own and open up catering businesses or sell pastries to existing caterers, bakeries, and restaurants.

Education and Training

Education and training requirements vary. Pastry Chefs often are graduates of culinary schools. Others have completed apprenticeships in restaurants, bakeries, or with other pastry chefs. Some talented individuals have taken numerous cooking and baking classes or are self-taught in this art.

Whatever the training is, it is mandatory that the Pastry Chef has the knowledge to prepare all the basics. As noted previously, the individual must also have the ability to work in chocolate, sugar, and pastillage.

Experience/Skills/Personality Traits

Pastry Chefs should have a vast amount of experience working with various types of pastries, chocolates, fillings, and sauces. This experience can be obtained through a job in a bakery or small restaurant.

A certain amount of skill and artistry sets one Pastry Chef apart from others. Individuals must be creative and artistic in this line of work.

Unions/Associations

Additional career information regarding Pastry Chefs may be obtained by contacting the American Culinary Federation (ACF), the International Association of Culinary Professionals (IACP), and the National Restaurant Association (NRA).

Tips for Entry

1. Get experience by working with a skilled pastry chef as a trainee or apprentice.
2. Positions in this field are advertised in the newspaper classified section under headings such as "Pastry Chef," "Casino Hotels," "Casino Restaurants," "Food Service," and "Riverboat Casinos."
3. Join trade associations. They often offer educational opportunities as well as conferences and professional guidance.
4. In many situations you will have to prepare samples of your work.
5. Take classes and workshops in pastry making, chocolate, and desserts.
6. Create your own special dessert. It might give you an edge over other applicants.

BAKER

Duties: Preparing bread, rolls, and additional baked products for use in restaurants and food outlets in casino hotel.

Alternative Titles(s): None

Salary Range: $25,000 to $40,000+

Employment Prospects: Fair

Best Geographical Location(s) for Position: Las Vegas, Reno, Laughlin, Lake Tahoe, Atlantic City, Biloxi, Baton Rouge, New Orleans, and Detroit offer most opportunities; other regions with land-based, riverboat, or Indian gaming facilities offer additional opportunities.

Prerequisites:
  Education or Training—High school diploma or equivalent; vocational trade school; apprentice program; see text.
  Experience and Qualifications—Experience in food service or bakery.
  Special Skills and Personality Traits—Baking skills; familiarity with variety of baking procedures and preparations; physical stamina.

```
┌─────────────────────────────────┐
│   Baker in Larger, More         │
│   Prestigious Casino Hotel,     │
│   Head Baker or Pastry Chef     │
└─────────────────────────────────┘

┌─────────────────────────────────┐
│            Baker                │
└─────────────────────────────────┘

┌─────────────────────────────────┐
│   Baker in Other Setting,       │
│   Baker's Helper or Apprentice  │
└─────────────────────────────────┘
```

Position Description

Casinos and casino hotels often have a great number of restaurants on their property. Bakers are responsible for preparing a variety of fresh bread and baked goods for these outlets on a daily basis.

Depending on the type of restaurants in the facility, Bakers make a wide array of baked goods. These can include rolls, bagels, croissants, muffins, biscuits, and scones. Various types of yeast breads might include corn, sourdough, rye, white, wheat, french, and pumpernickel. Some may be light and others dark and hearty.

The Baker is also responsible for preparing certain crossover items such as Danish pastries, sticky buns, sweet rolls, and other sweet breads. The individual may be required to bake quick breads prepared without yeast, as well as traditional breads. These might include specialties such as banana, lemon, orange, or nut breads or muffins. Bakers generally do not prepare desserts, since these are usually done by pastry chefs.

Bakers working in casino hotels usually prepare each bread product according to established recipe specifications. In this way, every product consistently tastes the same no matter which Baker prepares it.

When preparing baked goods, individuals must measure or weigh ingredients accurately before mixing and shaping. Yeast breads must be proofed so the bread can rise properly before baking the dough.

Other duties of Bakers in casino hotels may include:

• Specifying ingredients that need to be ordered
• Baking specialty breads at the request of the head baker, pastry chef, or executive chef

Salaries

Bakers working in casino hotels are usually paid an hourly wage ranging from $12.00 to $20.00 or more and may earn between $25,000 and $40,000 annually. In some settings, they might be compensated with a weekly salary instead.

Factors affecting earnings include the geographic location, size, and prestige of the specific casino hotel. Other variables include the experience, training, and responsibilities of the individual.

Employment Prospects

Employment prospects are fair for qualified individuals seeking to be Bakers. Restaurants in gaming areas are often open 24 hours a day. In order to keep fresh baked goods available, individuals may work various shifts.

Las Vegas, Reno, Laughlin, Lake Tahoe, Atlantic City, Biloxi, Baton Rouge, New Orleans, and Detroit offer the greatest number of job possibilities. Other employment settings include casinos and casino hotels in other areas of Nevada, Mississippi, New York, Louisiana, Colorado, Connecticut, Illinois, Arizona, and California.

Other regions hosting Indian gaming and land-based or riverboat gaming facilities offer additional opportunities. New casinos and casino hotels are constantly under construction. More casinos and casino hotels are also opening every year as areas legalize gambling.

Advancement Prospects

Bakers can advance their careers in a number of ways. With experience and training, some are promoted to head Bakers. Others find similar positions in larger or more prestigious casino hotels. This results in increased responsibilities and earnings. Bakers who wish to move into pastry baking should obtain additional training or education.

Education and Training

Casino hotels often prefer employees to have a high school diploma or the equivalent. Additional training may include courses or programs in professional bread baking offered at trade or vocational technical schools and community colleges. Other training is available at culinary schools, institutes, and academies throughout the country. Apprentice programs are also an excellent way to learn this trade.

Experience/Skills/Personality Traits

Experience in the preparation of bread and baked goods is necessary. This may be obtained through apprenticeships or jobs in restaurants or bakeries. Some Bakers worked as baker's helpers or assistants prior to being full-fledged Bakers.

Individuals must be able to stand for extended periods of time.

Unions/Skills

Depending on the location and specific casino or casino hotel, this may be a unionized position. In Atlantic City, for example, Bakers are represented by the Local 54 of the Hotel Employees and Restaurant Employees International Union.

Individuals interested in pursuing a career as Baker can obtain additional career information by contacting the human resources departments of casino hotels, the American Institute of Baking (AIB), and trade or vocational technical schools offering programs in bread and baked good production.

Tips for Entry

1. Visit the human resources departments of casino hotels to inquire about job openings.
2. Continue taking courses in baking a variety of baked goods. This will make you more marketable.
3. Contact a baker in a hotel or commercial bakery whose work you admire and inquire about apprenticeship possibilities.
4. Jobs may be advertised in the classified sections of newspapers in areas hosting gaming. Look under classifications such as "Baker," "Casino Hotels Opportunities," and "Food and Beverage."
5. Call casino hotels to get their job hotline numbers. Call often. They update job openings frequently. Contact each casino directly to get its job hotline phone number.

GARDE-MANGER

CAREER PROFILE

Duties: Preparing fresh, raw ingredients; handling creative presentations of cold foods.

Alternative Titles(s): Chef Garde-Manger

Salary Range: $12,000 to $32,000+

Employment Prospects: Good

Best Geographical Location(s) for Position: Las Vegas, Reno, Laughlin, Lake Tahoe, Atlantic City, Biloxi, Baton Rouge, New Orleans, and Detroit offer most opportunities; other regions with land-based, riverboat, or Indian gaming facilities offer additional opportunities.

Prerequisites:

Education or Training—Training requirements vary; see text.

Experience and Qualifications—Previous experience in food service preferred, but not always required.

Special Skills and Personality Traits—Creative; organized; ability to stand for extended periods of time; manual dexterity; physical stamina; ability to work quickly under pressure.

CAREER LADDER

```
┌─────────────────────────────────┐
│    Other Position in Kitchen    │
└─────────────────────────────────┘

┌─────────────────────────────────┐
│         Garde-Manger            │
└─────────────────────────────────┘

┌─────────────────────────────────┐
│    Entry Level or Apprentice    │
└─────────────────────────────────┘
```

Position Description

Casinos often mean bright lights and excitement. Casino restaurants often showcase some of the same pizazz through their elaborate and creative presentations of food. The person responsible for preparing cold foods in an attractive manner is called the Garde-Manger. Sometimes the individual may be referred to as the Chef Garde-Manger.

This individual prepares a wide variety of cold foods, including fruits, vegetables, salads, aspics, pates, and canapes.

The Garde-Manger must prepare foods in a decorative manner. For example, the individual may mold egg, tuna, chicken, or shrimp salad into various shapes, or create crudités that resemble huge bouquets of flowers. He or she might also carve fruits into decorate bowls or style fruit into impressive-looking animals, vehicles, and vessels. These may then be filled with cut-up fruits, spreads, or vegetables.

A creative Garde-Manger Chef takes a simple platter of cold meats, cheeses, vegetables, or fruits and makes it an artistic masterpiece.

The Garde-Manger may prepare cold garnishes for plates, or large decorations out of cold foods for guest rooms. The elaborate ice carvings the Garde-Manger prepares are often the items many guests remember at buffets and in banquet rooms. The Garde-Manger must be able to carve and design different creations depending on the theme of the banquet or buffet.

Other responsibilities of the Garde-Manger may include:

• Preparing cold buffets in an attractive manner
• Making sure cold foods are prepared to minimize waste

Salaries

Garde-Mangers usually earn an hourly wage ranging from $6.00 to $16.00 or more and may earn $12,000 to

$32,000 annually. Factors affecting earnings include the geographic location, size, and prestige of the casino or casino hotel, as well as the experience and responsibilities of the individual.

Employment Prospects

Employment prospects are good for Garde-Mangers seeking employment in casinos or casino hotels. Individuals may work full- or part-time in casino or casino hotel restaurants or their banquet facilities.

Las Vegas, Reno, Laughlin, Lake Tahoe, Atlantic City, Biloxi, Baton Rouge, New Orleans, and Detroit offer the greatest number of job possibilities. Other employment settings include casino hotels in other areas of Nevada, Mississippi, New York, Louisiana, Colorado, Connecticut, Illinois, Arizona, and California.

Other regions hosting Indian gaming and land-based or riverboat gaming facilities offer additional opportunities. New casinos and casino hotels are constantly under construction. More casinos and casino hotels are also opening every year as areas legalize gambling.

Advancement Prospects

When training to work in the kitchen, the Garde-Manger is usually the position at which individuals start. From there, with experience and training, they can be promoted to other stations in the kitchen.

Education and Training

Educational requirements for Garde-Mangers vary. A high school diploma or the equivalent is usually preferred by most casinos and casino hotels. Facilities often assist those without the minimum education get a GED.

The Garde-Manger Chef may either obtain training in a vocational technical school or receive on-the-job training.

Many casinos and casino hotels offer training and apprentice programs in which individuals learn various aspects of food preparation.

Experience/Skills/Personality Traits

Garde-Mangers interested in working in casino hotel restaurants should have prior experience in food service.

Individuals should be creative and enjoy working around food. Physical stamina is necessary as Garde-Mangers often must stand for extended periods of time. Manual dexterity is also essential, as is the ability to work quickly under pressure.

Unions/Associations

Individuals interested in pursuing careers in this area can obtain additional information by contacting the Educational Foundation of the National Restaurant Association (EFNRA), the Council on Hotel, Restaurant and Institutional Education (CHRIE), the American Culinary Federation (ACF), and the International Association of Culinary Professionals (IACP).

Tips for Entry

1. Stop by the human resources departments of casino and casino hotels to inquire about job openings.
2. Look for new casinos under construction. Apply early.
3. Jobs are often advertised in the classified sections of newspapers in areas hosting gaming. Look under classifications such as "Restaurants," "Casino/Hotel Opportunities," "Garde-Manger," "Casino Hotel Restaurants," or "Food and Beverage."
4. Training programs are excellent ways to get experience in this field.

CASINO OR CASINO HOTEL RESTAURANT MANAGER

CAREER PROFILE

Duties: Overseeing restaurant operation; training, supervising, and scheduling employees; setting service standards; dealing with customer service problems.

Alternative Titles(s): Restaurant Outlet Manager

Salary Range: $25,000 to $55,000+

Employment Prospects: Good

Best Geographical Locations(s) for Position: Las Vegas, Reno, Laughlin, Lake Tahoe, Atlantic City, Biloxi, Baton Rouge, New Orleans, and Detroit offer most opportunities; other regions with land-based, riverboat, or Indian gaming facilities offer additional opportunities.

Prerequisites:

Education or Training—Educational requirements vary; associate's or bachelor's degree in restaurant management preferred; see text.

Experience and Qualifications—Supervisory experience in restaurant outlets.

Special Skills and Personality Traits—Supervisory skills; management skills; communication skills; business skills; organization.

CAREER LADDER

```
┌─────────────────────────────────────┐
│   Restaurant Manager in Larger, More │
│   Prestigious Casino/Casino Hotel    │
│   Restaurant or Manager of           │
│   Restaurant Operations              │
└─────────────────────────────────────┘

┌─────────────────────────────────────┐
│        Casino or Casino Hotel        │
│          Restaurant Manager          │
└─────────────────────────────────────┘

┌─────────────────────────────────────┐
│       Assistant Restaurant Manager   │
└─────────────────────────────────────┘
```

Position Description

Casinos and casino hotels host a variety of restaurant outlets. Each outlet has a Restaurant Manager responsible for an array of duties overseeing the restaurant operation.

The Restaurant Manager may be in charge of interviewing, hiring, and training restaurant employees. Often the original recruitment and interviewing is done by the casino or casino hotel human resources department. However, the Manager usually has a say in the hiring process. Restaurant personnel may include assistant managers, hosts, hostesses, waiters, waitresses, and bus people. Chefs are usually hired by the executive chef of the casino hotel.

The Restaurant Manager supervises employees and explains restaurant procedures, rules, and regulations. The individual also oversees the training of new employees.

The Restaurant Manager may be expected to keep track of invoices from suppliers for food, equipment, and services. He or she may be responsible for ordering supplies and scheduling repair calls for restaurant equipment. In some situations, these tasks may be handled by others.

The Restaurant Manager makes sure the restaurant and its employees comply with health and safety rules and regulations as well as with local liquor laws. Other important functions of the individual include maintaining food quality and assuring prompt, courteous service.

The Restaurant Manager handles customer complaints and problems. When dealing with these situations, the Manager must try to solve problems quickly and calmly.

Other responsibilities of the Restaurant Manager may include:

- Scheduling employees
- Counting cash and charge receipts at the end of the shift
- Balancing cash against sales receipts
- Meeting financial goals
- Evaluating performance of staff

Salaries

Annual earnings for Restaurant Managers in casinos and casino hotels range from $25,000 to $55,000 or more depending on a number of factors, including the geographic location, size, and prestige of the specific casino or casino hotel, as well as the restaurant itself.

Other variables include the experience, education, and responsibilities of the individual. Those working in more prestigious, full-service restaurants in larger casinos or casino hotels in the gambling capitals usually earn more than their counterparts in other areas.

Employment Prospects

Employment prospects are good for Restaurant Managers seeking employment in casinos and casino hotels. Depending on the facility, restaurants may have one Manager or a day Manager and a night Manager.

Restaurant Manager positions vary in different types of restaurant settings, including gourmet restaurants, full-service restaurants, buffet-style restaurants, specialty restaurants, family restaurants, ethnic food restaurants, and coffee shops.

A trend has emerged in many larger, luxury casinos, which import famous-name eateries in an effort to entice more patrons. For example, Mandalay Bay in Las Vegas features the famous Border Grill Restaurant. The Venetian Casino Resort features Emeril Lagasse's Delmonico Steak House. The MGM Grand showcases Wolfgang Puck's Cafe. Such restaurants offer many opportunities for employment and advancement.

Las Vegas, Reno, Laughlin, Lake Tahoe, Atlantic City, Biloxi, Baton Rouge, New Orleans, and Detroit offer the greatest number of job possibilities. Other employment settings include casino hotels in other areas of Nevada, Mississippi, New York, Louisiana, Colorado, Connecticut, Illinois, Arizona, and California.

Other regions hosting Indian gaming and land-based or riverboat gaming facilities offer additional opportunities. New casinos and casino hotels are constantly under construction. More casinos and casino hotels are also opening every year as areas legalize gambling.

Advancement Prospects

Restaurant Managers can advance their careers in a number of ways. Individuals may obtain experience and land jobs in larger or more prestigious restaurants or casinos, resulting in increased responsibilities and earnings. Depending on experience, education, and career aspirations, individuals may also be promoted to other administrative positions such as manager of restaurant operations, food and beverage manager, or assistant manager.

Education and Training

Educational requirements vary from job to job. Positions, especially in prestigious, full-service restaurants, often require either a two- or four-year degree in restaurant and food service management or a related field. In some cases, experience is accepted in lieu of education requirements.

Some facilities also offer extensive training programs in which individuals learn every aspect of restaurant operations.

Experience/Skills/Personality Traits

Restaurant Managers in casinos and casino hotels should have at least two years supervisory experience in the food and beverage industry. Experience in gourmet or fine restaurant management may be required.

Restaurant Managers should be well-spoken, articulate people with good communication skills. Complete understanding of the operation of restaurants in essential.

The Educational Foundation of the National Restaurant Association (EFNRA) offers voluntary certification for individuals working in food service management. Those who complete classes, pass a written exam, and meet standards of work experience in the field can earn the designation of Foodservice Management Professional (FMP).

Unions/Associations

Individuals interested in pursuing careers in this field can obtain additional information by contacting the Educational Foundation of the National Restaurant Association (EFNRA) and the Council on Hotel, Restaurant and Institutional Education (CHRIE).

Tips for Entry

1. Training programs can offer excellent experience.
2. Send your résumé to the human resources departments of casinos and casino hotels.
3. Jobs are often advertised in the classifieds in areas hosting gaming. Look under "Restaurant Manager," "Restaurant Outlet Manager," "Casino Hotels," "Casino Hotel Restaurants," "Casinos," or "Food Service."
4. Casinos like to promote from within. Get your foot in the door and move up the career ladder.

MAITRE D'HOTEL

CAREER PROFILE

Duties: Managing dining room of fine restaurant; assisting manager in training and scheduling wait staff; handling customer service problems.

Alternative Titles(s): Maitre d'

Salary Range: $25,000 to $48,000+

Employment Prospects: Fair

Best Geographical Location(s) for Position: Las Vegas, Reno, Laughlin, Lake Tahoe, Atlantic City, Biloxi, Baton Rouge, New Orleans, and Detroit offer most opportunities; other regions with land-based, riverboat, or Indian gaming facilities offer additional opportunities.

Prerequisites:

Education or Training—Training requirements vary; see text.

Experience and Qualifications—Experience in dining room of fine restaurant is required.

Special Skills and Personality Traits—Personable; supervisory skills; organized; communication skills; articulate; well-groomed.

CAREER LADDER

```
┌─────────────────────────────────────┐
│ Maitre d' in Larger, More Prestigious │
│   Casino Restaurant or Restaurant     │
│              Manager                  │
└─────────────────────────────────────┘

┌─────────────────────────────────────┐
│           Maitre d'Hotel              │
└─────────────────────────────────────┘

┌─────────────────────────────────────┐
│   Maitre d' in Non-Casino Restaurant  │
└─────────────────────────────────────┘
```

Position Description

When visiting a casino, in addition to gambling, many people look forward to dining in a nice restaurant with good food, service, and atmosphere. While casinos and casino hotels often offer a variety of restaurants, usually at least one is a fine dining establishment. While the manager is responsible for overseeing the entire restaurant operation, fine dining estalishments also may employ a Maitre d'Hotel. These individuals, often referred to as Maitre d's, are responsible for managing the front of the house in the restaurant.

The Maitre d', working under the supervision of the restaurant manager, assists in setting the standards and style for service in the dining room. The individual assists in the training of the wait staff as well as bus people, hosts, hostesses, and others who work in the dining room. The individual oversees and supervises these employees.

Fine restaurants usually have reservation books. The Maitre d' is responsible for keeping abreast of reservations

to make sure there is enough staff scheduled during busy times. Because many casino restaurants have walk-ins, the individual also often forecasts business.

The Maitre d' greets customers and welcomes them to the dining establishment. The individual sometimes escorts patrons to tables, assisting the hosts or hostesses when they are busy with other guests. The Maitre d' tells patrons about specials and makes sure a wine steward or member of the wait staff is sent over in timely fashion.

The Maitre d' is responsible for arranging seating for large groups of guests. He or she accommodates any special seating requests. The Maitre d' may handle other special needs at the request of patrons, for example, champagne with an engagement ring in the glass for a couple about to become engaged or a birthday cake complete with candles and singing waiters.

The Maitre d' makes sure everything in the front of the house is in order, including making sure fresh flowers are in place, candles lit, napkins folded, and tables set.

The Maitre d' often walks around the dining room, stopping at tables to ask patrons if they need anything and making sure everyone is pleased with the service and the food. If they are any problems, the Maitre d' makes every effort possible to correct them to the guests' satisfaction.

When guests are done with their meal and ready to leave, the Maitre d' assists them with their coats and thanks them for visiting the establishment.

Other responsibilities of the Maitre d' may include:

- Acting in capacity of wine steward
- Recommending and serving wines to patrons
- Scheduling front of the house employees
- Evaluating the performance of front of the house staff

Salaries

Annual earning for Maitre d's in casinos and casino hotels range from $25,000 to $48,000 or more depending on a number of factors, including the geographic location, size, and prestige of the casino or casino hotel, as well as the specific restaurant. Other variables include the experience and responsibilities of the individual. Maitre d's may also receive tips from patrons.

Employment Prospects

Employment prospects are fair for Maitre d's seeking employment in casinos and casino hotel fine restaurants. Positions may be found in a variety of eateries, including gourmet restaurants, full-service restaurants, specialty restaurants, and ethnic restaurants.

Las Vegas, Reno, Laughlin, Lake Tahoe, Atlantic City, Biloxi, Baton Rouge, New Orleans, and Detroit offer the greatest number of job possibilities. Other employment settings include casinos and casino hotels in other areas of Nevada, Mississippi, New York, Louisiana, Colorado, Connecticut, Illinois, Arizona and California.

Other regions hosting Indian gaming and land-based or riverboat gaming facilities offer additional opportunities. New casinos and casino hotels are constantly under construction. More casinos and casino hotels are also opening every year as areas legalize gambling.

Advancement Prospects

Maitre d's can advance their careers in a number of ways. Individuals may obtain experience and locate similar jobs in larger or more prestigious restaurants, resulting in increased earnings.

Depending on experience, education, and career aspirations, some Maitre d's may also be promoted to positions such as restaurant managers.

Education and Training

Educational requirements for Maitre d's in casino and casino hotel restaurants vary from job to job. In many cases, experience is accepted in lieu of education requirements. Most facilities require applicants to hold a high school diploma or the equivalent.

Some casino hotel restaurants prefer that applicants complete courses in dining room management, wine service, and hospitality from two- or four-year colleges or vocational technical schools. Others accept on-the-job training. Many casinos and casino hotels offer training programs in which individuals learn various aspects of restaurant operations.

Experience/Skills/Personality Traits

Maitre d's working in casinos and casino hotels should have experience working in a fine restaurant. Most start their careers as waitpersons. Many casino restaurants require prior experience as a Maitre d'.

Maitre d's should be neatly groomed individuals. They must be well-spoken and articulate with good communication skills. Individuals should enjoy being around others and providing good customer service. Understanding of restaurant "front of the house" operation is mandatory.

Unions/Associations

Individuals interested in pursuing a career in this area can obtain additional information by contacting the Educational Foundation of the National Restaurant Association (EFNRA) and the Council on Hotel, Restaurant and Institutional Education (CHRIE).

Tips for Entry

1. Visit the human resources departments of casinos and casino hotels to inquire about job openings.
2. Also fax or send your résumé and a short cover letter to human resources departments.
3. Stop by privately owned restaurants in casino facilities. These might also offer additional opportunities.
4. Jobs are often advertised in the classified sections of newspapers in areas hosting gaming. Look under classifications such as "Restaurants," "Maitre D'," "Casino/Hotel Opportunities," "Food Service," "Fine Restaurant," "Casino Hotel Restaurants," or "Food and Beverage."
5. Training programs can offer excellent experience in this field.

RESTAURANT HOST/HOSTESS

CAREER PROFILE

Duties: Welcoming patrons to restaurant; assigning tables to customers; escorting patrons to tables; providing menus.

Alternative Titles(s): None

Salary Range: $12,000 to $21,000+; see text.

Employment Prospects: Good

Best Geographical Location(s) for Position: Las Vegas, Reno, Laughlin, Lake Tahoe, Atlantic City, Biloxi, Baton Rouge, New Orleans, and Detroit offer most opportunities; other regions with land-based, riverboat, or Indian gaming facilities offer additional opportunities.

Prerequisites:

Education or Training—Minimum of high school diploma or GED; no specific training requirements.

Experience and Qualifications—Experience working in service, food, or hospitality industry useful, but not always required.

Special Skills and Personality Traits—Interpersonal skills; customer service skills; pleasant; organized.

CAREER LADDER

```
┌─────────────────────────────────────┐
│  Restaurant Host/Hostess in Larger,  │
│  More Prestigious Restaurant or      │
│  Maitre d'Hotel, Dining Room         │
│  Supervisor or Restaurant Manager    │
└─────────────────────────────────────┘

┌─────────────────────────────────────┐
│     Restaurant Host/Hostess          │
└─────────────────────────────────────┘

┌─────────────────────────────────────┐
│  Entry Level or Host/Hostess in      │
│  Non-Casino Restaurant Setting       │
└─────────────────────────────────────┘
```

Position Description

Casinos and casino hotels usually have a number of restaurants, each with its own personality and flavor. The casino or casino hotel restaurant Host or Hostess is responsible for giving patrons their first impression of the restaurant. This individual greets and welcomes patrons. Functions include making sure that patrons have a pleasant and enjoyable meal and ensuring that service is prompt and courteous.

After the Host or Hostess greets patrons, the individual escorts them to their seats and provides menus. Sometimes the restaurant is busy and the Host or Hostess takes the name and number of people in the party and puts the information on a waiting list. The individual informs the people the approximate time it will take for a table to be ready. He or she may also direct the patrons to a lounge or other area to wait until their table is available.

Other functions of the Host or Hostess may include:

- Answering the restaurant telephone
- Scheduling dining reservations
- Handling complaints of dissatisfied patrons
- Organizing special services that may be required
- Acting as cashier

Salaries

Restaurant Hosts and Hostesses generally are paid an hourly wage. In some dining establishments they receive tips. Individuals may earn between $6.00 and $10.00 per hour or more or approximately $10,000 to $21,000 per year depending on a number of factors, including the geographic location, size, and prestige of the specific casino or casino hotel. Other variables include the size, prestige, and type of restaurant.

Generally, Hosts or Hostesses working in fine restaurants have higher earnings than their counterparts working in other types of dining establishments.

Employment Prospects

Employment opportunities are abundant for restaurant Hosts and Hostesses. Individuals work various hours depending on the specific job. Casinos and casino hotels often feature a wide variety of restaurants, including fine dining restaurants, coffee shops, family-style restaurants, buffet-style restaurants, and ethnic eateries, among others.

Las Vegas, Reno, Laughlin, Lake Tahoe, Atlantic City, Biloxi, Baton Rouge, New Orleans, and Detroit offer the greatest number of job possibilities. Other employment settings include casino hotels in other areas of Nevada, Mississippi, New York, Louisiana, Colorado, Connecticut, Illinois, Arizona, and California.

Other regions hosting Indian gaming and land-based or riverboat gaming facilities offer additional opportunities. New casinos and casino hotels are constantly under construction. More casinos and casino hotels are opening every year as areas legalize gambling.

Advancement Prospects

Restaurant Hosts and Hostesses can climb the career ladder by locating similar positions in better or more prestigious facilities. In larger establishments, they may also advance to supervisory jobs, including maitre d'hotel, dining room supervisor, or restaurant manager. Experience and/or additional training may be required.

Education and Training

Training requirements vary from job to job. Some positions do not require any type of prior training, while others provide on-the-job training.

Most restaurants in the casino and casino hotel industry prefer to hire high school graduates or those with the GED equivalent.

Experience/Skills/Personality Traits

Experience requirements also vary. In some restaurants, this is an entry-level position. In others, prior experience in the hospitality, service, or food and beverage industries is required or preferred.

Hosts and Hostesses should be friendly, well-spoken people with a neat and clean appearance. Customer service skills are mandatory. Individuals should also be organized and have the ability to prioritize.

Unions/Associations

Individuals interested in pursuing a career as a Host or Hostess should contact the National Restaurant Association (NRA) for more information.

Tips for Entry

1. Stop by human resources departments to inquire about job openings.
2. Check out openings in privately owned restaurants located in casino complexes.
3. Jobs are often advertised in the classified sections of newspapers in areas hosting gaming. Look under classifications such as "Host/Hostess," "Restaurant Host/Hostess," "Food Service," "Casino Restaurant," and "Casinos."
4. Jobs may also be listed on casino job hotlines. These are frequently updated messages listing jobs available. You can call each casino directly to get its job hotline phone number.

SERVER

CAREER PROFILE

Duties: Taking patrons' orders; serving food and beverages; preparing check.

Alternative Titles(s): Food Server; Waiter; Waitress

Salary Range: $11,000 to $18,000+ plus tips

Employment Prospects: Excellent

Best Geographical Location(s) for Position: Las Vegas, Reno, Laughlin, Lake Tahoe, Atlantic City, Biloxi, Baton Rouge, New Orleans, and Detroit offer most opportunities; other regions with land-based, riverboat, or Indian gaming facilities offer additional opportunities.

Prerequisites:

Education or Training—Minimum of high school diploma or GED; see text.

Experience and Qualifications—Prior experience waiting tables may be required for some positions; health certificate may be required.

Special Skills and Personality Traits—Good memory; math skills; pleasant; personable; customer service skills; ability to carry heavy trays.

CAREER LADDER

```
┌─────────────────────────────────────┐
│ Dining Room Supervisor, Maitre d'Hotel,│
│      or Server in Larger, More        │
│        Prestigious Eatery             │
└─────────────────────────────────────┘

┌─────────────────────────────────────┐
│              Server                   │
└─────────────────────────────────────┘

┌─────────────────────────────────────┐
│  Server in Other Setting or Entry Level│
└─────────────────────────────────────┘
```

Position Description

Servers are the food service workers who deal with customers in restaurants. They may also be referred to as Waiters or Waitresses. The service patrons receive when visiting restaurants often determines whether or not they will return.

Servers work in a variety of settings in casino and casino hotel restaurants—small, informal cafes or large, elegant restaurants. Whatever the setting, individuals are responsible for making the patron's gastronomic visit an enjoyable experience.

While specific duties are similar for all Servers, they are often performed differently, depending on the type of establishment in which the individual works. Those working in coffee shops in the hotel provide fast, efficient, and courteous service. However in the hotel's fine restaurants, the wait staff must be more attentive. Meals in these settings are served in a more leisurely manner, and servers offer more personal attention to patrons. Individuals working in these settings may, for example, recommend wines or explain how various items are prepared. They may also prepare certain dishes at tableside, such as salads or flaming desserts.

Servers take customers' orders and tell patrons about specials. When orders are ready, individuals bring the food and beverages from the kitchen and serve the customers. After the meal, Servers prepare an itemized check, manually or by computer.

Servers must be able to stand for long periods of time and carry heavy trays of food and dishes. Many people, however, enjoy such work as it affords individuals the opportunity to meet a large number of people, often on a flexible work schedule.

Usually larger or more prestigious fine restaurants employ special people to handle specific projects. Individuals working in smaller restaurants may handle more generalized tasks. In some settings Servers are required to perform duties associated with other food and beverage service jobs. These may include the following:

- Acting as a host or hostess
- Escorting patrons to tables
- Setting up and clearing tables
- Waiting on customers at counters
- Taking payment from customers

Salaries

Earnings for Servers in this industry vary tremendously. As a rule, earnings are a combination of hourly wages and tips from customers. Hourly earnings vary depending on the type of establishment in which the individual works.

Base wages range from approximately $5.50 to $8.50 or more per hour. With tips, Servers earn between $15 and $30 per hour or more. Tips generally average between 10 percent and 20 percent of a patron's check. Therefore, those working in expensive, fine restaurants usually earn more than their counterparts in other types of eateries.

Employment Prospects

There are unlimited opportunities for both full- and part-time employment. Servers work in a variety of settings, including coffee shops, casino hotel fine restaurants, on-site casino restaurants, ice-cream parlors, fast food eateries, family restaurants, and buffet-style restaurants.

Las Vegas, Reno, Laughlin, Lake Tahoe, Atlantic City, Biloxi, Baton Rouge, New Orleans, and Detroit offer the greatest number of job possibilities. Other employment settings include casino hotels in other areas of Nevada, Mississippi, New York, Louisiana, Colorado, Connecticut, Illinois, Arizona, and California.

Other regions hosting Indian gaming and land-based or riverboat gaming facilities offer additional opportunities. New casinos and casino hotels and constantly under construction. More casinos and casino hotels are opening every year as areas legalize gambling.

Advancement Prospects

Some individuals look on this position as a job, not a career. It offers immediate income and flexible hours. Others who enjoy the flexibility and the opportunity of meeting different people see it as a career choice. Opportunities for advancement in this career are often limited. Individuals may, however, increase earnings and tips by locating similar positions in better, more expensive restaurants. Some Servers advance to supervisory positions such as dining room supervisor or maitre d'hotel.

Education and Training

While there are usually no formal educational requirements, most food establishments in the gaming industry prefer applicants to have at least a high school diploma or GED.

Some restaurants provide on-the-job training so that Servers have the ability to wait on customers in a manner specified by the individual restaurant.

Experience/Skills/Personality Traits

Experience as a Server is required by some fine restaurants, especially those with rigid table service standards. In others, there may be no experience requirement.

Individuals in this line of work should be pleasant and well spoken with a neat and clean appearance. They should enjoy dealing with others. The ability to carry heavy trays is often needed. A good memory is also useful, as are math skills.

Many states require employees working in the food or beverage industry to provide a health certificate showing they are free of contagious diseases.

Unions/Associations

Depending on the location and specific casino, this may or may not be a unionized position. For example, in unionized casinos and casino hotels in Las Vegas, Servers might be members of the Culinary Workers Local #225. In Atlantic City Servers are represented by the Local 54 Hotel Employees and Restaurant Employees International Union.

Additional career information may be obtained by contacting the National Restaurant Association (NRA) and the Council on Hotel, Restaurant and Institutional Education (CHRIE).

Tips for Entry

1. If you have no experience and are interested in working in a fine restaurant, find a short-term job as a Server in another type of eatery first to get experience.
2. Positions in this field are advertised in newspaper classified sections under headings such as "Waiter," "Waitress," "Food Server," Server," "Casino Hotels," "Casino Restaurants," "Food Service," and "Riverboat Cruises."
3. Stop by the employment office of a casino or casino hotel. There is often a great deal of turnover in these positions.
4. Check casino job hotlines. These are frequently updated messages listing jobs available. Call each casino directly to get its job hotline phone number.

NIGHTCLUB MANAGER

CAREER PROFILE

Duties: Managing the operations of a club.

Alternative Titles(s): Club Manager

Salary Range: $25,000 to $60,000+

Employment Prospects: Fair

Best Geographical Location(s) for Position: Las Vegas, Reno, Laughlin, Lake Tahoe, Atlantic City, Biloxi, Baton Rouge, New Orleans, and Detroit offer most opportunities; other regions with land-based, riverboat, or Indian gaming facilities offer additional opportunities.

Prerequisites:

Education or Training—Formal or informal on-the-job training.

Experience and Qualifications—Experience in casinos, clubs, or entertainment industry useful; knowledge of food and beverage industry, entertainment and music business.

Special Skills and Personality Traits—Supervisory skills; business skills; interpersonal skills; aggressive; management skills; communication skills; organization.

CAREER LADDER

```
┌─────────────────────────────────┐
│ Nightclub Manager in Larger, More│
│   Prestigious Club or Showroom   │
└─────────────────────────────────┘

┌─────────────────────────────────┐
│        Nightclub Manager         │
└─────────────────────────────────┘

┌─────────────────────────────────┐
│    Assistant Nightclub Manager   │
└─────────────────────────────────┘
```

Position Description

Casinos and casino hotels feature a variety of nightclubs for their patrons. Nightclub Managers are in charge of managing the operation of the club. They handle the day-to-day running of the establishment. Individuals have varied responsibilities within the scope of the job, depending on the type of establishment, its size, and structure.

Other sections of this book discuss hotel casino entertainment. In some cases the facility hosts big showrooms in addition to nightclubs. In other situations, the nightclub is the focus of the hotel's entertainment.

Many larger casino hotels host special attractions and a theme that surrounds every aspect of the property, including the nightclub. In many cases the theme determines the type of entertainment behind the club's success. A club might use live entertainment, employ DJs, or a combination of both.

The Nightclub Manager is in charge of determining what type of entertainment the club wants to use as well as what type of patrons the club wants to attract—people who prefer

to drink, eat, dance, listen to music, see comedy shows, or just plain relax. Managers must often research other clubs in the area in order to decide the direction their clubs should take.

Responsibilities of the job include auditioning talent, such as comedians, bands, singers, musicians, and DJs. In some situations, the individual negotiates and signs contracts. In others, this function falls to someone else in the casino hotel.

The Nightclub Manager may also be in charge of hiring and training other key personnel, including bartenders, waitresses, waiters, hosts and hostesses, chefs, security guards, or lighting and sound people, sometimes in conjunction with other hotel departments.

The Nightclub Manager must see to it that all state and local alcohol laws are adhered to. Clubs can be closed down if there are infractions. Depending on the size and structure of the club, the Manager might also be responsible for the purchase and control of food and/or alcoholic beverages. In some clubs, the Manager oversees a food and beverage manager who handles this function.

During the day the Manager may be in charge of developing budgets, bookkeeping, checking receipts, and paying bills. The individual may also be responsible for determining the type of advertising campaign that will be most effective. In addition, he or she may implement advertising programs and develop special promotions. In some situations, the Nightclub Manager works with the hotel's marketing and advertising departments on these functions.

Many of the duties of the Nightclub Manager are handled at night when the club is open. Some of these duties include:

- Handling problems that crop up during the evening
- Dealing with customer complaints
- Totaling nightly receipts
- Putting nightly receipts in safe or making night deposit

Salaries

Earnings for Nightclub Managers range from $25,000 to $60,000 or more annually depending on the size, location, popularity, and type of club. Other factors include the experience and responsibilities of the individual.

Generally, the larger and more prestigious the casino hotel and club, the higher the earning potential of the Manager. Nightclub Managers in entertainment gaming capitals such as Las Vegas and Atlantic City usually earn more than their counterparts in gaming establishments in other parts of the country.

Employment Prospects

Employment prospects for Nightclub Managers in the gaming industry are fair. Employment settings range from very small clubs to large entertainment showrooms, depending on the type of facility. Individuals may be Managers of clubs specializing in a variety of types of entertainment, including piano bars, rock and roll, country music, jazz, blues, comedy, musical productions, show groups, or magic acts.

Las Vegas, Reno, Laughlin, Lake Tahoe, Atlantic City, Biloxi, Baton Rouge, New Orleans, and Detroit offer the greatest number of job possibilities. Other employment settings include casinos and casino hotels in other areas of Nevada, Mississippi, New York, Louisiana, Colorado, Connecticut, Illinois, Arizona, and California.

Other regions hosting Indian gaming and land-based or riverboat gaming facilities offer additional opportunities. New casinos and casino hotels are constantly under construction. More casinos and casino hotels are opening every year as areas legalize gambling.

Advancement Prospects

Nightclub Managers with experience can advance to similar jobs in larger, more prestigious facilities. This results in increased earnings and responsibilities. Nightclub Managers may climb the career ladder by starting at a smaller hotel nightclub, obtain experience, and then be promoted to the Manager of a large showroom. Some Nightclub Managers strike out in their own and open up their own clubs.

Education and Training

There is no formal educational requirement for Nightclub Managers. Some facilities prefer or require training in food service or the hospitality industry. Others require that Managers participate in either formal or informal on-the-job training programs.

Experience/Skills/Personality Traits

Experience requirements vary for Nightclub Managers. Some facilities prefer that a candidate have previously worked as an assistant manager in a club. Others may accept experience in various facets of business or the entertainment industry. Experience working in casino hotels in any capacity is helpful.

Individuals should have basic knowledge of the food and beverage and entertainment and/or music business. They should be cognizant of drawing up contracts, negotiating, and booking talent. The ability to supervise others is mandatory. Nightclub Managers must be able to handle a great many projects at the same time and still keep a cool head.

Unions/Associations

Additional information regarding careers in this area may be obtained by contacting the National Restaurant Association (NRA) or the human resources departments of casino hotels.

Tips For Entry

1. Job openings are often advertised in newspaper classified sections in areas hosting casino hotels. Look under headings such as "Nightclub Manager," "Club Manager," "Nightclub," "Manager," "Management," "Entertainment," "Hospitality," "Music Club Manager," "Comedy Club Manager," "Casino Club Manager," or "Hotel Club Manager."
2. If you do not live in a gaming area and are interested in working in this environment, obtain short-term subscriptions to newspapers in geographic areas you are considering.
3. Send your résumé and a short cover letter to the human resources departments of casino hotels, inquiring about openings. Ask that your résumé be kept on file.
4. Turnover is high in this field. You might start out working as a host or hostess in a club, learn the ropes, them move up the career ladder to become the Nightclub Manager.

BARTENDER/FRONT OF HOUSE

CAREER PROFILE

Duties: Mixing and serving alcoholic and nonalcoholic drinks for patrons.

Alternative Titles(s): None

Salary Range: $13,000 to $28,000+ plus tips

Employment Prospects: Excellent

Best Geographical Location(s) for Position: Las Vegas, Reno, Laughlin, Lake Tahoe, Atlantic City, Biloxi, Baton Rouge, New Orleans, and Detroit offer most opportunities; other regions with land-based, riverboat, or Indian gaming facilities offer additional opportunities.

Prerequisites:

Education or Training—High School diploma or equivalent usually required; training at bartending school or vocational-technical school; see text.

Experience and Qualifications—Prior experience as bartender in club, bar, or restaurant; certification and state licensing may be required.

Special Skills and Personality Traits—Interpersonal skills; customer service skills; drink mixing skills.

CAREER LADDER

```
┌─────────────────────────────────────┐
│  Bartender in Larger, More Prestigious │
│  Casino or Casino Hotel or Assistant  │
│         Beverage Manager              │
└─────────────────────────────────────┘

┌─────────────────────────────────────┐
│     Bartender-Front of the House      │
└─────────────────────────────────────┘

┌─────────────────────────────────────┐
│       Bartender in Other Setting      │
└─────────────────────────────────────┘
```

Position Description

Jobs in casinos and casino hotels are generally separated into front-of-the-house and back-of-the-house categories. The front of the house is the section of the hotel or casino that is accessible to the public. The back of the house is the section of the facility where employees work that is not accessible to the public.

Bartenders working in casinos and casino hotels can work either in the front of the house or the back of the house. Individuals working in the front of the house usually have more contact with patrons than their counterparts.

Bartenders in the front of the house may work in the hotel or casino bar, lounge restaurant, or banquet area. They are responsible for mixing and serving both alcoholic and nonalcoholic drinks for patrons.

Bartenders fill drink orders for customers sitting at the bar, as well as orders taken by waiters and waitresses from patrons seated in the restaurant, club, or bar.

Bartenders must know how to mix a great variety of drink recipes. They must have the ability to accomplish this quickly and accurately. Bartenders must also be able to mix drinks in the specific ways customers request. Many bartenders develop or concoct their own specialty drinks.

Successful Front-of-the-House Bartenders often socialize with patrons by listening to them and having light conversation. Bartenders are responsible for informing the beverage manager or assistant beverage manager of needed inventory of liquor, mixes, or other necessary bar supplies.

Other functions of the Front-of-the-House Bartender may include:

- Arranging bottles and glassware into attractive displays
- Serving snacks or food items to patrons seated at bar
- Collecting payments from patrons and operating the cash register
- Cleaning up the bar after patrons have left
- Monitoring liquor inventory

Salaries

Front-of-the-House Bartenders working in casinos and casino hotel facilities usually earn an hourly wage ranging from $6.50 to $14.00 or more plus tips and may make between $13,000 and $28,000 annually. Factors affecting earnings include the geographic location, size, type, and prestige of the specific casino, hotel, restaurant, bar, club, and/or lounge. Other variables may include the experience and duties of the individual.

In unionized settings, the union may negotiate minimum earnings.

Employment Prospects

Employment opportunities are abundant for qualified Bartenders. Individuals may work in a variety of settings, including casino hotels, casino nightclubs, casino and casino hotel restaurants, and casino bars and lounges.

Las Vegas, Reno, Laughlin, Lake Tahoe, Atlantic City, Biloxi, Baton Rouge, New Orleans, and Detroit offer the greatest number of job possibilities. Other employment settings include casino hotels in other areas of Nevada, Mississippi, New York, Louisiana, Colorado, Connecticut, Illinois, Arizona, and California.

Other regions hosting Indian gaming and land-based or riverboat gaming facilities offer additional opportunities. New casinos and casino hotels are constantly under construction. More casinos and casino hotels are opening every year as areas legalize gambling.

Advancement Prospects

Bartenders working in the front of the house may advance their careers in a number of ways. Some individuals enjoy the social contact of bartending. These people may climb the career ladder by locating similar jobs in larger or more prestigious facilities. This usually results in increased earnings and tips.

Others advance their careers by becoming an assistant or full-fledged beverage manager, or bar, lounge, or nightclub manager. This career move often requires additional experience and/or training.

Education and Training

Training requirements vary from job to job. Most casinos and casino hotels prefer individuals to be high school graduates or have the equivalent. Experienced bartending may often be substituted for education. Facilities also require individuals to have some sort of formal training, accomplished by attending bartending schools, vo-tech schools, or academies. These schools often provide certification in bartending.

Experience/Skills/Personality Traits

Experience requirements, like training, vary. Most casino and casino hotel positions in this area prefer applicants to have prior bartending experience. Many casinos require individuals to be certified.

Bartenders should be friendly and well spoken with a neat and clean appearance. Customer service skills are mandatory. The ability to remember cocktail recipes as well as mix drinks quickly and accurately is essential.

Unions/Associations

Depending on the specific casino or casino hotel and its location, this may be a unionized position. In unionized situations in Las Vegas, for example, individuals may be members of the Bartenders & Beverage Local #165. In Atlantic City, Bartenders are represented by Local 54 of the Hotel Employees and Restaurants Employees International Union.

Individuals interested in pursuing a Bartender career can obtain additional information by contacting the National Restaurant Association (NRA), local bartending schools, or vo-tech schools offering courses and programs in bartending.

Tips for Entry

1. Bartending schools, especially those in areas hosting gaming and gaming hotels, often offer job placement possibilities.
2. Jobs may be advertised on casino job hotlines. These are frequently updated messages listing jobs available. Call each casino directly to get its job hotline phone number.
3. Stop by human resources departments to inquire about job openings.
4. Jobs are often advertised in the classified sections of newspapers in areas hosting gaming. Look under classifications such as "Bartenders," "Restaurant/Lounge Bartender," "Food and Beverage," "Front Of The House Jobs," and "Casino."

BARTENDER/BACK OF HOUSE

CAREER PROFILE

Duties: Mixing alcoholic and nonalcoholic beverages in service bars.

Alternative Titles(s): None

Salary Range: $18,000 to $31,000; may share tips.

Employment Prospects: Good

Best Geographical Location(s) for Position: Las Vegas, Reno, Laughlin, Lake Tahoe, Atlantic City, Biloxi, Baton Rouge, New Orleans, and Detroit offer most opportunities; other regions with land-based, riverboat, or Indian gaming facilities offer additional opportunities.

Prerequisites:

Education or Training—High school diploma or equivalent usually required; training at bartending school or vocational-technical school; see text.

Experience and Qualifications—Prior experience as bartender in club, bar, or restaurants; certification and state licensing may be required.

Special Skills and Personality Traits—Drink mixing skills; organization; good memory.

CAREER LADDER

```
┌──────────────────────────────────────┐
│  Front-of-the-House Bartender or     │
│   Assistant Beverage Manager         │
└──────────────────────────────────────┘

┌──────────────────────────────────────┐
│     Bartender/Back of the House      │
└──────────────────────────────────────┘

┌──────────────────────────────────────┐
│     Bartender in Other Setting       │
└──────────────────────────────────────┘
```

Position Description

Most casinos and casino hotels employ Back-of-the-House Bartenders. The back of the house is the section of the facility where employees work that is not accessible to the public.

Bartenders working in casinos and casino hotels work either in the front of the house or the back of the house. The Bartender in the front of the house has contact with patrons. The individual working in the back of the house usually has no contact with patrons, but deals with waiters and waitresses bringing drink orders.

Bartenders in the back of the house usually work at the service bar in the hotel showroom, restaurant, club, or banquet area. They are responsible for mixing and preparing alcoholic and nonalcoholic drinks in service bars. Bartenders fill drink orders for customers seated at tables in the hotel's showroom, restaurant, or lounge.

As with Front-of-the-House Bartenders, those working the back of the house must know how to mix a great variety

of drink recipes. They must have the ability to accomplish this quickly and accurately. Bartenders must also be able to mix drinks in the specific ways customers request.

Other functions of the Back-of-the-House Bartender may include:

- Informing beverage manager or assistant beverage manager of needed inventory of liquor, mixes, or other necessary bar supplies
- Monitoring liquor inventory

Salaries

Back-of-the-House Bartenders working in casinos and casino hotel facilities usually earn an hourly wage ranging from $8.50 to $16.00 or more and may earn $18,000 to $31,000 per year. They often also share tips with cocktail servers, waiters, and waitresses. This may be done with a tip pool. The reason Back-of-the-House Bartenders may receive higher hourly earnings than their counterparts in the front of the house is that the ratio of tips is often different because it is shared.

Factors affecting earnings include the geographic location, size, type, and prestige of the specific casino, hotel, restaurant, or showroom. Other variables include the experience of the individual.

In unionized settings, the union may negotiate minimum earnings.

Employment Prospects

Employment opportunities are good for qualified Bartenders. Individuals work in a variety of settings, including casino hotels, casino nightclubs, casino showrooms, and casino and casino hotel restaurants.

Las Vegas, Reno, Laughlin, Lake Tahoe, Atlantic City, Biloxi, Baton Rouge, New Orleans, and Detroit offer the greatest number of job possibilities. Other employment settings include casino hotels in other areas of Nevada, Mississippi, New York, Louisiana, Colorado, Connecticut, Illinois, Arizona, and California.

Other regions hosting Indian gaming and land-based or riverboat gaming facilities offer additional opportunities. New casinos and casino hotels are constantly under construction. More casinos and casino hotels are opening every year as areas legalize gambling.

Advancement Prospects

Bartenders working in the back of the house may advance their careers in a number of ways. Some individuals want to earn more tips or want the socializing aspect of the job and move to a position in the front of the house. Others may climb the career ladder by locating similar jobs in larger or more prestigious facilities.

Some Bartenders advance their careers by becoming assistant beverage managers. This career move often requires additional experience and/or training.

Education and Training

Training requirements vary from job to job. Most facilities require individuals to be high school graduates or have the equivalent. They may accept bartending experience in lieu of education.

Some employers require that individuals be certified, accomplished through formal training in bartending at appropriate schools or academies.

Experience/Skills/Personality Traits

Experience requirements, like training vary. Most casinos and casino hotels prefer applicants with bartending experience. As noted previously, many casinos also require that individuals be certified.

Back-of-the-House Bartenders need the ability to remember a variety of cocktail recipes, as well as the ability to mix drinks quickly and accurately.

Unions/Associations

Depending on the specific casino or casino hotel and its location, this may be a unionized position. In unionized situations in Las Vegas, for example, individuals may be members of the Bartenders & Beverage Local #165. In Atlantic City, Bartenders are represented by Local 54 of the Hotel Employees and Restaurant Employees International Union.

Individuals interested in pursuing careers as Bartenders can obtain additional career information by contacting the National Restaurant Association (NRA), local bartending schools, or vo-tech schools offering courses and programs in bartending.

Tips for Entry

1. Bartending schools, especially those in areas hosting gaming and gaming hotels, often offer job placement possibilities.
2. Jobs are often advertised in the classified sections of newspapers in areas hosting gaming. Look under classifications such as "Bartenders," "Restaurant/Lounge Bartender," "Food and Beverage," "Back-Of-The-House Jobs," and "Casinos."
3. Stop by the human resources departments of casinos and casino hotels to inquire about job openings.
4. These jobs are often advertised on casino job hotlines, frequently updated messages listing jobs available. Call each casino directly to get its job hotline phone number.

COCKTAIL SERVER

CAREER PROFILE

Duties: Serving cocktails and nonalcoholic drinks to patrons.

Alternative Titles(s): Cocktail Waitress; Cocktail Waiter

Salary Range: $10,000 to $17,000+ plus tips

Employment Prospects: Excellent

Best Geographical Locations(s) for Position: Las Vegas, Reno, Laughlin, Lake Tahoe, Atlantic City, Biloxi, Baton Rouge, New Orleans, and Detroit offer most opportunities; other regions with land-based, riverboat, or Indian gaming facilities offer additional opportunities.

Prerequisites:

Education or Training—High school diploma or equivalent required or preferred; see text.

Experience and Qualifications—Prior experience working in food or beverage industry helpful, but not always required; state licensing may be required.

Special Skills and Personality Traits—Customer service skills; interpersonal skills; friendly.

CAREER LADDER

```
┌─────────────────────────────────────┐
│   Cocktail Server in Larger, More   │
│  Prestigious Casino/Casino Hotel or │
│    Cocktail Server Coordinator      │
│          or Supervisor              │
└─────────────────────────────────────┘

┌─────────────────────────────────────┐
│          Cocktail Server            │
└─────────────────────────────────────┘

┌─────────────────────────────────────┐
│   Cocktail Server in Other Setting  │
│           or Entry Level            │
└─────────────────────────────────────┘
```

Position Description

The main function of Cocktail Servers working in casinos and casino hotels is to serve alcoholic and nonalcoholic beverages to patrons. They may work in areas such as the showroom or clubs where patrons are seated. Individuals may also work in the casino area where customers are gambling.

Cocktail Servers take patrons' drink orders. They write down the drink order for each table or patron. Individuals then bring the order to the bar for a bartender to fill. Drinks are put on a tray, and the Cocktail Server brings them back and serves them to the customers.

Cocktail Servers ask patrons if they want refills. They also compute the bill when patrons are finished.

Cocktail Servers working in large showrooms are often assigned areas to work. They must take drink orders and fill them in crowded rooms. These individuals, however, may have the opportunity to see shows as they are working.

Cocktail Servers working in the gaming area are responsible for serving individuals who are gambling, some of whom may be high roller customers.

Other functions of Cocktail Servers may include:

- Keeping tables clear of used drink glasses
- Providing clean ashtrays
- Taking payments from patrons

Salaries

Cocktail Servers working in casinos and casino hotels earn an hourly wage ranging from minimum wage to $9.00 or more plus tips. They share tips in a tip pool with bartenders and may earn between $10,000 and $17,000 annually.

Factors affecting earnings include the geographic location, size, type, and prestige of the specific casino, hotel, restaurant, showroom, or lounge.

In unionized settings, the union may negotiate minimum earnings.

Employment Prospects

Employment opportunities are excellent for Cocktail Servers interested in working in casinos and casino hotels. Individuals may work throughout the property, including the gaming floor, nightclubs, showrooms, restaurants, lounges, and bars.

Las Vegas, Reno, Laughlin, Lake Tahoe, Atlantic City, Biloxi, Baton Rouge, New Orleans, and Detroit offer the greatest number of job possibilities. Other employment settings include casino hotels in other areas of Nevada, Mississippi, New York, Louisiana, Colorado, Connecticut, Illinois, Arizona, and California.

Other regions hosting Indian gaming and land-based or riverboat gaming facilities offer additional opportunities. New casinos and casino hotels are constantly under construction. More casinos and casino hotels are opening every year as areas legalize gambling.

Advancement Prospects

Cocktail Servers may advance their careers in a number of ways. Those interested in staying Cocktail Servers may find similar positions in larger or more prestigious facilities, usually resulting in increased tip earning.

Others may climb the career ladder by being promoted to supervisory positions such as cocktail server coordinator or cocktail server supervisor. These career moves may require additional experience and/or training.

Education and Training

Many positions in casinos and casino hotels require individuals to be high school graduates or have the equivalent. They may take job experience in lieu of the educational requirement.

Training is not required for employment in this field. However, for those who are interested, these are academies and vocational technical schools offering training for Cocktail Servers.

Experience/Skills/Personality Traits

Prior experience as a Cocktail Server may or may not be required. Knowledge and understanding of beverage service is preferred.

Individuals should be personable people who enjoy interacting with others. They should be well spoken with a neat appearance. A good memory is helpful for remembering who ordered what drink.

Unions/Associations

Depending on the location and specific casino, this may or may not be a unionized position. For example, in unionized casinos and casino hotels in Las Vegas, Cocktail Servers might be members of the Culinary Workers Local #225. In Atlantic City, Cocktail Servers are represented by Local 54 Hotel Employees and Restaurant Employees International Union.

Individuals interested in pursuing a career as a Cocktail Server can obtain additional career information by contacting the National Restaurant Association (NRA) or vo-tech schools offering courses in this area.

Tips for Entry

1. Schools in areas with casinos and casino hotels offering programs for Cocktail Servers usually have job placement services.
2. Jobs are often advertised in the classified sections of newspapers in areas hosting gaming. Look under classifications such as "Cocktail Servers," "Restaurant/Lounge Cocktail Server," "Food and Beverage," "Casino Showroom," and "Casinos."
3. Check casino job hotlines, frequently updated messages listing jobs available. Call each casino directly to get its job hotline phone number.
4. Stop by the human resources departments of casinos and casino hotels to inquire about job openings.

CAREER OPPORTUNITIES IN CASINO AND CASINO HOTEL HUMAN RESOURCES DEPARTMENTS

DIRECTOR OF HUMAN RESOURCES

CAREER PROFILE

Duties: Directing operations of human resources department; supervising and monitoring department employees; developing and administering policies; recruitment; overseeing employee relations.

Alternative Titles(s): Human Resources Director, H.R. Director

Salary Range: $35,000 to $85,000+

Employment Prospects: Fair

Best Geographical Location(s) for Position: Las Vegas, Reno, Laughlin, Lake Tahoe, Atlantic City, Biloxi, Baton Rouge, New Orleans, and Detroit offer the greatest number of opportunities; other regions hosting Indian gaming and land-based or riverboat gaming facilities offer additional opportunities.

Prerequisites:

Education or Training—Bachelor's degree preferred; see text.

Experience and Qualifications—Five to 10 years' experience in human resources.

Special Skills and Personality Traits—Communication skills; interpersonal skills; management skills; knowledge of federal and state employment laws; writing skills; organized.

CAREER LADDER

```
┌─────────────────────────────────────┐
│ Director of Human Resources in Larger,│
│ More Prestigious Casino or V.P.       │
│ of Human Resources                    │
└─────────────────────────────────────┘

┌─────────────────────────────────────┐
│ Director of Human Resources          │
└─────────────────────────────────────┘

┌─────────────────────────────────────┐
│ Personnel Director or Director of Human│
│ Resources in Other Industry           │
└─────────────────────────────────────┘
```

Position Description

Casinos and casino hotels employ large numbers of people. The department that handles employment is called the human resources department. In some facilities it may also be referred to as the personnel or employment department. The individual in charge of overseeing the department is called the Director of Human Resources.

This is a very important position. At one time or another, everyone who is hired must go through the human resources department. The individual directs the operation of the department. The Director is responsible for planning, organizing, and controlling everything that happens within the human resources department.

The Director of Human Resources develops, writes, and administers policies. These policies have a direct impact on the employees who are hired and the manner in which they are expected to work. They also have a great impact on the atmosphere and the way the casino or casino hotel functions.

The Director of Human Resources oversees several departments headed by other managers. Each of these departments specializes in a personnel activity. These may include employment, compensation, benefits, training and development, employee relations, and employee licensing.

The Director is in charge of strategic planning as it relates to human resources. The individual may develop programs designed to enhance training, provide internship opportunities, and create career development within the property.

Other duties of the casino or casino hotel Director of Human Resources may include:

- Overseeing special projects and promotional events such as job fairs to stimulate recruitment of potential employees
- Building employee relations programs
- Developing and coordinating personnel programs

Salaries

The Director of Human Resources in casino and casino hotels earns between $35,000 and $85,000 or more annually. Factors affecting earnings include the geographic location, size, and prestige of the specific casino or casino hotel, as well as the education, experience, and responsibilities of the individual. Generally, those with the most education and experience working in larger facilities in the gambling capitals earn the highest salaries.

Employment Prospects

While employment opportunities are not plentiful, they are available for qualified individuals. Those seeking jobs in this area may have to relocate. As gaming moves into additional areas, there will be even more opportunities.

Las Vegas, Reno, Laughlin, Lake Tahoe, Atlantic City, Biloxi, Baton Rouge, New Orleans, and Detroit offer the greatest number of opportunities. Other regions hosting Indian gaming and land-based or riverboat gaming facilities offer additional opportunities.

Advancement Prospects

The Director of Human Resources may climb the career ladder in a number of ways. The individual may locate a similar position in a larger or more prestigious facility, resulting in increased responsibilities and earnings. He or she might also be promoted to a position such as vice president of human resources.

Education and Training

Generally, most casinos and casino hotels prefer that their Directors of Human Resources hold a minimum of a bachelor's degree. The best major is one earned in human resources. However, majors in other areas are often acceptable with work experience.

Additional courses, workshops, and seminars in human resources, labor relations, personnel, compensation, employee relations, gaming, and the hospitality industry are very helpful.

Experience/Skills/Personality Traits

Five to 10 years' experience working in human resources and related areas is usually necessary for this position. Individuals often have worked in the human resources department in various positions. Many have been personnel directors or the Director of Human Resources in areas other than gaming. Experience working in human resources in the hospitality industry, hotels, or casinos is preferred in most instances.

Human Resources Directors should have supervisory and administrative skills. Writing and communication skills are also necessary. Individuals must have total knowledge of all federal and state employment laws.

Unions/Associations

Those interested in learning more about careers in this field should contact the Society for Human Resources Management (SHRM).

Tips for Entry

1. Get your foot in the door of a casino hotel. Most promote from within. If you have experience in human resources, see what positions are open and then move up the career ladder.
2. Jobs may be advertised in the classified sections of newspapers in areas hosting gaming. Look under classifications such as "Casino/Hotel Director of Human Resources," "Casino Human Resources Director," "Human Resources," or "Casino/Hotel Opportunities."
3. Openings are often advertised on the Internet. They may be located via the home pages of casino hotels. They may also be found doing a search of "Casino" or "Casino Hotel Job Opportunities."

HUMAN RESOURCES CLERK

CAREER PROFILE

Duties: Greeting applicants; scheduling pre-employment job interviews; screening applicants; checking references; evaluating applicants.

Alternative Titles(s): Human Resources Interviewer; Human Resources Coordinator

Salary Range: $20,000 to $32,000+

Employment Prospects: Good

Best Geographical Location(s) for Position: Las Vegas, Reno, Laughlin, Lake Tahoe, Atlantic City, Biloxi, Baton Rouge, New Orleans, and Detroit offer the greatest number of opportunities; other regions hosting Indian gaming and land-based or riverboat gaming facilities offer additional opportunities.

Prerequisites:

Education or Training—College degree preferred; see text.

Experience and Qualifications—Experience in recruiting, counseling, or interviewing helpful.

Special Skills and Personality Traits—Interpersonal skills; customer service skills; communication skills; interviewing skills; objective.

CAREER LADDER

```
┌─────────────────────────────────┐
│  Human Resources Clerk in Larger, │
│  More Prestigious Casino or Casino │
│  Hotel or Other Human Resources   │
│  Department Position              │
└─────────────────────────────────┘

┌─────────────────────────────────┐
│     Human Resources Clerk        │
└─────────────────────────────────┘

┌─────────────────────────────────┐
│  Human Resources or Personnel    │
│  Clerk in Other Industry         │
└─────────────────────────────────┘
```

Position Description

Casinos and casino hotels employ a great many people. Prior to becoming employed, each individual must be recruited, screened, and interviewed. The Human Resources Clerk has an array of duties depending on the specific job. The individual, who may also be called an interviewer or human resources coordinator, is responsible for greeting applicants upon arrival at the casino hotel for the initial interview.

The Human Resources Clerk schedules pre-employment job interviews with applicants. He or she is responsible for conducting pre-interviews with potential employees to determine their qualifications, as well as for seeing if they match those of job openings. The individual ascertains the skills, personality traits, education, and training of applicants. In this manner, the Human Resources Clerk can determine what other jobs the potential employee may be qualified for.

The Human Resources Clerk must also screen applicants. There may be a number of people for each job opening. The Clerk weeds out those who do not have the proper qualifications or might not fit into the casino hotel environment.

Other duties of the casino or casino hotel Human Resources Clerk may include:

- Making sure potential employees can meet necessary licensing requirements
- Assisting applicants with applications
- Checking references
- Handling administrative functions

Salaries

Human Resources Clerks earn between $10.00 and $16.00 per hour or more or between $20,000 to $32,000 annually. Factors affecting earnings include the geographic location, size, and prestige of the specific facility, as well as the experience, education, and responsibilities of the individual. Generally, those with the most education and experience working in larger casino hotels in the gambling capitals earn the highest salaries.

Employment Prospects

Employment prospects for Human Resources Clerks aspiring to work in casinos and casino hotels are good.

Las Vegas, Reno, Laughlin, Lake Tahoe, Atlantic City, Biloxi, Baton Rouge, New Orleans, and Detroit offer the greatest number of opportunities. Other regions hosting Indian gaming and land-based or riverboat gaming facilities offer additional opportunities.

Advancement Prospects

Individuals may climb the career ladder in a number of ways. Some people obtain experience and locate similar positions in larger or more prestigious facilities. This results in increased responsibilities and earnings. Others who have the proper education and training may eventually be promoted to different positions in the human resources department.

Education and Training

Casinos and casino hotels prefer, but may not always require, Human Resources Clerks to have a college degree. Good majors include human resources, liberal arts, public relations, marketing, communications, and hotel management. Experience working in human resources may be accepted in lieu of education.

Courses, workshops, and seminars in interviewing, recruiting, vocational counseling, and human resources will be useful.

Experience/Skills/Personality Traits

Experience working in human resources, recruiting, or vocational counseling is usually required. Some individuals may have worked in public or private personnel offices or departments prior to being hired at the casino or casino hotel. Others may have moved up the ranks in the human resources department of the casino.

Knowledge and understanding of the gaming and hospitality industries is necessary. Individuals should be objective and articulate with good communication skills. The ability to make people comfortable is useful. Interviewing skills are essential.

Unions/Associations

Those interested in learning more about careers in human resources in casino hotels should contact the human resources departments of casinos and casino hotels.

Tips for Entry

1. Get your foot in the door of a casino or casino hotel human resources department. Start as a secretary or administrative assistant if there are no current openings as a Human Resources Clerk. Most casinos promote from within, and you can move up the career ladder.

2. Jobs may be advertised in the classified sections of newspapers in areas hosting gaming. Look under classifications such as "Casino/Gaming," "Human Resources," "Human Resources Clerk," "Interviewer," or "Casino/Gaming Opportunities."

3. Visit the human resources departments of casinos and inquire about job openings. You might also consider sending or faxing a résumé and a short cover letter.

4. Most casinos also have job hotlines, frequently updated messages listing jobs available. You can call each casino directly to obtain its job hotline phone number.

5. Openings are often advertised on the Internet. They may be located via the home pages of casino hotels. They may also be found by doing a search of casino, casino hotel, or gaming job opportunities.

TRAINING MANAGER

CAREER PROFILE

Duties: Developing and facilitating classes, seminars, workshops, and other training programs for casino and casino hotel employees.

Alternative Titles(s): Training and Development Manager

Salary Range: $23,000 to $52,000+

Employment Prospects: Fair

Best Geographical Location(s) for Position: Las Vegas, Reno, Laughlin, Lake Tahoe, Atlantic City, Biloxi, Baton Rouge, New Orleans, and Detroit offer the greatest number of opportunities; other regions hosting Indian gaming and land-based or riverboat gaming facilities offer additional opportunities.

Prerequisites:

Education or Training—Educational requirements vary; see text.

Experience and Qualifications—Human resources or training background.

Special Skills and Personality Traits—Communication skills; interpersonal skills; writing skills; ability to speak in public; creative; organized.

CAREER LADDER

```
┌─────────────────────────────────────┐
│   Training Manager in Larger, More   │
│      Prestigious Casino or           │
│      Human Resources Director        │
└─────────────────────────────────────┘

┌─────────────────────────────────────┐
│          Training Manager            │
└─────────────────────────────────────┘

┌─────────────────────────────────────┐
│        Training Coordinator          │
└─────────────────────────────────────┘
```

Position Description

Casinos and casino hotels employ large staffs. Training Managers are employed by these facilities to develop programs for employees in a multitude of areas and a variety of subjects, depending on the needs of the specific casino or casino hotel. In some facilities, the individual may be called the training and development manager.

The Training Manager has a great deal of responsibility. The individual facilitates all classes personally or works with a staff. Staff members may include a training coordinator and other trainers to handle this task.

The Training Manager works with the director of human resources, who writes and administers policies. These policies have a direct impact on the way employees are expected to work. The human resources director may, at his or her discretion, ask the Training Manager to develop programs designed to enhance training within the property, as well as to provide internship opportunities.

The Training Manager develops and facilitates orientation programs for new employees. During orientation, employees learn the policies of the casino as well as any governmental regulations that may affect their job performance. The orientation program also explains to staff members how they are expected to act on the job. The program also alerts employees to situations that are acceptable as well as unacceptable.

As customer service is mandatory to the success of casinos and casino hotels, it is essential that every employee treat every guest in a courteous and gracious manner. An important function of Training Managers in casinos is teaching employees about good customer service and how it should be provided to guests.

The Training Manager may offer classes in interactive management, also known as IM. These classes assist management in learning how to better communicate with their employees. Other subjects covered in this type of class often include acceptable methods for staff member discipline and how to speak to subordinates without coming across abruptly.

The Training Manager may design TIPS classes, which are offered to employees who work around alcohol, such as bartenders, cocktail servers, dealers, and floorperons. TIPS classes teach these employees how to deal properly with customers who are intoxicated—the signs to look for in those who have had enough alcohol and how to stop serving patrons without causing a scene.

To those working in the casino area, Training Managers offer classes covering governmental regulations. For example, employees may need to learn how to fill in currency transaction reports (CTR). These are needed whenever customers win over $10,000 in a 24-hour period.

Other duties of the casino or casino hotel Training Manager may include:

- Creating and directing programs to teach department directors, managers, and supervisors methods of conducting training within their departments
- Teaching department directors, managers, and supervisors proper procedures for interview techniques and employment reviews
- Training employees in team building so that managers, supervisors, and subordinates all work together

Salaries

Training Managers in casinos and casino hotels earn between $23,000 and $52,000 or more annually. Factors affecting earnings include the geographic location, size, and prestige of the specific casino or casino hotel, as well as the education, experience, and responsibilities of the individual. Generally, those with the most education and experience working in larger facilities earn the highest salaries.

Employment Prospects

Employment prospects for Training Managers aspiring to work in casinos or casino hotels are fair. Most employment opportunities for Training Managers are located in areas hosting a large number of casinos. Las Vegas, Reno, Laughlin, Lake Tahoe, Atlantic City, Biloxi, Baton Rouge, New Orleans, and Detroit offer the greatest number of opportunities. Other regions hosting Indian gaming and land-based or riverboat gaming facilities offer additional opportunities.

As gaming moves into additional areas, there will be even more jobs.

Advancement Prospects

Training Managers working in casinos and casino hotels may advance their careers by locating similar positions in larger or more prestigious facilities. Individuals might also climb the career ladder by obtaining additional experience and training and becoming director of human resources.

Education and Training

Educational requirements vary from casino to casino for Training Managers. Some facilities require or prefer individuals to hold a bachelor's degree in human resources, communications, the hospitality industry, or a related field. Others may accept those with a high school diploma with a background and experience in training, human resources, and/or the hospitality industry.

Experience/Skills/Personality Traits

As noted, experience in human resources, training, and the hospitality industry are needed. Training Managers usually have worked as training coordinators or trainers prior to their appointment.

This is a highly visible position. Almost everyone in the casino knows the Training Manager. The individual must have excellent interpersonal and employee relations skills. Training Managers must also have both verbal and written communication skills. The ability to speak effectively in front of groups of people is essential to this position.

Unions/Associations

Those interested in learning more about careers in this field should contact the American Society of Training Developers (ASTD).

Tips For Entry

1. Become either an active or affiliate member of ASTD. This may give you the edge over another applicant with the same qualifications.
2. Get your foot in the door of a casino hotel. Most promote from within. If you have experience in training, see if a position exists as a trainer. Get experience and climb the career ladder.
3. Openings are often advertised on the Internet. They may be located via the home pages of casino hotels. They may also be found doing a search of casino or casino hotel job opportunities.
4. Jobs may be advertised in the classified sections of newspapers in areas hosting gaming. Look under classifications such as "Casino/Hotel Director Training Manager," "Training and Development Manager," "Casino Training and Development Manager," "Casino/Hotel Opportunities," or "Human Resources."
5. You may be asked to conduct an impromptu training presentation as part of your interview process. Develop a sample program ahead of time and rehearse it before the interview.

COMPENSATION AND BENEFITS MANAGER

Duties: Overseeing and coordinating employee wage, salary, and benefits programs in casino or casino hotel; supervising compensation and benefits office employees.

Alternative Titles(s): Benefits Manager; Compensation Manager

Salary Range: $30,000 to $53,000+

Employment Prospects: Fair

Best Geographical Location(s) for Position: Las Vegas, Reno, Laughlin, Lake Tahoe, Atlantic City, Biloxi, Baton Rouge, New Orleans, and Detroit offer the greatest number of opportunities; other regions hosting Indian gaming and land-based or riverboat gaming facilities offer additional opportunities.

Prerequisites:

Education or Training—Educational requirements vary; see text.

Experience and Qualifications—Experience in human resources, benefits, or labor relations.

Special Skills and Personality Traits—Communication skills; interpersonal skills; computer skills; patience; familiarity with and understanding of compensation and benefits programs in the industry.

```
┌─────────────────────────────────────────┐
│ Compensation and Benefits Manager in     │
│ Larger, More Prestigious Casino or        │
│ Director of Compensation and Benefits     │
└─────────────────────────────────────────┘

┌─────────────────────────────────────────┐
│ Compensation and Benefits Manager         │
└─────────────────────────────────────────┘

┌─────────────────────────────────────────┐
│ Benefits Coordinator                       │
└─────────────────────────────────────────┘
```

Position Description

Casinos, like many other large businesses, have many employees. In most casinos and casino hotels, employees receive a variety of benefits in addition to their compensation. The person in charge of overseeing and directing the various benefit plans and compensation packages of employees is called the Compensation and Benefits Manager. The individual has a variety of responsibilities.

The Compensation and Benefits Manager is in charge of overseeing the employees in the benefits and compensation office. These may include a benefits coordinator who works under the Compensation and Benefits Manager administering the health insurance and other benefit plans, compensation and benefits analysts, and benefit clerks.

The Compensation and Benefits Manager tracks employee evaluations often to determine employee raises.

The Compensation and Benefits Manager may also determine raise amounts by the length of time employees are in service, the amount of training, grade levels, or promotions. Raise amounts usually must be placed within the policy set by management.

The Compensation and Benefits Manager is usually one of the checkpoints an employee must go through when hired by a casino or casino hotel. The Manager is in charge of discussing the type of compensation the employee will receive for the job. Depending on the specific job, the employee may be paid hourly or receive a set weekly salary. The Compensation and Benefits Manager may also explain to the employee whether he or she will be paid on a weekly or bi-weekly basis.

At this time, the Compensation and Benefits Manager also explains the benefits that are offered as part of the job. These may include, but are not limited to, health insurance, life insurance, pension plans, profit sharing, child care, educational reimbursement, paid holidays, and vacations.

The Compensation and Benefits Manager is responsible for answering any questions regarding compensation or benefits. The individual may refer employees to others working in the department for answers or assistance.

The Compensation and Benefits Manager gathers information regarding salaries, wages, and benefits offered within the industry, as well as in the area in which the casino or casino hotel is located. The individual uses this information to analyze the casino's programs and make recommendations for new programs.

Other duties of the casino or casino or casino hotel Compensation and Benefits Manager may include:

• Ensuring that employees meets the proper employment requirements
• Making sure accurate files are maintained on all employees, as well as the benefits and compensation they receive

Salaries

The Compensation and Benefits Manager in a casino or casino hotel earns between $30,000 and $53,000 or more annually. Factors affecting earnings include the geographic location, size, and prestige of the specific casino or casino hotel, as well as the education, experience, and responsibilities of the individual.

Individuals with a great deal of experience working with large numbers of employees in casino hotels earn the highest salaries.

Employment Prospects

Most casinos and casino hotels have Compensation and Benefits Managers. The greatest number of employment opportunities exist in areas hosting gaming with large numbers of casinos.

Las Vegas, Reno, Laughlin, Lake Tahoe, Atlantic City, Biloxi, Baton Rouge, New Orleans, and Detroit offer the greatest number of opportunities. Other regions hosting Indian gaming and land-based or riverboat gaming facilities offer additional opportunities. As gaming moves into additional areas, there will be even more jobs available.

Advancement Prospects

Casino and casino hotel Compensation and Benefits Managers may take a number of paths toward career advancement. Individuals may be promoted to the job of director of compensation and benefits in larger facilities where the position exists. Others may locate similar positions in larger facilities, resulting in increased responsibilities and earnings.

Compensation and Benefits Managers with experience in additional areas of human resources may also advance to positions such as the assistant director of human resources or, in some facilities, the director of the department.

Education and Training

Educational requirements vary for Compensation and Benefits Managers. College is often required or preferred with a degree in human resources, personnel management, labor relations, compensation and benefits, business management, or economics.

For those who have moved up the ranks in the compensation and benefits area, a high school diploma or its equivalent and experience may be acceptable.

Experience/Skills/Personality Traits

Experience in human resources, personnel administration, labor relations, insurance administration, benefits, or compensation is necessary. As noted previously, some individuals have obtained experience by moving up the ranks. They began as benefit clerks or had prior experience as benefits coordinators.

Individuals must have knowledge and understanding of insurance programs, retirement plans, labor relations, and wage and benefit trends. Compensation and Benefit Managers should have excellent communication and interpersonal skills. Management, administrative, and supervisory skills are also needed.

Unions/Associations

Those interested in learning more about careers in this field should contact the International Foundation of Employee Benefit Plans (IFEBP) and the American Compensation Association (ACA).

Tips for Entry

1. Jobs may be advertised in the classified sections of newspapers in areas hosting gaming. Look under classifications such as "Casino/Hotel Opportunities," "Casino/Gaming," "Benefits and Compensation," or "Benefits and Compensation Manager."
2. Look for jobs in casinos and casino hotels on the Internet. They may be located via the home pages of casino hotels. They may also be found doing a search of casino or casino hotel job opportunities.
3. Visit the human resources departments of casinos and casino hotels to see what employment opportunities are available.
4. Fax or send your résumé to human resources departments.
5. Casinos often promote from within. Get your foot in the door and move up the ranks.

BENEFITS COORDINATOR

CAREER PROFILE

Duties: Handling casino's or casino hotel's employee benefits program; administering health insurance and pension plans; signing up employees to proper plans.

Alternative Titles(s): None

Salary Range: $24,000 to $35,000+

Employment Prospects: Fair

Best Geographical Location(s) for Position: Las Vegas, Reno, Laughlin, Lake Tahoe, Atlantic City, Biloxi, Baton Rouge, New Orleans, and Detroit offer the greatest number of opportunities; other regions hosting Indian gaming and land-based or riverboat gaming facilities offer additional opportunities.

Prerequisites:

Education or Training—High school diploma or equivalent and on-the-job training; see text.

Experience and Qualifications—Experience working in human resources department preferred.

Special Skills and Personality Traits—Communication skills; interpersonal skills; computer skills; patience; familiarity and understanding of insurance programs and pension plans.

CAREER LADDER

```
┌─────────────────────────────────────┐
│  Compensation and Benefits Manager   │
└─────────────────────────────────────┘

┌─────────────────────────────────────┐
│         Benefits Coordinator          │
└─────────────────────────────────────┘

┌─────────────────────────────────────┐
│            Benefits Clerk             │
└─────────────────────────────────────┘
```

Position Description

Employees working in casinos and casino hotels receive a variety of benefits. While these vary in each facility, they often include health insurance, life insurance, pension plans, profit sharing, child care, educational reimbursement, paid holidays, and vacations.

The Benefits Coordinator works in the casino's employee benefits office. This is usually a subdivision of the human resources department. In some facilities, the Benefits Coordinator also handles the duties of the compensation coordinator or manager.

Great benefits are a major advantage to employees working in casinos. The Benefits Coordinator is responsible for making sure employees not only know what is offered and what they are entitled to, but understand how to take advantage of these benefits as well.

One of the major benefits of working in most casinos is health insurance. This may include a variety of plans, including major medical, dental, and vision. The Benefits Coordinator is in charge of explaining what each plan entails and helping employees determine which plan is best for them. The Benefits Coordinator administers the health insurance plan on behalf of the casino and its employees.

The individual signs up employees and assists them in participating in applicable plans. The Coordinator is also responsible for making insurance forms available and helping employees fill them in when necessary. As part of this function, the Benefits Coordinator acts as a liaison between the insurance company and the casino to ensure that employees receive reimbursement or other benefits.

The Benefits Coordinator is responsible for answering any questions from employees regarding their benefits. Individuals may have questions about their health insurance, pension plan, or other benefits provided to them.

The Benefits Coordinator gathers necessary information from employees for the records. The individual must maintain accurate files on all employees and the benefits they receive.

Other duties of the casino or casino hotel Benefits Coordinator may include:

- Administering pension and other retirement plans
- Explaining educational reimbursement policies
- Handling compensation responsibilities
- Making sure payments are made in a timely fashion to correct parties

Salaries

The Benefits Coordinator in a casino or casino hotel earns between $24,000 and $35,000 or more annually. Factors affecting earnings include the geographic location, size, and prestige of the specific casino or casino hotel, as well as the education, experience, and responsibilities of the individual.

Experienced individuals handling the benefits of large numbers of employees earn the highest salaries. Earnings will also be at the higher end of the scale in facilities where the benefits coordinator also handles compensation responsibilities.

Employment Prospects

Employment prospects are fair for people seeking this position. Almost every casino and casino hotel has a Benefits Coordinator or someone who handles the responsibilities. The greatest number of employment opportunities for these individuals exist in areas hosting gaming with large numbers of casinos.

Las Vegas, Reno, Laughlin, Lake Tahoe, Atlantic City, Biloxi, Baton Rouge, New Orleans, and Detroit offer the greatest number of opportunities. Other regions hosting Indian gaming and land-based or riverboat gaming facilities offer additional opportunities.

As gaming moves into additional areas, there will be even more jobs available.

Advancement Prospects

There are a number of advancement paths for Benefits Coordinators. Some individuals obtain experience and locate similar positions in larger facilities. Others may be promoted to benefits and compensation managers or directors.

Benefits Coordinators aspiring to move out of the benefits area, but still desiring to work in human resources, may become a human resources generalist or a supervisor in other areas of the human resources department.

Education and Training

Educational requirements vary for Benefits Coordinators. A high school diploma or its equivalent is usually required, along with on-the-job training.

A bachelor's degree may be preferred and is helpful in climbing the career ladder. Colleges and universities offer programs leading to degrees in compensation and benefits, personnel, and human resources.

Any courses, workshops, and seminars completed in insurance, profit sharing, or pension plan administration will be helpful.

Experience/Skills/Personality Traits

Experience in human resources, personnel administration, insurance administration, benefits, or compensation is necessary. Many individuals obtain experience by working as a benefits clerk in the compensation and benefits office.

Understanding of insurance programs and pension plans is helpful. Benefits Coordinators need excellent communication and interpersonal skills. Patience is also essential so as to be able to explain hard-to-understand plans and benefits.

Unions/Associations

Those interested in learning more about careers in this field should contact the International Foundation of Employee Benefit Plans (IFEBP) and the American Compensation Association (ACA).

Tips for Entry

1. Most casinos promote from within. If you are interested in this career and don't have experience, see if positions are open as benefits clerks. Learn what you can and climb the career ladder.
2. Jobs may be advertised in the classified sections of newspapers in areas hosting gaming. Look under classifications such as "Casino/Hotel Opportunities," "Casino/Gaming," "Benefits Coordinator," or "Benefits Department."
3. Openings are often advertised on the Internet. They may be located via the home pages of casino hotels. They may also be found doing a search of casino or casino hotel job opportunities.
4. Stop by the human resources departments of casinos and casino hotels to see what employment opportunities are available.
5. Fax or send your résumé to the human resources departments.

EMPLOYEE RELATIONS MANAGER

CAREER PROFILE

Duties: Creating and planning employee events and functions; developing and editing employee publications; handling employee grievances.

Alternative Titles(s): None

Salary Range: $30,000 to $50,000+

Employment Prospects: Fair

Best Geographical Location(s) for Position: Las Vegas, Reno, Laughlin, Lake Tahoe, Atlantic City, Biloxi, Baton Rouge, New Orleans, and Detroit offer the greatest number of opportunities; other regions hosting Indian gaming and land-based or riverboat gaming facilities offer additional opportunities.

Prerequisites:

Education or Training—Bachelor's degree; see text.

Experience and Qualifications—Experience in human resources.

Special Skills and Personality Traits—Communication skills; organization; detail-oriented; interpersonal skills; knowledge of negotiation and arbitration.

CAREER LADDER

```
┌─────────────────────────────────────┐
│  Employee Relations Manager in      │
│  Larger, More Prestigious Casino or │
│  Casino Hotel or Personnel or       │
│  Human Resources Director           │
└─────────────────────────────────────┘

┌─────────────────────────────────────┐
│  Employee Relations Manager         │
└─────────────────────────────────────┘

┌─────────────────────────────────────┐
│  Human Resources Clerk or Other     │
│  Position in Human Resources        │
└─────────────────────────────────────┘
```

Position Description

Casinos and casino hotels need a wide variety of employees in order to run efficiently. Some casinos have over 1,000 employees; larger ones may employ 2,500 people or more. The Employee Relations Manager usually works in the human resources department. The individual makes sure employees are kept abreast of what's happening within the casino. The Employee Relations Manager also helps keep employees satisfied with their jobs.

The Employee Relations Manager acts as a liaison between management and employees, bringing employee problems to the attention of management, and, conversely, explaining management policies to employees. In order to do this, the individual must meet with management to learn about new policies or changes in existing ones.

The Employee Relations Manager is responsible for handling staff communications. This may include developing and writing letters, memos, flyers, posters, and employee newsletters. In some settings, the Manager hands some of these duties on to an assistant. In this event, the individual is responsible for editing and checking the written communications.

Many feel that one of the plusses of working in a casino environment is that it is somewhat like an extended family. The Employee Relations Manager is responsible for the development and implementation of employee events. These activities not only boost morale, but help everyone relax while getting to know one another on a different basis. The Employee Relations Manager may develop functions such as picnics, parties, dances, and basketball or softball games.

The Employee Relations Manager may be responsible for working with union shop stewards. The individual must attend their meetings and relay information to management. In some cases, he or she works with other management people negotiating union requests.

Other duties of the Employee Relations Manager working in a casino or casino hotel may include:

- Conducting training seminars and workshops for employees
- Investigating and answering employee grievances
- Negotiating with employees regarding grievances
- Arranging events to recognize casino employees for long or outstanding service
- Supervising others in the department

Salaries

Employee Relations Managers earn salaries ranging from $30,000 to $50,000 annually. Factors affecting earnings include the geographic location, size, and prestige of the specific casino or casino hotel, as well as the education, experience, and responsibilities of the individual. Generally, those working in larger facilities who are responsible for greater numbers of employees earn higher salaries.

Employment Prospects

Employment prospects for Employee Relations Managers are fair. They generally can be found in mid-sized and larger facilities. In smaller properties, the director of human resources or personnel director may handle the functions of the Employee Relations Manager. Individuals usually work normal business hours. They may be required to work overtime or on weekends when emergencies arise, during negotiations, or when employee events are scheduled.

Advancement Prospects

Employee Relations Managers may advance their careers by locating similar positions in larger casinos. Individuals climb the career ladder by being promoted to human resources or personnel director. There are also Employee Relations Managers who go into public relations as well.

Education and Training

A bachelor's degree is usually required to become an Employee Relations Manager in a casino or casino hotel. Work experience may sometimes be accepted in lieu of formal education.

A broad educational background with courses in group dynamics, negotiation, arbitration, labor relations, human resources, personnel, public relations, marketing, communications, journalism, English, business, writing, and psychology will be useful.

Experience/Skills/Personality Traits

Individuals interested in becoming Employee Relations Managers should have experience in the human resources field.

Employee Relations Managers should be personable people who genuinely like others. Individuals need good communication skills with the ability to speak articulately to groups of people. They must be able to write clearly and accurately.

Employee Relations Managers additionally must have good understanding of the attitudes of both employees and those in management. General knowledge of group dynamics, negotiations, and arbitration is also needed.

Unions/Associations

Those interested in learning more about careers as Employee Relations Managers may obtain information from the Society for Human Resources Management (SHRM) or the Public Relations Society of America (PRSA), as well as the human resources departments in casinos and casino hotels.

Tips for Entry

1. Visit the human resources departments of casinos and inquire about job openings. Send or fax a résumé and a short cover letter.
2. Many casinos have job hotline numbers. These offer current job opportunities available at the facility.
3. Openings are often advertised on the Internet. They may be located via the home pages of casino hotels. They may also be found by doing a search of "Casino," "Casino Hotel," or "Gaming Job Opportunities."
4. Jobs may be advertised in the classified sections of newspapers in areas hosting gaming. Look under classifications such as "Casino/Gaming Opportunities," "Employee Relations Manager," "Employee Relations," or "Casinos/Casino Hotels."

CASINO OR CASINO HOTEL PAYROLL CLERK

CAREER PROFILE

Duties: Ensuring that employees' paychecks are correct; calculating earnings and deductions; computing pay; maintaining backup files; researching payroll records.

Alternative Titles(s): Payroll Specialist

Salary Range: $12,000 to $30,000+

Employment Prospects: Good

Best Geographical Location(s) for Position: Las Vegas, Reno, Laughlin, Lake Tahoe, Atlantic City, Biloxi, Baton Rouge, New Orleans, and Detroit offer the greatest number of opportunities; other regions hosting Indian gaming and land-based or riverboat gaming facilities offer additional opportunities.

Prerequisites:

Education or Training—High school diploma or equivalent.

Experience and Qualifications—Accounting or payroll background preferred, but not always required.

Special Skills and Personality Traits—Detail-oriented; organized; ability to work accurately with numbers; data-entry skills.

CAREER LADDER

```
┌─────────────────────────────────┐
│      Payroll Supervisor         │
└─────────────────────────────────┘

┌─────────────────────────────────┐
│        Payroll Clerk            │
└─────────────────────────────────┘

┌─────────────────────────────────┐
│  Entry Level or Payroll Clerk in │
│        Other Industry           │
└─────────────────────────────────┘
```

Position Description

Casinos and casino hotels employ large numbers of staff members. Payroll Clerks, also called payroll specialists, help ensure that employees' paychecks are correct. Specific responsibilities depend on the specific facility and the manner in which payroll is handled. Generally, Payroll Clerks are responsible for inputting data regarding employees' pay, as well as maintaining and researching these records.

Payroll Clerks are responsible for calculating the earnings of employees, including regular and overtime hours. Individuals must also calculate deductions such as income tax withholdings, social security, credit union payments, and insurance. This task may be accomplished by computers.

Hourly employees of the casino and casino hotel punch time cards. At the end of the pay period, Payroll Clerks are responsible for screening time cards to make sure there are no calculating, coding, or other types of errors. Pay is then computed by subtracting allotments such as retirement, federal and state taxes, and insurance from employees' gross earnings. When a computer performs these calculations, it alerts the Payroll Clerk to problems or errors in data. The individual can then adjust the errors.

Payroll Clerks enter the correct data on checks, check stubs, and master payroll sheets, or more commonly on forms for computer preparation of checks. Individuals are also expected to prepare and distribute pay envelopes.

Payroll Clerks correct any problems in employees' checks or explain calculations. These may include adjusting monetary errors or incorrect amounts of vacation time.

Other responsibilities of Payroll Clerks working at casinos and casino hotels may include:

- Typing, checking, and filing wage information forms
- Keeping wage and fringe benefit information on employees
- Maintaining records of employee sick leave pay and non-taxable wages
- Performing additional clerical tasks

Salaries

Payroll Clerks working at casinos and casino hotels are paid on an hourly basis. Earnings range from $6.00 to $15.00 per hour or more or up to $12,000 to $30,000 annually. Factors affecting earnings include the experience, level of training, and responsibilities of the individual, as well as the geographic location, size, and prestige of the specific casino or casino hotel.

Employment Prospects

Employment prospect are good for Payroll Clerks in casinos and casino hotels. All casinos and casino hotels employ Payroll Clerks. This is generally a day-shift position. Individuals can find employment on either a full-time or part-time basis.

Las Vegas, Reno, Laughlin, Lake Tahoe, Atlantic City, Biloxi, Baton Rouge, New Orleans, and Detroit offer the greatest number of opportunities. Other regions hosting Indian gaming and land-based or riverboat gaming facilities offer additional opportunities.

Advancement Prospects

Payroll Clerks can advance their careers by obtaining experience and advancing to positions such as payroll supervisors.

Education and Training

A high school diploma or the equivalent is the minimum required for this position in most casinos and casino hotels. While no specific training may be necessary, individuals must have the ability to use adding machines, calculators, computers, and word processors. Knowledge of office machinery use may be self-taught or learned in high school or business courses in vo-tech schools, community colleges, or adult education classes. Some casinos and casino hotels also offer on-the-job training.

Experience/Skills/Personality Traits

In some facilities Payroll Clerk may be an entry-level job, while in others it may require a background in accounting or payroll.

Payroll Clerks must be detail-oriented, organized individuals who enjoy working with numbers. Accuracy as well as the ability to find and correct math errors is essential. Data-entry skills are mandatory.

Unions/Associations

Those interested in learning more about careers in this area should contact the human resources departments of casinos and casino hotels.

Tips for Entry

1. Jobs are often advertised in the classified sections of newspapers in areas hosting gaming. Look under classifications such as "Payroll Clerk," "Payroll Specialist," "Casinos," "Casino Hotels," "Payroll," or "Casino Opportunities."
2. Visit the human resources departments of casino and casino hotels to see if there are any job openings in this area.
3. Get experience working in the payroll department in any industry, even for a short time. This will make you more marketable when seeking a job in casinos.
4. Most casinos have job hotlines. These are frequently updated messages listing jobs available. You can call each casino directly to get its job hotline phone number.

CAREER OPPORTUNITIES
IN CASINO HOTEL
HEALTH CLUBS AND SPAS

HEALTH CLUB MANAGER

CAREER PROFILE

Duties: Hiring, training, supervising, and coordinating activities of staff; attending to day-to-day activities of health club.

Alternative Titles(s): Spa Manager

Salary Range: $20,000 to $45,000+

Employment Prospects: Fair

Best Geographical Location(s) for Position: Las Vegas, Reno, Laughlin, Lake Tahoe, Atlantic City, Biloxi, Baton Rouge, New Orleans, and Detroit offer the greatest number of opportunities; other regions hosting Indian gaming and land-based or riverboat gaming facilities offer additional opportunities.

Prerequisites:

Education or Training—Educational requirements vary; see text.

Experience and Qualifications—Experience in health club or spa management or administration preferred; knowledge of exercise and exercise equipment; certification may be required.

Special Skills and Personality Traits—Management skills; supervisory skills; detail-oriented; personable; communication skills; organized; physically fit; energetic.

CAREER LADDER

```
┌─────────────────────────────────┐
│   Health Club Manager in Larger, │
│   More Prestigious Casino Hotel  │
└─────────────────────────────────┘

┌─────────────────────────────────┐
│       Health Club Manager        │
└─────────────────────────────────┘

┌─────────────────────────────────┐
│   Assistant Health Club Manager  │
└─────────────────────────────────┘
```

Position Description

Many casino hotels host health clubs and spas as amenities for guests. Health Club Managers in casino hotels have a number of responsibilities. First and foremost, they attend to the day-to-day activities of the health club.

Most health club guests in casino hotels are transient. Many guests, however, return to the same hotel to gamble on a regular basis and therefore may become members of the hotel's health club as well. Hotels may also sell health club memberships to people who live in the local area. Entrance requirements to hotel health clubs vary. In some, individuals must just be a guest of the hotel. In others, the Health Club Manager sells memberships or charges entrance fees to patrons. The individual is responsible for keeping records of the club's clientele and any payments received.

The Health Club Manager may also be in charge of developing promotions to bring people into the club. The individual works on this responsibility with the hotel's advertising and marketing departments.

The Manager is expected to meet guests and make sure they are pleased with the club's services. The individual shows them around and tells them what services are available. Being accessible to patrons is essential to this type of job.

Depending on the facility, health clubs offer pools, saunas, Jacuzzis, whirlpools, exercise classes, and a variety of exercise equipment. Some health clubs offer an array of other amenities, including facials and massages.

The Health Club Manager is an administrative position. The individual is in charge of hiring and firing personnel within the facility. The Manager also trains and supervises employees. Other staff members may include assistant managers, receptionists, exercise directors, aerobic instructors, lifeguards, masseurs, masseuses, and pool attendants. The Manager is in charge of assigning and scheduling workers to meet the needs of guests.

The Health Club Manager must be able to fully explain the operation and purpose of equipment within the club to both employees and clientele.

The Manager notifies health care personnel and hotel administration regarding any accidents within the club. He or she is also responsible for making sure reports are written and filed regarding accidents or mishaps.

The Health Club Manager is responsible for making sure that the club facility is kept in good order and run in a safe and efficient manner. If equipment breaks down, the individual must make sure it is either fixed or replaced. Facilities must be kept immaculate.

Other responsibilities of the Health Club Manager may include:

- Running exercise classes
- Filling in for staff members
- Handling customer complaints
- Solving any problems

Salaries

Earnings for Health Club Managers in casino hotels range from $20,000 to $45,000 or more depending on a number of variables, including the specific facility, type, size, and geographic location. Other factors affecting earnings include the responsibilities, training, and experience of the individual.

Employment Prospects

Health clubs and spas are not found in every casino hotel. They are, however, usually located in most of the larger or more prestigious casino hotels in Las Vegas, Reno, Laughlin, Lake Tahoe, and Atlantic City. Other opportunities may be located in Biloxi, Baton Rouge, New Orleans, and Detroit, as well as in other regions hosting Indian gaming and land-based or riverboat gaming facilities.

Advancement Prospects

Health Club Managers can advance their careers by locating similar positions in larger or more prestigious facilities. In some cases, individuals find jobs in health clubs outside of the hospitality industry. Some Health Club Managers climb the career ladder by opening up their own health club facility.

Education and Training

Education and training requirements vary depending on the specific job. Some facilities require their Managers to be college graduates. A degree in business, physical education, or a related field is preferred.

Hotels may hire individuals without college, however, if they possess work experience.

Experience/Skills/Personality Traits

Individuals should have some background in management or administration. Prior work in a health club or spa is usually preferred.

Health Club Managers deal with a variety of people and circumstances on different levels. They should be organized and detail-oriented. Administrative, management, and supervisory skills are necessary. Problem-solving skills are mandatory.

Health Club Managers should be friendly people who enjoy working with others.

Unions/Associations

Additional career information for those aspiring to become Health Club Managers can be obtained by contacting the Aerobics Center or the Association For Fitness In Business (AFFIB).

Tips for Entry

1. Get a job working in a local health club in any capacity. This will look good on your résumé and give you experience working in health clubs.
2. Positions in this field are advertised in the newspaper classified section in areas hosting casinos. Look under the headings of "Health Club Manager," "Casino Hotels," "Cruise Ships Jobs," Health Clubs," or "Hotel Spa."
3. Send your résumé to casino hotel human resources departments.
4. Casino job hotlines may advertise job openings in this area. These are frequently updated messages listing jobs available. You can call each casino directly to get its job hotline phone number.
5. Check out the home pages of casino hotels on the Internet. Many have employment opportunities listed on their site.

HEALTH CLUB INSTRUCTOR

CAREER PROFILE

Duties: Assisting in supervising health club guests; leading exercise and aerobics classes; instructing individuals in use of exercise equipment.

Alternative Titles(s): Exercise Instructor; Aerobic Instructor

Salary Range: $15,000 to $30,000+

Employment Prospects: Good

Best Geographical Location(s) for Position: Las Vegas, Reno, Laughlin, Lake Tahoe, Atlantic City, Biloxi, Baton Rouge, New Orleans, and Detroit offer the greatest number of opportunities; other regions hosting Indian gaming and land-based or riverboat gaming facilities offer additional opportunities.

Prerequisites:

Education or Training—Educational requirements vary; see text.

Experience and Qualifications—Knowledge of exercise and exercise equipment; certification may be required; see text.

Special Skills and Personality Traits—Physically fit; energetic; personable; communication skills.

CAREER LADDER

```
┌─────────────────────────────────────┐
│ Health Club Instructor in Larger,   │
│ More Prestigious Casino Hotel or    │
│ Assistant Health Club Manager       │
└─────────────────────────────────────┘

┌─────────────────────────────────────┐
│      Health Club Instructor         │
└─────────────────────────────────────┘

┌─────────────────────────────────────┐
│ Health Club or Exercise Instructor in│
│         Different Setting            │
└─────────────────────────────────────┘
```

Position Description

Casino hotels usually host health clubs and spas that offer guests pools, saunas, whirlpools, massages, beauty treatments, exercise classes, and an array of exercise equipment. They may also have employees to pamper guests, including hairstylists, manicurists, skin care specialists, and makeup artists.

The casino hotel Health Club Instructor has a wide array of responsibilities depending on the structure of the specific facility. The individual assists in the supervision of health club guests. When guests visit, Health Club Instructors welcome them, showing them the facilities and what services are offered.

Instructors may also be required to lead exercise classes. Individuals must understand how all the exercise equipment in the facility work and have the ability to illustrate to guests how to use them properly.

Instructors help the assistant manager and manager of the club when needed. They are responsible for reporting accidents to them, as well as for making out accident reports.

The Health Club Instructor may be required to perform minor first aid on guests. In emergencies, if qualified, individuals may have to perform CPR on guests in need. While Instructors are not usually hired to act as pool lifeguards, they may, on occasion, pinch hit.

Other responsibilities of the casino hotel Health Club Instructor may include:

- Reporting malfunctioning equipment to management
- Keeping club area neat and clean
- Explaining benefits of exercise equipment

Salaries

Casino hotel Health Club Instructors are usually paid an hourly wage. This can range from $7.00 to $15.00 or more per hour or about $15,000 to $30,000 annually. Factors affecting earnings include the experience, training, and responsibilities of the individual, as well as the geographic location, size, and prestige of the specific casino hotel.

Employment Prospects

Employment prospects for casino hotel Health Club Instructors are good. The greatest number of opportunities are located in large casino hotels hosting spas and health clubs. Las Vegas, Reno, Laughlin, Lake Tahoe, Atlantic City, Biloxi, Baton Rouge, New Orleans, and Detroit offer most opportunities. Other regions hosting Indian gaming and land-based or riverboat gaming facilities offer additional prospects.

Advancement Prospects

There are a number of different advancement opportunities for Health Club Instructors working in casino hotel spas and health clubs. Individuals may obtain experience and locate similar positions in larger or more prestigious facilities. Health Club Instructors may also be promoted to the position of assistant health club manager.

Education and Training

Educational requirements vary from job to job. Many casino hotels prefer or require that Health Club Instructors hold a college degree in physical education or a related field. Some colleges now offer degrees in exercise and fitness. Work experience will often be accepted by many facilities in lieu of education requirements. Some casino hotels may not require college, but may require training in exercise, aerobics, and related areas. Additional courses and seminars in aerobics techniques, exercise physiology, exercise biochemistry, and exercise science will also be helpful.

Experience/Skills/Personality Traits

Experience requirements, like education and training requirements, vary. Some casino hotel health clubs require

or prefer that individuals have experience working in other health clubs or spas.

Health Club Instructors working in casino hotel health clubs and spas are usually required to hold Red Cross or National Safety Council Lifeguard Certification. They may also be required to hold the Red Cross Water Safety Instructors Certification. Some states may also mandate that health club workers have CPR (Cardio Pulmonary Resuscitation) training.

Unions/Associations

Individuals interested in pursuing careers in health clubs can obtain additional information by contacting the American Red Cross, National Safety Council, or American Heart Association. They may also contact the Aerobics and Fitness Association of America (AFAA).

Tips for Entry

1. Jobs are often advertised in the classified sections of newspapers in areas hosting gaming. Look under classifications such as "Health Club Instructor," "Health Club," "Spa," "Casino Hotel Spa," or "Casino Hotel Health Club."
2. Obtain training and experience by contacting corporate headquarters of health and fitness clubs and gyms that are franchise operations. These groups often offer training programs and job placement.
3. Call casino job hotlines to see if jobs are open in this area. Job hotlines are frequently updated messages listing jobs available. You can call each casino directly to get its job hotline phone number.
4. Send your résumé and a short cover letter to the human resources departments of casinos and casino hotels, as well as to their corporate offices to inquire about job openings.
5. Look for new casinos being built. Apply early for the best positions.

CAREER OPPORTUNITIES IN CASINO AND CASINO HOTEL RETAIL SHOPS

RETAIL SUPERVISOR/STORE MANAGER

CAREER PROFILE

Duties: Providing day-to-day management of casino hotel shop; supervising and training sales associates; scheduling employees; providing accounting of sales; assisting customers; overseeing loss prevention.

Alternative Titles(s): None

Salary Range: $16,000 to $37,000+; see text.

Employment Prospects: Excellent

Best Geographical Location(s) for Position: Las Vegas, Reno, Laughlin, Lake Tahoe, Atlantic City, Biloxi, Baton Rouge, New Orleans, and Detroit offer the greatest number of opportunities; other regions hosting Indian gaming and land-based or riverboat gaming facilities offer additional opportunities.

Prerequisites:

Education or Training—High school diploma or equivalent; on-the-job training.

Experience and Qualifications—Prior experience in retail store management or retailing.

Special Skills and Personality Traits—Supervisory skills; customer service skills; sales ability; communication skills; pleasant.

CAREER LADDER

```
┌─────────────────────────────────┐
│   Store Manager in Larger, More │
│     Prestigious Store or Shop   │
└─────────────────────────────────┘

┌─────────────────────────────────┐
│   Retail Supervisor/Store Manager│
└─────────────────────────────────┘

┌─────────────────────────────────┐
│      Assistant Store Manager    │
└─────────────────────────────────┘
```

Position Description

Casinos and casino hotels like to keep customers on the property once they arrive. Management, therefore, tries to have as many amenities as possible on-site. These facilities have a wide array of restaurants for all tastes and pocketbooks. Many also host a variety of on-site retail shops.

The individual who provides the day-to-day management of the casino hotel shop is called the Store Manager or Retail Shop Supervisor.

Store Managers have a number of responsibilities. They establish and implement policies, goals, objectives, and procedures for the specific shop. This may be done in conjunction with other casino administrators.

Store Managers supervise the sales associates working in the store. As part of this function, they must train associates in all necessary areas. This includes writing sales slips, using the cash register, processing credit cards, and approving checks.

The Store Manager is responsible for scheduling employees. The individual must take into account the days and hours the store is expected to be busiest to make sure enough employees are on hand to adequately service customers.

Store Managers assign duties and oversee the activities of sales associates, including pricing and ticketing goods, placing them on display, and cleaning and organizing shelves, displays, and inventory in stockrooms.

In order for merchandise to sell, the Store Manager makes sure it is displayed in an attractive manner. Store Managers may handle this duty themselves or assign it to other employees.

The Store Manager is ultimately responsible for everything that occurs in the store. The Manager maintains customer satisfaction, sometimes working on the sales floor greeting and assisting customers with purchases.

Other duties of the casino or casino hotel Retail Store Manager may include:

- Developing and coordinating sales promotions
- Overseeing loss prevention
- Reviewing sales records and accounting for sales
- Keeping track of inventory
- Ordering merchandise

Salaries

Retail Store Managers working in casinos and casino hotels are paid an hourly wage ranging between $8.00 and $18.00 or more per hour or between $16,000 and $37,000 annually. They may also earn commissions on sales in addition to their hourly salary. In some settings, individuals are paid a weekly salary.

Factors affecting earnings include the geographic location, size, and prestige of the casino or casino hotel, as well as the specific type of shop. Other variables include the experience and responsibilities of the individual.

Employment Prospects

Employment prospects are excellent for qualified individuals aspiring to be Retail Store Managers in casinos and casino hotels. Most facilities have one or more shops. Individuals work various shifts, including daytime and swing shift. Casinos that are open 24 hours a day may require a Supervisor or Manager to work the graveyard shift.

Employment opportunities depend on the type of shops in the casino—sundry shops, boutiques, souvenir shops, gift shops, floral shops, candy stores, and jewelry stores.

Many of the new multimillion-dollar casino hotels also have large upscale shopping areas filled with exclusive stores.

Advancement Prospects

With experience and/or additional training, Store Managers working in casinos or casino hotels may be promoted to management positions in larger or more prestigious stores in the facility.

Education and Training

Casinos and casino hotels generally prefer Store Managers to have a high school diploma or the equivalent. Many facilities assist individuals who do not have this education in obtaining a GED. Work experience is often accepted in lieu of education.

While there is not usually any formal training requirement for this position, any training individuals have received in buying, retailing, or store management will be useful. Many Store Managers have moved up the career ladder by starting as sales associates and learning as they go.

Experience/Skills/Personality Traits

This is not an entry-level position. Experience in retail sales and management is usually required.

Store Managers must have supervisory and administrative skills. They should be personable people with good customer service skills. Sales ability and merchandising skills are necessary.

Unions/Associations

Those interested in learning more about careers in retailing can obtain information from the National Retail Federation (NRF).

Tips for Entry

1. Visit the human resources departments of casinos and casino hotels to learn about job openings.
2. Check with stores directly to see if they have openings, then fill out applications.
3. Jobs are often advertised in the classified sections of newspapers in areas hosting gaming. Look under classifications such as "Casinos/Gaming," "Casinos/Hotels," "Retail Opportunities," "Casino Shop Manager," or "Casino Hotel Shops."
4. Most casinos have job hotlines. These are frequently updated messages listing jobs available. You can call each casino directly to get its job hotline phone number.

SALES ASSOCIATE—RETAIL

CAREER PROFILE

Duties: Working in casino hotel shops; assisting customers; selling merchandise; handling cashier duties.

Alternative Titles(s): Sales Clerk

Salary Range: $12,000 to $22,000+

Employment Prospects: Excellent

Best Geographical Location(s) for Position: Las Vegas, Reno, Laughlin, Lake Tahoe, Atlantic City, Biloxi, Baton Rouge, New Orleans, and Detroit offer the greatest number of opportunities; other regions hosting Indian gaming and land-based or riverboat gaming facilities offer additional opportunities.

Prerequisites:

Education or Training—High school diploma or equivalent; on-the-job training.

Experience and Qualifications—Sales experience helpful, but not always required.

Special Skills and Personality Traits—Customer service skills; sales ability; communication skills; pleasant; money-handling skills.

CAREER LADDER

```
┌─────────────────────────────────┐
│  Assistant Store Manager or     │
│        Store Manager            │
└─────────────────────────────────┘

┌─────────────────────────────────┐
│   Sales Associate—Retail Shop   │
└─────────────────────────────────┘

┌─────────────────────────────────┐
│   Sales Associate in Other      │
│   Setting or Entry Level        │
└─────────────────────────────────┘
```

Position Description

Casinos and casino hotels are often like small cities. In addition to the gaming area and hotel, there are restaurants, spas, and shops. Depending on the specific casino, there may be a variety of retail establishments. These can include newspaper and sundry shops, souvenir stores, kiosks, clothing stores, boutiques, and gift shops.

Every store and shop in the casino needs Sales Associates, also referred to as sales clerks.

Sales Associates assist customers. They must determine what each customer's needs are. Customer service is extremely important in this job. Sales Associates must make every person who comes into the retail establishment feel comfortable, whether they just are browsing or want to buy.

Sales Associates must know the stock in their store and be able to answer questions regarding merchandise. Individuals offer suggestions to customers regarding purchase possibilities.

Once patrons decide what they want to purchase, Sales Associates are responsible for taking payment. Individuals must know how to ring up purchases and make correct change if people are paying with cash. They must also know the proper procedure for accepting checks, charging items to guest's rooms, or processing credit card charges.

Sales Associates stock, price, and ticket merchandise. They are responsible for putting merchandise out in displays. Sales Associates also are expected to clean and organize shelves, as well as keep the shop neat and orderly.

Other duties of the casino or casino hotel shop Sales Associate include:

- Handling loss prevention
- Accounting for sales
- Putting out and displaying merchandise

Salaries

Sales Associates working in casinos and casino hotels earn between $6.00 and $10.50 per hour or more or about $12,000 to $22,000 per year. Factors affecting earnings include the geographic location, size, and prestige of the casino or casino hotel, as well as the specific type of shop. Other variables include the experience and responsibilities of the individual. In some stores Sales Associates earn a commission in addition to the hourly wage.

Employment Prospects

Employment prospects are excellent for Sales Associates in casinos and casino hotels. Most facilities have one or more shops. Individuals work in various shifts, including daytime and swing shift. In casinos that are open 24 hours a day, shops also need employees for the graveyard shift.

Advancement Prospects

With experience and/or additional training, Sales Clerks may be promoted to supervisory retail positions, including assistant manager or manager.

Education and Training

Most casinos and casino hotels prefer Sales Associates to have a high school diploma or the equivalent. Many facilities assist individuals who do not have this education in obtaining a GED.

On-the-job training in handling customers with sales, as well as using the cash register and credit card machines, is usually provided.

Experience/Skills/Personality Traits

In some establishments entry-level positions may be open. Many facilities, however, prefer that individuals have some type of retail sales experience.

Sales Associates must be courteous and pleasant. Customer service skills, sales ability, and money-handling skills are essential.

Unions/Associations

Those interested in learning more about careers as Sales Associates can obtain information from the National Retail Merchants Association (NRMA).

Tips for Entry

1. While retail experience is not always needed, it is usually preferred. Remember to include any prior retail experience on your job application or résumé.
2. Jobs are often advertised in the classified sections of newspapers in areas hosting gaming. Look under classifications such as "Casinos/Gaming," "Casinos/Hotels," "Retail Opportunities," "Sales Associates," "Sales Clerks," or "Casino Hotel Shops."
3. Most casinos have job hotlines. These are frequently updated messages listing jobs available. You can either call each casino directly to obtain its job hotline phone number or obtain a copy of "Casino Job Hotline Phone Number Directory." The address is in the resource section of this book.
4. Stop by the human resources departments of casinos and casino hotels to learn about job openings.

CAREER OPPORTUNITIES IN CASINO AND CASINO HOTEL SUPPORT PERSONNEL

EXECUTIVE SECRETARY

CAREER PROFILE

Duties: Handling secretarial duties for casino or hotel executive; answering telephones; scheduling appointments; typing; routing mail; greeting people in office.

Alternative Titles(s): Confidential Secretary

Salary Range: $23,000 to $30,000+; see text.

Employment Prospects: Good

Best Geographical Location(s) for Position: Las Vegas, Reno, Laughlin, Lake Tahoe, Atlantic City, Biloxi, Baton Rouge, New Orleans, and Detroit offer the greatest number of opportunities; other regions hosting Indian gaming and land-based or riverboat gaming facilities offer additional opportunities.

Prerequisites:

Education or Training—High school diploma or equivalent.

Experience and Qualifications—Secretarial experience necessary.

Special Skills and Personality Traits—Office skills; phone skills; typing skills; computer skills; ability to handle multiple tasks; communication skills; ability to take and transcribe dictation; good judgment.

CAREER LADDER

```
┌─────────────────────────────┐
│  Administrative Assistant   │
└─────────────────────────────┘

┌─────────────────────────────┐
│    Executive Secretary      │
└─────────────────────────────┘

┌─────────────────────────────┐
│        Secretary            │
└─────────────────────────────┘
```

Position Description

Casinos and casino hotels have many executives, many of whom have executive secretaries. Executive Secretaries are responsible for many of the duties of general office secretaries. However, they often have additional responsibilities.

Executive Secretaries type a wide array of correspondence and reports. While general office secretaries just type this correspondence, Executive Secretaries are often responsible for composing some of it. For example, the individual may answer letters for the executive or compose memos on his or her behalf. These will usually be approved by the executive.

The Executive Secretary is responsible for necessary computer software programs. The Executive Secretary often takes and transcribes dictation from a transcription machine or directly from the executive.

The Executive Secretary oversees other secretaries and clerks in the office. The individual instructs these employees to photocopy documents, file, collate papers and reports, send faxes, and input information into the computer.

The Executive Secretary is often privy to confidential conversations and information that must remain within the office. To maintain confidentiality, the Executive Secretary may be required to handle personally certain files that contain this type of information.

Other duties of the Executive Secretary working in a casino or casino hotel may include:

• Returning phone calls for the executive
• Scheduling appointments for meetings
• Screening calls and visitors
• Taking notes at meetings

Salaries

Executive Secretaries working in casinos and casino hotels earn between $10.00 and $18.00 or more per hour. Some Executive Secretaries are paid a yearly salary ranging from $23,000 to $30,000 plus instead of an hourly wage.

Factors affecting earnings include the geographic location, size, and prestige of the specific facility, as well as the experience, education, and responsibilities of the individual.

Employment Prospects

Employment prospects for casino and casino hotel Executive Secretaries are good. Individuals may work for executives of the hotel or casino in various areas, including but not limited to casino management, marketing, legal affairs, hotel management, casino operations, and public relations.

Las Vegas, Reno, Laughlin, Lake Tahoe, Atlantic City, Biloxi, Baton Rouge, New Orleans, and Detroit offer the greatest number of opportunities. Other regions hosting Indian gaming and land-based or riverboat gaming facilities offer additional opportunities.

Advancement Prospects

Executive Secretaries often advance their careers by becoming administrative assistants to casino or casino hotel executives. In some instances, with additional training, Executive Secretaries may also move into other areas of casino employment.

Education and Training

Casinos and casino hotels usually require Executive Secretaries to hold a high school diploma or the equivalent. Secretarial school or secretarial courses are useful.

Experience/Skills/Personality Traits

Executive Secretaries working in casinos and casino hotels must have at least two or three years of prior office experience. Individuals must be well-groomed and articulate with excellent communication skills. Understanding of the workings of the specific casino or hotel department is useful.

Executive Secretaries should accurately type between 65 and 80 words a minute accurately. Word processing and computer skills are necessary. The abilities to take dictation is usually required.

Individuals need interpersonal skills and a pleasant phone manner. Good judgment is essential. The ability to keep office matters confidential is mandatory.

Unions/Associations

Those interested in learning more about careers as Executive Secretaries should contact the human resources departments of casinos and casino hotels. Individuals may also contact Professional Secretaries International (PSI) for additional information.

Tips for Entry

1. Check the job hotlines of casinos and casino hotels to see what openings are available. Call each casino directly to get its job hotline phone number.
2. Jobs may be advertised in the classified sections of newspapers in areas hosting gaming. Look under classifications such as "Casino/Gaming," "Executive Secretary," or "Casino Opportunities."
3. Visit the human resources departments of casinos to inquire about job openings. Send or fax a résumé and a short cover letter to the director of human resources.
4. Make sure you are up to date on software by taking courses. This will make you more marketable.
5. Casinos like to promote from within. Get your foot in the door and move up to this position.

SECRETARY/VARIOUS DEPARTMENTS

CAREER PROFILE

Duties: Answering telephones; filing; typing; routing mail; greeting people.

Alternative Titles(s): None

Salary Range: $14,000 to $25,000+

Employment Prospects: Good

Best Geographical Location(s) for Position: Las Vegas, Reno, Laughlin, Lake Tahoe, Atlantic City, Biloxi, Baton Rouge, New Orleans, and Detroit offer the greatest number of opportunities; other regions hosting Indian gaming and land-based or riverboat gaming facilities offer additional opportunities.

Prerequisites:

Education or Training—High school diploma or equivalent

Experience and Qualifications—Secretarial or office experience preferred.

Special Skills and Personality Traits—Office skills; phone skills; typing skills; computer skills; communication skills; ability to take and transcribe dictation.

CAREER LADDER

```
┌─────────────────────────────┐
│    Executive Secretary       │
└─────────────────────────────┘

┌─────────────────────────────┐
│         Secretary            │
└─────────────────────────────┘

┌─────────────────────────────┐
│  Secretary in Other Industry │
└─────────────────────────────┘
```

Position Description

The gaming industry, like many other industries, requires secretaries. These people help casino and hotel departments and offices run smoothly. Secretaries handle a wide array of clerical duties. They type a variety of correspondence, envelopes, and reports. Specific typing responsibilities depend on the department in which the individual is working. Typing is done on a word processor or computer. Individuals might additionally be required to use various computer software programs necessary to the department.

A Secretary might be required to take and transcribe dictation, as well as to take shorthand. The Secretary must photocopy documents, file, maintain files, collate reports, sort mail, answer phones, and send faxes.

Secretaries working in various gaming departments may handle additional duties. For example, the Secretary working in the slot office may assist in coordinating small slot tournaments. A great many duties of Secretaries working in the casino area depend on the specific department in which the individual works.

Other duties of the Secretary working in a casino or casino hotel may include:

- Answering letters and other correspondence
- Returning phone calls
- Making appointments for meetings
- Screening calls and visitors

Salaries

Secretaries working in casinos and casino hotels earn between $7.00 and $12.00 per hour or more or about $15,000 to $25,000 annually.

Factors affecting earnings include the geographic location, size, and prestige of the specific facility, as well as the experience, education, and responsibilities of the individual.

Employment Prospects

Employment prospects for casino and casino hotel Secretaries are excellent. Individuals may be employed in any department of the hotel or casino, including human resources, marketing, public relations, or administration.

Las Vegas, Reno, Laughlin, Lake Tahoe, Atlantic City, Biloxi, Baton Rouge, New Orleans, and Detroit offer the greatest number of opportunities. Other regions hosting Indian gaming and land-based or riverboat gaming facilities offer additional opportunities.

Advancement Prospects

One of the advantages about working as a Secretary in a casino or casino hotel is that promotion is usually done from within. Secretaries who want to remain in administrative work may move up to executive secretaries or administrative assistants.

Those who want to move out of secretarial work may obtain training and locate positions in other departments in either the administrative area, the casino, or hotel.

Education and Training

Casinos and casino hotels usually require that Secretaries and executive secretaries have a high school diploma or the equivalent. Secretarial courses as well as those in computers and various software packages are helpful.

Experience/Skills/Personality Traits

Experience working in an office is preferred. Secretaries should accurately type between 55 and 65 words per minute. Word processing and computer skills are usually necessary. The ability to take dictation is often required or preferred.

Individuals should have interpersonal skills with a pleasant telephone manner. Good judgment is also needed.

Unions/Associations

Those interested in learning more about careers as Secretaries should contact the human resources departments of casinos and casino hotels. Individuals may also write to Professional Secretaries International (PSI) for additional information.

Tips for Entry

1. Jobs may be advertised in the classified sections of newspapers in areas hosting gaming. Look under classifications such as "Casino/Gaming," "Secretary," or "Casino Opportunities-Secretarial."
2. This is a good job to get your foot in the door of a casino or casino hotel. Learn what you can and work hard. You will have a good chance of moving up the career ladder.
3. Stop by the human resources departments of casinos and inquire about job openings. Send or fax a résumé and a short cover letter.
4. Most casinos also have job hotlines that tell about current job openings. You can call each casino directly to get its job hotline phone number.

APPENDIXES

APPENDIX I
GAMING ACADEMIES
AND DEALER SCHOOLS

The following is a listing of gaming academies and dealer schools. Before enrolling in any school you are not familiar with, check the school's reputation and credentials with the local Better Business Bureau and/or the specific state's licensing organization.

Gaming academies and dealer schools are located in many areas hosting gaming. Some are affiliated with local vo-tech schools, universities, or community colleges. Others are privately owned. Many casinos themselves also have their own training schools.

New gaming academies open as more areas legalize gambling. Casino human resources departments may know of additional schools or training facilities.

The author does not endorse any one school and provides this list as a beginning to get you started.

ARIZONA

Mojave Community College
1971 Jagerson Avenue
Kingman, AZ 86401
602-757-4331

CALIFORNIA

Casino Career Center
28780 Front Street, Suite B-3
Temecula, CA 92590
909-506-3119

FLORIDA

Casino Training Academy
Port of Miami
Terminal No 1, First Floor
1265 S. America Way
Miami, FL 33132
305-371-3325

International Casino Institute
4401 Stirling Road
Hollywood, FL 33314
954-587-3325

**National Bartenders, Casino Games
and Hospitality School**
2502 Second Street
Ft. Meyers, FL 33901
941-334-6300

LOUISIANA

**Crescent City School of Gaming
and Bartending**
209 North Broad Avenue
New Orleans, LA 70119
504-822-3362

Jefferson College
P.O. Box 1040
12 Westbank Expressway
Gretna, LA 70054
504-362-5787

MISSISSIPPI

Academy of Casino Training, Inc. (ACT)
213 Pass Road
Gulfport, MS 39507
228-864-7133
800-8DEALER

Crescent School
1205 25th Avenue
Gulfport, MS 39501
228-822-2444

NEVADA

Las Vegas

Casino Gaming School
900 East Karen Avenue
Las Vegas, NV 89109
702-893-1788

CDF Gaming Machine Repair School
1111 Grier Drive
Las Vegas, NV 89119
702-361-8828

**Community College of Southern
Nevada**
3200 East Cheyenne
North Las Vegas, NV 89030
702-651-4579

International Dealers School
503 East Fremont Street
Las Vegas, NV 89101
702-385-7665

JTC Training School
953 East Sahara Avenue
Las Vegas, NV 89104
702-893-0885

**Las Vegas Gaming and Technical
School**
3033 South Highland
Las Vegas, NV 89109
702-733-3030

Las Vegas School of Dealing
3850 South Valley View Boulevard
Las Vegas, NV 89103
702-368-1717

National Academy for Casino Dealers
557 East Sahara Avenue # 108
Las Vegas, NV 89104
702-735-4884

Nevada School of Dealing
4132 South Rainbow Boulevard
Las Vegas, NV 89103
702-382-9128

Paramount Dealers Academy
3280 East Tropicana
Las Vegas, NV 89121
702-897-2940

Personalized Casino Instruction
920 South Valley View
Las Vegas, NV 89107
702-877-4724

UNLV International Gaming Institute
4505 Maryland Parkway
Box 456037
Las Vegas, NV 89154
702-895-3412

Vegas Career School
3333 South Maryland Parkway
Las Vegas, NV 89109
702-792-6299

Reno

Academy of Casino Careers
99 North Virginia Street
Reno, NV 89501
775-786-7713

Morisson College
140 Washington Street
Reno, NV 89501
775-323-3145

Reno-Tahoe Gaming Academy
300 East First Street #103
Reno, NV 89501
775-329-5665

University of Nevada - Reno
Reno, NV 89557

NEW JERSEY

Atlantic Cape Community College's Casino Career Institute
1535 Bacharach Boulevard
Atlantic City, NJ 08401
609-343-4848

CANADA

Canadian School of Gaming
Pyramid Place
Career Opp. In Casinos
5400 Robinson Street
Niagara Falls, Ontario L2G 4P1
Canada
905-374-8933

Casino City Training Centre
6710 Drummond Road-Unit #8
Niagara Falls, Ontario L2G 4P1
Canada
905-371-3002

Casino Excellence
6278 Lundy's Lane
Niagara Falls, Ontario L2G 4P1
Canada

Gamex Gaming Consultants Inc. Casino Training School
47 Carlisle Street, Unit D
St. Catharines, Ontario L2R 4H5
Canada
905-688-2011

International Casino Games
6689 Lundy's Lane
Niagara Falls, Ontario L2G 1V4
Canada
905-374-4777

Niagara College Casino Training School
300 Woodlawn Road
P.O. Box 1005
Welland, Ontario L3B 5S2
Canada
905-735-2211

National Casino Academy
4680 Queen Street
Niagara Falls, Ontario L2E 2L8
Canada
905-354-3661

Robby Robertson's Winning Touch Casino Training School
4685 Queen Street
Niagara Falls, Ontario L2E 2L9
Canada
905-357-7333

APPENDIX II
DEGREE PROGRAMS

A. COLLEGES AND UNIVERSITIES OFFERING MAJORS IN HOSPITALITY ADMINISTRATION AND MANAGEMENT

Casinos and casino hotels often accept experience in lieu of formal college education. However, many facilities maintain that a college background gives an applicant an edge in marketability and advancement prospects, as well as providing experiences not otherwise available.

The following is a selected list of four-year schools granting degrees with majors in hospitality administration and management. They are grouped by state.

More colleges are beginning to grant degrees in this area every year. Check the newest copy of *Lovejoy's* (found in the reference section of libraries or in guidance counseling centers) for additional schools offering degrees in this field.

ALABAMA

Alabama A & M University
P.O. Box 284
Normal, AL 35762

Tuskegee University
Tuskegee, AL 36088

The University of Alabama
Tuscaloosa, AL 35487

ARKANSAS

Arkansas Tech University
Caraway Hall
Russelville, AR 72801

CALIFORNIA

California State Polytechnic University–Pomona
3801 West Temple Avenue
Pomona, CA 91768

San Jose State University
One Washington Square
San Jose, CA 95192

University of San Francisco
2130 Fulton Street
San Francisco, CA 94117

COLORADO

Metropolitan State College of Denver
1006 11th Street
Denver, CO 80204

CONNECTICUT

Teikyo Post University
800 Country Club Road
Waterbury, CT 06723

DISTRICT OF COLUMBIA

George Washington University
2300 I Street, NW
Washington, DC 20060

Howard University
2400 Sixth Street, NW
Washington, DC 20059

FLORIDA

Bethune-Cookman College
640 Second Avenue
Daytona, FL 32015

Florida Institute of Technology
150 West University Boulevard
Melbourne, FL 32901

Florida International University
University Park
Miami, FL 33199

Florida Southeastern University
111 Lake Hollingsworth Drive
Lakeland, FL 33801

Florida State University
Tallahassee, FL 32306

Nova Southeastern University
3301 College Avenue
Fort Lauderdale, FL 33314

St. Thomas University
16400 Northwest 32nd Avenue
Miami, FL 33054-6459

University of Central Florida
4000 Central Florida Boulevard
Orlando, FL 32816

GEORGIA

Morris Brown College
643 Martin Luther King Jr. Drive, NW
Atlanta, GA 30314

IDAHO

Idaho State University
741 South 7th Avenue
Pocatello, ID 83209

ILLINOIS

Chicago State University
95th Street at King Drive
Chicago, IL 60628

Kendall College
2408 Orrington Avenue
Evanston, IL 60201-2899

Roosevelt University
430 South Michigan Avenue
Chicago, IL 60605-1394

INDIANA

**Indiana University–Purdue University
Indianapolis**
355 North Lansing
Indianapolis, IN 46202

KENTUCKY

University of Kentucky
100 Funkhouser Building
Lexington, KY 40506

LOUISIANA

University of Southwestern Louisiana
104 University Circle
Lafayette, LA 70504

MAINE

Husson College
One College Circle
Bangor, ME 04401

MARYLAND

Morgan State University
Cold Spring Lane and Hillen Road
Baltimore, MD 21239

MASSACHUSETTS

Boston University
121 Bay State Road
Boston, MA 02215

MICHIGAN

Baker College of Flint
1050 West Bristol Road
Flint, MI 48507

Central Michigan University
100 Warriner Hall
Mount Pleasant, MI 48859

Ferris State University
901 State Street
Big Rapids, MI 49307

Grand Valley State University
1 Seidman House
Allendale, MI 49401

Madonna University
36600 Schoolcraft Road
Livonia, MI 48150

Michigan State University
Administration Building
East Lansing, MI 48824

University of Detroit–Mercy
4001 West McNicholls Road
Detroit, MI 48221

MISSOURI

St. Louis University
221 North Grand Boulevard
St. Louis, MO 65211

Southwest Missouri State University
901 South National
Springfield, MO 65854

NEBRASKA

University of Nebraska-Lincoln
14th and R Streets
Lincoln, NE 68588

NEW HAMPSHIRE

New Hampshire College
2500 North River Road
Manchester, NH 03106

NEW YORK

New York Institute of Technology
P.O. Box 8000
Old Westbury, NY 11568

St. John's University
8000 Utopia Parkway
Jamaica, NY 11439

SUNY–Oneonta
Ravine Parkway
Oneonta, NY 13820

NORTH CAROLINA

Appalachian State University
Boone, NC 28608

East Carolina University
Greenville, NC 27834

Western Carolina University
520 H.F. Robinson Administration
Building
Cullowhee, NC 28723

OHIO

Bowling Green State University
1100 McFall Center
Bowling Green, OH 43403

Central State University
Brush Row Road
Wilberforce, OH 45384

Ohio State University–Columbus
1800 Cannon Drive-Lincoln Tower
Columbus, OH 43210

Tiffin University
155 Miami Street
Tiffin, OH 44883

University of Akron
381 East Buchtel Common
Akron, OH 44325

Youngstown State University
1 University Plaza
Youngstown, OH 44555

PENNSYLVANIA

East Stroudsburg University of Pennsylvania
200 Prospect Street
East Stroudsburg, PA 18301

Mercyhurst College
Glenwood Hills
Erie, PA 16546

Robert Morris College
Narrows Run Road
Coraopolis, PA 15108

University of Pennsylvania
200 Prospect Street
East Stroudsburg, PA 18301

Widener University
One University Place
Chester, PA 19013

RHODE ISLAND

Johnson & Wales University
8 Abbott Park Place
Providence, RI 02903

TENNESSEE

Belmont University
1900 Belmont Boulevard
Nashville, TN 37212

VERMONT

Johnson State College
RR2, Box 75
Johnson, VT 05656

VIRGINIA

James Madison University
Harrisonburg, VA 22807

WEST VIRGINIA

Davis and Elkins College
Elkins, WV 26241

University of Charleston
2300 MacCorkle Avenue, SE
Charleston, WV 25304

WISCONSIN

Lakeland College
P.O. Box 359
Sheboygan, WI 53082

University of Wisconsin-Stout
Menomonie, WI 54751

B. COLLEGES AND UNIVERSITIES OFFERING MAJORS IN HOTEL AND RESTAURANT MANAGEMENT

Casinos and casino hotels often accept experience in lieu of formal college education. However, many facilities maintain that a college background gives an applicant an edge in marketability and advancement prospects, as well as providing experiences not otherwise available.

The following is a selected list of four-year schools granting degrees with majors in hotel and restaurant management. They are grouped by state.

More colleges are beginning to grant degrees in these areas every year. Check the newest copy of *Lovejoy's* (found in the reference section of libraries or in guidance counseling centers) for additional schools offering degrees in this field.

ALABAMA

Auburn University
Auburn University, AL 36849-0001

University of Alabama
Tuscaloosa, AL 35487

ARIZONA

Northern Arizona University
P.O. Box 4132
Flagstaff, AZ 86011

ARKANSAS

Arkansas Tech University
Caraway Hall
Russelville, AR 72801

University of Arkansas at Pine Bluff
1200 North University Drive
Pine Bluff, AR 71601-2799

CALIFORNIA

California State Polytechnic University–Pomona
3801 West Temple Avenue
Pomona, CA 91768

California State University–Chico
Chico, CA 95929

Golden Gate University
536 Mission Street
San Francisco, CA 94105

United States International University
10455 Pomerado Road
San Diego, CA 92131

University of San Francisco
2130 Fulton Street
San Francisco, CA 94117

COLORADO

Colorado State University
Fort Collins, CO 80523

Denver Institute of Technology
7350 North Broadway
Denver, CO 80221

Mesa State College
P.O. Box 2647
Grand Junction, CO 81502

National College
2577 North Chelton Road
Colorado Springs, CO 80909

University of Denver
University Park
Denver, CO 80208

CONNECTICUT

Teikyo Post University
800 Country Club Road
Waterbury, CT 06723

University of New Haven
300 Orange Avenue
West Haven, CT 06516

DELAWARE

Delaware State University
Dover, DE 19901-2277

University of Delaware
Newark, DE 19716

DISTRICT OF COLUMBIA

Howard University
2400 Sixth Street, NW
Washington, DC 20059

Southeastern University
501 I Street, SW
Washington, DC 20024

FLORIDA

Bethune-Cookman College
640 Dr. Mary McLeod Bethune Boulevard
Daytona Beach, FL 32114

Florida Institute of Technology
150 West University Boulevard
Melbourne, FL 32901

Florida International University
University Park
Miami, FL 33199

Florida Southern College
111 Lake Hollingsworth Drive
Lakeland, FL 33801

Florida State University
Tallahassee, FL 32306

Fort Lauderdale College
1040 Bayview Drive
Fort Lauderdale, FL 33304

Lynn University
3601 North Military Trail
Boca Raton, FL 33431

Northwood University–Florida Campus
2600 North Military Trail
West Palm Beach, FL 33409

Saint Leo College
P.O. Box 2008
Saint Leo, FL 33574

St. Thomas University
16400 Northwest 32nd Avenue
Miami, FL 33054

University of Central Florida
4000 Central Florida Boulevard
Orlando, FL 32816

Webber College
P.O. Box 96
Babson Park, FL 33827

GEORGIA

Berry College
P.O. Box 490159
Mount Berry, GA 30149

Clark Atlanta University
James P. Brawley Drive at Fair Street, SW
Atlanta, GA 30314

Georgia Southern University
Landrum Box 8027
Statesboro, GA 30460

Georgia State University
University Plaza
Atlanta, GA 30303

Morris Brown College
643 Martin Luther King Jr. Drive, NW
Atlanta, GA 30314

University of Georgia
Athens, GA 30602

HAWAII

Brigham Young University–Hawaii Campus
55-220 Kulanui Street
Laie, Oahu, HI 96762

ILLINOIS

Chicago State University
9501 South King Drive
Chicago, IL 60628

Kendall College
2408 Orrington Avenue
Evanston, IL 60201

Southern Illinois University At Carbondale
Carbondale, IL 62901

University of Illinois At Urbana–Champaign
601 East John Street
Champaign, IL 61820

Western Illinois University
900 West Adams Street
Macomb, IL 61455

INDIANA

Indiana University–Purdue University Indianapolis
355 North Lansing
Indianapolis, IN 46202

Purdue University
West Lafayette, IN 47907

Purdue University–Calumet
Hammond, IN 46323

Purdue University North Central
1401 South US Highway 421
Westville, IN 46391

University of Indianapolis
1400 East Hanna Avenue
Indianapolis, IN 46227

IOWA

Iowa State University
100 Alumni Hall
Ames, IA 50011

KANSAS

Kansas State University
Anderson Hall, Room 1
Manhattan, KS 66506

KENTUCKY

Berea College
Berea, KY 40404

Morehead State University
Morehead, KY 40351

Sullivan College
Sullivan Centre
P.O. Box 33-308
Louisville, KY 40232

Western Kentucky University
One Big Red Way
Bowling Green, KY 42101

LOUISIANA

Grambling State University
P.O. Box 607
Grambling, LA 71245

University of New Orleans
Lakefront
New Orleans, LA 70148

University of Southwestern Louisiana
104 University Circle
Lafayette, LA 70504

MAINE

University of Southern Maine
96 Falmouth Street
P.O. Box 9300
Portland, ME 04104

MARYLAND

Morgan State University
Cold Spring Lane and Hillen Road
Baltimore, MD 21239

University of Maryland Eastern Shore
Princess Anne, MD 21853

MASSACHUSETTS

Becker College–Leicester Campus
3 Paxton Street
Leicester, MA 01524

Boston University
Boston, MA 02215

Endicott College
376 Hale Street
Beverly, MA 01915

Laseli College
1844 Commonwealth Avenue
Auburndale, MA 02166

Northeastern University
360 Huntington Avenue
Boston, MA 02115

University of Massachusetts–Amherst
Amherst, MA 01003

MICHIGAN

Baker College of Flint
1050 West Bristol Road
Flint, MI 48507

Baker College of Muskegon
123 East Apple Avenue
Muskegon, MI 49442

Baker College of Owosso
1020 South Washington Street
Owosso, MI 48867

Baker College of Port Huron
3403 Lapeer Road
Port Huron, MI 48060

Central Michigan University
Mount Pleasant, MI 48859

Davenport College of Business
415 East Fulton
Grand Rapids, MI 49503

Grand Valley State University
1 Campus Drive
Allendale, MI 49401

Michigan State University
East Lansing, MI 48824

Northern Michigan University
Cohodas Administration Center
Marquette, MI 49855

Northwood University
3225 Cook Road
Midland, MI 48640

Siena Heights University
1247 East Siena Heights Drive
Adrian, MI 49221

MINNESOTA

Southwest State University
1501 State Street
Marshall, MN 56258

University of Minnesota–Crookston
Crookston, MN 56716

MISSISSIPPI

University of Southern Mississippi
P.O. Box 5001
Hattiesburg, MS 39406

MISSOURI

Central Missouri State University
Warrensburg, MO 64093

College of the Ozarks
Point Lookout, MO 65726

Southwest Missouri State University
901 South National
Springfield, MO 65804

University of Missouri–Columbia
305 Jesse Hall
Columbia, MO 65211

NEBRASKA

University of Nebraska–Omaha
60th and Dodge Streets
Omaha, NE 68182

NEVADA

Sierra Nevada College
800 College Drive
P.O. Box 4269
Incline Village, NV 89450

University of Nevada–Las Vegas
4505 Maryland Parkway
Las Vegas, NV 89154

NEW HAMPSHIRE

New Hampshire College
2500 North River Road
Manchester, NH 03106

University of New Hampshire
Garrison Avenue
Grant House
Durham, NH 03824

NEW JERSEY

Fairleigh Dickinson University
1000 River Road
Teaneck, NJ 07666

Thomas Edison State College
101 West State Street
Trenton, NJ 08608

NEW MEXICO

National College
1202 Pennsylvania Avenue, NE
Albuquerque, NM 87110

New Mexico State University
P.O. Box 30001
Las Cruces, NM 88003

NEW YORK

Canisius College
2001 Main Street
Buffalo, NY 14208

Cornell University
Ithaca, NY 14853

Keuka College
Keuka Park, NY 14478

New York Institute of Technology
P.O. Box 8000
Old Westbury, NY 11568

New York University
70 Washington Square South
New York, NY 10012

Niagara University
Niagara University, NY 14109

Pace University
Pace Plaza
New York, NY 10038

Rochester Institute of Technology
One Lomb Memorial Drive
Rochester, NY 14623

SUNY–Plattsburgh
101 Broad Street
Plattsburgh, NY 12901

Syracuse University
201 Tolley Administration Building
Syracuse, NY 13244

NORTH CAROLINA

Appalachian State University
Boone, NC 28608

Barber-Scotia College
145 Cabarrus Avenue, West
Concord, NC 28025

North Carolina Wesleyan College
3400 North Wesleyan Boulevard
Rocky Mount, NC 27804

**University of North
   Carolina–Greensboro**
1000 Spring Garden Street
Greensboro, NC 27412

NORTH DAKOTA

North Dakota State University
Fargo, ND 58105

OHIO
Ashland University
401 College Avenue
Ashland, OH 44805

Bowling Green State University
Bowling Green, OH 43403

Central State University
1400 Brush Row Road
Wilberforce, OH 45384

Kent State University
P.O. Box 5190
Kent, OH 44242

Ohio State University
Columbus, OH 43210

Tiffin University
155 Miami Street
Tiffin, OH 44883-2161

University of Akron
302 Buchtel Common
Akron, OH 44325-0001

OKLAHOMA

Oklahoma State University
Stillwater, OK 74078

University of Central Oklahoma
100 North University Drive
Edmond, OK 73034

OREGON

Southern Oregon State College
Siskiyou Boulevard
Ashland, OR 97520

PENNSYLVANIA

Cheyney University of Pennsylvania
Cheyney, PA 19319

Drexel University
32nd and Chestnut Streets
Philadelphia, PA 19104

Indiana University of Pennsylvania
Indiana, PA 15705

Lebanon Valley College
P.O. Box R
Annville, PA 17003

Marywood College
2300 Adams Avenue
Scranton, PA 18509

Mercyhurst College
Glenwood Hills
Erie, PA 16546

**Pennsylvania State
    University–University Park**
201 Old Main
University Park, PA 16802

Widener University
One University Place
Chester, PA 19013

RHODE ISLAND

Johnson & Wales University
8 Abbott Park Place
Providence, RI 02903

SOUTH CAROLINA

Johnson & Wales University
PCC Box 1409, 701 East Bay Street
Charleston, SC 29403

University of South Carolina
Columbia, SC 29208

SOUTH DAKOTA

Black Hills State University
College Station Box 9501
Spearfish, SD 57799

National College–Sioux Falls Branch
2801 South Kiwanis Avenue
Sioux Falls, SD 57105

Presentation College
1500 North Main Street
Aberdeen, SD 57401

TENNESSEE

Belmost University
1900 Belmont Boulevard
Nashville, TN 37212

Tennessee State University
3500 John Merritt Boulevard
Nashville, TN 37203

University of Tennessee–Knoxville
Knoxville, TN 37996

TEXAS

Huston-Tillotson College
900 Chicon Street
Austin, TX 78702

Stephen F. Austin State University
1936 North Street
Nacogdoches, TX 75962

Texas A&M University–Kingsville
West Santa Gertrudis
Kingsville, TX 78363

Texas Tech University
P.O. Box 45005
Lubbock, TX 79409

University of Houston
4800 Calhoun
Houston, TX 77204

University of Incarnate Word
4301 Broadway
San Antonio, TX 78209

Wiley College
711 Wiley Avenue
Marshall, TX 75670

VERMONT

Johnson State College
Johnson, VT 05656

Southern Vermont College
Monument Avenue
Bennington, VT 05201

VIRGINIA

Hampton University
Hampton, VA 23668

Virginia State University
Petersburg, VA 23806

WASHINGTON

Washington State University
Pullman, WA 99164

WEST VIRGINIA

Concord College
Vermillion Street
P.O. Box 1000
Athens, WV 24712

Glenville State College
200 High Street
Glenville, WV 26351

Shepherd College
Shepherdstown, WV 25443

West Virginia State College
Post Office Box 1000
Institute, WV 25112

WISCONSIN

Lakeland College
P.O. Box 359
Sheboygan, WI 53082

Mount Mary College
2900 North Menomonee River Parkway
Milwaukee, WI 53222

University of Wisconsin-Stout
Menomonie, WI 54751

APPENDIX III
TRADE ASSOCIATIONS, UNIONS, AND OTHER ORGANIZATIONS

The following is a listing of trade associations, unions, and organizations discussed in this book. There are also a number of other associations listed that might be of use to you.

The names, addresses, phone numbers, fax numbers, Web addresses, and e-mail addresses are included so that you can get in touch with any of the associations or unions for information.

Many of the organizations have branch offices located throughout the country. Organization headquarters can get you the phone number and address of the closest local branch.

Advertising Club of New York (ACNY)
235 Park Avenue South, 6th Floor
New York, NY 10003
Phone: 212-533-8080
Fax: 212-533-1929

Advertising Research Foundation (ARF)
641 Lexington Avenue
New York, NY 10022
Phone: 212-751-5656
Fax: 212-319-5265
E-Mail: email@arfsite.org
www.arfsite.org

Advertising Women of New York (AWNY)
153 E. 57th Street
New York, NY 10022
Phone: 212-593-1950
Fax: 212-759-2865
E-Mail: awny85@aol.com

Aerobics Center
(Now known as Cooper Aerobics Center)

Aerobics and Fitness Association of America (AFAA)
15250 Ventura Boulevard, Suite 200
Sherman Oaks, CA 91403
Phone: 818-905-0040
Fax: 818-990-5468
Toll-Free: 800-446-AFAA
www.afaa.com

Affiliated Advertising Agencies International (AAAI)
2289 South Zanadu Way
Aurora, CO 80014
Phone: 303-671-8551

American Advertising Federation (AAF)
1101 Vermont Avenue, NW, Suite 500
Washington, DC 20005
Phone: 202-898-0089
Fax: 202-898-0159
www.aaf.org

American Assembly of Collegiate Schools of Business (AACSB)
AACSB-The International Association for Management Education
600 Emerson Road, Suite 300
St. Louis, MO 63141-6762
Phone: 314-872-8481
Fax: 314-872-8495
www.aacsb.edu

American Association for Adult and Continuing Education (AAACE)
1200 19th Street, NW, Suite 300
Washington, DC 20036
Phone: 202-429-5131
Fax: 202-223-4579
www.albany.edu/aaace

American Association of Advertising Agencies (AAAA)
405 Lexington Avenue, 18th Floor
New York, NY 10174-1801
Phone: 212-682-2500
Fax: 212-682-8391
www.commercepark.com/AAAA/index.html

American Compensation Association (ACA)
14040 N. Northsight Boulevard
Scottsdale, AZ 85260 USA

Phone: 602-951-9191
Fax: 602-483-8352
E-Mail: aca@acaonline.org
www.acaonline.org

American Culinary Federation (ACF)
10 San Bartola Drive
P.O. Box 3466
St. Augustine, FL 32085-3466
Phone: 904-824-4468
Fax: 904-825-4758

American Federation of Musicians of the United States and Canada (AFM)
1501 Broadway, Suite 600
New York, NY 10036
Phone: 212-869-1330
Fax: 212-764-6134

American Gaming Association (AGA)
555 13th Street, NW
Suite 1010 East
Washington, DC 20004-1109
Phone: 202-637-6500
Fax: 202-637-6507
www.americangaming.org/

American Hotel & Motel Association (AH&MA)
1201 New York Avenue, NW, Suite 600
Washington, DC 20005-3931
Phone: 202-289-3100
Fax: 202-289-3199
E-Mail: info@ahma.com
www.ahma.com

American Institute of Baking (AIB)
1213 Bakers Way
P.O. Box 3999
Manhattan, KS 66505-3999

Phone: 785-537-4750
Fax: 785-537-1493
E-Mail: mailbox@aibonline.org
www.aibonline.org

American Institute of Certified Public Accountants (AICPA)

1211 Avenue of the Americas
New York, NY 10036-8775
Phone: 212-596-6200
Fax: 212-596-6213
Toll-Free: 800-862-4272
www.aicpa.org

American Institute of Graphic Arts (AIGA)

164 Fifth Avenue
New York, NY 10010
Phone: 212-807-1990
Fax: 212-807-1799
Toll-Free: 800-548-1634

American Marketing Association (AMA)

250 S. Wacker Drive, Suite 200
Chicago, IL 60606
Phone: 312-648-0536
Fax: 312-993-7542
Toll-Free: 800-262-1150
E-Mail: info@ama.org
www.ama.org

American Nurses Association (ANA)

600 Maryland Avenue SW, Suite 100 W.
Washington, DC 20024-2571
Phone: 202-651-7000
Fax: 202-651-7001
Toll-Free: 800-637-0323
www.nursingworld.org

American Occupational Therapy Association (AOTA)
American Red Cross National Headquarters (ARC)

8111 Gatehouse Road
Falls Church, VA 22042
Phone: 202-737-8300

American Society of Heating, Air Conditioning, and Refrigeration

1105 Nothingham Hill
Round Rock, TX 78681
Phone: 512-255-3146

American Society for Training and Development (ASTD)

Box 1443
1640 King Street

Alexandria, VA 22313
Phone: 703-683-8100
Fax: 703-683-8103

American Society of Travel Agents (ASTA)

1101 King Street
Alexandria, VA 22314
Phone: 703-739-2782
Fax: 703-684-8319
www.astanet.com

Art Directors Club (ADC)

250 Park Avenue South
New York, NY 10003-1402
Phone: 212-674-0500
Fax: 212-460-8506
E-Mail: adcny@interport.net
www.adcny.org

Association for Business Communication (ABC)

Baruch College
17 Lexington Avenue
New York, NY 10010
Phone: 212-387-1620
Fax: 212-387-1655

Association of Computer Professionals (ACP)

9 Forest Drive
Plainview, NY 11803
Phone: 516-938-8223
Fax: 516-938-3073
www.acp-inter.org

Association for Computing Machinery (ACM)

One Astor Plaza
1515 Broadway
New York, NY 10036
Phone: 212-869-7440
Fax: 212-944-1318
E-Mail: ACMHELP@acm.org
www.acm.org

Association for Computing Machinery, Special Interest Groups On Programming Languages (SIGPL)

One Astor Plaza
1515 Broadway
New York, NY 10036
Phone: 212-869-7440
Fax: 212-944-1318
E-Mail: ACMHELP@acm.org
www.acm.org

Association for Women In Communications

1244 Ritchie Highway, Suite 6
Arnold, MD 21012-1887
Phone: 410-544-7442
Fax: 410-544-4640
E-Mail: pat@womcom.org

Bartenders & Beverage Local #165

1630 South Commerce Street
Las Vegas, NV 89102
702-384-7774

British Casino Association

29 Castle Street
Reading RG1 57B, England
Phone: 44 0118 9589191
Fax: 44 0118 9590592
www.british-casinos.co.uk

Career College Association (CCA)

750 1st Street NE, Suite 900
Washington, DC 20002
Phone: 202-336-6700
Fax: 202-336-6828
E-Mail: cca@career.org
www.career.org

Casino Customer Care

P.O. Box 711
Monticello, NY 12701
914-794-7312

Casino Management Association

3172 N. Rainbow, Suite 254
Las Vegas, NV 89108-4534
Phone: 702-593-5477
Fax: 702-837-5353
E-Mail: lasvegascma@juno.com
www.cmaweb.org

Casino and Theme Party Operators Association

P.O. Box 1686
Las Vegas, NV 89125-1686
Phone: 702-385-2963
Fax: 702-385-6963
E-Mail: gameco@vegas.quik.com

Central City Casino Association

P.O. Box 773
Central City, CO 80427-0773
Phone: 303-582-5322
Fax: 303-582-5326

Communications Workers of America, Local 4478 (CWA)

1464 Temple Road
Bucyrus, OH 44820
Phone: 419-562-3535

Computer and Communications Industry Association (CCIA)
666 11th Street, NW, Suite 600
Washington, DC 20001
Phone: 202-783-0070
Fax: 202-783-0534
E-Mail: ccianet@gte.net
www.ccianet.org

Cooper Aerobics Center
12200 Preston Road
Dallas, TX 75230
Phone: 214-239-7223
E-Mail: coopermail@cooperaerobics.com
www.coopercenter.com

Council on Hotel, Restaurant, and Institutional Education (CHRIE)
1200 17th Street, NW
Washington, DC 20036-3097
Phone: 202-331-5990
Fax: 202-785-2511
E-Mail: alliance@access.digex.net

Culinary Institute of America (CIA)
433 Albany Post Road
Hyde Park, NY 12538
Phone: 914-452-9600

Culinary Workers Local #226
1630 South Commerce
Las Vegas, NV 89102
702-385-2131

Direct Marketing Association (DMA)
1120 Avenue of the Americas
New York, NY 10036-6700
Phone: 212-768-7277
Fax: 212-768-7353
E-Mail: dma@the-dma.org
www.the-dma.org

Educational Foundation of the National Restaurant Association (EFNRA)
1200 17th Street, NW, No. 1400
Washington, DC 20036-3097
Phone: 202-331-5900
Toll-Free: 800-765-2122
E-Mail: isal@restaurant.org
www.restaurant.org

Educational Institute of the American Hotel & Motel Association (AH&MA)
1201 New York Avenue, NW, Suite 600
Washington, DC 20005-3931
Phone: 202-289-3100
Fax: 202-289-3199
E-Mail: info@ahma.com
www.ahma.com

Gaming and Economic Development Institute
121 Main Street
Annapolis, MD 21401-2002

Graphic Artists Guild (GAG)
90 John Street, Suite 403
New York, NY 10038-3202
Phone: 212-791-3400
Fax: 212-791-0333
E-Mail: paulatgag@aol.com
www.gag.org

Hotel Employees, Restaurant Employees AFL-CIO, Culinary & Casino
1632 Highway 95, P.O. Box 21825
Bullhead City, AZ 86442

Institute for Certification of Computing Professionals (ICCP)
2200 E. Devon Avenue, Suite 247
Des Plaines, IL 60018
Phone: 847-299-4227
Fax: 847-299-4280
Toll-Free: 800-U-GET-CCP
E-Mail: 74040.3722@compuserve.com
www.iccp.org

Institute of Certified Travel Agents (ICTA)
148 Linden Street
P.O. Box 812059
Wellesley, MA 02482
Phone: 781-237-0280
Fax: 781-237-3860
Toll-Free: 800-542-4282

Institute of Internal Auditors (IIA)
249 Maitland Avenue
Altamonte Springs, FL 32701-4201
Phone: 407-830-7600
Fax: 407-831-5171
E-Mail: iia@theiia.org
www.theiia.org

International Alliance of Theatrical Stage Employees (IATSE)
1515 Broadway, Suite 601
New York, NY 10036
Phone: 212-730-1770
Fax: 212-921-7699

International Association of Business Communicators (IABC)
1 Hallidie Plaza, Suite 600
San Francisco, CA 94102

Phone: 415-433-3400
Fax: 415-362-8762
E-Mail: leader-centre@iabc.com
www.iabc.com

International Association for Computer Information Systems (IACIS)
c/o Dr. G. Daryl Nord
Oklahoma State University
College of Business Administration
Stillwater, OK 74078
Phone: 405-744-8632
Fax: 405-744-5180
E-Mail: dnord@okway.okstate.edu
www.iacis.org

International Association of Culinary Professionals (IACP)
304 W. Liberty Street, Suite 201
Louisville, KY 40202
Phone: 502-581-9786
Fax: 502-589-3602
Toll-Free: 800-928-4227
E-Mail: iapl@hqtrs.com
www.iacp-online.org

International Association of Culinary Professionals Foundation (IACP)
304 W. Liberty Street, Suite 201
Louisville, KY 40202 USA
Phone: 502-587-7953
Fax: 502-589-3602
E-Mail: ellenm@hqtrs.com
www.gstis.net/epicure

International Brotherhood of Electrical Workers (IBEW)
1125 15th Street, NW
Washington, DC 20005
Phone: 202-833-7000
Fax: 202-467-6316
www.ibew.org

International Dance-Exercise Association (IDEA)
6190 Cornerstone Court E
San Diego, CA 92121
Phone: 619-535-8979

International Executive Housekeepers Association (IEHA)
1001 Eastwind Drive, Suite 301
Westerville, OH 43081-3361
Phone: 614-895-7166
Fax: 614-895-1248
Toll-Free: 800-200-6342
E-Mail: excel@ieha.org
www.ieha.org

International Foundation of Employee Benefit Plans (IFEBP)
18700 W. Bluemound Road
P.O. Box 69
Brookfield, WI 53008
Phone: 414-786-6700
Fax: 414-786-8670
Toll-Free: 888-334-3327
E-Mail: pr@ifebp.org
www.ifebp.org

Internet Professionals Association (IPA)
P.O. Box 92
Passumpsic, VT 05861

Mail Advertising Service Association International (MASA)
1421 Prince Street
Alexandria, VA 22314
Phone: 703-836-9200
Fax: 703-548-8204
Toll-Free: 800-333-6272

Marketing Research Association (MRA)
1344 Silas Deane Highway, Suite 306
P.O. Box 230
Rocky Hill, CT 06067-0230
Phone: 860-257-4008
Fax: 860-257-3990
E-Mail: email@mra-net.org

Massachusetts Gaming Association
c/o Gerard Mazzola
100 Boylston Street, Suite 1050
Boston, MA 02116-4610
Phone: 617-426-6400

Missouri Riverboat Gaming Association
6609 Clayton Road, Suite 2 W
St. Louis, MO 63117-1641
Phone: 314-721-7704

Missouri River Casino Security Association
c/o Shay East
4443 NW Gateway
Riverside, MO 64150-0000

Musicians Local #369
3701 Vegas Drive
Las Vegas, NV 89108
702-647-3690

National Association of Personnel Services (NAPS)
3133 Mt. Vernon Avenue
Alexandria, VA 22305
Phone: 703-684-0180
Fax: 703-684-0071
E-Mail: info@napsweb.org
www.napsweb.org

National Association of Webmasters (NAW)
9580 Oak Parkway, Suite 7-177
Folsom, CA 95630 USA
Phone: 916-929-6557
Fax: 916-929-1721
E-Mail: wbc@naw.org
www.naw.org

National Cosmetology Association (NCA)
3510 Olive Street
St. Louis, MO 63103
Phone: 314-534-7982
Fax: 314-534-8618
Toll-Free: 800-527-1683
E-Mail: nca-now@primary.net
www.nca-now.com

National Indian Gaming Association (NIGA)
c/o Richard G. Hill
224 Second Street SE
Washington, DC 20003
Phone: 202-546-7711
Fax: 202-546-1755
Toll-Free: 800-286-6442

National Restaurant Association (NRA)
1200 17th Street, NW
Washington, DC 20036
Phone: 202-331-5900
Fax: 202-331-2429
E-Mail: isal@restaurant.org
www.restaurant.org

National Retail Federation (NRF)
325 7th Street, NW, Suite 1000
Washington, DC 20004-2802
Phone: 202-783-7971
Fax: 202-737-2849
Toll-Free: 800-NRF-HOW2
E-Mail: nrf@nrf.com
www.nrf.com

National Safety Council (NSC)
1121 Spring Lake Drive
Itasca, IL 60143-3201
Phone: 630-285-1121
Fax: 630-285-1315
www.nsc.org

National Society of Professional Engineers (NSPE)
1420 King Street
Alexandria, VA 22314
Phone: 703-684-2800
Fax: 703-836-4875
Toll-Free: 888-285-6773
E-Mail: customer.service@nspe.org
www.nspe.org

National Society of Public Accountants (NSPA)
1010 N. Fairfax Street
Alexandria, VA 22314-1574
Phone: 703-549-6400
Fax: 703-549-2984
Toll-Free: 800-966-6679
E-Mail: NSA@wizard.net
www.nsa.org

Nevada Association Race and Sports Book Operators (NARASO)
37-65 Central Park Circle, No. 8
Las Vegas, NV 89109
Phone: 702-731-0749

Nevada Casino Dealers Association
1120 Fremont Street
Las Vegas, NV 89101-5406

North American Gaming Regulators Association (NAGRA)
P.O. Box 21886
Lincoln, NE 68542-1886
Phone: 402-474-4261
Fax: 402-474-2426
www.nagra.org

The One Club
32 East 21st Street
New York, NY
www.oneclub.com/

Passenger Vessel Association (PVA)
1600 Wilson Boulevard, Suite 1000-A
Arlington, VA 22209
Phone: 703-807-0100
Fax: 703-807-0103
E-Mail: pasvessl@msn.com

Professional Secretaries International
10502 NW Ambassador Drive
P.O. Box 20404
Kansas City, MO 64195-0404
Phone: 816-891-6600
Fax: 816-891-9118
www.main.org/psi/

Promotion Marketing Association of America (PMAA)
257 Park Avenue South, 11th Floor
New York, NY 10010-7304
Phone: 212-420-1100
Fax: 212-533-7622
E-Mail: pmaa@pmaalink.org
www.pmaalink.org

Public Relations Society of America (PRSA)
33 Irving Place, 3rd Floor
New York, NY 10003-2376
Phone: 212-995-2230
Fax: 212-995-0757
Toll-Free: 800-WER-PRSA
www.prsa.org

Refrigeration Service Engineers Society (RSES)
1666 Rand Road
Des Plaines, IL 60016-3552
Phone: 847-297-6464
Fax: 847-297-5038
E-Mail: rses@starnetinc.com
www.rses.org

River Boat Casino Association of Louisiana
301 Main Street
Baton Rouge, LA 70801

Sales and Marketing Executives International (SMEI)
5500 Interstate North Parkway #545
Atlanta, GA 30328
Phone: 770-661-8500
Fax: 770-661-8512
E-mail: smeihq@smei.org
www.smei.org

Shelly Field Organization Motivational Speeches & Seminars
P.O. Box 711
Monticello, NY 12701
Phone: 914-794-7312
www.shellyfield.com

Society of Actuaries (SOA)
475 N. Martingale Road, Suite 800
Schaumburg, IL 60173-2226
Phone: 847-706-3500
Fax: 847-706-3599
www.soa.org

Society for Human Resource Management (SHRM)
1800 Duke Street
Alexandria, VA 22314-3499
Phone: 703-548-3440
Fax: 703-836-0367
Toll-Free: 800-283-7476
E-Mail: shrm@shrm.org

Society of Illustrators (SI)
128 E. 63rd Street
New York, NY 10021
Phone: 212-838-2560
Fax: 212-838-2561
E-Mail: society@societyillustrators.org
www.societyillustrators.org

Society for Technical Communication (STC)
901 N. Stuart Street, Suite 904
Arlington, VA 22203-1854
Phone: 703-522-4114
Fax: 703-522-2075
E-Mail: stc@stc-va.org
www.stc-va.org

Society of Wine Educators (SWE)
8600 Foundry Street Mill 2044
Savage, MD 20763
Phone: 301-776-8569
Fax: 301-776-8578
E-Mail: vintage@erols.com

Society of Women Engineers
120 Wall Street, 11th Floor
New York, NY 10005-3902
Phone: 212-509-9577
E-Mail: hq@swe.org
www.swe.org

STRESS-BUSTERS: Casino Customer Care
P.O. Box 107
Monticello, NY 12701
914-794-7312
www.shellyfield.com

Teamsters Local #995
300 Shadow Lane
Las Vegas, NV 89106
702-385-0995

Texas Casino Development Association
1108 Lavaca Street
Austin, TX 78701-2125

United Food and Commercial Workers International Union (UFCW)
1775 K Street, NW
Washington, DC 20006
Phone: 202-223-3111
Fax: 202-466-1562
www.ufcw.org

United Scenic Artists (USA)
16 W. 61st Street, 11th Floor
New York, NY 10023
Phone: 212-581-0300
Fax: 212-977-2011

United States Department of Labor
200 Constitution Avenue, NW,
    Room S-1032
Washington, DC 20210
Phone: 202-693-4650
www.dol.gov

U.S. Office of Personnel Management and the Veterans Administration
1900 E Street, NW
Washington, DC 20415-0001
Phone: 202-606-1800
www.opm.gov/veterans/index.htm

Veterans Administration
810 Vermont Avenue
Washington, DC 20420
Phone: 202-233-2741
www.va.gov

Women In Communications, Inc. (Now known as Association for Women In Communications)
1244 Ritchie Highway, Suite 6
Arnold, MD 21012-1887
Phone: 410-544-7442
Fax: 410-544-4640
E-Mail: pat@womcom.org

APPENDIX IV
DIRECTORY OF AMERICAN CASINOS

The following is a directory of American casinos. It includes those that are land-based, floating and docked riverboats, daily gaming cruises sailing territorial waters, and Indian gaming facilities.

Names, addresses, phone numbers, toll-free numbers, and Web addresses are included. Casinos are listed alphabetically by state. In areas where there are a number of cities or areas hosting casinos, they have been additionally separated by area.

ARIZONA

Apache Gold Casino
P.O. Box 1210
San Carlos, AZ 85550
520-425-7692
800-APACHE-3

Blue Water Casino
119 W. Riverside Drive
Parker, AZ 85344
520-669-7777
800-747-8777
www.bluewatercasino.com

Bucky's Casino & Resort
530 E. Merrit
Prescott, AZ 86301
520-776-1666
www.buckyscasino.com

Casino Arizona
524 North 92nd Street
Scottsdale, AZ 85256
602-850-7777
877-724-HOUR

Casino of the Sun
7406 South Camino De Oeste
Tucson, AZ 85746
520-883-1700
800-344-9435
www.casinosun.com

Cliff Castle Casino
353 Middle Verde Road
Campe Verde, AZ 86322
520-567-9031
800-381-SLOT
www.cliffcastle.com

Cocopah Casino & Bingo
15136 South Avenue B
Somerton, AZ 85350
520-726-8066
800-23-SLOTS

Desert Diamond Casino
7350 South Old Nogales Highway
Tucson, AZ 85734
520-294-7777

Fort McDowell Casino
P.O. Box 18539
Fountain Hills, AZ 85269
602-837-1424
800-THE-FORT
www.fortmcdowellcasino.com

Gila River Casino–Vee Quiva
6443 North Komarke Lane
Leveen, AZ 85339
520-796-7777
800-WIN-GILA

Gila River Casino–Wild Horse
5512 West Wild Horse Pass
Chandler, AZ 85226
520-796-7727
800-WIN-GILA

Harrah's Ak-Chin Casino
15406 Maricopa Road
Maricopa, AZ 85239
602-802-5000
800-HARRAHS
www.harrahs.com

Hon Dah Casino
P.O. Box 3250
Pinetop, AZ 85835
520-369-0299
800-WAY-UPHI

Mezzatzal Casino
P.O. Box 1820
Payson, AZ 85547
520-474-6044
800-777-7529

Paradise Casino
450 Quechan Drive
Yuma, AZ 85364

760-572-7777
888-777-4946

Spirit Mountain Casino
8555 South Highway 95
Mohave Valley, AZ 86440
520-346-2000

Yavapai Casino
1501 East Highway 69
Prescott, AZ 86301
520-445-5767
800-SLOTS-44
www.buckyscasino.com

CALIFORNIA

Barona Casino
1000 Wildcat Canyon Road
Lakeside, CA 92040
619-443-2300
800-7-BARONA
www.barona.com

Black Bart Casino
P.O. Box 1177
Willits, CA 95490
707-459-7330

Cache Creek Indian Bingo & Casino
14455 Highway 16
Brooks, CA 95606
530-796-3118
800-452-8181

Cahuilla Creek Restaurant & Casino
P.O. Box 390845
Anza, CA 92539
909-763-1200

Casino Morongo
49750 Seminole Drive
Cabazon, CA 92230
909-849-3080
800-252-4499

Cher-Ae Heights Casino
P.O. Box 635
Trinidad, CA 95570
707-677-3611
800-684-BINGO

Chicken Ranch Bingo
16929 Chicken Ranch Road
Jamestown, CA 95327
209-984-3000
800-752-4646

Chumash Casino
3400 Highway 246
Santa Ynez, CA 93460
805-686-0855
800-728-9997
www.casinocity.com/us/ca/santayne

Colusa Casino & Bingo
P.O. Box 1267
Colusa, CA 95932
530-458-8844
800-655-U-WIN

Crystall Mountain Casino
5200 Honpie Road
Shingle Springs, CA 95682
530-676-8010

Eagle Mountain Casino
P.O. Box 1659
Porterville, CA 93258
209-788-6220
800-903-3353

Elk Valley Casino
2500 Howland Hill Road
Crescent City, CA 95531
707-464-1020

Fantasy Springs Casino
82-245 Indio Springs Drive
Indio, CA 92203
760-342-5000
800-827-2WIN
www.cabazonindians.com

Feather Falls Casino
3 Alverda Drive
Oronville, CA 95966
530-533-3885
877-OK-BINGO

Gold Country Casino
4020 Olive Highway
Oronville, CA 95966
530-538-4560

Golden Bear Casino
54 East Klamath Beach Road
Klamath, CA 95546
707-482-5501

Havasu Landing Casino & Resort
P.O. Box 1707
Havasu Lake, CA 92363
707-858-4593

Hopland Sho-Ka-Wah Casino
13101 Nakomis Road
Hopland, CA 95440
707-744-1395

Jackson Rancheria Casino & Hotel
12222 New York Ranch Road
Jackson, CA 95642
209-223-1677
800-822-WINN
www.jacksoncasino.com

Konocti Vista Casino
2755 Mission Rancheria Road
Lakeport, CA 95453
707-262-1900
800-FUN-1950

Lucky Bear Casino
P.O. Box 1348
Hoopa, CA 95546
530-625-4048

Lucky 7 Casino
350 North Indian Road
Smith River, CA 95567
707-487-7777

Mono Win Casino
37302 Rancheria Lane, Box 1060
Auberry, CA 93602
209-855-4350

Paiute Palace Casino
P.O. Box 1325
Bishop, CA 93154
760-873-4150

Palace Indian Gaming Center
17225 Jersey Avenue
Lemoore, CA 93245
209-924-7751
800-942-6886

Paradise Casino
350 Picado Road
Winterhaven, CA 92283
760-572-7777
888-777-4946

Pechango Entertainment Center
45000 Pala Road
Temecula, CA 92592
909-693-1819

Pit River Casino
20265 Tamarack Avenue
Burney, CA 96013
530-335-2334
888-245-2992

Red Fox Casino & Bingo
300 Cahto Drive
Laytonville, CA 95454
707-984-6800
888-4-RED-FOX

Robinson Rancheria Bingo & Casino
1545 East Highway 20
Nice, CA 95464
707-275-9000
800-809-3636

San Manuel Indian Bingo & Casino
5797 North Victoria Avenue
Highland, CA 92346
909-864-5050
800-359-2464
www.sanmanuel.com

Shokakai Casino
P.O. Box 320
Calpella, CA 94581
707-485-0700

Soboba Casino
2333 Soboba Road
San Jacinto, CA 92583
909-654-2883
800-618-7774

Spa Casino
140 North Indian Canyon Drive
Palm Springs, CA 92262
760-323-5865
800-258-2WIN

Spotlight 29 Casino
46200 Harrison Place
Coachella, CA 92236
760-775-5566

Susanville Casino
900 Skyline Drive
Susanville, CA 96130
530-252-1100

Sycuan Casino
5469 Dehesa Road
El Cajon, CA 92019
619-445-6002
800-279-2826
www.sycuancasino.com

Table Mountain Casino & Bingo
8184 Table Mountain Road
Friant, CA 93626
209-822-2485
800-541-3637

Twin Pines Casino
22223 Highway 29 at Rancheria Road
Middletown, CA 95461
707-987-0197
800-564-4872
www.twinpine.com

Viejas Casino & Turf Club
5000 Willows Road
Alpine, CA 91901
619-445-5400
800-84-POKER
www.viejasnet.com

Win-River Casino
2100 Redding Rancheria Road
Redding, CA 96001
530-243-3377
800-280-8946

COLORADO

Black Hawk

Black Hawk Sation
141 Gregory Street
Black Hawk, CO 80422
303-582-5582

Bull Durham Saloon & Casino
110 Main Street
Black Hawk, CO 80422
303-582-0810

Bullwhackers Black Hawk Casino
101 Gregory Street
Black Hawk, CO 80422
303-764-1600
800-GAM-BULL

Bullwhackers Silver Hawk
100 Chase Street
Black Hawk, CO 80422
303-764-1400
800-GAM-BULL

Canyon Casino
131 Main Street
Black Hawk, CO 80422
303-777-1111

Colorado Central Station Casino
340 Main Street
Black Hawk, CO 80422
303-582-3000

Crook's Palace Saloon & Casino
200 Gregory Street
Black Hawk, CO 80422
303-582-5094

Eureka Casino
211 Gregory Street
Black Hawk, CO 80422
303-582-1040

Fitzgeralds Casino
101 Main Street
Black Hawk, CO 80422
303-582-6162
800-538-5825

Gilpin Hotel Casino
111 Main Street
Black Hawk, CO 80422
303-582-1133

Gold Mine Casino
130 Clear Creek
Black Hawk, CO 80422
303-582-0711

Golden Gates Casino
261 Main Street
Black Hawk, CO 80422
303-582-1650

Isle of Capri-Black Hawk
451 Main Street
Black Hawk, CO 80422
303-998-7777
800-THE-ISLE

Jazz Alley Casino
321 Main Street
Black Hawk, CO 80422
303-582-1125

The Lodge Casino at Blackhawk
240 Main Street
Black Hawk, CO 80422
303-582-1117
877-711-1177

Otto's Casino at the Black Forest Inn
260 Gregory Street
Black Hawk, CO 80422
303-642-0415

Red Dolly Casino
530 Gregory Street
Black Hawk, CO 80422
303-582-1100

Richman Casino
101 Richman Street
Black Hawk, CO 80422
303-582-0400

Wild Card Saloon & Casino
112 Main Street
Black Hawk, CO 80422
303-582-3412

Central City

Bullwhackers Central City Casino
130 Main Street
Central City, CO 80427
303-271-2500
800-GAM-BULL

Central Palace Casino
132 Lawrence Street
Central City, CO 80427
303-477-7117
800-822-7466

Doc Holiday Casino
101 Main Street
Central City, CO 80427
303-582-1400

Dostal Alley Saloon & Gaming Emporium
1 Dostal Alley
Central City, CO 80427
303-582-1610

Famous Bonanza Lucky Strike Casino
107 Main Street
Central City, CO 80427
303-582-5914

Gold Coin Casino
120 Main Street
Central City, CO 80427
303-582-1990

Golden Rose Casino
102 Main Street
P.O. Box 157
Central City, CO 80427

303-582-5060
800-929-0255

Harvey's Wagon Wheel Hotel & Casino
321 Gregory Street
Central City, CO 80427
303-582-0800
800-WAGON-HO

Teller House Casino
120 Eureka Sreet
P.O. Box 8
Central City, CO 80427
303-582-3200

Cripple Creek

Black Diamond Silver Spur Casino
425 East Bennett Avenue
Cripple Creek, CO 80813
719-689-2898

Brass Ass Casino
264 East Bennett Avenue
Cripple Creek, CO 80813
719-689-2104

Bronco Billy's Sports Bar & Casino
300 East Bennett Avenue
Cripple Creek, CO 80813
719-689-2142
www.cripplecreek.com

Colorado Grande Gaming Parlor
300 East Bennett Avenue
Cripple Creek, CO 80813
719-689-3517

Crapper Jack's Casino
404 E. Bennett Avenue
Cripple Creek, CO 80813
719-689-9467

Creeker's Casino
272 East Bennett Avenue
Cripple Creek, CO 80813
719-689-3239

Double Eagle Hotel & Casino
442 East Bennett Avenue
Cripple Creek, CO 80813
719-689-5000
800-711-7234

Gold Rush Hotel & Casino
290 East Bennett Avenue
Cripple Creek, CO 80813
719-689-2646

800-235-8329
www.criple-creek.com.us/grush.htm

Imperial Casino Hotel
123 North Third Street
Cripple Creek, CO 80813
719-689-2922
800-235-2922

J. P. McGill's
232 East Bennett Avenue
Cripple Creek, CO 80813
719-689-2497

Johnny Nolon's Casino
301 East Bennett Avenue
Cripple Creek, CO 80813
719-689-2080

Jubilee Casino & Carnival
351 Myers Avenue
P.O. Box 610
Cripple Creek, CO 80813
719-689-2519
800-WIN-HERE

Maverick's Casino & Steak House
411 East Bennett Avenue
Cripple Creek, CO 80813
719-689-2737

Midnight Rose Hotel and Casino
256 East Bennett Avenue
Cripple Creek, CO 80813
719-689-2865
800-635-5825

Old Chicago Casino
419 East Bennett Avenue
Cripple Creek, CO 80813
719-689-7880

Palace Hotel & Casino
172 East Bennett Avenue
Cripple Creek, CO 80813
719-689-2993

Virgin Mule
259 East Bennett Avenue
Cripple Creek, CO 80813
719-689-2734

Womack's Legends Hotel & Casino
200-220 East Bennett Avenue
Cripple Creek, CO 80813
719-689-0333
888-WOMACKS

Ignacio

Sky Ute Casino and Lodge
14826 Highway 172 North
P.O. Box 340
Ignacio, CO 81137
800-876-7017
www.southern.ute.nsn.us/casino

Towaoc

Ute Mountain Casion & RV Park
3 Weeminuche Drive
P.O. Drawer V
Towaoc, CO 81334
970-565-8800
800-258-8007
www.utemountaincasino.com

CONNECTICUT

Foxwoods Resort Casino
Route 2
Ledyard, CT 06339
816-312-3000
800-PLAY-BIG

Mohegan Sun Casino
1 Mohegan Sun Boulevard
Uncasville, CT 06382
860-204-8000
888-226-7711
www.mohegan.nsn.us

DELAWARE

Delaware Park Racetrack & Slots
777 Delaware Park Boulevard
Stanton, DE 19804
302-994-2521
800-441-6587
www.delpark.com

Dover Downs
1131 N. Dupont Highway
Dover, DE 19901
302-674-4600
800-711-5882
www.doverdowns.com

Midway Slots & Simulcast
Delaware State Fairgrounds
U.S. 13 South
Harrington, DE 19952
302-398-4920
888-88-SLOTS
www.midwayslots.com

FLORIDA

Daytona Beach Area

SunCruz Casino-Daytona
4884 Front Street
Ponce Inlet, FL 32127
904-322-9000
800-474-DICE
www.suncruzcasino.com

Fort Lauderdale Area

Monte Carlo Casino Cruiser
101 N. Riverside Drive
Suite 210
Pompano Beach, FL 33062
954-785-5100

New Sea Escape
2701 West Oakland Park Boulevard
Fort Lauderdale, FL 33311
954-453-2200
800-327-2005

SunCruz Casino-Hollywood
647 East Dania Beach Boulevard
Dania, FL 33004
954-929-3800
800-474-DICE
www.suncruzcasino.com

Fort Myers Beach Area

Big M Casino
450 Harabor Court
Fort Myers Beach, FL 33931
941-463-6137

Europa SeaKruz
645 San Carlos Boulevard
Fort Myers Beach, FL 33931
941-463-5000
800-688-PLAY
www.europa-seakruz.com

Giordano International Casino
7181 College Parkway #30
Fort Myers, FL 33907
941-936-DICE
800-984-DICE
www.giordanocasinos.com

Fort Pierce

Midnight Gambler
1 Avenue A, Dock A
Fort Pierce, FL 34950
561-464-8694
888-777-8198

Hollywood

Hollywood Seminole Gaming
4150 N. State Road 7
Hollywood, FL 33201
954-961-3220
800-323-5452

Immokalee

Seminole Indian Casino
506 South 1st Street
Immokalee, FL 33934
941-658-1313
800-218-0007

Jacksonville Area

La Cruise Casino
4738 Ocean Street
Atlantic Beach, FL 32233
904-241-7200
800-752-1778

Key Largo

SunCruz Casino–Key Largo
99701 Overseas Highway
Key Largo, FL 33037
305-451-0000
800-474-DICE
www.suncruzcasino.com

Miami Area

Casino Miami
300 Biscayne Boulevard
Miami, FL 33131
305-577-7775

Casino Princesa
100 South Biscayne Boulevard
Miami, FL 33131
305-379-4422

Europa SeaKruz–South Beach
300 Alton Road, Pier A
Miami Beach, FL 33139
305-538-8300
800-688-PLAY
www.europa-seakruz.com

Miccosukee Indian Gaming
500 S.W. 177 Avenue
Miami, FL 33194
305-222-4600
800-741-4600
www.miccosukee.com

Palm Beach Area

Contessa Cruise & Casino
1201 U.S. Highway 1 #35
North Palm Beach, FL 33408
561-622-6744
888-711-8946

Palm Beach Princess
777 East Port Road
Riviera Beach, FL 33404
561-845-7447
800-841-7447

SunCruz Casino–Palm Beach
111 East 14th Street
Riviera Beach, FL 33404
561-863-9555
800-474-DICE
www.suncruzcasino.com

Panama City

Emerald Coast Cruise
4 Harrison Avenue
Panama City, FL 32401
850-873-9900

Port Canaveral Area

SunCruz Casino–Port Canaveral
620 Glen Cheeks Drive
Port Canaveral, FL 32920
407-799-3511
800-474-DICE
www.suncruzcasino.com

Sterling Casino Lines
101 George King Boulevard #3
Cape Canaveral, FL 32921
407-783-2212
888-81-LUCKY

Port Richey

SunCruz Casino–Port Richey
8715 Port Richey Village Loop
Port Richey, FL 34668
813-848-3423
800-474-DICE
www.suncruzcasino.com

St. Petersburg Area

SunCruz Casino–Clearwater
198 Seminole Street
Clearwater, FL 33757
813-895-3325
800-474-DICE
www.suncruzcasino.com

SunCruz Casino–John's Pass
12788 Kingfish Drive
Treasure Island, FL 33706
813-895-3325
800-474-DICE
www.suncruzcasino.com

Europa SeaKruz
150 153rd Avenue
Madeira Beach, FL 33708
813-393-2885
800-688-PLAY
www.europa-seakruz.com

Tampa

Seminole Indian Casino
5223 North Orient Road
Tampa, FL 33610
813-621-1302
800-282-7016
www.casino-tampa.com

Tarpon Springs

SunCruz Casino–Tarpon Springs
507 Ancolote Road
Tarpon Springs, FL 34689
813-848-3423
800-474-DICE
www.suncruzcasino.com

Venice

Vegas N'Venice
449 North Tamiami Trail
Venice, FL 34292
941-486-1118
888-VENICE-1

GEORGIA

Atlantic Star Cruise Line
P.O. Box 2117
Tybee Island, GA 31328
912-786-7827

Emerald Princess Dinner Cruise & Casino
One St. Andrews Court
Brunswick, GA 32034
912-265-3558
800-842-0115
www.emeraldprincesscasino.com

IDAHO

Clearwater River Casino
7463 North & South Highway 95
Lewiston, ID 83501
208-746-5733

Coeur D'Alene Tribal Bingo and Casino
U.S. Highway 95
P.O. Box 236
Worley, ID 83876
208-686-5106
800-523-BINGO
www.uslottery.com

It'se Ye-Ye Bingo and Casino
4040 Main Street
Kamiah, ID 85356
208-935-1019
www.idcasino.net

Kootenai River Inn & Casino
Kootenai River Plaza
Bonners Ferry, ID 83805
208-267-8511
800-346-5668

Sho-Bannock High Stakes Casino
P.O. Box 868
Fort Hall, ID 83203
208-237-8778

ILLINOIS

Alton Belle Riverboat Casino
219 Piasa Street
Alton, IL 62002
618-474-7500
800-336-SLOT
www.argosycasinos.com

Casino Queen
200 S. Front Street
East S. Louis, IL 62201
618-874-5000
800-777-0777
www.casinoqueen.com

Empress Casino–Joliet
2300 Empress Drive
Joliet, IL 60436
815-744-9400
800-4-EMPRESS
www.empresscasino.com

Grand Victoria Casino
250 South Grove Avenue
Elgin, IL 60120
847-888-1000
www.grandvictoria-elgin.com

Harrah's Joliet Casino
150 North Scott Street
Joliet, IL 60431
815-774-2610
800-HARRAHS
www.harrahs.com

Hollywood Casino–Aurora
1 New York Street Bridge
Aurora, IL 60506
630-801-7000
800-888-7777
www.hollywoodcasino.com

Jumer's Casino Rock Island
1735 First Avenue
Rock Island, IL 61201
309-793-4200
800-477-7747
www.jumers.com

Par-A-Dice Riverboat Casino
21 Blackjack Boulevard
East Peoria, IL 61611
309-698-7711
800-727-2342
www.par-a-dice.com

Players Island Casino–Metropolis
203 South Ferry Street
Metropolis, IL 62960
618-524-2628
800-935-7700
www.playersisland.com

INDIANA

Argosy Casino & Hotel–Lawarenceburg
777 Argosy Parkway
Lawarenceburg, IN 47025
812-539-8000
888-ARGOSY-7
www.argosycasinos.com

Blue Chip Casino
2 Easy Street
Michigan City, IN 46360
219-879-7711
888-879-7711

Casino Aztar
421 N.W. Riverside Drive
Evansville, IN 47708
812-433-4000
800-DIAL-FUN
www.casinoaztar.com

Ceasars Indiana
1355 Stucky Road
Elizabeth, IN 47117
812-738-3848
800-CEASARS

Empress Casino Hammond
One Empress Place
Hammond, IN 46320
219-473-7000
888-4-EMPRESS

Grand Victoria Casino and Resort
600 Grand Victoria Drive
Rising Sun, IN 47040
812-438-1234
800-GRAND-11

Majestic Star Casino
1 Buffington Harbor Drive
Gary, IN 46406
219-977-7777
888-2B-LUCKY

Showboat Casino–East Chicago
One Showboat Place
East Chicago, IN 46312
219-378-3000
800-SHOWBOAT
www.showboatcasino.com

Trump Hotel Casino
1 Buffington Harbor Drive
Gary, IN 46406
219-977-8980
888-218-7867
www.trump.com

IOWA

Ameristar Casino Council Bluffs
2200 River Road
Council Bluffs, IA 51501

712-328-8888
800-700-1012
www.ameristars.com

Bluffs Run Casino
2710 23rd Avenue
Council Bluffs, IA 51501
712-323-2500
800-BET-2-WIN

Belle of Sioux City
100 Chris Larsen Park
Sioux City, IA 51102
712-255-0080
800-424-0080
www.argosycasinos.com

Casino Omaha
1 Blackbird Bend, Box 89
Onawa, IA 51040
713-423-3700
800-858-U-BET

Catfish Bend Casino
902 Riverview Drive
Fort Madison, IA 52627
319-372-2946

Dubuque Diamond Jo Casino
3rd Street Ice Harbor
Dubuque, IA 52004
319-583-7005
800-LUCKY-JO
www.diamondjo.com

Havey's Casino Hotel–Council Bluffs
One Harvey's Boulevard
Council Bluffs, IA 51501
712-329-6000
800-HARVEYS
www.harveys.com

Lady Luck Casino Bettendorf
1821 State Street
Bettendorf, IA 52722
319-359-7280
800-742-5825
www.ladyluck.com

Meskwaki Bingo & Casino
1504 305th Street
Tama, IA 52339
515-484-2108
800-728-4263

Mississippi Belle II
Showboat Landing
Clinton, IA 52733

319-243-9000
800-457-9975

Miss Marquette Riverboat Casino
P.O. Box 460
Marquette, IA 52158
319-873-3431
800-4-YOU-BET
www.mismarquette.com

President Riverboat Casino
130 West River Drive
Davenport, IA 52801
319-328-8000
800-BOAT-711
www.prescasino.com

Winnevegas
1500 330th Street
Sloan, IA 51055
712-428-9466
800-468-9466

KANSAS

Casino White Cloud
777 Jackpot Drive
White Cloud, KS 66094
785-595-3430
877-652-6155

Golden Eagle Casino
Rt. 1, Box 149
Horton, KS 66439
785-486-6601
888-464-5825

Harrah's Prairie Band Casino
12305 150th Road
Mayetta, KS 66509
785-966-7777
800-HARRAHS
www.harrahs.com

Sac & Fox Casino
RR #1, Box 105-A, N. Highway 75
Powhattan, KS 66527
785-467-8000
800-990-2-WIN

LOUISIANA

Bally's Casino Lakeshore Resort
1 Stars & Stripes Boulevard
New Orleans, LA 70126

504-248-3200
800-57-BALLY
www.ballysno.com

Belle of Baton Rouge
103 France Street
Baton Rouge, LA 70802
504-378-6000
800-676-4847
www.argosycasinos.com

Boomtown Casino Westbank
4132 Peters Road
Harvey, LA 70058
504-366-7711
800-366-7711
www.boomtowncasinos.com

Casino Magic–Bossier City
300 Riverside Drive
Bossier City, LA 71111
318-746-0711
800-5-MAGIC-5
www.casinomagic.com

Casino Rouge
1717 River Road North
Baton Rouge, LA 70802
504-381-7777
800-44-ROUGE
www.casinorouge.com

Cypress Bayou Casino
P.O. Box 519
Charenton, LA 70523
318-923-7284
800-284-4386

Grand Casino Avoyelles
711 Grand Boulevard
Marksville, LA 71351
318-253-1946
800-WIN-1-WIN
www.grandcasino.com

Grand Casino Coushatta
777 Coushatta Drive
Kinder, LA 70648
318-738-7300
800-58-GRAND
www.grandcasino.com/coushatta

Harrah's Shreveport
315 Clyde Fant Parkway
Shreveport, LA 71101
318-424-7777
800-HARRAHS
www.harrahs.com

Horseshoe Casino Hotel–Bossier City
711 Horseshoe Boulevard
Bossier City, LA 71111
318-742-0711
800-895-0711
www.horseshoe.com

Isle of Capri Casino & Hotel–Bossier City
711 Isle of Capri Boulevard
Bossier City, LA 71111
318-678-7777
800-THE-ISLE
www.casinoamerica.com

Isle of Capri Casino & Hotel–Lake Charles
100 Westlake Avenue
Westlake, LA 70669
318-430-0711
800-THE-ISLE
www.casinoamerica.com

Players Island Hotel & Casino–Lake Charles
800 Bilbo Street
Lake Charles, LA 70601
318-437-1500
800-977-PLAY

Treasure Chest Casino
5050 Williams Boulevard
Kenner, LA 70065
504-443-8000
800-298-0711
www.treasurechest.com

MASSACHUSETTS

Leisure Casino Cruises
6 Rowe Square
Gloucester, MA 01830
978-282-3330
877-786-7827

MICHIGAN
Detroit

Bay Mills Resort & Casino
Lakeshore Drive, Box 249
Brimley, MI 49715
906-248-3715
800-386-2250

Big Bucks Casino
M-38 Route 1
Box 284A
Baraga, MI 49908
906-353-6333

Casino Windsor (over the Detroit border)
377 Riverside Drive East
Windsor, Ontario N9A 7H7
519-258-7878
800-991-7777
www.windsorcasino.com

Chip-In's Island Resort & Casino
P.O. Box 351
Harris, MI 49845
906-466-2941
800-682-6040
www.chipincasino.com

Eagle's View Casino
2521 N.W. Bayshore Drive
Suttons Bay, MI 49682
616-271-4104
800-922-2949

Greektown Casino
400 Monroe (Temporary Address)
Detroit, MI 48226
313-963-3357

Kewadin Casino–Christmas
N7761 Candy Cane Lane
Munising, MI 49862
906-387-5475
800-KEWADIN
www.kewadin.com

Kewadin Casino–Hessel
3 Mile Road, Box 789
Hessel, MI 49745
906-484-2903
800-KEWADIN
www.kewadin.com

Kewadin Casino–Manistique
US 2 East, Rte. 1, Box 1553D
Manistique, MI 49854
906-341-5510
800-KEWADIN
www.kewadin.com

Kewadin Casino Hotel–Sault Ste. Marie
2186 Shunk Road
Sault Ste. Marie, MI 49783
906-632-0530
800-KEWADIN
www.kewadin.com

Kewadin Shores Casino
3309 Mackinaw Trail
St. Ignace, MI 49781
906-643-7071
800-KEWADIN
www.kewadin.com

Kings Club Casino
12140 West Lakeshore Drive
Brimley, MI 49715
906-248-3227
800-575-5493

Las Viex Desert Casino
N 5384 US 45 North
Watersmeet, MI 49969
916-358-4226
800-583-3599

Leelanau Sands Casino
2521 Northwest Bayshore Drive
Sutton's Bay, MI 49682
616-271-4104
800-922-2946
www.casino2win.com

Leelanau Super Gaming Palace
2649 Northwest Bayshore Drive
Suttons Bay, MI 49682
616-271-6852
FAX: 616-271-4208

MGM Grand Detroit Casino
1553 Woodward Avenue (Temporary
    Address)
Detroit, MI 48232
877-888-2121

Motor City Casino
1922 Cass Avenue (Temporary Address)
Detroit, MI 48226
313-237-7711

Ojibwa Casino–Marquette
105 Acre Trail
Marquette, MI 49855
906-249-4200
www.ojibwacasino.com

Ojibwa Casino Resort
Rte. 1, Box 284A
Baraga, MI 49908
906-353-6333
800-323-8045
www.ojibwacasino.com

Soaring Eagle Casino & Resort
6800 East Soaring Eagle Boulevard
Mount Pleasant, MI 48858
517-775-5777
888-7-EAGLE-7
www.sagchip.com

Turtle Creek Casino
7741 M-72 East
Williamsburg, MI 49690
616-267-9574

888-777-8946
www.casino2win.com

MINNESOTA

Black Bear Casino & Hotel
1785 Highway 210
Carlton, MN 55718
218-878-2327
888-771-0777

Che-We Casino
Route 3, Box 100
Cass Lake, MN 56633
218-335-8338

Firefly Creek Casino
Route 2, Box 96
Granite Falls, MN 56241
320-564-2121

Fond-du-Luth Casino
129 East Superior Street
Duluth, MN 55802
218-722-0280
800-873-0283

Fortune Bay Resort & Casino
1430 Bois Forte Road
Tower, MN 55790
800-992-7529

Grand Casino Hinckley
777 Lady Luck Drive
Hinckley, MN 55037
800-GRAND-21

Grand Casino Mille Lacs
777 Grand Avenue
Omania, MN 56359
320-532-7777
800-626-LUCK

Grand Portage Lodge and Casino
P.O. Box 233
Grand Portage, MN 55605
218-475-2401
800-543-1384

Jackpot Junction Casino Hotel
P.O. Box 420
Morton, MN 56270
507-644-3000
800-WIN-CASH

Lake of the Woods Casino & Bingo
1012 East Lake Street
Warroad, MN 56763
218-386-3381
800-815-8293

Little Six Casino
2354 Sioux Trail N.W.
Prior Lake, MN 55372
612-445-8982

Mystic Lake Casino Hotel
2400 Mystic Lake Boulevard
Prior Lake, MN 55372
612-445-9000
800-262-7799

Northern Lights Casino
HCR73, Box 1003
Walker, MN 56484
218-547-2744
800-252-PLAY

Palace Casino Hotel
RR 3, Box 221
Casa Lake, MN 56633
218-335-7000
800-228-6676

Red Lake Casino & Bingo
Highway 1 East
Red Lake, MN 56671
218-679-2500
888-679-2501

River Road Casino & Bingo
RR 3, Box 168
Thief River Falls, MN 56701
218-681-4062
800-881-0712

Shooting Star Casino & Hotel
777 Casino Boulevard
Mahnomen, MN 56557
218-935-2701
800-453-STAR

Treasure Island Casino
5734 Sturgeon Lake Road
Red Wing, MN 55066
651-388-6300
800-222-7077

MISSISSIPPI

Bay St. Louis

Casino Magic–Bay St. Louis
711 Casino Magic Drive
Bay St. Louis, MS 39520
228-467-9257
800-5-MAGIC-5
www.casinomagic.com

Biloxi

Beau Rivage
875 Beach Boulevard
Biloxi, MS 39530
228-386-7171
888-56-ROOMS
www.mirageresorts.com

Boomtown Casino–Biloxi
676 Bayview Avenue
Biloxi, MS 39530
228-435-7000
800-627-0777
www.boomtowncasino.com

Casino Magic–Biloxi
195 East Beach Boulevard
Biloxi, MS 39530
228-467-9257
800-5-MAGIC-5
www.casinomagic.com

Grand Casino Biloxi
265 Beach Boulevard
Biloxi, MS 39530
228-436-2946
800-WIN-2-WIN
www.grandcasinos.com

Imperial Palace Hotel & Casino
850 Bayview Avenue
Biloxi, MS 39530
228-436-3000
800-436-3000
www.imperialpalace.com

Isle of Capri Casino–Biloxi
151 Beach Boulevard
Biloxi, MS 39530
228-435-5400
800-THE-ISLE
www.casinoamerica.com

New Palace Casino
158 Howard Avenue
Biloxi, MS 39530
228-432-8888
800-PALACE-9

President Casino Broadwater Resort
2110 Beach Boulevard
Biloxi, MS 39531
228-385-3500
800-THE-PRES
www.broadwater.com

Treasure Bay Casino Resort
1980 Beach Boulevard
Biloxi, MS 39531
228-385-6000
800-PIRATE-9
www.treasurebay.com

Greenville

Bayou Caddy's Jubilee Casino
Lake Fergueson Waterfront
Greenville, MS 38701
601-335-1111
800-WIN-MORE

Las Vegas Casino
Lake Fergueson Waterfront
Greenville, MS 38701
601-335-5800
800-VEGAS-21

Lighthouse Point Casino
199 North Lakefront Road
Greenville, MS 38701
601-334-7711
800-878-1777

Gulfport

Copa Casino
P.O. Box 1600
Gulfport, MS 39502
228-863-3330
800-WIN-COPA

Grand Casino Gulfport
3215 West Beach Boulevard
Gulfport, MS 39501
228-870-7777
800-WIN-7777
www.grandcasinos.com

Lula

Lady Luck Rhythm & Blues Casino
777 Lady Luck Parkway
Lula, MS 38644
601-363-4600
800-789-LUCK
www.ladyluck.com

Natchez

Lady Luck Casino Hotel–Natchez
53 Silver Street
Natchez, MS 39120

601-445-0605
800-722-LUCK
www.ladyluck.com

Philadelphia

Silver Star Resort & Casino
Highway 16 West
Philadelphia, MS 39350
601-650-1234
800-557-0711
www.silverstarcasino.com

Robinsonville

Bally's Saloon and Gambling Hall Hotel
1450 Bally's Boulevard
Robinsonville, MS 38664
601-357-1500
800-382-2559
www.ballysms.com

Fitzgerald's Casino Hotel
711 Lucky Lane
Robinsonville, MS 38664
601-363-5825
800-766-LUCK
www.fitzgeralds.com

Gold Strike Casino
100 Casino Center Drive
Robinsonville, MS 38664
601-357-1111
888-245-7829
www.goldstrikemississippi.com

Grand Casino Tunica
13615 Old Highway 61 North
Robinsonville, MS 38664
601-363-2788
800-946-4946
www.grandcasinos.com

Harrah's Tunica Mardi Gras Casino & Hotel
1100 Casino Strip Boulevard
Robinsonville, MS 38664
601-363-7777
800-HARRAHS
www.harrahs.com

Hollywood Casino Tunica
1150 Comerce Landing
Robinsonville, MS 38671
601-357-7700
800-871-0711
www.hollywoodcasino.com

Horseshoe Casino and Hotel
1021 Casino Center Drive
Robinsonville, MS 38664
601-357-5500
800-303-7463
www.horseshoe.com

Sam's Town Hotel & Gambling Hall
1477 Casino Strip Boulevard
Robinsonville, MS 38664
601-363-0711
800-456-0711
www.samstowntunica.com

Sheraton Casino & Hotel
1107 Casino Center Drive
Robinsonville, MS 38664
601-363-4900
800-391-3777

Vicksburg

Ameristar Casino–Vicksburg
4146 Washington Street
Vicksburg, MS 39180
601-638-1000
800-700-7770
www.ameristars.com

Harrah's Vicksburg Casino Hotel
1310 Mulberry Street
Vicksburg, MS 39180
601-636-DICE
800-HARRAHS
www.harrahs.com

Isle of Capri Casino–Vicksburg
3990 Washington Street
Vicksburg, MS 39180
601-636-5700
800-THE-ISLE
www.casinoamerica.com

Rainbow Casino
1380 Warrenton Road
Vicksburg, MS 39182
601-636-7575
800-503-3777

MISSOURI

Argosy Casino
777 N.W. Argosy Parkway
Riverside, MO 64150
816-746-7711
800-270-7711
www.argosycasinos.com

Casino Aztar
777 East Third
Caruthersville, MO 63830
573-333-6000

Flamingo Hilton Casino–Kansas City
1800 East Front Street
Kansas City, MO 64120
816-855-7777
800-946-8711

Harrah's St. Louis–Riverport Casino and Hotel
777 Casino Center Drive
Maryland Heights, MO 63043
800-HARRAHS
www.harrahs.com

Harrah's North Kansas City
One Riverboat Drive
Kansas City, MO 64116
816-472-7777
800-HARRAHS
www.harrahs.com

Players Island Casino–St. Louis
777 Casino Center Drive
St. Louis, MO 63043
314-209-3900
888-77-PLAYER
www.playersisland.com

President Casino by the Arch
800 North First Street
St. Louis, MO 63102
314-622-1111
800-772-3647

Station Casino Kansas City
3200 North Stanton Drive
Kansas City, MO 64161
816-414-7000
800-499-4961
www.stationkansascity.com

Station Casino St. Charles
P.O. Box 720
St. Charles, MO 63302
314-949-7777
800-325-7777
www.stationcasinos.com

St. Jo Frontier Casino
77 Francis Street
St. Joseph, MO 64501
816-279-7577
800-888-2WIN

MONTANA

Charging House Casino
P.O. Box 128
Lame Deer, MT 59043
406-477-6677

4C's Cafe and Casino
Rocky Boy Route, Box 544
Box Elder, MT 59520
406-395-4850

Kwa Taq Nuk Casino
303 Highway 93
East Polson, MT 59860
406-883-3636
800-882-6363

Little Big Horn Casino
P.O. Box 580
Crow Agency, MT 59022
406-638-4444

Silverwolf Casino
P.O. Box 726
Wolf Point, MT 59201
406-653-3476

NEVADA

Amargosa Valley

Stateline Saloon
Route 15
Amargosa Valley, NV 89020
775-372-5238

Battle Mountain

Owl Hotel and Casino
8 East Front Street
Battle Mountain, NV 89020
775-635-2453

Beatty

Burro Inn Motel and Casino
Highway 95 South
Beatty, NV 89003
775-553-2225
800-843-2078

Exchange Club Casino and Motel
P.O. Box 97
Beatty, NV 89003
775-553-2368

Stagecoach Hotel & Casino
P.O. Box 836
Beatty, NV 89003
775-553-2419
800-4BIG-WIN

Boulder City

Gold Strike Inn and Casino
U.S. Highway 93
Boulder City, NV 89005
702-293-5000

Carson City

Carson City Nugget
507 North Carson Street
Carson City, NV 89701
775-882-1626
800-426-5239
www.ccnugget.com

Carson Station Hotel and Casino
900 South Carson Street
Carson City, NV 89702
775-883-0900
800-528-1234

Ormsby House Hotel Casino
600 South Carson Street
Carson City, NV 89701
775-892-1890
800-662-1890

Pinon Plaza Casino Resort
2171 Highway 50 East
Carson City, NV 89701
775-885-9000
877-519-5567
www.pinonplaza.com

Elko

Commercial Casino
345 4th Street
Elko, NV 89801
775-738-3181
800-648-2345

Gold Country Motor Inn
2050 Idaho Street
Elko, NV 89801
775-738-8421
800-621-1332

Red Lion Inn & Casino
2065 Idaho Street
Elko, NV 89801
775-738-2111
800-545-0044

Stockmen's Hotel & Casino
340 Commercial Street
Elko, NV 89801
775-738-5141
800-648-2345

Ely

Hotel Nevada & Gambling Hall
501 Aulman Street
Ely, NV 89301
775-289-6665
888-406-3055
www.hotelnevada.com

Fallon

Bird Farm
128 East Williams Avenue
Fallon, NV 89406
775-423-7877

Bonanza Inn and Casino
855 West Williams Avenue
Fallon, NV 89406
775-423-6031

Depot Casino and Restaurant
875 West Williams Avenue
Fallon, NV 89406
775-423-2411

Fallon Nugget
70 South Maine Street
Fallon, NV 89406
775-423-3111

Headquarter's Bar & Casino
134 Main Street
Fallon, NV 89406
775-423-6355

Stockman's Casino
1560 West Williams Avenue
Fallon, NV 89406
775-423-2117

Gardnerville

Sharkey's Nugget
P.O. Box 625
Gardnerville, NV 89410
775-782-3133

Topez Lodge and Casino
1979 Highway 395 South
Gardnerville, NV 89410
775-266-3338
800-962-0732

Hawthorne

El Capitan Resort Casino
540 F Street
Hawthorne, NV 89415
775-945-3321

Henderson

Barley's Casino & Brewing Company
4500 East Sunset Road #30
Henderson, NV 89014
702-458-2739

Eldorado Casino
140 Water Street
Henderson, NV 89015
702-564-1811

Jokers Wild
920 North Boulder Highway
Henderson, NV 89015
702-564-8100

Pot O'Gold of Nevada
120 Market Street
Henderson, NV 89015
702-564-8488

Railroad Pass Hotel & Casino
2800 South Boulder Highway
Henderson, NV 89015
702-294-5000
800-654-0877

The Reserve Hotel & Casino
777 West Lake Mead Drive
Henderson, NV 89015
702-567-7000
888-899-7770
www.ameristars.com

Skyline Restaurant & Casino
1741 North Boulder Highway
Henderson, NV 89015
702-565-9116

Sunset Station
1301 West Sunset Road
Henderson, NV 89014
702-547-7777
888-786-7389
sunsetstation.com

Tom's Sunset Casino
444 West Sunset Road
Henderson, NV 89015
702-564-5551

Indian Springs

Indian Springs
372 Tonopah Highway
Indian Springs, NV 89018
702-879-3456

Jackpot

Barton's Club 93
Highway 93
Jackpot, NV 89825
775-755-2341
800-258-2937

Cactus Pete's Resort Casino
1385 Highway 93
Jackpot, NV 89825
775-755-2321
800-821-1103
www.ameristars.com

Horseshu Hotel & Casino
Highway 93
Jackpot, NV 89825
775-755-7777
800-432-0051
www.ameristars.com

Jean

Gold Strike Hotel & Gambling Hall
1 Main Street
P.O. Box 19278
Jean, NV 89019
702-477-5000
800-634-1359
www.goldstrike-jean.com

Nevada Landing Hotel & Casino
2 Goodsprings Road
P.O. Box 19728
Jean, NV 89019
702-477-5000
800-628-6682
www.nevadalanding.com

Lake Tahoe

Bill's Casino
U.S. Highway 50
P.O. Box 8
Stateline, NV 89449
775-588-2455
www.harrahslaketahoe.com

Caesars Tahoe
55 Highway 50
Stateline, NV 89449
775-588-3515
800-648-3353
www.caesars.com

Cal-Neva Lodge Resort Hotel, Spa & Casino
P.O. Box 368
Crystal Bay, NV 89402
775-832-4000
800-CAL-NEVA
www.calnevaresort.com

Crystal Bay Club Casino
14 Highway 28
Crystal Bay, NV 89402
775-831-0512

Harrah's Lake Tahoe
Highway 50
P.O. Box 8
Stateline, NV 89449
775-588-6611
800-HARRAHS
www.harrahstahoe.com

Harveys Resort Hotel and Casino– Lake Tahoe
P.O. Box 128, Highway 50
Stateline, NV 89449
775-588-2411
800-553-1022
www.harveys.com

Hyatt Regency Lake Tahoe Resort & Casino
P.O. Box 3239
Incline Village, NV 89450
775-832-1234
800-233-1234
www.hyatt.com

Lake Tahoe Horizon
50 Highway 50
P.O. Box C
Lake Tahoe, NV 89449
775-588-6211
800-322-7723
www.horizoncasino.com

Lakeside Inn & Casino
Highway 50 & Kingsbury Grade
Stateline, NV 89440
775-588-7777
800-523-1291
www.lakesideinn.com

Tahoe Biltmore Lodge & Casino
#5 Highway 28
P.O. Box 115
Crystal Bay, NV 89402
775-831-0660
800-BILTMOR
www.tahoebiltmore.com

Las Vegas

Arizona Charlie's Hotel & Casino
740 South Decateur Boulevard
Las Vegas, NV 89107
702-258-5200
800-342-2695
www.azcharlies.com

Bally's Las Vegas
3645 Las Vegas Boulevard South
Las Vegas, NV 89109
800-BALLYS-7
www.ballyslv.com

Barbary Coast Hotel & Casino
3595 Las Vegas Boulevard South
Las Vegas, NV 89109
702-737-7111
888-227-2279
www.barbarycoastcasino.com

Barcelona Hotel & Casino
5011 East Craig Road
Las Vegas, NV 89115
702-644-6300
800-223-6330

Bellagio
3600 Las Vegas Boulevard South
Las Vegas, NV 89109
702-693-7111
888-987-6667
www.mirageresorts.com

Binion's Horseshoe Casino and Hotel
128 East Fremont Street
Las Vegas, NV 89101
702-382-1600
800-622-6468

Boardwalk Casino–Holiday Inn
3750 Las Vegas Boulevard South
Las Vegas, NV 89109
702-735-2400
800-635-4581
www.hiboardwalk.com

Boulder Station Hotel & Casino
4111 Boulder Highway
Las Vegas, NV 89121
702-432-7777
800-981-5577
www.stationcasinos.com

Bourbon Street Hotel & Casino
120 East Flamingo Road
Las Vegas, NV 89109
702-737-7200
800-634-6956

Caesars Palace
1570 Las Vegas Boulevard South
Las Vegas, NV 89109
702-731-7110
800-634-6002
www.caesars.com

California Hotel & Casino
12 Ogden Avenue
Las Vegas, NV 89101
702-385-1222
800-634-6505
www.thecal.com

Casino Royale & Hotel
3411 Las Vegas Boulevard South
Las Vegas, NV 89109
702-737-3500
800-854-7666

Circus Circus Hotel & Casino
2880 Las Vegas Boulevard South
Las Vegas, NV 89109
702-734-0410
800-634-3450
www.circuscircus-lasvegas.com

Continental Hotel & Casino
4100 Paradise Road
Las Vegas, NV 89109
800-777-4844
www.continentalhotel.com

Days Inn Town Hall Casino-Hotel
4155 Koval Lane
Las Vegas, NV 89109
702-731-2111
800-634-6541

El Cortez Hotel & Casino
600 East Freemont Street
Las Vegas, NV 89101
702-385-5200
800-634-6703

Ellis Island Casino
4178 Koval Lane
Las Vegas, NV 89109
702-734-8638

Excalibur Hotel and Casino
3850 Las Vegas Boulevard South
Las Vegas, NV 89109
702-597-7777
800-937-7777
www.excaliburcasino.com

Fitzgeralds Casino & Holiday Inn
301 Fremont Street
Las Vegas, NV 89101
702-388-2400
800-274-5825
www.fitzgeralds.com

Flamingo Hilton Las Vegas
3555 Las Vegas Boulevard South
Las Vegas, NV 89109
702-733-3111
800-329-3232
www.hilton.com

Four Queens Hotel and Casino
202 Fremont Street
Las Vegas, NV 89101
702-385-4011
800-634-6045

Fremont Hotel & Casino
200 East Fremont Street
Las Vegas, NV 89101
702-385-3232
800-634-6460
www.fremontcasino.com

Gold Coast Casino & Hotel
4000 W. Flamingo Road
Las Vegas, NV 89103
702-367-7111
888-402-6278
www.goldcoastcasino.com

Golden Gate Hotel & Casino
One Fremont Street
Las Vegas, NV 89101
702-385-1906
800-426-1906

The Golden Nugget
129 East Fremont Street
Las Vegas, NV 89101
702-385-7111
800-634-3403
www.goldennugget.com

Gold Spike Hotel & Casino
400 East Ogden Avenue
Las Vegas, NV 89101
702-384-8444
800-634-6703

Hard Rock Hotel & Casino
4455 Paradise Road
Las Vegas, NV 89109
702-693-5000
800-HRD-ROCK
www.hardrockhotel.com

Harrah's Las Vegas
3475 Las Vegas Boulevard South
Las Vegas, NV 89109
702-369-5000
800-HARRAHS
www.harrahslv.com

Hotel San Remo Casino & Resort
115 East Tropicana Avenue
Las Vegas, NV 89109
702-739-9000
800-522-REMO
www.sanremolasvegas.com

Imperial Palace Hotel & Casino
3535 Las Vegas Boulevard South
Las Vegas, NV 89109
702-731-3311
800-634-6441
www.imperialpalace.com

Jackie Gaughan's Plaza Hotel & Casino
1 Main Street
Las Vegas, NV 89101
702-386-2110
800-634-6575

Lady Luck Casino Hotel
206 North Third Street
Las Vegas, NV 89101
702-477-3000
800-634-6580
www.ladyluck.com

Las Vegas Auto and Truck Plaza
8050 South Industrial Road
Las Vegas, NV 89118
702-361-1176

Las Vegas Club Hotel & Casino
18 East Fremont Street
Las Vegas, NV 89101
702-385-1664
800-634-6532

Las Vegas Hilton
3000 Paradise Road
Las Vegas, NV 89109
702-732-5111
800-732-7117
www.lv-hilton.com

Longhorn Casino
5288 Boulder Highway
Las Vegas, NV 89122
702-435-9170

Luxor Las Vegas
3900 Las Vegas Boulevard South
Las Vegas, NV 89119
702-262-4000
800-288-1000
www.luxor.com

Main Street Station Hotel & Casino
200 North Main Street
Las Vegas, NV 89101
702-387-1896
800-713-8933
www.mainstreetcasino.com

Mandalay Bay
3950 Las Vegas Boulevard South
Las Vegas, NV 89109
702-632-7777
877-632-7000

Maxim Hotel and Casino
160 East Flamingo Road
Las Vegas, NV 89109
702-731-4300
800-634-6987
www.maximhotel.com

MGM Grand Hotel Casino
3799 Las Vegas Boulevard South
Las Vegas, NV 89109
702-891-1111
800-929-1111
www.mgmgrand.com

The Mirage
3400 Las Vegas Boulevard South
Las Vegas, NV 89109
702-791-7111
800-627-6667
www.themirage.com

Monte Carlo Resort & Casino
3770 Las Vegas Boulevard South
Las Vegas, NV 89109
702-730-7777
800-311-8999
www.monte-carlo.com

Nevada Palace Hotel & Casino
5255 Boulder Highway
Las Vegas, NV 89122
702-458-8810
800-634-6283
www.lvcybermall.com/nevadapalace

New Frontier Hotel & Casino
3120 Las Vegas Boulevard South
Las Vegas, NV 89109
702-794-8200
800-634-6966

New York-New York Hotel & Casino
3790 Las Vegas Boulevard South
Las Vegas, NV 89109
702-740-6969
800-NY-FOR-ME
www.nynyhotelcasino.com

The Orleans Hotel & Casino
4500 West Tropicana Avenue
Las Vegas, NV 89103
702-365-7111
800-ORLEANS
www.orleanscasino.com

O'Shea's Casino
3555 Las Vegas Boulevard South
Las Vegas, NV 89109
702-697-2667
800-329-3232

Palace Station Hotel & Casino
2411 West Sahara Avenue
Las Vegas, NV 89102
702-367-2411
800-634-3101
www.stationcasinos.com

Paris Casino Resort
3655 Las Vegas Boulevard South
Las Vegas, NV 89109
702-967-4401
1-888-BONJOUR
www.paris-lv.com

Quality Inn & Key Largo Casino
377 East Flamingo Road
Las Vegas, NV 89109
702-733-7777
800-634-6617

Rio Suite Hotel & Casino
3700 West Flamingo Road
Las Vegas, NV 89103
702-252-7777
800-PLAYRIO
www.playrio.com

Riviera Hotel & Casino
2901 Las Vegas Boulevard South
Las Vegas, NV 89109
702-734-5110
800-634-3420
www.theriviera.com

Sahara Hotel & Casino
2535 Las Vegas Boulevard South
Las Vegas, NV 89109
702-737-2111
800-634-6645

Sam's Town Hotel & Gambling Hall
5111 Boulder Highway
Las Vegas, NV 89122
702-456-7777
800-897-8696
www.samstownlvnv.com

Sheraton Desert Inn
3145 Las Vegas Boulevard South
Las Vegas, NV 89109
702-733-4444
800-634-6906
www.thedesertinn.com

Showboat Hotel & Casino
2800 Fremont Street
Las Vegas, NV 89104
702-385-9123
800-826-2800

Silver City Casino
3001 Las Vegas Boulevard South
Las Vegas, NV 89109
702-732-4152

Silverton Hotel Casino & RV Resort
3333 Blue Diamond Road
Las Vegas, NV 89139
702-263-7777
800-588-7711

Slots-A-Fun
2890 Las Vegas Boulevard South
Las Vegas, NV 89109
702-794-3814

Sports World Casino
3049 Las Vegas Boulevard South
Las Vegas, NV 89109
702-796-1111

Stardust Resort & Casino
3000 Las Vegas Boulevard South
Las Vegas, NV 89109

702-732-6111
800-823-6033
www.vegas.com

Stratosphere Hotel & Casino
2000 Las Vegas Boulevard South
Las Vegas, NV 89117
702-383-7777
800-99-TOWER
www.stratlv.com

Treasure Island
3300 Las Vegas Boulevard South
Las Vegas, NV 89109
702-849-7111
800-944-7444
www.treasureislandlasvegas.com

Tropicana Resort & Casino
380 Las Vegas Boulevard South
Las Vegas, NV 89109
702-739-2222
800-634-4000
www.tropicana.lv.com

Vacation Village Hotel and Casino
6711 Las Vegas Boulevard South
Las Vegas, NV 89119
702-897-1700
800-658-5000

The Venetian Resort Hotel Casino
3355 Las Vegas Boulevard South
Las Vegas, NV 89109
702-733-5000
800-494-3556
www.venetian.com

Western Hotel & Casino
899 East Fremont Street
Las Vegas, NV 89101
702-384-4620
800-634-6703

Westward Ho Hotel & Casino
2900 Las Vegas Boulevard South
Las Vegas, NV 89109
702-731-2900
800-634-6803
www.westwardho.com

Wild Wild West Casino
3330 West Tropicana Avenue
Las Vegas, NV 89103
702-736-8988
800-634-3488

Laughlin

Avi Hotel & Casino
10000 Aha Macav Parkway
Laughlin, NV 89029
702-535-5555
800-AVI-2-WIN
www.aviresort.com

Colorado Belle Hotel & Casino
2100 South Casino Drive
Laughlin, NV 89029
702-298-4000
800-458-9500
www.coloradobelle.com

**Don Laughlin's Riverside Resort Hotel
    and Casino**
1650 South Casino Drive
Laughlin, NV 89029
702-298-2535
800-227-3849
www.riversideresort.net

Edgewater Hotel Casino
2020 South Casino Drive
Laughlin, NV 89029
702-298-2453
800-67-RIVER
www.edgewater-casino.com

Flamingo Hilton Laughlin
1900 South Casino Drive
Laughlin, NV 89029
702-298-5111
800-FLAMINGO
www.hilton.com

Golden Nugget Laughlin
2300 South Casino Drive
Laughlin, NV 89029
702-298-7111
800-237-1739
www.gnlaughlin.com

Harrah's Laughlin Casino & Hotel
2900 South Casino Drive
Laughlin, NV 89029
702-298-4600
800-HARRAHS
www.harrahs.com

Pioneer Hotel & Gamblin Hall
2200 South Casino Drive
Laughlin, NV 89029
702-298-2442
800-634-3469

Ramada Express Hotel & Casino
2121 South Casino Drive
Laughlin, NV 89029
702-298-4200
800-243-6846
www.ramadaexpress.com

Regency Casino
1950 Casino Way
Laughlin, NV 89029
702-298-2439

River Palms Resort & Casino
2700 South Casino Drive
Laughlin, NV 89029
702-298-2242
800-835-7903

Lovelock

Sturgeon's Casino
1420 Cornell Avenue
Lovelock, NV 89419
702-273-2971
888-234-6835
www.ramadainn.com

McDermitt

Say When Casino
P.O. Box 375
McDermitt, NV 89421
702-532-8515

Mesquite

Casablanca Resort & Casino
P.O. Box 2727
Mesquite, NV 89024
702-346-PLAY
800-896-4567
www.casablancaresort.com

**Rancho Mesquite Casino and Holiday
    Inn**
275 Mesa Boulevard
Mesquite, NV 89024
702-346-4600
800-346-4611

Si Redd's Oasis Resort Hotel & Casino
P.O. Box 360
Mesquite, NV 89024
702-346-5232
800-621-0187
www.siredd.com/oasis

Stateline Casino
490 West Mesquite Boulevard
Mesquite, NV 89024
702-346-5752

Virgin River Hotel & Casino
100 Pioneer Boulevard
Mesquite, NV 89027
702-346-7777
800-346-7721
www.virginriver.com

Minden

Carson Valley Inn
1627 Highway 395 North
Minden, NV 89423
702-782-9711
800-321-6983
www.cvinn.com

North Las Vegas

Bighorn Casino
3016 East lake Mead Boulevard
North Las Vegas, NV 89030
702-642-1940

Fiesta Casino Hotel
2400 North Rancho Drive
North Las Vegas, NV 89130
702-631-7000
800-731-7333

Jerry's Nugget
1821 Las Vegas Boulevard North
North Las Vegas, NV 89030
702-399-3000
www.jerrysnugget.com

Mahoney's Silver Nugget
2140 Las Vegas Boulevard North
North Las Vegas, NV 89030
702-399-2222

Opera House Saloon and Casino
2542 Las Vegas Boulevard North
North Las Vegas, NV 89030
702-649-8801

The Poker Palace
2757 Las Vegas Boulevard North
North Las Vegas, NV 89030
702-649-3799

Santa Fe Hotel & Casino
4949 North Rancho Drive
North Las Vegas, NV 89130
702-658-4900
800-872-6823
www.santafecasino.com

Texas Station
2101 Texas Star Lane
North Las Vegas, NV 89102
702-631-1000
800-654-8804
www.texasstation.com

Pahrump

Saddle West Hotel, Casino and RV Park
1220 South Highway 160
Pahrump, NV 89048
800-GEDDY-UP
www.saddlewest.com

Terrible's Town Casino
751 South Highway 160
Pahrump, NV 89048
702-751-7777

Primm

Buffalo Bill's Resort & Casino
1-15 South
Primm, NV 89019
702-382-1212
800-FUN-STOP
www.primadonna.com

Primm Valley Resort & Casino
1-15 South
Primm, NV 89019
702-382-1212
800-FUN-STOP
www.primadonna.com

Whiskey Pete's Hotel & Casino
1-15 South
Primm, NV 89019
702-382-1212
800-FUN-STOP
www.primadonna.com

Reno

Atlantis Casino Resort
3800 South Virginia Street
Reno, NV 89502
775-825-4700

800-723-6500
www.atlantiscasino.com

Bonanza Casino
4720 North Virginia Street
Reno, NV 89503
775-323-2724
www.bonanzacasino.com

Bordertown
19575 Highway 395
North Reno, NV 89506
775-972-1309
800-443-4383

Circus Circus Hotel Casino–Reno
500 North Sierra Street
Reno, NV 89503
775-329-0711
800-648-5010
www.circusreno.com

Club Cal-News
38 East Second Street
Reno, NV 89505
775-323-1046
www.nevadnet.com/cal-news

Colonial Casino
250 North Arlington Avenue
Reno, NV 89501
775-323-2039
800-336-7366

Comstock Hotel Casino
200 West Second Street
Reno, NV 89501
775-329-1880
800-COM-STOC

Diamond Casino at Holiday Inn
1010 East 6th Street
Reno, NV 89512
775-323-4183
800-648-4877

Eldorado Hotel and Casino
345 North Virginia Street
Reno, NV 89501
775-786-5700
800-777-5825
www.eldoradoreno.com

Fitzgeralds Casino Hotel–Reno
255 North Virginia Street
Reno, NV 89504
775-785-3300

800-648-5022
www.fitzgeralds.com

Flamingo Hilton Reno
255 North Sierra Street
Reno, NV 89501
775-322-1111
800-648-4882
www.hilton.com

Harrah's Reno Casino Hotel
219 North Center Street
Reno, NV 89501
775-786-3232
800-HARRAHS
www.harrahs.com

Holiday Hotel and Casino
111 Mill Street
Reno, NV 89501
775-329-0411
800-648-5431

Nevada Club
224 North Virginia Street
Reno, NV 89501
775-329-1721

The Nugget
233 North Virginia Street
Reno, NV 89501
775-323-0716

Peppermill Hotel Casino–Reno
2707 South Virginia Street
Reno, NV 89502
775-826-2121
800-648-6992
www.peppermillcasino.com

Pioneer Inn Hotel Casino
221 South Virginia Street
Reno, NV 89501
775-324-7777
800-879-9979
www.travelbase.com/pioneer-inn.

Reno Hilton
2500 East Second Street
Reno, NV 89595
775-789-2000
800-648-5080
www.renohilton.net

Riverboat Hotel & Casino
34 West Second Street
Reno, NV 89501

775-323-8877
800-888-5525

Sands Regency Hotel Casino
345 North Arlington Avenue
Reno, NV 89501
775-348-2200
800-648-3553
www.sandsregency.com

Silver Legacy Resort Casino
407 North Virginia Street
Reno, NV 89501
775-329-4777
800-687-8733
www.silverlegacy.com

Sundowner Hotel Casino
450 North Arlington Avenue
Reno, NV 89503
775-786-7050
800-648-5490

Searchlight

Searchlight Nugget Casino
100 North Highway 95
Searchlight, NV 89046
702-297-1201

Sparks

Alamo Travel Center
1959 East Greg Street
Sparks, NV 89431
775-355-8888

Baldini's Sports Casino
865 South Rock Boulevard
Sparks, NV 89431
775-358-0116
www.baldinis.com

John Ascuaga's Nugget
1100 Nugget Avenue
Sparks, NV 89431
775-356-3300
800-468-4388
www.jnugget.com

Rail City Casino
2121 Victorian Avenue
Sparks, NV 89431
775-359-9440

Silver Club Hotel Casino
1040 Victorian Avenue
Sparks, NV 89432

775-358-4771
800-905-7774

Western Village Inn & Casino
815 Nichols Boulevard
Sparks, NV 89432
775-331-1069
800-648-1170

Tonopah

Station House
P.O. Box 1351
Tonopah, NV 89049
702-482-9777

Verdi

Boomtown Hotel and Casino
P.O. Box 399
Verdi, NV 89439
775-345-6000
800-648-3790
www.boomtowncasinos.com

Gold Ranch Casino
P.O. Box 160
Verdi, NV 89439
775-345-6789

Wells

Four Way Bar and Casino
U.S. 93 & Interstate 80
Wells, NV 89835
775-752-3344

West Wendover

Peppermill Inn & Casino
680 Wendover Boulevard
West Wendover, NV 89883
775-664-2255
800-648-9660
www.peppermillcasinos.com

Rainbow Hotel & Casino
1045 Wendover Boulevard
West Wendover, NV 89883
775-664-4000
800-217-0049

Red Garter Hotel & Casino
P.O. Box 2399
West Wendover, NV 89883
775-664-3315
800-982-2111

Silver Smith Hotel Casino
100 Wendover Boulevard
West Wendover, NV 89883
775-664-2231

State Line Hotel Casino
100 Wendover Boulevard
West Wendover, NV 89883
775-664-2221
800-848-7300
www.statelinenv.com

Winnemucca

Model T Casino Hotel & RV Park
1130 West Winnemucca Boulevard
Winnemucca, NV 89446
775-623-2588
800-645-5658
www.modelt.com

Red Lion Inn and Casino
741 Winnemucca Boulevard
Winnemucca, NV 89445
775-623-2565
800-633-6435

Winners Hotel Casino
185 West Winnemucca Boulevard
Winnemucca, NV 89445
775-623-2511
800-648-4770
www.winnerscasino.com

Yerington

Casino West
11 North Main Street
Yerington, NV 89447
775-463-2481
800-227-4661

Dini's Lucky Club
45 North Main Street
Yerington, NV 89447
775-463-2868

NEW JERSEY

Atlantic City Hilton Casino Resort
Boston & Boardwalk
Atlantic City, NJ 08402
609-347-7111
800-HILTONS
www.ballysac.com

Bally's Park Place
Park Place & Boardwalk
Atlantic City, NJ 08401
609-340-2000
800-HILTONS
www.ballysac.com

Ceasars Atlantic City
2100 Pacific Avenue
Atlantic City, NJ 08401
609-348-4411
609-443-0104
www.caesars.com

Clarridge Casino Hotel
Boardwalk & Park Place
Atlantic City, NJ 08401
609-340-3400
800-257-8585

Harrah's Casino Hotel
777 Harrah's Boulevard
Atlantic City, NJ 08401
609-441-5000
800-HARRAHS
www.harrahs.com

Resorts Casino Hotel
North Carolina Avenue & Boardwalk
Atlantic City, NJ 08401
609-344-6000
800-336-6378
www.resortsac.com

Sands Hotel & Casino
Indiana Avenue & Brighton Park
Atlantic City, NJ 08401
609-441-4000
800-257-8580
www.acsands.com

Showboat Casino Hotel
801 Boardwalk
Atlantic City, NJ 08401
609-343-4000
800-621-0200

Tropicana Casino Resort
Brighton Avenue & Boardwalk
Atlantic City, NJ 08401
609-340-4000
800-THE-TROP
www.tropicana.net

Trump Marina Hotel Casino
Huron Avenue & Brigantine Boulevard
Atlantic City, NJ 08401
609-441-2000
800-365-8786
www.trumpmarina.com

Trump Plaza Hotel and Casino
Boardwalk at Mississippi Avenue
Atlantic City, NJ 08401
609-441-6000
800-677-7376
www.trumptaj.com

Trump Taj Mahal Casino Resort
1000 Boardwalk at Virginia Avenue
Atlantic City, NJ 08401
609-449-1000
800-TAJ-TRUMP
www.trumptaj.com

NEW MEXICO

Apache Nugget Casino
P.O. Box 650
Dulce, NM 87528
505-759-3777

Camel Rock Casino
Route 11, Box 3A
Santa Fe, NM 87501
505-984-8414
800-GO-CAMEL

Casino Apache
Route 4 Carizo Canyon Road
Mescalero, NM 88340
505-257-5141
800-545-9011

Cities of Gold Casino Hotel
Route 11, Box 21-B
Santa Fe, NM 87505
505-455-3313
800-455-3313

Isleta Gaming Palace
11000 Broadway S.E.
Albuquerque, NM 87022
800-460-5686

Ohkay Casino
P.O. Box 1270
San Juan Pueblo, NM 87566
505-747-1668
800-PLAY-AT-OK

Sandia Casino
P.O. Box 10188
Albuquerque, NM 87184
505-897-2173
800-526-9366

Santa Ana Star Casino
54 Jeme Dam Canyon Road
Bernalilo, NM 87004
505-867-0000

Sky City Casino
P.O. Box 519
San Fidell, NM 87049
505-552-6017
www.skycitycasino.com

Taos Mountain Casino
P.O. Box 1477
Taos, NM 87571
505-758-4460
888-WIN-TAOS

NEW YORK

Manhattan Cruises
3202 Emmons Avenue
Brooklyn, NY 11235

Turning Stone Casino Resort
Patrick Road
Verona, NY 13478
315-361-7711
800-771-7711

NORTH CAROLINA

Harrah's Cherokee Casino
P.O. Box 1959
Cherokee, NC 28719
800-HARRAHS
www.harrahs.com

NORTH DAKOTA

Dakota Magic Casino
16849 102nd Street SE
Hankinson, ND 58041
701-634-3000
800-325-6824

Four Bears Casino & Lodge
HC3, 2-A
New Town, ND 58763
701-627-4018
800-294-5454

Prairie Knights Casino and Lodge
HC 1, Box 26-A
Fort Yates, ND 58538
701-854-7777

800-425-8277
www.prairieknights.com

Spirit Lake Casino & Resort
Highway 57
Spirit Lake, ND 58370
701-766-4747
800-WIN-U-BET

Turtle Mountain Chippewa Casino
P.O. Box 1449, Highway 5 West
Belcourt, ND 58316
701-477-3281
800-477-3497

Turtle Mountain Chippewa Mini Casino
P.O. Box 1449, Highway 5 West
Belcourt, NDX 58316
701-477-6438

OREGON

Chinook Winds Gaming Center
1777 N.W. 44th Street
Lincoln City, OR 97367
541-996-5825
888-CHINOOK

Indian Head Casino
P.O. Box 1240
Warm Springs, OR 97761
541-553-6123
800-BET-N-WIN

Kis-Mo-Ya Casino
34333 Highway 97 North
Chiloquin, OR 97624
541-783-7529
888-552-6692

The Mill Resort & Casino
3201 Tremont Avenue
North Bend, OR 97459
541-756-8800
800-953-4800
www.themillcasino.com

Old Camp Casino
2205 West Monroe Street
Burns, OR 97720
541-573-1500

Seven Feathers Hotel & Casino Resort
146 Chief Miwaleta Lane
Canyonville, OR 97417

541-839-1111
800-548-8461
www.sevenfeathers.com

Spirit Mountain Casino
P.O. Box 39
Grand Ronde, OR 97343
503-879-2350
800-760-7977
www.spirit-mountain.com

Wild Horse Gaming Resort
72777 Highway 331
Pendleton, OR 97801
541-278-2274
800-654-9453
www.wildhorseresort.com

RHODE ISLAND

Lincoln Park
1600 Louisquissert Pike
Lincoln, RI 02865
401-723-3200
800-720-7275
www.trackinfo.com

Newport Grand Jai-Alai
150 Admiral Kalbfus Road
Newport, RI 02840
401-849-5000
800-451-2500
www.newportgrand.com

SOUTH DAKOTA

Deadwood

B.B. Cody's
681 Main Street
Deadwood, SD 57732
605-578-3430

Best Western Hickok House
137 Charles Street
Deadwood, SD 57732
605-578-1611
800-528-1234

Bodega Bar
662 Main Street
Deadwood, SD 57732
605-578-1996

Buffalo Saloon
658 Main Street
Deadwood, SD 57732
605-578-9993

Bullock Hotel
633 Main Street
Deadwood, SD 57732
605-578-1745
800-336-1876
www.bullock-hotel.com

Celebrity Hotel & Casino
629 Main Street
Deadwood, SD 57732
605-578-1909
888-399-1886

Dakota Territory Saloon
652 Main Street
Deadwood, SD 57732
605-578-3566

Deadwood Dick's Saloon & Nickel Dick's
51-55 Sherman Street
Deadwood, SD 57732
605-578-3224
www.deadwood.netbbbrew

Deadwood Gulch Resort
Highway 85 South
P.O. Box 643
Deadwood, SD 57732
605-578-1294
800-695-1876
www.deadwoodgulch.com

Deadwood Gulch Saloon
560 Main Street
Deadwood, SD 57732
605-578-7770

Depot Motherlode
155 Sherman Street
Deadwood, SD 57732
605-578-2699
800-31-DEPOT
www.deadwood.net/depot

Double Diamond
29 Lee Street
Deadwood, SD 57732
605-578-3546

Elk's Lodge
696 Main Street #508
Deadwood, SD 57732
605-578-1333

First Gold Hotel & Gaming
270 Main Street
Deadwood, SD 57732
605-578-9777

800-274-1876
www.firstgold.com

Four Aces
531 Main Street
Deadwood, SD 57732
605-578-2323

Gold Country Inn
801 Main Street
Deadwood, SD 57732
605-578-2393
800-287-1251

Gold Dust Gaming & Entertainment Complex
688 Main Street
Deadwood, SD 57732
605-578-2100
800-456-0533

Goldberg's Old San Francisco Mint
670 Main Street
Deadwood, SD 57732
605-578-1515

Hickok's Saloon
685 Main Street
Deadwood, SD 57732
605-578-2222

Historic Franklin Hotel
777 Main Street
Deadwood, SD 57732
605-578-2242
800-688-1876
www.deadwood.net/franklin

Lady Luck
660 Main Street
Deadwood, SD 57732
605-578-1162

Lariat Motel
360 Main Street
Deadwood, SD 57732
605-578-1500

Midnight Star
677 Main Street
Deadwood, SD 57732
605-578-1555
800-999-6482
www.themidnightstar.com

Mineral Palace Hotel & Gaming Complex
601 Main Street
Deadwood, SD 57732

605-578-2036
800-84-PALACE

Mustang Sally's
634 Main Street
Deadwood, SD 57732
605-578-2025

Miss Kitty's Gaming Emporium Days Inn
647 Main Street
Deadwood, SD 57732
605-578-1811
800-668-8189
www.deadwood.net/mskitty

Old Style Saloon #10
657 Main Street
Deadwood, SD 57732
605-578-3346
800-952-9398

Oyster Bay Fairmont Hotel
628 Main Street
Deadwood, SD 57732
605-578-2205

76 Motel & Restaurant
68 Main Street
Deadwood, SD 57732
605-578-3476
800-526-8277

Silverado Gaming
709 Main Street
Deadwood, SD 57732
605-578-3670
800-584-7005

Super 8 Lodge Lucky 8 Gaming Hall
196 Cliff Street
Deadwood, SD 57732
605-578-2535
800-800-8000

Thunder Cove Inn
Highway 85 South
Deadwood, SD 57732
605-578-3045
800-209-7361

Tin Lizzie Gaming
555 Main Street
Deadwood, SD 57732
605-578-1715
800-643-4490

Wild Bill Bar and Gambling Hall
608 Main Street
Deadwood, SD 57732
605-578-2177
800-873-1876

Wild West Winners Casino
622 Main Street
Deadwood, SD 57732
605-578-1100
888-500-7711

Wooden Nickel
9 Lee Street
Deadwood, SD 57732
605-578-1952

Other South Dakota. Areas

Dakota Connection
RR 1, Box 177-B
Sisseton, SD 57602
605-698-4273
800-542-2876

Dakota Sioux Casino
16415 Sioux Conifer Road
Watertown, SD 57201
605-882-2051
800-658-4717

Fort Randall Casino
West Highway 46 R.R. 1, Box 46
Wagner, SD 57380
605-487-7871
800-362-6333
www.ftrandalcasino.com

Golden Buffalo Casino
P.O. Box 204
Lower Brule, SD 57548
605-473-5577

Grand River Casino
P.O. Box 639
Mobridge, SD 57601
605-845-7104
800-475-3321

Lode Star Casino
P.O. Box 140
Fort Thompson, SD 57339
605-245-6000

Prarie Wind Casino
HC 49, Box 10
Pine Ridge, SD 57770
605-533-6300
800-705-WIND

Rosebud Casino
P.O. Box 21
Mission, SD 57555

Royal River Casino & Bingo
Veterans Street, Box 326
Flanxdreau, SD 57028
605-977-3746
800-833-8666

TEXAS

Kikapoo Lucky Eagle Casino
Rt. 1, Box 7777
Eagle Pass, TX 78852
830-758-1995
888-255-8299

Speaking Rock Casino
122 South Old Pueblo Road
El Paso, TX 79907
915-860-7777
800-77-BINGO

WASHINGTON

Coulee Dam Casino
515 Birch Street
Coulee Dam, WA 99155
509-633-0766
800-556-7492

Double Eagle Casino
2539 Smith Road
Chewelah, WA 99109
509-935-4406

Emerald Queen Casino
2102 Alexander Avenue
Tacoma, WA 98421
206-594-7777
888-831-7655

Little Chiefs Casino
P.O. Box 130
Wellpinit, WA 99040
509-258-4544

Little Creek Casino
West 91 Highway 108
Shelton, WA 98584
360-427-7711
800-667-7711

Lucky Eagle Casino
12888 188th Road SW
Rochester, WA 98579

360-273-2000
800-720-1788

Mill Bay Casino
455 East Wapato Lake Road
Manson, WA 98871
509-687-2102
800-648-2946

Muckleshoot Indian Casino
P.O. Box 795
2402 Auburn Way South
Auburn, WA 98002
206-804-4444
800-804-4444
www.muckleshoot.nsn.com

Nooksack River Casino
5048 Mt. Baker Highway
Deming, WA 98244
360-592-5472
800-233-2573

Okanogan Bingo and Casino
41 Appleway Road
Okanogan, WA 98840
509-422-4646
800-559-4643

Red Wind Casino
12919 Yelm Highway
Olympia, WA 98513
360-412-5000

Seven Cedars Casino
27056 Highway 101
Sequim, WA 98382
360-683-7777
800-4-LUCKY-7

Shoalwater Casino
4112 Highway 105
Tokeland, WA 98590
360-267-2046
800-801-3401

Skagit Valley Casino
590 Dark Lane
Bow, WA 98232
360-724-7777

Spokane Indian Bingo and Casino
P.O. Box 1106
Chewelah, WA 99109
509-935-6167
800-322-2788

Suquamish Clearwater Casino
15347 Suquamish Way NE
Box 1210
Suquamish, WA 98392
360-598-6889
800-375-6073
www.clearwatercasino.com

Swinomish Casino and Bingo
837 Casino Drive
Anacortes, WA 98221
360-293-2691
www.swinomishcasino.com

Tulalip Casino
6410 33rd Avenue NE
Marysville, WA 98271
888-272-1111

Two Rivers Casino
6828-B Highway 25 South
Davenport, WA 99122
509-772-4000
800-722-4031

Yakama Nation Legends Casino
580 Fort Road
Toppenish, WA 98948
509-865-8800
877-7-COME-11

WEST VIRGINIA

Charles Town Races
P.O. Box 551
Charles Town, WV 25414
304-723-7001
800-795-7001
www.clownraces.com

Mountaineer Park and Gaming Resort
State Route #2
Chester, WV 26034
304-387-2400
800-804-0468
www.mtrgaming.com

Tri-State Greyhound Park & Video Lottery
1 Greyhound Lane
Cross Lanes, WV 25356
304-776-1000
800-224-9683

Wheeling Downs Race Track & Gaming Center
1 South Stone Street
Wheeling, WV 26003

304-232-5050
877-WIN-HERE
www.wheelingdowns.com

WISCONSIN

Bad River Lodge and Casino
Highway 2, P.O. Box 11
Odanah, WI 54861
715-682-6102
800-777-7449

Grindstone Creek Casino
13767 West Country Road B
Hayward, WI 54843
715-634-2430

Ho Chunk Casino
S3214A Highway 12
Baraboo, WI 53913
608-356-6210
800-HO-CHUNK
www.ho-chunk.com

Hole In The Wall Casino & Hotel
P.O. Box 98
Highway 35 & 77
Danbury, WI 54830
715-656-3444
800-BET-U-WIN

Isle Vista Casino
Highway 13 North
Box 1167
Bayfield, WI 58414
715-779-3712
800-226-8478

Lake of the Torches Resort Casino
510 Old Abe Road
Lac du Flambeau, WI 54538
715-588-7070
800-25-TORCH

LCO Casino, Lodge and Convention Center
13767 West Country Road B
Hayward, WI 54843
715-634-5643
800-LCO-CASH

Majestic Pines Bingo & Casino
W9010 Highway 54 East
Black River Falls, WI 54615
715-284-9098
800-657-4621
www.ho-chunk.com/majestic.htm

Menominee Casino, Bingo and Hotel
P.O. Box 760
Highway 47 & 55
Keshena, WI 54135
715-799-3600
800-343-7778

Mohican North Star Casino
W12180A Country Road A
Bowler, WI 54416
715-787-3110
800-952-0195

Mole Lake Regency Casino
Highway 55
Mole Lake, WI 54520
715-478-5290
800-236-WINN

Oneida Bingo & Casino
2020/2100 Airport Drive
Green Bay, WI 54313
414-494-4500
800-238-4263

Potawatomi Bingo Casino
1721 West Canal Street
Milwaukee, WI 53233
414-645-6888
800-755-6171
www.paysbig.com

Potawatomi Bingo/Northern Lights Casino
P.O. Box 140
Highway 32
Carter, WI 54566
715-473-2021
800-487-9522
www.wisconsingaming.com

Rainbow Casino & Bingo
949 Country Road G
Nekoosa, WI 54457
715-886-4560
800-782-4560
www.ho-chunk.com

St. Croix Casino & Hotel
777 US Highway 8
Turtle Lake, WI 54889
715-986-4777
800-U-GO-U-WIN
www.stcroixcasino.com

APPENDIX V
DIRECTORY OF CANADIAN CASINOS

The following is a directory of Canadian casinos. Names, addresses, phone numbers, toll-free numbers, and Web addresses are included when available.

BRITISH COLUMBIA

Billy Barker Casino Hotel
308 Maclean Street
Quesnel, British Columbia V2J 2N9
Canada
250-992-5533
888-992-4255 (US)

Gateway Casino–New Westminster
140 6th Street
New Westminster, British Columbia V3M
1J4
Canada
604-521-3262

Grand Casino
206-5050 Kingsway
Burnaby, British Columbia VH5 4H2
Canada
604-437-1696

**Great Canadian Casino–Holiday Inn
on Broadway**
709 West Broadway
Vancouver, British Columbia V5Z 4H3
Canada
604-303-100
www.gcgaming.com

**Great Canadian Casino–Mayfair
Casino**
3075 Douglas Street
Victoria, British Columbia V8T 4N3
Canada
604-303-1000
www.gcgaming.com

Great Canadian Casino–Nanaimo
115 Chapel Street
Nanaimo, British Columbia V9R 5H3
Canada
604-303-1000

Great Canadian Casino–Red Lion Inn
3366 Douglas Street
Victoria, British Columbia V8Z 3L3
Canada
604-303-1000
www.gcgaming.com

**Great Canadian Casino–Renaissance
Hotel Downtown**
1133 West Hastings Street
Vancouver, British Columbia V6E 3T3
Canada
604-303-1000
www.gcgaming.com

Great Canadian Casino–Surrey
13538 73rd Avenue
Surrey, British Columbia V6V 2V4
Canada
604-303-1000

Lake City Casinos–Kelowna
1300 Water Street
Kelowna, British Columbia V1Y 1P6
Canada
250-860-9467

Lake City Casinos–Vernon
4801 27th Street
Vernon, British Columbia V1T 5S9
Canada
250-545-3505
www.lakecitycasinos.com

Royal Diamond Casino
B106-750 Pacific Boulevard South
Plaza of Nations
Vancouver, British Columbia V6B 5E7
604-685-2340

**Royal Towers Hotel and Casino
WWW Link:**
http://www.royaltowers.com

New Westminster, British Columbia
V3M 1J4
Canada
604-528-7353
800-663-0202 (Canada)

MANITOBA

Club Regent
1425 Regent Avenue West
Winnipeg, Manitoba R2C 3B2
Canada
204-957-2700

McPhillips Street Station
484 McPhillips Street
Winnipeg, Manitoba R2X 2H2
Canada
204-957-3900
800-265-3912 (US)
800-265-3912 (Canada)

The Crystal Casino
10th Floor
222 Broadway
Winnipeg, Manitoba R3C 0R3
Canada
204-957-2500
800-265-3912 (US)
www.users.aol.com/casinonews/crystal.htm

NOVA SCOTIA

Sheraton Casino Nova Scotia–Halifax
1969 Upper Water Street
Halifax, Nova Scotia B3J 3R7
Canada
902-425-7777

Sheraton Casino Nova Scotia–Sydney
525 George Street
Sydney, Nova Scotia B1P 1K5
Canada
902-563-7777

Ontario

Casino Niagara
5705 Falls Avenue
Niagara Falls, Ontario L2E 6T3
Canada
905-374-3598
888-946-3255 (US)
www.casinoniagara.com

Casino Rama Resort
Orillia, Ontario L0K 1T0
Canada
705-329-3325
www.arcos.org/ernie/casino.html

Casino Windsor
377 Riverside Drive East
Windsor, Ontario N9A 6T3
Canada
519-258-7878
800-991-7777 (US)
www.casinowindsor.com

Klondike Casino
Thunder Bay, Ontario L0K 1T0
Canada
807-626-2548

Klondike Casino
Sudbury, Ontario L0K 1T0
Canada
705-670-4333

QUEBEC

Casino de Charlevoix
183 Avenue Richelieu
Pointe-Au-Pic, Quebec G0T 1M0
Canada
418-665-5300
800-665-2274
www.casinos-quebec.com

Casino de Montréal
1 Avenue du Casino
Montreal, Quebec H3C 4W7
Canada
514-392-2746
800-665-2274 (US)
800-665-2274 (Canada)
www.casinos-quebec.com/MontreaA.htm

Hull Casino/Casino de Hull
1 Boul du Casino
Hull, Quebec J8Y 6W3
Canada
819-772-2100
800-665-2274 (Canada)
www.casino-quebec.com/Hull.htm

SASKATCHEWAN

Bear Claw Casino
Highway 9
Whitebear Reserve, Saskatchewan
    S0C 0R0
Canada
306-577-4577

Casino Regina
1880 Saskatchewan Drive
Regina, Saskatchewan S4P 0B2
Canada
306-565-3000
800-555-3189 (US)
www.casinoregina.com/

Digger's Territorial Casino
Exhibition Grounds

North Battleford, Saskatchewan S9A 2Y9
Canada
306-445-2024

Emerald Casino
Saskatoon Praireland Exhibition Centre
Lorne Ave & Ruth Street
Saskatoon, Saskatchewan S7K 4E4
Canada
306-931-7149

Gold Eagle Casino
11906 Railway Avenue
North Battleford, Saskatchewan S7K 4E4
Canada
306-446-3833

Golden Nugget Casino
250 Thatcher Drive East
Moose Jaw, Saskatchewan S6H 4R3
Canada
306-692-2723

Northern Lights Casino
44 Marquis Road W.
Prince Albert, Saskatchewan S6V 7L7
Canada
306-764-4777

Painted Hand Casino
30 3rd Avenue North
Yorkton, Saskatchewan S6V 7L7
Canada
306-786-6777

Silver Stage Casino
1800 Elphinstone Street
Regina, Saskatchewan S4P 2Z6
Canada
306-781-9200

APPENDIX VI
DIRECTORY OF CRUISE LINES

The following is a selected listing of cruise lines hosting cruises with onboard casinos. Contact the human resources department of each line to inquire about openings and opportunities. While you will have the opportunity to travel in this type of position, don't forget that when working in casinos on cruise ships you will be away from home for periods of time.

Carnival Cruise Lines
3655 N.W. 87th Avenue
Miami, FL 33178
305-599-2600
800-438-6744

Celebrity and Fantasy Cruise
5201 Blue Lagoon Drive
Miami, FL 33126
305-262-6677
800-437-3111

Commodore Cruise Lines
4000 Hollywood Boulevard
Suite 385
Hollywood, FL 33021
305-967-2100
800-538-1000

Costa Cruise Lines
Brickell Bay View Center
80 Southwest 8th Street
Miami, FL 33130
305-358-7325
800-662-6782

Crystal Cruises
2121 Avenue of the Stars
Los Angeles, CA 90067
310-785-9300
800-446-6620

Cunard Line/Crown Cruise Lines
555 5th Avenue
New York, NY 10017
212-880-7500
800-5-CUNARD

Holland America Line
300 Elliot Avenue West
Seattle, WA 98119
206-281-3535
800-426-0329

Norwegian Cruise Line
7665 Corporate Center Drive
Miami, FL 33126
800-327-7030

Premier Cruise Lines
400 Challenger Road
Cape Canaveral, FL 32920
407-783-5061
800-327-7113

Princess Cruises
10100 Santa Monica Boulevard
Los Angeles, CA 90067
310-553-1770
800-421-1700

Radisson Seven Seas Cruise Line
600 Corporate Drive
Ft. Lauderdale, FL 33334
954-776-6123

Regency Cruises
260 Madison Avenue
New York, NY 10016
212-972-4774

Royal Caribbean Cruises
1050 Caribbean Way
Miami, FL 33132
305-539-6000

Royal Cruise Lines
1 Maritime Plaza
San Francisco, CA 93111
415-956-7200

Royal Viking Line
95 Merrick Way
Coral Gables, FL 33134
305-447-9660

Windstar Cruises
300 Elliott Avenue West
Seattle, WA 98119
206-281-3535

APPENDIX VII
GAMING CONFERENCES AND EXPOS

Conferences and expos are a great way to learn about new trends in the gaming industry, as well as to attend seminars and network. This is a listing of some of the more prominent conferences.

Use this list as a beginning. To find additional conferences, contact industry trade associations.

**AMERICAN GAMING
LODGING & LEISURE SUMMIT**
Held annually in Las Vegas, NV, and produced by *Casino Journal;* features seminars and programs for those working in the gaming and hospitality industries.

For more information contact:
Casino Journal Gaming Summits
8025 Black Horse Pike
Suite 470
West Atlantic City, NJ 08232
609-484-8866

BINGO WORLD
Held annually in Las Vegas, NV, Bingo World is produced by Gem Communications. It is the only event of its kind for the bingo industry and features seminars and exhibits of interest to those involved in all aspects of the bingo industry.

For more information contact:
Gem Communications
888 Seventh Avenue
New York, NY 10106
212-636-2960

**CALIFORNIA INDIAN GAMING
SUMMIT**
Held annually in Palm Springs, CA, this summit is produced by Gem Communications. It is strictly educational with informative seminars focusing on the ever-changing and trend-setting Indian Gaming market in California.

For more information contact:

Gem Communications
888 Seventh Avenue
New York, NY 10106
212-636-2960

CASINO OPS
Held annually in Las Vegas, NV and produced by *Casino Journal* in association with UNVL's Gaming Institute, this show features exhibits, educational and informational seminars, and great networking opportunities.

For more information contact:
Casino Journal Gaming Summits
8025 Black Horse Pike
Suite 470
West Atlantic City, NJ 08232
609-484-8866

**GREATER ATLANTIC CITY
CHAMBER BUSINESS EXPO**
Held annually in Atlantic City, NJ, this exposition hosts exhibitors and seminars. It is produced by *Casino Journal.*

For more information contact:
Casino Journal Gaming Summits
8025 Black Horse Pike
Suite 470
West Atlantic City, NJ 08232
609-484-8866

**MID-ATLANTIC GAMING AND
ENTERTAINMENT CONGRESS**
Held annually in Atlantic City, NJ, the Mid-Atlantic Gaming and Entertainment Congress is produced by Gem Communications. This summit

focuses on gaming issues east of the Mississippi.

For more information contact:
Gem Communications
888 Seventh Avenue
New York, NY 10106
212-636-2960

**NATIONAL GAMING
CONFERENCE**
Held annually in Las Vegas, NV, and produced by the Nevada Society of Certified Public Accountants, this show highlights seminars and programs on financial and internal control issues for high-level financial and gaming professionals.

For more information contact:
The Nevada Society of Certified Public
    Accountants
5250 Neil Road
Suite 205
Reno, NV 89502
800-554-8254

**NATIONAL AMERICAN INDIAN
ASSOCIATION CONVENTION
AND TRADE SHOW**
Held annually, the National American Indian Association Convention and Trade Show deals with the Indian Gaming Industry and hosts exhibits, seminars, and workshops.

For more information contact:
The National Indian Gaming Association
    Convention and Trade Show
224 Second Street, SE
Washington, DC 20003
202-546-7711

NORTHERN GAMING SUMMIT

Held in Detroit, MI, and produced by *Casino Journal* with Fraser Trebilcock Davis & Foster, P.C., the Northern Gaming Summit highlights exhibits and informational seminars.

For more information contact:
Casino Journal Gaming Summits
8025 Black Horse Pike
Suite 470
West Atlantic City, NJ 08232
609-484-8866

SLOT MANAGER INSTITUTES

Slot Manager Institutes are produced by Gem Communications and are held just prior to the World Gaming Congress and Expo, the Mid-Atlantic Gaming And Entertainment Congress, and the Western Gaming Summit Congress and Expo. They feature educational programs focusing on the latest developments relating to the slot industry.

For more information contact:

Gem Communications
888 Seventh Avenue
New York, NY 10106
212-636-2960

SOUTHERN GAMING SUMMIT

Held annually in Biloxi, MS, and produced by *Casino Journal* in association with the Mississippi Casino Operators Association, this show hosts exhibits, seminars, and networking opportunities.

For more information contact:
Casino Journal Gaming Summits
8025 Black Horse Pike
Suite 470
West Atlantic City, NJ 08232
609-484-8866

WESTERN GAMING SUMMIT CONGRESS AND EXPO

Held annually in Las Vegas, NV, and produced by Gem Communications, this show spotlights exhibits, informational and educational seminars, and great networking opportunities.

For more information contact:
Gem Communications
888 Seventh Avenue
New York, NY 10106
212-636-2960

WORLD GAMING CONGRESS AND EXPO

Held annually in Las Vegas, NV, and produced by Gem Communications, the World Gaming Congress and Expo is the largest and most prestigious gaming show in the world. It features an extensive array of exhibits and seminars of interest to those working in the gaming industry, as well as offering networking opportunities.

For more information contact:
Gem Communications
888 Seventh Avenue
New York, NY 10106
212-636-2960

APPENDIX VIII
SEMINARS AND WORKSHOPS

The following is a listing of associations and companies that offer workshops, seminars, and courses. This is by no means a complete listing. Many associations, schools, agencies, and companies offer other seminars and workshops. Because subject matter changes frequently, many of the organizations running these workshops and seminars did not wish to have their programs listed.

This listing is for your information. It is offered to help you find programs of interest. The author does not endorse any specific program and is not responsible for subject content.

The Advertising Research Foundation (ARF)
3 East 54th Street
New York, NY 10022
212-751-5656

The Advertising Research Foundation conducts a number of conferences and seminars throughout the year on advertising and marketing research.

Casino Customer Care Seminars
Shelly Field Organization
Booking Office
P.O. Box 711
Monticello, NY 12701
914-794-7312

Customer service is essential in the gaming industry. Casino Customer Care Seminars offer a variety of training programs to casinos for their employees in the hospitality and casino industry.

Casino Management Association
2172 North Rainbow Boulevard
Las Vegas, NV 89108
702-593-5477

The Casino Management Association offers seminars and a certification program in Las Vegas to casino professionals in a variety of areas of the gaming industry. These include operations, gaming law, finance, marketing, and human resources.

Direct Marketing Association (DMA)
11 West 42nd Street
New York, NY 10036
212-768-7277

The Direct Marketing Association (DMA) offers educational programs, seminars, and workshops in direct marketing.

Shelly Field Motivational Programs and Seminars
Shelly Field Organization
Booking Office
P.O. Box 711
Monticello, NY 12701
914-794-7312

Shelly Field offers a variety of motivational programs, seminars, and keynote presentations to casinos, conventions, and corporations throughout the country in areas including careers, human resources, employee recruitment and retention, customer service, motivation, empowerment, stress management, and gaming.

Stress Busters: Beating The Stress In Your Work and Your Life Seminars and Keynote Presentations
Shelly Field Organization
Booking Office
P.O. Box 711
Monticello, NY 12701
914-794-7312

Stress is a fact of life and a key issue in today's work environment, and casinos are no exception. Stressed employees are never the casino's best employees. Managing stress on a daily basis is a big step toward managing overall stress. Stress Busters Seminars offers programs, workshops, and keynote presentations to casinos, conventions, and corporations throughout the country on busting the stress out of life and work. This results in less stressed-out employees who are more productive and ready to offer the best customer service to guests.

The Public Relations Society of America (PRSA)
33 Irving Place
New York, NY 12003
212-995-2230

The Public Relations Society of America offers seminars, conferences, and workshops on a variety of public relations–oriented subjects.

UNLV International Gaming Institute
4505 Maryland Parkway
Las Vegas, NV 89154
702-895-3412

The UNLV International Gaming Institute, one of the most recognized gaming schools in the world, offers casino management seminars, certificate programs, and lecture series in all facets of the gaming industry.

APPENDIX IX
GAMING INDUSTRY WEB SITES

The Internet hosts a wealth of information on gaming, casinos, and industry news. The following is a selected listing of Web sites related to the gaming industry. Use this list as a beginning. There are many more sites on the World Wide Web to explore.

American Gaming Association
(The trade association for the gaming
    industry)
www.americangaming.org

Michigan Gaming
(Michigan gaming news)
www.michigangaming.com

Casino Center
(Information on casinos, gaming,
    publications, etc.)
www.casinocenter.com.

Casino City
(Casino directory and other casino
    information)
www.casinocity.com.

Casino Journal
(Monthly gaming periodical)
www.casinocenter.com/journal

Casino Management Association
(Las Vegas based association comprised
    of professionals in the casino industry)
www.cmaweb.org

Casino Net
(Gaming information)
www.thecasinonet.com/

Casino Wire
(Casino news)
www.casinowire.com

Detroit Free Press Casino Page
(Casino related articles appearing in the
    Detroit Free Press)
www.freep.com/index/casinos.htm

Detroit News Casino Guide
(Information on casinos and gaming in
    Michigan)
www.detnews.com/CASINO

Indian Gaming
(Information on Indian Gaming)
www.indian-gaming.com

**International Gaming & Wagering
    Business**
(Gaming industry publication)
www.gemcommunications.com

Las Vegas.com
(Information on Las Vegas area)
www.lasvegas.com/

Las Vegas Corner
(Gaming news and information for on-
    line gaming sites)
www.vegascorner.com

Michigan Gaming Control Board
(Information on the gaming industry in
    Michigan)
www.state.mi.us/mgcb/

National Indian Gaming
(National Indian Gaming Association
    Site)
www.indiangaming.org

Rolling Good Times Online
(Industry news)
www.rgtonline.com/

Shellyfield.com
(Information on careers, stress
    management, seminars, training
    programs, gaming, etc.)
www.shellyfield.com/

Yahoo Gaming News Update Page
www.biz.yahoo.com/news/gambling.html

APPENDIX X
BIBLIOGRAPHY

A. BOOKS

There are thousands of books on all aspects of the gaming and hospitality industries. The books listed below are separated into general categories, but subjects often overlap.

These books can be found in bookstores or libraries. If your local library does not have the ones you want, ask your librarian to order them for you through the interlibrary loan system.

This list is meant as a beginning. For other books that might interest you, look in the business, hospitality, travel, and gaming sections of bookstores and libraries. You can also check *Book In Print* (found in the reference section of libraries) for other books on the subject.

ACCOUNTING & FINANCIAL MANAGEMENT

Coltman, Michael M. *Hospitality Management Accounting.* John Wiley & Sons: New York, 1997.

Gray, William S. *Hospitality Accounting.* Prentice Hall College Div.: Upper Saddle River, NJ, 1996.

Greenlees, Malcolm. *Casino Accounting & Financial Management.* University of Nevada Press: Reno, NV, 1998.

ADVERTISING

Field, Shelly. *Career Opportunities In Advertising and Public Relations.* Facts On File: New York, 1996.

BARTENDING

Egerton-Thomas, Christopher. *How to Manage a Successful Bar.* John Wiley & Sons: New York, 1994.

Farrell, Ronald A. *The Black Book and the Mob: The Untold Story of the Control of Nevada's Casinos.* University of Wisconsin Press: Madison, WI, 1995.

Harvard Student Agencies. Macdonald, Ellen (Editor). *The Official Harvard Student Agencies Bartending Course.* St. Martin's Press: New York, 1994.

Katsigris, Costas & Porter, Mary. *The Bar and Beverage Book: Basics of Profitable Management.* John Wiley & Sons: New York, 1991.

Marcus, Lori. *Bartending Inside-Out, The Guide To Profession, Profit & Fun.* Cadillac Press: Crystal Bay, NV, 1997.

Plotkin, Robert. *501 Questions Every Bartender Should Know How to Answer: A Unique Look at the Bar Business.* P.S.D. Pub. Co.: Tucson, AZ, 1993.

CASINO DESIGN

Casino Design. *Resorts, Hotels, and Themed Entertainment Spaces.* Rockport Publishers, Gloucester, MA, 1999.

Meyer-Arendt, Klaus & Hartmann, Rudi. *Casino Gambling in America: Origins, Trends, & Impacts.* Cognizant Communication Corporation: Elmsford, NY, 1998.

CASINO MARKETING

Romero, John S. & Quiroga, Robin M. *Casino Marketing.* American Eagle Arts & Letters: Parker, CO, 1994.

Walker, Terry C. & Miller, Richard K. *The 1997 Casino & Gaming Market Research Handbook.* Richard K. Miller & Associates: Norcross, GA, 1997.

CASINO OPERATIONS AND MANAGEMENT

Eade, Vincent H. & Eade, Raymond H. *Introduction to the Casino Entertainment Industry.* Prentice Hall College Div.: Upper Saddle River, NJ, 1996.

Eadington, William R. *The Business of Gaming: Economic and Management Issues.* University of Nevada Press: Reno, NV, 1999.

Fenich, George & Hashimoto, Kathryn, *Casino Dictionary.* Kendall/Hunt Publishing Company: Dubuque, IA, 1995.

Friedman, Bill. *Casino Management.* Carol Publishing Group: Secaucus, NJ, 1982.

Gallion. *Hotel & Casino Operations.* Delmar Publishers: Albany, NY, 2001.

Hashimoto, Kathryn. *Casino Management for the '90s.* Kendall/Hunt Publishing Company: Dubuque, IA, 1997.

Kilby, Jim & Fox, Jim. *Casino Operations Management.* John Wiley & Sons: New York, 1998.

Marshall, Lincoln H. & Rudd, Denis. *Introduction to Casino & Gaming Operations.* Prentice Hall: Upper Saddle River, NJ, 1995.

Martinez, Ruben. *Managing Casinos: A Guide for Entrepreneurs, Management Personnel and Aspiring Managers.* Barricade Books: New York, 1995.

Tracy, Mark. *The Casino Management Handbook: A Practical Guide for Increasing Casino Profits.* Preston Publishing: Las Vegas, NV, 1995.

CASINO SECURITY

McDowell, Marcia A. *Techniques of Casino Surveillance.* Candlelight Publishing: Las Vegas, NV, 1995.

Williams, John J. *Casino Security.* Consumertronics: Albuquerque NM, 1999.

Zender, Bill. *How to Detect Casino Cheating at Blackjack.* RGE Publishing: Oakland, CA, 1999.

CONCIERGE

Bryson, McDowell & Ziminski, Adele. *The Concierge: Key to Hospitality: A Training Manual.* John Wiley & Sons: New York, 1992.

CONFERENCES & CONVENTIONS

Dodson, Dorian. *How to Put on a Great Conference: A Straightforward, Friendly and Practical Guide.* Adolfo Street Publications: Santa Fe, NM, 1992.

Montgomery, Rhonda J. & Strick, Sandra K. *Meetings, Conventions, and Expositions: An Introduction to the Industry.* John Wiley & Sons: New York, 1994.

Voso, Michele. *The Convention and Meeting Planners Handbook: A Step-By-Step Guide to Making Your Event a Success.* Lexington Books: New York, 1990.

CUSTOMER SERVICE

Vavra, Terry G. *Aftermarketing: How to Keep Customers for Life Through Relationship Marketing.* Homewood, IL: Irwin Professional Publishing 1995.

Barlow, Janelle & Moller, Claus. *A Complaint Is a Gift: Using Customer Feedback As a Strategic Tool.* Berrett-Koehler Publishing: San Francisco, CA, 1996.

Davidoff, Donald M. *Contact: Customer Service in the Hospitality and Tourism Industry.* Prentice Hall College Div.: Upper Saddle River, NJ, 1994.

Dutka, Alan. *AMA Handbook for Customer Satisfaction: A Complete Guide to Research, Planning, & Implementations.* NTC Publishing Group: Lincolnwood, IL, 1995.

Peppers, Don & Rogers, Martha. *The One to One Future: Building Relationships One Customer at a Time.* Currency/Doubleday: New York, 1997.

Wing, Michael J & Andersen Arthur, Llp. *The Arthur Andersen Guide to Talking With Your Customers: What They Will Tell You About Your Business: When You Ask the Right Questions.* Upstart Publishing Co.: Dover, NH 1997.

FOOD SERVICE

Axler, Bruce H. *Food and Beverage Service.* John Wiley & Sons: New York, 1990.

McDowell, Milton C. *Math Workbook for Foodservice/Lodging.* John Wiley & Sons: New York, 1988.

Restaurant & Institute Council. *A Guide to College Programs in Hospitality and Tourism.* John Wiley & Sons: New York, 1997.

FRONT OFFICE MANAGEMENT

Deveau, Linsley T., de Portocarrero, Nestor and Deveau, Patricia. *Front Office Management and Operations.* Prentice Hall College Div.: Upper Saddle River, NJ, 1997.

Picot, Derek. *Hotel Reservations.* Parkwest Pubs: Jersey City, NJ, 1995.

HOSPITALITY INDUSTRY

Powers, Thomas F. *Introduction to Management in the Hospitality Industry.* John Wiley & Sons: New York, 1999.

Solomon, Ed, Prueter, Shelley, Solomon, Edward & Solomon, Lorin. *Serve 'Em Right: The Complete Guide to Hospitality Service.* Oak Hill Press: Greensboro, NC, 1997.

Stefanelli, John M. *Purchasing: Selection and Procurement for the Hospitality Industry.* John Wiley & Sons: New York, 1997.

GAMBLING & GAMING

Consumer Guide Editors. *Winning Tips for Casino Games.* NAL/Dutton: New York, 1995.

Glazer, Andrew N.S. *Casino Gambling the Smart Way: How to Have More Fun and Win More Money.* Career Press: Hawthorne, NJ, 1999.

Griffin, Peter A. *The Theory of Blackjack: The Complete Card Counter's Guide to the Casino Game of 21.* Huntington Press: Las Vegas, NV, 1996.

Herczog, Mary & Garman, Rick. *Frommer's Las Vegas 98: With Insider Tips on Casino Gambling.* Alpha Books: New York, 1997.

Malone, Myrtle D. *MGM Grand Hotel, Inc. Hotel-Casino-Theme Park: Grand Opening Commemorative.* Pioneer Publications, Incorporated: Houston, TX, 1993.

Ortiz, Darwin. *Casino Gambling for the Clueless: A Beginner's Guide to Playing & Winning.* Carol Publishing Group: Secaucus, NJ, 1998.

———— *Darwin Ortiz on Casino Gambling: The Complete Guide to Playing & Winning.* Carol Publishing Group: Secaucus, NJ, 1990.

Pileggi, Nicholas. *Casino: Love & Honor in Las Vegas.* Pocket Books: New York, 1996.

Renneisen, Robert M. & Patrick, John. *How to Be Treated Like a High Roller: . . . Even Though You're Not One.* Lyle Stuart: Secaucus, NJ, 1996.

Silberstang, Edwin. *The Winner's Guide to Casino Gambling.* Signet: New York, 1998.

Spector, Susan & Wong, Stanford. *Complete Idiot's Guide to Gambling.* Macmillan Publishing Company: New York, 1999.

Trebor, Bob. *Casino Gambling: How to Maximize Your Winnings & Minimize Your Losses.* Bob Trebor: Springboro, OH, 1997.

Vinson, Barney & Tarino, David. *Casino Secrets.* Huntington Press: Las Vegas, NV, 1997.

Vinson, Barney. *Las Vegas Behind the Tables.* Gollehon Press: Grand Rapids, MI, 1998.

Vinson, Barney. *Casino Secrets.* Huntington Press: Las Vegas, NV, 1997.

Wong, Stanford. *Casino Tournament Strategy.* Pi Yee Press: La Jolla, CA, 1997.

GAMING INDUSTRY

Edwards, Jerome E. & Kofoed, Leslie S. *Kofoed's Meanderings in Lovelock Business, Nevada Government, the U. S. Marshal's Office, & the Gaming Industry.* University of Nevada: Reno, NV, 1972.

International Gaming Institute. *The Gaming Industry: Introduction and Perspectives.* John Wiley & Sons: New York, 1996.

Lynch, Don, Thompson, David, Bean, James H. & Horton, Verne. *Battle Born Nevada: People History Stories.* Dangberg, Grace Foundation, Incorporated: Carson City, NV, 1998.

Money Laundering: *Rapid Growth of Casinos Makes Them Vulnerable.* Diane Publishing Company: Upland, PA, 1996.

Thompson, David, Dickerson, Donald & Barker, Bill. *Nevada: A History of Changes.* Dangberg, Grace Foundation: Carson City, NV, 1986.

Universal International Gaming Institute Staff. *The Gaming Industry: Introduction and Perspectives.* John Wiley & Sons: New York, 1996.

HOSPITALITY BUSINESS, MANAGEMENT & OPERATIONS

Brotherton, Bob (Editor). *The Handbook of Contemporary Hospitality Management Research.* John Wiley & Sons: New York, 1999.

Medlik, S. *The Business of Hotels.* Butterworth-Heinemann: Newton, MA, 1995.

Powers, Thomas F. *Introduction to Management in the Hospitality Industry.* John Wiley & Sons: New York, 1999.

Riley, Michael. *Managing People: A Guide for Managers in the Hotel and Catering Industry.* Butterworth-Heinemann: Newton, MA, 1995.

Rutherford, Denney G. (Editor). *Hotel Management and Operations.* John Wiley & Sons: New York, 1997.

HUMAN RESOURCES

Drummond, Karen Eich. *Human Resource Management for the Hospitality Industry.* John Wiley & Sons: New York, 1997.

Jerris, Linda A. *Human Resources Management for Hospitality.* Prentice Hall: Upper Saddle River, NJ, 1999.

INDIAN GAMING

Ganson, Harriet, Perez, Nilsa I., Steck, Keith & Gordon, Bryon. *Tax Policy: A Profile of the Indian Gaming Industry.* Diane Publishing: Upland, PA, 1998.

Practicing Law Institute. *The Gaming Industry on American Indian Lands: The Profit-Making Opportunities.* Practicing Law Institute: New York, 1994.

LAS VEGAS

Smith, John, L. *No Limit: The Rise and Fall of Bob Stupak and Las Vegas.* Huntington Press: Las Vegas, NV, 1997.

Smith, John & Hinton, William. *Running Scared: The Life and Treacherous Times of Las Vegas Casino King Steve Wynn.* Barricade Books: New York, 1995.

Sheehan, Jack (Editor). *The Players: The Men Who Made Las Vegas.* University of Nevada Press: Reno, NV, 1997.

Cannon, David Jack & Yenne, Bill. *The Illustrated History of Las Vegas.* Book Sales Inc.: Edison, NJ, 1997.

PUBLIC RELATIONS

Field, Shelly. *Career Opportunities In Advertising and Public Relations.* Facts On File: New York, 1996.

RESTAURANT MANAGEMENT & SERVICE

Marvin, Bill. *The Foolproof Foodservice Selection System: The Complete Manual for Creating a Quality Staff.* John Wiley & Sons: New York, 1993.

———. *From Turnover to Teamwork: How to Build and Retain a Customer-Oriented Foodservice Staff.* John Wiley & Sons: New York, 1994.

———. *Restaurant Basics: Why Guests Don't Come Back . . . and What You Can Do About It.* John Wiley & Sons: New York, 1992.

Mill, Robert Christe. *Restaurant Management: Customers, Operations and Employees.* Prentice Hall College Div.: Upper Saddle River, NJ, 1997.

Scanlon, Nancy Loman. *Quality Restaurant Service Guaranteed: A Training Outline.* John Wiley & Sons: New York, 1998.

SALES & MARKETING

Gordon, Ian & Gordon, Alan. *Relationship Marketing: New Strategies, Techniques and Technologies to Win the Customers You Want and Keep Them Forever.* John Wiley & Sons: New York, 1998.

Kotler, Philip, Bowen, John & Makens, James. *Marketing for Hospitality and Tourism.* Prentice Hall College Div.: Upper Saddle River, NJ, 1998.

Lewis, Robert C. *Cases in Hospitality Marketing and Management. John Wiley & Sons: New York, 1997.*

Morrison, Alastair M. *Hospitality and Travel Marketing.* Delmar Pub.: Albany, NY, 1996.

Newell, Frederick. *The New Rules of Marketing: How to Use One-To-One Relationship Marketing to Be the Leader in Your Industry.* Irwin Professional Pub.: Homewood, IL, 1997.

Nykiel, Ronald A. *Marketing in the Hospitality Industry.* Educational Institute of the American Hotel Motel Assoc.: Washington, DC, 1997.

Wolosz, Joe. *Hotel & Motel Sales, Marketing & Promotion: Strategies to Impact Revenue & Increase Occupancy for Smaller Lodging Properties.* Infinite Corridor Pub: 1997.

SPECIAL EVENTS & EVENT MANAGEMENT

Catherwood, Dwight W., Van Kirk, Richard L. & Ernest, Young. *The Complete Guide to Special Event Management: Business Insights, Financial Advice, and Successful Strategies from Ernst & Young.* John Wiley & Sons: New York, 1992.

Getz, Donald. *Event Management & Event Tourism.* Cognizant Communication Corp.: Elmsford, NY, 1997.

Goldblatt, Joe. *Special Events: Best Practices in Modern Event Management.* John Wiley & Sons: New York, 1997.

Malouf, Lena. *Behind the Scenes at Special Events: Flowers, Props, and Design.* John Wiley & Sons: New York, 1999.

TOURISM

Collin, P. H. *Dictionary of Hotels, Tourism and Catering Management.* Peter Collin Pub. Ltd.: Middlesex, U.K., 1997.

Tribe, John. *The Economics of Leisure and Tourism.* Butterworth-Heinemann: Newton, MA, 1996.

B. PERIODICALS

Magazines, newspapers, membership bulletins, and newsletters may be helpful in finding information about a specific job category, finding a job in a specific field, or giving you insight into what certain jobs entail.

As with the books in the previous section, this list should serve as a beginning. There are many periodicals that are not listed because of space limitations. Periodicals also tend to come and go. Look in your local library or in the newspaper and magazine shop for other periodicals that might interest you.

The gaming industry, like others, has trade publications as well as consumer publications. This listing includes both.

CASINOS & GAMING

Atlantic City Action
33 S. Presbyterian Ave.
Atlantic City, NJ 08404
609-347-1225

Atlantic City Insider
8025 Black Horse Pike, Suite 470
West Atlantic City, NJ 08232
609-641-3200
609-645-1661

Baccarat Quarterly Newsletter
309 Orizaba Avenue
Long Beach, CA 90814
562-434-7348

Bingo Manager
P.O. Box 720
Wayzata, MN 55391
612-473-5088

Bingo Bugle Newspaper Group
3127 South Industrial Road
Las Vegas, NV 89109
702-893-7774

Bingo News & Gaming Hi-Lites
101, 10171 Saskatchewan Dr.
Box 106
Edmonton, Alberta T6E 4R5
Canada
403-986-5088

Blackjack Forum
414 Santa Clara Avenue
Oakland, CA 94610
510-465-6452

Blackjack Review
P.O. Box 541967
Merritt Island, FL 32954
407-452-2957

Canadian Casino News
2100 Hartington Court
Mississauga, Ontario L5J 2G9
Canada
905-855-1869

Card Player Magazine
3140 South Polaris, Suite 8
Las Vegas, NV 89102
702-871-1720

Casino Boat News & Gaming Report
14 Carteret Street
Staten Island, NY 10307
718-984-8710

Casino Chronicle
10880 Crescendo Circle
Boca Raton, FL 33498
407-477-3082

Casino Executive
50 South Ninth Street, Suite 200
Minneapolis, MN 55402
612-338-1578

Casino Games Magazine
1009 Nawkee Drive, Suite 711
North Las Vegas, NV 89031
702-399-3998

Casino Gaming International
4020 Lake Washington Boulevard, N.E.,
   Suite 100
Kirkland, WA 98033

Casino Journal
8025 Black Horse Pike, Suite 470
West Atlantic City, NJ 08232
609-484-8866

Casino Player
8025 Black Horse Pike, Suite 470
West Atlantic City, NJ 08232
609-641-3200

Casino World
The Maltings, 50 Bath Street
Gravesend, Kent DA11 0DF
United Kingdom
+44 (0) 1474 335-087

Chance the Best of Gaming
125 East 12th Street, Suite 2C
New York, NY 10003
212-505-9854

The Crapshooter
P.O. Box 421440
San Diego, CA 92142
619-571-1346

Current Blackjack News
Pi Yee Press
7910 Ivanhoe Ave., No. 34
La Jolla, CA 92037
619-456-4080

EuroSlot
Daltry Street
Oldham, Lancashire, OL1 4BB
United Kingdom
+44 (0) 161 624 3687

Fun & Gaming
P.O. Box 6448
Reno, NV 89503
702-786-3594

Fun 'N' Games
1075 North Albany Avenue
Atlantic City, NJ 08401
609-345-6623

Gaming for Africa
P.O. Box 2561
North Riding, Johannesburg, 2162
South Africa
+27 (11) 704 3147

The Gaming Industry Daily Report
177 Main Street, Suite 312
Fort Lee, NJ 07024
201-947-4642

The Gaming Industry Weekly Report
177 Main Street, Suite 312
Fort Lee, NJ 07024
201-947-4642

Gaming Law Review
2 Madison Ave.
Larchmont, NY 10538
914-834-3100

Gaming Products & Services
P.O. Box 720
Wayzata, MN 55391
612-473-5088

Gaming Systems Source Directory
Box 600927
N. Miami Beach, FL 33160

Gaming Times
4089 Spring Mountain Road
Las Vegas, NV 89102
702-876-6020

Gaming Today
P.O. Box 93116
Las Vegas, NV 89193

Grogan Gaming Report
P.O. Box 359, 2620 South Maryland
　　Parkway
Las Vegas, NV 89109
702-737-7005

Indiana Gaming Insight
Box 383
Noblesville, IN 46061
317-817-9997

Indian Gaming Magazine
4020 Lake Washington Boulevard
　　Northeast, Suite 10
Kirkland, WA 98033
425-803-2900

Indian Gaming News
Seven Penn Plaza
New York, NY 10001
212-594-4120

International Gaming & Wagering
Business
Seven Penn Plaza
New York, NY 10001
212-594-4120

Las Vegas Insider
P.O. Box 1144
Buffalo, NY 14220
520-636-1649

Las Vegas Informer
3540 West Sahara, Suite 164
Las Vegas, NV 89102
702-648-7709

Las Vegas Sporting News
850 3rd Street
Whitehall, PA 18052
800-325-8259

Las Vegas Style Magazine
5087 South Arville, Suite F
Las Vegas, NV 89118
702-871-6040

Las Vegas Today
4440 South Arville, Suite 12
Las Vegas, NV 89103
702-221-5000

Laughlin, Nevada Entertainer
2075 Miracle Mile
P.O. Box 1209
Bullhead City, AZ 86442
602-763-2505

Lottery & Casino News
321 New Albany Rd
Moorestown, NJ 08057
609-778-8900

Lottery, Parimutuel & Casino
Regulation – State Capitals
300 N. Washington St.
Alexandria, VA 22314
703-549-8606

National Gaming Summary
Bayport One Suite 470
8025 Black Horse Pike
West Atlantic City, NJ 08232
800-486-7529

Nevada Gaming News
Seven Penn Plaza
New York, NY 10001
212-594-4120

The Nevada Gaming Newsletter
95 Wells Avenue, Suite 3
Newton Centre, MA 02159
617-964-6250

Nevada Hospitality
5230 South Eastern
Las Vegas, NV 89119
702-736-8886

New Jersey State Bar Association
Casino Law
1 Constitution Square
New Brunswick, NJ 08901
908-249-5000

New Jersey Casino Control Commission
Annual Report
Public Information Assistant
Arcade Building Tennessee Avenue &
　　Boardwalk
Atlantic City, NJ 08401
609-441-3749

Passenger Vessel News
P.O. Box 8662
Metairie, LA 70011
504-455-9758

Poker World
An Internet Magazine on the Poker World.
www.pokerworld.com/

Riverboat Gaming News
Seven Penn Plaza
New York, NY 10001
212-594-4120

Rolling Good Times Online
The Premier Gambling 'Zine On The Net.
www.rgfonline.com/

Showbiz Weekly
800 South Valley View
Las Vegas, NV 89107
702-383-7185

Showtime
2303 Kietzke Lane, Suite 18
Reno, NV 89504
702-827-5400

Today in Las Vegas
3626 Pecos McLeod, Suite 14
Las Vegas, NV 89121
702-385-2737

What's on in Las Vegas
4425 South Industrial Road
Las Vegas, NV 89103
702-891-8811

Winning Times
10507 Gravelly Lake Drive SW, Suite #4
Tacoma, WA 98499
206-584-1212

HOSPITALITY, HOTELS & FOOD SERVICE MANAGEMENT

Foodservice and Hospitality
23 Les Mill Road, Suite 101
Don Mills, Ontario M3B 3P6
Canada
416-447-0888

Hospitality Manager
120 Hayward
Ames, IA 50010
515-296-2400

Inn Business
65 St. John Side Road East
Aurora, Ontario L4G 3G8

Canada
905-841-8753

Official Guide to Food Service and
Hospitality Management Careers
665 La Villa Drive
Miami Springs, FL 33166
305-887-1700

Restaurant Hospitality
1100 Superior Avenue
Cleveland, OH 44114
216-696-7000

ABOUT THE AUTHOR

Shelly Field is a nationally recognized motivational speaker, career expert, and author of more than 20 best-selling books in the business and career fields.

Her books instruct people on how to obtain jobs in a wide array of areas, including the hospitality, music, sports, and communications industries; casinos and casino hotels; advertising; public relations; theater; the performing arts; entertainment; animal rights; health care; writing; and art, as well as how to choose the best career for the new century.

She is a frequent guest on local, regional, and national radio, cable, and television talk, information, and news shows and she also does numerous print interviews and personal appearances.

Field is a featured speaker at casinos, conventions, expos, corporate functions, employee training and development sessions, career fairs, spouse programs, and events nationwide. She speaks on empowerment, motivation, gaming, careers, human resources; attracting, retaining, and motivating employees; customer service; and stress reduction. Her popular seminar, "STRESS BUSTERS: Beating the Stress in Your Work and Your Life" is a favorite around the country.

Field is a career consultant to businesses, educational institutions, employment agencies, women's groups, and individuals. She is a corporate consultant to casinos throughout the country, appearing at job fairs and providing assistance with human resources issues, such as attracting, retaining, and motivating employees, customer service training, and stress management in the workplace.

President and CEO of The Shelly Field Organization, a public relations and management firm handling national clients, she also does corporate consulting and has represented celebrities in the sports, music, and entertainment industries, as well as authors, businesses, and corporations.

For information about personal appearances or seminars contact The Shelly Field Organization at P.O. Box 711, Monticello, NY 12701 or log on to www.shellyfield.com.

INDEX

E

F

W